CRICKET 2.0

CRICKET 2.0

INSIDE THE T20 REVOLUTION

TIM WIGMORE · FREDDIE WILDE

POLARIS
PUBLISHING

This edition first published in 2020 by

POLARIS PUBLISHING LTD
c/o Aberdein Considine
2nd Floor, Elder House
Multrees Walk
Edinburgh
EH1 3DX

www.polarispublishing.com

First published 2019

Distributed by

ARENA SPORT
An imprint of Birlinn Limited

ISBN: 9781913538071
eBook ISBN: 9781788851886

British Library Cataloguing-in-Publication Data
A catalogue record for this book is available on request from the British Library.

Designed and typeset by Polaris Publishing, Edinburgh

Printed in Great Britain by MBM Print SCS Limited, East Kilbride

CONTENTS

To my dad for indulging my cricket obsession,
and my mum and Fay, my partner, for tolerating it
Tim Wigmore

To my dad for introducing me to cricket, a constant
source of joy for both of us, and for encouraging my T20 focus.
I have been fortunate that I have never had to look far for inspiration
Freddie Wilde

AUTHORS' NOTE

Over the last few years, Freddie and I have had many – too many, others would doubtless say – conversations about Twenty20. For all that has been written and said about the game, we would often have questions that remained unanswered: about the skills of the game, culture and tactics, or how it was changing cricket off the field.

We wanted to read a book that would address these questions. As we couldn't find it, we decided to try and write it ourselves. Over the last couple of years, we have interviewed more than 50 players, coaches and administrators involved in T20 in search of answers about everything from the art and science of batting and bowling in T20, where matches are won and lost, how T20 has democratised the game, how the West Indies built a T20 dynasty, and what the future will hold. This book is the result.

It is not a definitive history of T20 cricket, but the story of how T20 has changed cricket and our attempts to get inside, and deconstruct, the T20 revolution. We feel that now is the perfect time for this book –16 years since T20 was created at professional level – allowing us to reflect on all the changes it has wrought with the benefit of perspective.

So swiftly has T20 become part of cricket's fabric that it is easy to ignore that, in terms of its global impact and fanbase, it is the most successful new professional sport to have been created this century, and for many years before. Yet we believe that T20 – its skills and strategies, and the opportunities and challenges it presents to cricket worldwide – remain poorly understood. *Cricket 2.0* is our attempt to change that as T20 reaches a new level of maturity.

This book is solely on men's T20 cricket. T20 has transformed women's cricket too – quite possibly even more so – but that story deserves its own full telling, and there are others better qualified than us to do it justice.

Before we decided to work together, neither of us had considered writing a book like this individually. But we believe that collaborating together – combining Freddie's experience of working with T20 teams as well as analysing the game in his writing, and my experience as a journalist writing about T20 both on and off the field – will make for a more rewarding book for readers. We have learned a huge amount in our interviews, research and writing of this book, sometimes reinforcing what we thought we knew, and other times challenging it and leading us to think anew. This is a book designed to be accessible both to T20 devotees and those with little previous knowledge of, or interest in, the game. We hope that, whichever applies to you, you enjoy reading it as much as we enjoyed writing it.

Tim Wigmore and Freddie Wilde

FOREWORD

BY HARSHA BHOGLE

There is a custom in almost all Indian families that parents bear the cost of their children's education, their marriage, sometimes the honeymoon and, wherever possible, do what it takes to set them up in life. Without quite being stated, this comes with the assumption that when the parents are much older, having to live off their pension (if there is one), the children start looking after them. The power structure might change but through the harmony of the parent-child relationship, the cycle continues.

So what is this nugget of Indian culture doing in this foreword? T20 cricket benefited from the family of Test and One Day International (ODI) cricket it was born in, but it has grown and become rich and successful and the time has come for it to carry its ageing Test match parents along to extend their twilight years. If you live in England or Australia you might try me for treason – but you live in a little island of joy in a vast ocean. T20 has changed the way the game is played and taught, has altered lives dramatically, has welcomed more players into its fold and given them sustenance, and it has unlocked the value that lay dormant in cricket.

A year ago, I asked a senior executive in one of the leading stakeholders in Indian cricket what percentage of the total bid they would consider if they had to bid for Test match cricket alone. He let me finish my sentence and then said, 'You mean, *if* we bid.' I often wonder where our game would have been if T20 hadn't appeared. It wouldn't have been dead –

cricket is far too resilient for that – but antibiotics and painkillers would have been bedside.

So is T20 really cricket? With its outrageous hitting and quirky bowling styles, is it the enemy of cricket as we knew it or is it the saviour of our game? I met a young man, representing a generation that will take our world forward, at a discussion on whether T20 would ruin our cricket, on how it needed to be curtailed to allow Test cricket to prosper and he rolled his eyes and said, 'Your generation, na! When will you realise that the challenge to Test cricket comes not from T20 but from Netflix, from having the world at your fingertips on a handset?'

I love T20 cricket. I have ever since I first heard about it and a year later, in 2006, when I saw my first game. I wrote on 21 January 2005 that it was time to feel the fresh breeze blowing our way, that our generation had to embrace it or it would leave us behind. I loved the fact that it demanded different skills from its participants, not inferior skills. I was fascinated by the new mindset where getting out might be tactically better than hanging on, I enjoyed seeing a new generation of players recalibrate risk and I was particularly enamoured by match-ups and the chess-like manoeuvring of pieces.

Not surprisingly, existing thought was being challenged, leading to thrilling results. Getting out if your strike rate was suboptimal was but one. Players questioned why the space behind the wicketkeeper couldn't be seen as a scoring area. The scoop to the yorker arrived, the foot began moving towards midwicket rather than towards the pitch of the ball. The bowlers responded with loopy bouncers and wider yorkers and a bewildering variety of slower balls. Catching around the boundary rope was revolutionised and 100 in the last ten overs stopped intimidating batsmen in a run chase because their mind now saw possibilities, not constraints. Entrepreneurs think like that. It is no coincidence that India's young population has me enthralled by its approach to life.

In India we were lucky to see all this being played out before our eyes. The Indian Premier League (IPL) is a giant laboratory where innovations are being studied. Some have likened it to a giant concert where the best musicians come, not just to play, but to jam with colleagues. The IPL made cricket outward-looking where it once prided itself on being exclusive and closed. For all its reliance on analytics, the IPL was also easy to understand and it took everyone along with it. More women started watching cricket, for example, and it became a festival with cricket at its core. The new demographics brought new advertisers and we grew aware of the value that lay within, much like an oil well that was deeper and richer than imagined. The rights went up from $900 million for ten years in 2008, to $1.6 billion for nine years in 2009 (when Sony bought the rights from World Sports Group, the original buyers) and then, from 2018, to $2.5 billion for just five years.

But something else happened. 'Where Talent Meets Opportunity', the IPL said about itself and that is exactly what started happening. Where the opportunity to play at an exalted level was confined to 20 players, now 75 or 80 could. If you had a skill you were noticed, sometimes for a hundred thousand dollars, sometimes for half a million, sometimes, unbelievably, for a million. Beautiful stories of players lifting their families out of poverty emerged. The IPL changed people's lives. Test cricket could never have done that.

It has had side effects. Not everyone wants to bat for a day in tough conditions when they can earn enough by biffing the ball for 20 minutes. Playing for the country is a dream but playing for a high-profile franchise is not a bad alternative. The lure of riches has parents going to coaches and asking that their children be made good enough to play in the IPL. Coaches aren't quite sure whether to tell their wards to take their front foot to the pitch of the ball or away from it to open up the body to more hitting zones.

Other players are teammates one day and rivals the next; strengths are circulated, weaknesses analysed. Conversations, and analytics, mean there are no secrets any more. And in a world where a corporate executive is your boss, your post-tournament appraisal might lead to the sack. Insecurity has taken a step closer. Dare I say it, franchise cricket is more football than Test cricket.

Will it survive? Will people find one game is like another, will monotony creep in? Will the lure of the extra buck in a shortened game draw all kinds into its fold? As ownership gets fuzzier, who controls the sanctity of our game? Who are its parents? I am not worried about the first – tennis and football have survived and thrived – but I am very concerned by the second. Not all that we hear is noble, not all countries have laws to deal with malpractices.

T20 cricket, at the moment, is similar to what we see as soon as the lights turn green in India. Everyone wants to move ahead immediately, there is honking and jostling for territory but amidst the turbulence, everyone seems to find space. Within a couple of hundred metres, laminar flow is re-established. T20 cricket seeks that laminar flow. It needs regulation, it needs vigilance.

But it is a fascinating sport, it will keep cricket alive and having drawn people into its fold, will introduce them to the many joys of Test cricket too. T20 is a proud young adult and if we nurture it, it will carry its ageing parents further.

It is entirely appropriate that two young men tell this story. Both have grown up hearing of the mysteries of Test cricket but they are not bound by it and that allows them to explore T20 cricket with an open mind. Tim and Freddie are the torchbearers of tomorrow, we must listen to them.

FOREWORD

BY MICHAEL VAUGHAN

In the early years of T20 many thought, 'Wow this is amazing for the game – but it'll just be a flash in the pan.' But I could clearly see that it was going to be a long-term success. When you've got India – with their passion for the game and the billions who follow it there – and the kind of people that were getting involved in the franchises, it was only ever going to continue on an upward trajectory. It seemed obvious to me that if anyone had ever played cricket, it was likely that they played a T20 game and they would therefore be able to readily relate to this project.

On the flip side, I could never understand why those in England, in particular, were reluctant to back a game we had created. I couldn't understand why we weren't open to giving England players the opportunity to play in the IPL.

Only the best will survive on the T20 circuit. It's very difficult to come back from disappointing at a franchise. If you fail at one, you almost lose the trust of all the franchises. Particularly in the IPL. If you have one bad year you just get lobbed on the scrapheap.

When it first came to the fore, T20 was seen as a crash-bang-wallop format where players didn't really have to think. People said it was basically baseball in 20 overs and that only sloggers would flourish. I think it's been proven over the years that you need a lot of nous. You need a lot of skill. You need a really strong cricket brain because you are under the ultimate pressure. Test match cricket is the ultimate test but if you find yourself in trouble, you often get a period of time to work your way out of the problem. In T20, if you find yourself in trouble, you're out, you're gone.

T20 has brought pressure and exposure to players. The levels and the standard has risen because all players now know they have a great opportunity to earn a lot of money.

If I was playing now I'd go and make sure that I was a 360-degree player. So I'd need the ramps, the tricks, the reverse sweeps, the reverse ramps, I'd learn to manoeuvre my feet more at different times to the different bowlers. Create different angles. But you can still be very effective and have a strike rate of 130-plus by being a classical player. Not everyone can hit the ball like Andre Russell. Not everyone has the power and muscles that he has, but there are ways and means of making yourself into a really good 360-degree player who can time the ball, finesse and manoeuvre it into gaps and I think that's what the best-quality players do. You wouldn't say that Virat Kohli is a power hitter, but he times the ball so well he can hit it over the boundary. That's the style of player I would try to be.

I think the old-fashioned player and fan would say the T20 stars are just sloggers but actually in order to hit it hard you have to have amazing technique. You have to have a great base to play those shots. Your head position has to be strong. You have to be still on the release of the ball. That's a technical side of the game that doesn't get spoken about enough – and T20 players have incredible techniques.

These players work very, very hard and they get rewards for it but I think – and where T20 is clever – you need different styles of player in different positions throughout the different overs. It's the skill of the captain and the coaches to provide their team with these options in order to be successful.

Anyone who looks down on T20 should try it themselves. You try to hit a ball miles out of the ground on a regular basis with such clean, consistent striking as these players do. Go into a field and get someone to throw you balls and try to do it – it's nigh-on impossible, yet these guys make it look so easy and do it on such a consistent basis. I think that's the biggest compliment I can give: players of this era that can strike the ball out of the ground make it look so easy. Like a golfer hitting a drive 330 yards, a cover drive played beautifully by a quality player makes it look easy. It's not. And like an elite golfer, they've worked incredibly hard to get there. They've trained their brain, they've trained their eye, they've trained their technique and they've trained their mindset to be able to deliver under pressure on a regular basis. Any skill at the highest level doesn't just happen. These guys have put thousands of hours of effort and time and hard work into getting their skill levels up so they can produce those flamboyant strokes under the pressure of a quality game.

You are always going to get the odd dinosaur who will say these big smashes to the boundary are down to the bats, that the boundaries are shorter and the bowling is not as good as in Test cricket. Well I disagree. The bowling in T20 is right up there. Sometimes you might see the bowlers flapping and flipping a little bit but that's because the batsmen are putting them under so much pressure with the power and variation of their shots. I think we should be really promoting the fact that if a bowler's numbers are up there, they must be among the best of all time because of the pressure they're being put under by the power, variation and fitness of the batsmen. We don't mention fitness enough. How fit these players are, how strong they are, is phenomenal. I guess it's partly to do with the opportunities they've been given with training facilities, coaching, strength and conditioning, nutritional advice and so on, but we have to give them credit for the amount of work they put in off the field. It's a remarkable level of dedication.

T20 is here to stay and we should celebrate and cherish all the skills involved. As long as we are on this globe it's a brand of cricket that we are going to be watching. And it is only going to get bigger.

ACRONYMS

ACU (Anti-Corruption Unit [of the International Cricket Council (ICC)])

BBL (Big Bash League)

BCCI (Board of Control for Cricket in India)

BPL (Bangladesh Premier League)

CSK (Chennai Super Kings)

CPL (Caribbean Premier League)

DRS (Decision Review System)

ECB (England & Wales Cricket Board)

FICA (Federation of International Cricketers Association)

ICC (International Cricket Council)

ICL (Indian Cricket League)

IPL (Indian Premier League)

KKR (Kolkata Knight Riders)

MCC (Marylebone Cricket Club)

NBA (National Basketball Association)

ODI (One Day International)

PSL (Pakistan Super League)

RCB (Royal Challengers Bangalore)

T20 (Twenty20)

TKR (Trinbago Knight Riders)

WADA (World Anti-Doping Agency)

WICB (West Indies Cricket Board)

WT20 (World T20)

PROLOGUE

THE GIMMICK

'I think it's difficult to play seriously'
Australia captain Ricky Ponting, 2005

On a sultry evening at The Oval cricket ground in London in June 2003, Surrey's captain Adam Hollioake won the toss against Middlesex. 'We're going to bowl first,' he announced, 'because I haven't got a clue what's going to happen.'

This was how professional T20 cricket began, in a spirit of ignorance, innocence and sheer bedlam. Professional sport fleetingly became a world of children playing a game for the first time. No room for tactical smarts here. Just figuring out the new rules – the threat of an incoming batsman being 'timed out' if they took more than 90 seconds to take guard at the crease, and the need to bowl all 20 overs within 75 minutes or be penalised six runs for every over unbowled – was challenging enough.

'Like many, we took it as a bit of a joke to begin with,' Hollioake later admitted. Alex Tudor, who played for Surrey at the time, recalled before the tournament, 'I remember Keith Medlycott, our coach at the time, was saying, "Who wants to play?" I was very much a longer formats player . . . so I couldn't care less about it.'

Surrey were the Twenty20 Cup's first champions. This was largely a triumph for simply having the best players, though Hollioake immediately grasped that T20 was not merely a shorter version of one-day cricket so much as a drastically different game. Before the tournament, he addressed the side, saying, 'Lads, we're not going to worry too much about ones and twos, we're just going to try and hit more sixes than the other team.'

In this way, Hollioake stumbled on an essential truth about the nature of T20, and how it diverged from the longer formats. 'We went in with the theory that basically a one run here and there in a T20 game isn't a big deal but if you had a six it's a big chunk. You hit a couple of sixes and that could be 10% of your total – that's a big swing. We went in to bat with the mentality of hitting sixes.'

In many ways the point of T20 was to make people forget they were watching cricket at all. In that first, heady summer of 2003, evenings at the cricket were about pitchside Jacuzzis, bouncy castles, cheerleaders, speed dating and copious alcohol, with the cricket itself incidental. This was very deliberate; the very point of T20 was to create a product that appealed to those who would never normally go to cricket.

At the start of the new century, the English game seemed moribund: domestic attendances fell 17% in the five years to 2001. John Carr, director of cricket operations for the England and Wales Cricket Board (ECB), gave Stuart Robertson, the marketing manager, £250,000 to undertake the biggest consumer survey in cricket history.

'We specifically wanted to ask people who were non-cricket fans but we felt might be convertible why they weren't attending – we spoke to young people, children, ethnic minorities, inner-city communities, women,' Robertson recalled. 'The key reason why people weren't attending cricket was summed up in a word: inaccessible. The game was perceived as being socially inaccessible. Some people thought it was a posh sport and they had to go to county games in a suit and tie.' Over the course of their research, the ECB found that one-third of the population, were 'cricket tolerators'. They neither disliked the game nor attended matches.

The research made clear what this demographic wanted: a condensed format of the game on midweek evenings or weekends, lasting no more than three hours. 'The killer finding was we found 19 million people who were there for convincing,' Robertson said. 'The format that they were keen about and would come along to was the 20-over format.'

The concept was not new – T20 was a staple of club cricket around the country – but it had never been played at professional level before. The ECB executives, in need of a cure for the ailing summer game, were ardently in favour. The trouble was, those with the votes – the county chairmen – were not.

On the morning of 21 April 2002, English cricket was on the brink of rejecting T20. As the vote at Lord's loomed, the ECB's chairman Lord MacLaurin – whose cricketing instincts were always far more radical than might have been expected of a Conservative member of the House of Lords – decided to 'flatter the fuck' out of the county chairmen, as one observer recalled.

Some were wooed, but it did not look like enough, as became apparent in the meeting of the county chairmen immediately prior to the vote. Minutes before the vote, Bill Midgley, the 60-year-old Durham chairman who had previously opposed T20, gave a speech likening the debate to the staunch opposition to the creation of one-day cricket 40 years earlier. It proved decisive: the vote of the counties and the Marylebone Cricket Club (MCC) was won 11-7, with the MCC abstaining. T20 cricket was born.

For all the gimmicks, T20 looked just enough like cricket that it was still recognisable. Cricket remained an 11-a-side game, played with six-ball overs; a mooted 'golden over', in which the batting side would choose an over for runs to count double, was rejected as too manufactured. Earlier innovations – Cricket Max, an abbreviated form of the game, designed by the former New Zealand batsman Martin Crowe; and the Hong Kong Sixes, a five-overs-a-side game played by teams of six – had been a qualified success without taking off, and were considered to have deviated too much from the sport's underlying norms.

The first-ever delivery in a professional T20 match – between Hampshire and Sussex on 13 June 2003 – was a wide, from Sussex's James Kirtley. Thereafter the first year of English domestic T20 was a resounding success. The notorious English rain stayed away: all 48 games in 2003 were completed and the 20-over format produced an accelerated form of the game, with all the action of a 50-over match crammed into less than half the time. Over 18 exhilarating days, Robertson's target of an average attendance of 5,000 was cleared; it would have been considerably higher than 5,300 had county grounds had greater capacity. No county chief executive would ever again question whether they should play T20. *Wisden Cricketers' Almanack*, regarded as the sport's bible, noted that the competition 'struck the motherlode of public affection for cricket that runs just below the surface crust of apparent indifference'. The ECB had got very lucky, but they had also got a lot right.

Even as the game's popularity snowballed – South Africa immediately launched a domestic T20 competition of their own, to great acclaim, and a swathe of other countries, including Pakistan, Australia and New Zealand, soon followed, its fundamental image, as nothing more than frivolous fun, remained.

When New Zealand hosted Australia in the inaugural T20 international in 2005, the match drew more resemblance to a charity fundraiser than elite-level sport. The New Zealand players dressed up in retro kits and outfits – batsman Hamish Marshall wore frizzy hair more at home in a 1970s disco, and Australian fast bowler Glenn McGrath did an impersonation of Trevor Chappell's notorious underarm delivery. The sport itself was a sideshow. Australian captain Ricky Ponting scored 98 not out in his side's victory yet, after the game, regarded the whole spectacle as a gimmick. 'I think it's difficult to play seriously. If it does become an international game then I'm sure the novelty won't be there all the time.'

***

Because of its brevity, T20 completely transformed how risk was conceived in cricket. In longer formats, the number of balls available to a batting team compelled batsmen to manage risk, to ensure that the team were not bowled out prematurely. In T20 the number of balls available to a batting team (120) was under half that in 50-over cricket (300) – but they still possessed 11 batsmen. A team could lose a wicket every 12 balls and still bat out their full allocation of 20 overs. Even Chris Martin, the New Zealand bowler regarded as the worst Test batsman of the 21st century, was only dismissed every 11.82 balls in Test cricket. In T20, then, defence virtually ceased to matter.

Defence had historically formed the bedrock of batting because the tactical and technical foundation of cricket was the first-class game – the oldest format played at professional level. That first-class cricket was played across multiple days placed an emphasis on wicket preservation to enable batsmen to bat for as long as possible and steadily accumulate runs. Traditional cricket coaching has therefore always prescribed the foundation of a strong batting technique to be a solid defence.

In Test cricket, the bowlers were charged with attacking – to take wickets – while batsmen traditionally emphasised defence. The framework of T20 cricket inverted this relationship – suddenly batsmen were the offence as they looked to score as quickly as possible and bowlers the defence as they looked to prevent batsmen from doing so.

This was a paradigm shift. T20 was not merely a shorter version of one-day cricket; the difference was altogether more profound, necessitating a wholly different approach to playing.

The format's incipient years were defined by an underlying tactical anarchy. 'Nobody knows anything,' the screenwriter William Goldman once said of the entertainment industry. So it was in the first skirmishes of T20.

Worcestershire began the first summer by virtually inverting their batting order, aiming to use their bowlers' big hitting to exploit the fielding restrictions in the first six overs. They even signed a big-hitting club player, David Taylor, on a specialist T20 contract, a harbinger of how T20 would encourage specialisation. Yet such attempts to innovate looked more like over-complication; Taylor harrumphed 46 on his debut, but averaged 11.71 in seven county T20 matches. The promoted bowlers, meanwhile, set about proving that uncultured hoicking was no way to score runs in T20. On the second day of professional T20, Matt Mason, a hulking Australian fast bowler, was sent in to bat at four, imbued with intent to clear the ropes. Every ball he swung, with ever more ferocity. Every ball he missed, until he was caught for nought off ten balls; Worcestershire's were left with insufficient time and the team stumbled to 122 all out. It was a salutary lesson in the pitfalls of wrong-headed strategy in T20.

Yet even in the bedlam of T20's first years, there were glimpses of sides succeeding through recognising what could be achieved by taking the game a little more seriously. John Inverarity, the coach of Warwickshire, used to bellow 'two' to his players, reflecting a belief that the side who scored the most twos would win. His side reached the final in 2003. Derbyshire, convinced that the six Powerplay overs – with only two fielders permitted outside the 30-yard circle – were pivotal and that batsmen were more dangerous if they could line up a particular bowler, used six different bowlers across the six overs.

Leicestershire were the first to succeed through embracing how, for all that T20 is seen as the most instinctive, spontaneous format of the game, it also lends itself best to planning. They overcame the limitations of a small playing squad and budget to triumph in the Twenty20 Cup in 2004 and 2006, giving a glimpse of what was possible.

'No one had really decided how to play it. They basically just thought it was "slog it as far as you can and that's it", and that spinners wouldn't even be a factor in the game,' recalled fast bowler Charles Dagnall. Leicestershire took a different approach. 'We weren't great in other competitions, and we thought we've got a chance here.'

'We were ahead of our time as far as planning and game management,' remembered the wicketkeeper Paul Nixon. 'Having the right opportunities at the right times, reading pitches, knowing the right times for hitters, the right times to be able to box clever, and save hitters for the end, to get a new batsman in, not losing two wickets together, change of orders, having certain batsmen that can target spin – certain things that you can really latch on to that you can take on most pitches.'

Leicestershire managed the pace of the game intelligently, slowing things down when they were batting to help them think and speeding things up when they were bowling, to rush the opposition batsmen.

At a time when many teams experimented opening with pinch-hitters – weaker batsmen with a penchant for scoring quickly – their batting followed a simple mantra. Leicestershire put their best batsman, Brad Hodge, at the top of the order so he could face the most balls. They planned where they wanted to be after the end of the six-over Powerplay and mapped out the progression of their innings. They emphasised having partnerships between a hitter and a player who would rotate the strike. They believed this combination meant they avoided a build-up of dot balls if two hitters struggled to get going or avoided falling behind the required rate if they had two strike rotators at the crease. The top eight batsmen were always padded up and ready to go, enabling Leicester to have a flexible batting order. They would send in players to target certain bowling types; the earliest intimation of a team playing to match-ups, well before the advent of data analysis elevated it to become a major part of the game.

With the ball, Leicestershire attacked early on, even if it meant leaking boundaries, believing that ultimately the best way to contain a T20 innings was to take regular wickets. They played with two frontline spinners – Claude Henderson and Jeremy Snape – with Hodge offering an extra spin option, and extended the boundaries at Grace Road to make the spinners harder to hit; sometimes, Hodge would even open the bowling with his off spin. They put mandatory men in the 30-yard circle to save one, rather than leaving them on the edge of the circle, reasoning that they could not afford to let the opposition score off every ball of the innings. They used Dagnall's inswing in the middle overs, believing that it was harder for batsmen to free their arms than against outswingers.

And they innovated. At T20 practice sessions, bowlers experimented audaciously – running in, stopping again, and then restarting; bowling with no front arm; looking away as they ran in – to try to put batsmen off. Bowlers were encouraged to master not just one slower ball, but several. Tweaks were made to the field before a bowler delivered a slower ball.

Now, none of these steps look revolutionary or, perhaps, anything more than an implementation of the obvious. But low-budget Leicestershire's triumphs were a hint of what it was possible to achieve by embracing T20 not simply as an abridged version of limited overs cricket, but an entirely different sport.

'Everyone knew their specific roles and despite looking like a pretty unfashionable team we had some players that were sort of humble enough to play for the team and play the role,' recalled Snape. 'We were in the first four finals and in such a volatile tournament to be in four finals and win two of them is a pretty good effort. So that's not a fluke. That's not chaos, that's a strategy and we knew how to manage risk.'

***

The nature of T20's inception, as a marketing tool as much as a serious sporting contest, and the complexities of the game itself, informed the early coverage of it. Lots was said about T20's impact on the sport; very little was said about the game itself, and coverage was almost infantilised. 'Very few writers have tried to get under the bonnet of T20,' the former England captain Michael Atherton noted in *The Times* in 2016. 'What T20 means for cricket as a sport has been the prevailing narrative, while there has been precious little writing about the game itself.'

Traditional forms of cricket, played over days rather than hours, more obviously lent themselves to considered analysis. And so an image was created that T20 – while popular and fun – was somehow lacking in sporting integrity. Such was the inherent snobbery and conservatism of those within the sport that T20 was treated with little more than casual disregard. That much was embodied by the way in which the T20 World Cup was created.

For the International Cricket Council (ICC), a T20 world championship held obvious appeal. They were about to go out to tender on commercial rights for 2007 to 2015 and believed that a T20 World Cup would add significant value. And the ICC feared that, if they did not take ownership of a world championship, somebody else would try to, raising the spectre of a schism in cricket, like that caused by the Australian mogul Kerry Packer's World Series Cricket in the 1970s when he lured players away from the international game with comparably vast sums of money. 'There were entrepreneurs, broadcasters, sponsors and multinational businesses that would seek to claim the right to run the international version of T20 if the ICC did not stake its claim and actually hold the first event,' ICC chief executive Malcolm Speed wrote in *Sticky Wicket: A Decade of Change in World Cricket*.

Before an ICC board meeting in March 2006, Speed prepared a paper arguing that there was 'first-mover advantage' for the ICC in organising an international T20 tournament before anyone else. But, just like the ECB had found four years earlier, other administrators were not natural supporters of the concept.

Two countries stood out in their opposition: India and Pakistan, the two nations with the most cricket fans. The Pakistan Cricket Board's chairman Shahryar Khan said that he had never been to a T20 match and never would; awkward, then, when a PowerPoint presentation later showed him presenting the trophy at the final of Pakistan's domestic tournament.

Most problematic of all was India's stance. 'T20? Why not ten-ten or five-five or one-one?' So Niranjan Shah, the honorary secretary of the Board of Control for Cricket in India (BCCI), thundered, endlessly repeating one mantra: 'India will never play T20.' Eventually India and Pakistan agreed to the creation of the World T20 (WT20) from 2007, but only on the condition that participation in 2007 was not obligatory. The ICC's decision to initially call the tournament the World T20 – rather than the T20 World Cup, as they would later brand it – reflected a certain uncertainty about how the tournament would go. In the ICC commercial rights contracts for the 2007 to 2015 period, there was only a stipulation of one WT20 every four years. A second planned edition of the tournament each four-year cycle was marked as either a WT20 or a Champions Trophy (a 50-over ODI tournament billed as a mini World Cup), leaving the ICC scope to row back from the WT20 if it was not successful.

India and Pakistan only made it to South Africa, for the inaugural event, because of shrewd politicking from Speed and Ehsan Mani, the ICC president. While discussions about the tournament's creation were taking place, the ICC was inviting countries to make submissions for hosting the 2011 and 2015 ICC World Cups. The bid submitted by the four Asian Test nations – Bangladesh, India, Pakistan and Sri Lanka – did not comply with ICC requirements, but there were no alternatives; Speed and Mani persuaded England to bid too, to give the ICC more clout.

Initially, the ICC rejected the Asian bid on account of it being non-compliant. The Asian nations were shocked. At a subsequent private meeting, Mani offered to allow Bangladesh, India, Pakistan and Sri Lanka to submit another bid if they all agreed to participate in the inaugural WT20. The BCCI reluctantly agreed.

Preparation for the tournament was scarcely less slapdash than before Hollioake chose to bowl on T20's first night. The ICC didn't even bother to organise a qualifying tournament, instead inviting non-Test nations based on their ODI performances. Only a two-week window could be found to squeeze in the tournament. But there was a happy by-product of this bedlam, making the tournament feel breezy and fun, and an antidote to the bloated, torturously long and over-corporatised 50-over World Cup in the West Indies earlier that year.

Unlike that event, teams did not prioritise the T20 World Cup. England and India did not even bother to organise any warm-up matches, because their own series in England did not finish in time. That was not the only indication of India's disinterest. Legendary players Sachin Tendulkar, Sourav Ganguly, Anil Kumble, V.V.S. Laxman and Rahul Dravid were all left out of the squad. No one was quite sure who to choose in their place; India's first domestic T20 tournament only began in April 2007, later than any other Test nation, and matches were not even televised. India were the last Test nation to play a T20 international, and had only played one before the WT20.

Yet the two teams who did not want to contest the tournament – two teams preoccupied with one-day internationals, but who had both crashed out of that year's 50-over World Cup at the first stage – would end up being the best two. This quirk of fate would have extraordinary consequences for the sport.

Pakistan sent a full-strength team to South Africa and, given the presence of Shahid Afridi, a prototype T20 cricketer before anyone had created the format, their success was not overly surprising. More unexpected – and *transformative* – was India's performance.

At 26, Mahendra Singh Dhoni was appointed captain, the first time he had ever led India in any format, embodying the sense that the nation was treating the WT20 as little more than glorified exhibition matches.

Two rousing weeks ensued. India won a bowl-out – T20's version of a penalty shootout – with Pakistan. Yuvraj Singh thrashed six sixes in an over off Stuart Broad. An epic semi-final, still one of the finest games in T20 history, was played out against Australia. And on 24 September 2007, Dhoni entrusted the medium-pacer Joginder Sharma to defend 13 from the last over of the final against Pakistan.

Sharma's first delivery betrayed the tension in Johannesburg. It was hurled so far away wide of the off stump that it ended up off the pitch altogether. Pakistan's fans responded to the umpire's signal with an outcry of delight.

Now Dhoni ran to calm down his bowler. Sharma responded with a delivery that swung away outside off stump. Misbah-ul-Haq could only swing and miss. Now, Indian supporters were rapt.

Not for long. The next delivery was an egregious full toss. Misbah, already striding down the wicket, harrumphed it straight down the ground for six.

A repeat would clinch the first World T20 for Pakistan. Dhoni lost his impenetrable demeanour, furrowing his brow as he returned from talking to Sharma. Perhaps he regretted asking him, and not the more experienced Harbhajan Singh, to bowl the final over.

The next ball, once again, was well outside off stump. There was no reason for Misbah to digress from what had worked so well the previous delivery. Instead, he shuffled across his crease and attempted to scoop the ball over fine leg, a shot he had played with distinction throughout the tournament.

Yet Sharma was too slow to play the shot against; there was not enough pace on the ball. So, rather than hurtle towards the fine leg boundary, the ball remained marooned in the air. Sreesanth grasped the catch with a nonchalance that defied the pressure of the moment. Misbah slouched to his knees in despair, unable to rag himself away from the ground; India's entire support staff ran on to the field in their joy, and the players were soon embraced by Bollywood star Shah Rukh Khan. In a format India did not care for a fortnight earlier, Indian tricolours were now ubiquitous in the crowd and far beyond.

Sharma would never play international cricket again. He would become Deputy Superintendent of Police in Haryana. But he helped usher in a revolution that transformed the sport forever.

***

In most major international sports, the game's beating heart – the source of most matches and cash – has long been at club level. Before T20, cricket was the major exception. Since the first Ashes Test match between England and Australia in 1877, cricket's pinnacle has been at international level. Club matches were widely viewed as subsidiary to the international game; more a tool to produce international players than a rival attraction to marquee nation against nation fixtures. Before T20 was created, only around 10% of the sport's total wealth came from club matches. In football, about 80% of the sport's wealth came from club games.

The difference reflected cricket's roots and individual development. Yet it also amounted to an enormous missed opportunity. Anyone who could turn domestic cricket from an addendum to the international game to the main event could bring a huge influx of cash to the sport.

Lalit Modi, an Indian businessman who had made millions selling cigarettes, and a cricketing fanatic, had a plan. He believed that cricket did not need to be dominated by international matches alone. After spending much of his youth in America he sensed that India was ripe for an American-style sports league too – with privately owned domestic teams and the competition featuring the best players, both from India and overseas. So he proposed an inter-city cricket league, to be played over four to six weeks each year, under floodlights at the country's best cricket grounds. Like an Indian soap opera, the league would draw in fans to return night after night.

The plan failed. The BCCI, perhaps loath to give up control to individual franchises, did not agree to Modi's idea for a 50-over franchise competition. That was in 1996. Twelve years later, everything was different.

It would be easy to say that the BCCI's new embrace of domestic franchise cricket, in the T20 format, owed to their vision, awareness of dwindling attention spans and sense of cricket's shifting sands. Certainly, it owed something to all of these. But, more than anything else, the IPL, the glitziest club competition that the sport had ever known, was born out of fear.

On 3 April 2007, Subhash Chandra, an Indian billionaire who pioneered cable television in India in the 1990s, announced the creation of the Indian Cricket League (ICL). Zee TV, the cable network Chandra founded, had been outbid for rights to broadcast Indian internationals. So Chandra hatched a plan: he would organise his own private league to provide content for Zee TV to broadcast. That way, he would never need to worry about being outbid for rights ever again.

The ICL would be a T20 tournament, owned by Zee, consisting of six city-based teams. Zee's ICL board comprised former international players including Kapil Dev, one of the enduring icons of Indian cricket. Dev's home town, Chandigarh, provided the tournament with a stadium. When the tournament was officially launched, in August 2007, it revealed that it had signed leading Pakistan players Inzamam-ul-Haq and Mohammad Yousuf, West Indies great Brian Lara and a number of other internationals from India and the rest of the world.

The ICL amounted to a profound threat to the Indian board. Effectively it challenged their monopoly on scheduling cricket in the country, just as Kerry Packer's World Series Cricket had in Australia 30 years earlier. Realisation of how the ICL imperilled their position drove the BCCI to confront it.

First came a brutal clampdown. Any player who signed with the league was threatened to be banned for life from cricket organised by the BCCI. 'Our stand is very clear,' said the BCCI secretary Niranjan Shah. 'Players who take part in the ICL will never be eligible to play for the country again. It is up to the players to decide what they want to do.' The BCCI pressurised the ICC, and then other national boards, not to recognise the competition. Anyone who signed up risked never being able to play international cricket again.

Second came imitation, and an embrace of Modi's plan. Two days after the inaugural T20 World Cup began in South Africa, the BCCI announced that they would launch the IPL the following April. For the first time in cricket, this would comprise privately owned teams. At the official launch of the IPL in September 2007 Modi was named as the league's convener. Now he could make good on the vision he had outlined two years earlier, when he declared, 'Cricket in India is a $2 billion-a-year market. We are sitting on a gold mine. Our players should be paid on a par with international footballers and NBA stars, in millions of dollars and not measly rupees.'

In the months ahead, Modi relentlessly signed up dozens of the world's greatest players to agree to join the league. Given that players stood to earn up to £1 million for six weeks, this proved little challenge.

India's victory in Johannesburg had spurred interest in the country in T20, leading Modi to seal a £500 million broadcasting deal, over ten years, even before the identity of any of the teams was known. The eight teams were sold for a total of £367 million, payable to the BCCI over a decade. The owners included film stars Shah Rukh Khan, Preity Zinta and Shilpa Shetty, ensuring a perfect synergy of cricket and Bollywood. The BCCI had made almost £1 billion even before a ball had been bowled in the IPL, one of the most audacious inceptions to any sporting league in history.

On 20 February 2008, a collection of India's richest businessmen and biggest Bollywood stars lined up at the Hilton Towers Hotel on Mumbai's western waterfront at 11 a.m. By the time they left that afternoon, they had spent £21 million on contracting 78 players for a seven-week tournament – and cricket had entered a new age.

The auction was not just designed to distribute players between teams. It was designed to be 'the opening episode in the new series of the soap opera', recalled Andrew Wildblood, the joint architect of the IPL alongside Modi. 'The auction is the best possible trailer for the new series.'

ONE

NEVER FEAR THE AIR

'You have to travel at such speeds that you're
going to come off the road occasionally'
Brendon McCullum

After facing five of the first six balls of the match, Brendon McCullum had still not scored a run. In T20 cricket – he would later acknowledge – that is almost worse than getting out. The first over had been bowled by Praveen Kumar, an intelligent seam bowler who bowled a tight line and had given McCullum no room to free his arms and attack.

'I was swinging at every one of them but I was missing every one by a foot,' he recalled. 'I don't normally get nervous but for that innings I really was. I was batting with Sourav Ganguly and Ricky Ponting was at three. There were 45,000 people in an atmosphere I've never experienced anything like before.'

McCullum, a New Zealander renowned for his ebullient approach, had been in terrible form in the nets in the lead-up to the start of the inaugural IPL season. Sharing a dressing room with legends of the game such as Ganguly and Ponting after being sold at the player auction for the life-changing fee of £355,000, the 26-year-old felt an unusual pressure to justify both his presence and his price tag. He would be playing for the Kolkata Knight Riders (KKR), one of the most glamorous teams, owned by the Bollywood actor Shah Rukh Khan.

As the first match of the season drew nearer, McCullum had been so out of sync that Matthew Mott, Kolkata's assistant coach, decided to have some one-on-one time with him in the nets, feeding him balls from a bowling machine in an effort to help him regain some rhythm.

After an hour of fruitless effort Mott decided to abandon the session and instead took McCullum to the hotel bar for a beer. That seemed to relax him and he scored 40 and 50 in consecutive warm-up matches over the next few days. Suddenly he felt like he belonged at the crease again.

One over into the first IPL match, that feeling of belonging had deserted him once more. The IPL had been launched earlier that evening with a dazzling opening ceremony featuring lasers, fireworks and Bollywood stars but the quiet start to the match had sucked energy from the stadium.

There was more to this match than the result. Despite the millions of dollars of investment and despite there being one billion cricket fans in India, until that night the IPL was little more than a concept. 'We really needed that one spark which would set the IPL's inaugural season alight,' said the league's impresario Lalit Modi in James Astill's book *The Great Tamasha*. 'I was sceptical, I had my doubts, I was always afraid deep down. At the end of the day, if the consumer didn't buy it, there was nothing more we could do.'

McCullum played and missed at the first ball of the second over, too: he was now on nought off six balls. 'It was swing out or get out,' said McCullum, who recognised that he would be more use to his team sitting back in the dugout than staying out in the middle using up valuable balls. This enlightened approach demonstrated an intricate understanding of the nature of T20. It was about to define the most critical innings of his life.

'If it's not meant to be then it's not meant to be,' McCullum recalled thinking. 'Just keep swinging.' That the next ball was full and in McCullum's arc was essentially irrelevant; he was attacking anyway and slogged across the line of the ball. McCullum regularly cited the role of luck in a game with margins as fine as T20; his shot was one that could have lobbed to the fielder just as easily as it could have cleared him. He got just enough on the ball to get it over the fielder's head and score four. The crowd roared; McCullum – and the IPL – had their first boundary. 'I just kept swinging and something clicked. I don't know what it was but suddenly I calmed down a lot and then I was able to do what I did which pretty much changed my life.'

What followed in the next hour and a half was one of the most significant and spectacular innings in cricket history. McCullum, clad in the space-age black and gold livery of the Knight Riders, blazed an absurd 158 not out off 73 balls – an individual score that would remain a world record for five years.

McCullum's innings contained 13 sixes, each shot like fireworks into the night sky. The Royal Challengers Bangalore (RCB) bowling attack comprised international standard bowlers but McCullum treated them with disdain – brazenly charging out from his crease, carving the ball over the off side and heaving it over the leg side. This was batting that propelled cricket into a new age. 'To score a hundred in a T20 game was an amazing achievement,' recalled John Buchanan, the Knight Riders' head coach. 'But to score 158 . . . He certainly redefined or at least told everybody what T20 cricket could be if you took in the right mindset, were aggressive, had a bit of luck and just had the courage and bravery to keep going.'

For Modi and the IPL it was the perfect beginning. The stadium was in a frenzy. It didn't matter that McCullum was playing for the away team – this was an innings of the purest entertainment. The runs surged and the music blared – Kolkata's owner Shah Rukh Khan was dancing in the aisles. 'It was when Brendon hit what he hit that I knew it [the IPL] would work,' Modi told Astill. 'It was slam-dunk cricket. The ball was being hit out over the ropes, you had people screaming and shouting and jumping. The next day I went to Brendon and said thank you very much for making my tournament a success. To me he was my hero. The man who fast-tracked my dream into a reality.'

In truth the IPL would have worked anyway. The power in cricket had been shifting eastwards from England – the cradle of the game – to India – the sport's financial behemoth – for decades. The IPL, with its heady cocktail of money, cricket and Bollywood, was the distillation of this change. McCullum's impudent 158 not out was the emblem of a new age.

The inaugural IPL was a runaway success: television ratings were huge and stadiums were packed. 'Although it is impossible to be sure from such a recent perspective,' wrote Scyld Berry in his Editor's Notes of the 2009 *Wisden Cricketers' Almanack*, 'it looks as though the supranational IPL is the single biggest change in cricket not merely since the advent of the limited-overs game in the 1960s but of fixtures between countries in the 19th century: that is, since the invention of international or Test cricket.' Berry was right; the IPL was a tournament that would change cricket forever.

Instantly, the IPL recalibrated the entire economics of the sport. Until the IPL, cricket had been a game dominated and entirely funded by international competition. This was in contrast to the world's other major sports – football, basketball and baseball – where club competition was predominant. Cricket's reliance on international competition left it vulnerable to the natural imbalance of nation against nation contests, with talent restricted by borders.

Although T20 leagues had existed before the IPL they were comparatively tame, featuring almost exclusively local domestic players and none of the razzmatazz. The nature of the IPL – with private ownership, celebrity influence and vast sums of money – changed everything. The IPL alerted cricket boards to the potential value of their domestic game. Within ten years major leagues with the potential to attract the world's best players had been established in Australia, Bangladesh, Pakistan, the Caribbean and England. Together with the IPL these six leagues established a year-round T20 circuit, running parallel to, and in direct competition with, the international game and sometimes each other.

It was apt that McCullum played that momentous innings, for very few other players have so embodied T20 cricket's essence. Here was cricket – compressed and radicalised, heightened and elevated. And here was McCullum – a hurricane of a cricketer, fiercely competitive, a stunningly audacious batsman, an all-action wicketkeeper or fielder, depending on his team's needs, and a sportsman who conceived of himself as an entertainer. 'You literally feel like a gladiator in a coliseum. There's 35,000 people, they've all turned up to watch you play and wishing you well but if it doesn't work, then it doesn't work but you still get up and go again . . . T20 definitely aligned with my style of cricket.'

***

Growing up in the 1980s McCullum's hero was the legendary West Indian batsman Viv Richards. Richards was one of the first players to reconfigure cricket's traditional approach to batting by eschewing defence in favour of attack.

'The big change really came from a mindset point of view,' explained Simon Katich, who played 56 Test matches for Australia and enjoyed T20 success as a player and a coach. 'We were always taught to value our wicket, but in T20 you need to play with no fear of losing your wicket.'

This attitude was wound deep into the fabric of the game. In the book *The Game of Life*, Berry wrote: 'When a batsman has been dropped by a fielder we say he was "given a life". We are saying that a batsman is alive when he is at the wicket. When he is out, therefore, he is dead, killed by the bowler, perhaps aided and abetted by the fielders. If the batsman makes a false stroke, it can be a "fatal" mistake. Thus a dismissal in cricket can be equated to death.' This elegiac assessment of a wicket distils the psychological depth and weight of batting, and the importance traditionally placed on defence and on wicket preservation.

Across history Test batting has generally become increasingly attacking. But it wasn't until the advent of limited overs cricket in the 1960s – with various competitions ranging from 40 overs up to 65 overs – that the game's tempo began to change. Once the number of deliveries available to a batting team was restricted, as was the case in limited overs matches, batsmen were compelled to place a greater emphasis on run scoring which in turn forced them to compromise their wicket.

Richards, who made his debut for the West Indies in 1974, was a trailblazer for this aggressive mentality. 'The first thing that came to mind was the need to attack,' he explained in an interview with ESPNcricinfo. 'Sometimes some of us just look to defend. When we think of defending, sometimes we get deliveries that need to be dealt with, and we haven't quite dealt with them the way we should because we are in such a defensive mode.' Across his ODI career Richards scored at a rate of 90 runs per 100 balls in an era when players typically scored around 65 runs per 100 balls. Years after he had retired Richards fittingly reversed the defensive foundation of batting by saying in an interview, 'I would rather have a guy who can play the shots and teach him the defence than a guy who doesn't have any shots.' This implied that attacking batting was the more valuable skill, something that went against mainstream opinion in the sport. Attacking batting – often described as slogging – was widely considered uncouth compared to the more noble art of defence and steady accumulation. Hitting across the line was viewed as an indulgence to be resisted until a batsman had played himself in.

'There are good balls and there are bad balls and any time you get a bad ball you've got to hit it for runs,' said the former England batsman Geoffrey

Boycott in a masterclass on BT Sport. 'But you've got to remember that in Test cricket there are good bowlers who are going to bowl you good balls so you can't hit every ball. So you have to learn to stay in.'

Richards' approach was partly enabled by his role as a middle order batsman. During his career the typical pattern of a team innings in ODIs was for the opening batsmen – tasked with facing the new ball and the opposition's best bowlers – to bat cautiously at the start of the innings and lay a platform for the more aggressive players, such as Richards, to capitalise on and accelerate from later. This pattern was inverted at the 1992 World Cup by the moustachioed New Zealander Mark Greatbatch, another player who would leave an indelible mark on the game and on attacking batting.

The 1992 World Cup, played in Australia and New Zealand, was a modernising tournament. It saw the introduction of new rules to the ODI format including teams wearing coloured clothing and playing with a white ball, but more pertinently it signalled the introduction of fielding restrictions which permitted only two fielders outside a 30-yard circle around the 22-yard strip in the first 15 overs. New Zealand's coach Warren Lees and captain Martin Crowe – open to innovations to reinvigorate their struggling team – recognised that the fielding restrictions provided an opportunity for quick runs. They asked Greatbatch – despite him playing all 39 of his ODI innings until then in the middle order and being in terrible form before the tournament – to open. Lees and Crowe wanted Greatbatch to bat positively and try to get New Zealand ahead of the game early on.

That's exactly what he did. Rather than batting cautiously in the manner of other specialist openers of the era, Greatbatch instead attacked the opening bowlers. In his first innings of the tournament New Zealand were only chasing a modest target of 191 but Greatbatch batted aggressively, flaying the hard new ball against South Africa's vaunted pace attack. 'There was a fair bit of adrenaline pumping,' Greatbatch remembered in an interview on ESPNcricinfo. 'In those days four an over at the start of the innings was quick. The norm was about three. We were scoring at five or six an over and that was a real shift in momentum.' Greatbatch continued in a similar vein through the rest of the tournament, blitzing three rapid fifties in all and finishing with 313 runs at a strike rate of 88. New Zealand, riding on the wave of Greatbatch's early aggression, exceeded expectations and reached the semi-finals. Greatbatch had done more than take his country deep into the World Cup; he had transformed the role of the one-day opener.

New Zealand's success emboldened others to adopt similar tactics. Sri Lanka were shock winners of the 1996 ODI World Cup thanks largely to their explosive opening partnership of Sanath Jayasuriya and Romesh Kaluwitharana who took Greatbatch's aggression to another level, both scoring well above a run a ball across the competition. Jayasuriya, whose flashy upper cuts and pick-up pulls expertly cleared the inner ring and exploited the fielding restrictions, racked up 221 runs off just 168 deliveries in another step change for batting. Jayasuriya was awarded man of the tournament despite 16 players scoring more runs than him; how quickly he had scored mattered more than how many he had scored.

By the turn of the century attacking the new ball and taking advantage of the early fielding restrictions became the new norm. The late 1990s and early 2000s gave birth to a coterie of attacking openers in ODIs: Matthew Hayden and Adam Gilchrist for Australia, Sachin Tendulkar and Virender Sehwag for India, Marcus Trescothick for England, Herschelle Gibbs for South Africa, Nathan Astle for New Zealand and Shahid Afridi for Pakistan. The arrival of T20 would galvanise attacking batting once more – but its icons were standing on the shoulders of giants.

***

McCullum's batting, inspired by Richards and infused with the spirit of his countryman Greatbatch, was perfectly aligned with T20. Like Greatbatch, McCullum was an aggressive shot-maker and like Greatbatch, his role was to take advantage of the Powerplay fielding restrictions, which in T20 lasted just six overs.

McCullum's IPL century launched an iconic T20 career. In the decade after 2008 arguably the only batsman to overshadow McCullum's impact on the format was the monolithic West Indian Chris Gayle. While Gayle's brilliance was defined by his colossal power, McCullum's contribution was more profound. McCullum was blessed with rapid hand speed and a wonderful eye, but his defining feature was his mind. If Gayle was T20's gunslinger, McCullum was its philosopher king.

There was a critical difference between T20 and longer forms of cricket and McCullum immediately grasped it. His recognition in his autobiography that his five scoreless balls at the start of his totemic IPL century were 'almost as bad as getting out' cut straight to the heart of batting in the 20-over format. Even ODI revolutionaries like Richards at least had some flexibility; the framework of the game encouraged them to attack, but the length of the contest allowed them time to pick their moment. It was a luxury not afforded to T20 batsmen.

The length of T20 represented a tipping point in the precarious relationship between attack and defence. Now, defence virtually ceased to matter; the overwhelming focus was on attacking. T20 reduced batting to a simple credo, perfectly encapsulated in the immortal words of the Indian opener Sehwag: 'See ball, hit ball.' According to the data analytics company CricViz, between 2010 and 2018, batsmen in T20 attempted to score off 91% of deliveries compared to 79% in 50-over cricket and 52% in first-class cricket. Naturally, scoring rates in T20 were markedly higher than in other formats – on average teams scored at 7.84 runs per over compared to 5.28 in ODIs and 3.21 in Tests in this time.

Scoring Attempts (2010–2018)		
First-Class Cricket	**List A Cricket**	**T20 Cricket**
52%	79%	91%

For McCullum, as for Sehwag, this aggressive approach came entirely naturally. In longer forms of cricket he had to hold himself back, but in T20, it was ideal: 'I always wanted to play in a free-spirited manner and that aligned with T20.' McCullum's attitude towards attacking batting was shaped by his acceptance that it was an inconsistent, but essential, approach in the shortest form of the game. 'T20 forced the issue a bit because you have to travel at such speeds that you're going to come off the road occasionally.'

At every turn T20's new framework challenged cricket's old understanding which was shackled by conservatism.

Conventional wisdom prescribed that batsmen should take time to 'play themselves in' when they first arrived at the crease by getting used to the pace of the pitch and the nature of the bowlers. This method did have value, but in T20, with a premium on quick runs, batsmen had less time to do this. Batting in the Powerplay against the hard new ball and with just two fielders outside the circle certainly helped, but McCullum wasted very little time in getting going even by the standards of other openers. Between 2008 and 2018 he was one of only a dozen players who scored at more than a run a ball in the first over of the innings.

Another conservative trope of cricket was that it was considered 'smart cricket' if a batsman followed hitting a boundary by taking a single off the next ball – the implication being the batsman should be commended for resisting the temptation to get greedy and hit another boundary. McCullum despised such an approach. 'Nothing shits me more than boundary-one – and everyone claps and it's the old-school thinking . . . But to me you've passed up your opportunity to be able to win the game in that moment.'

Such was the scope of longer forms of cricket, changes in the direction of the match were obvious; major events were more spread out and therefore more discernible. But in T20 so much happened so fast it was hard to identify those that mattered and those that didn't. McCullum saw inactivity as the biggest crime. 'You have opportunities through a T20 game – and it might be in the fifth, sixth over – where your team is flying and you can put the opposition away. So you need to identify when that moment is and take the risk. If you get out doing it, then the other guys will then have another opportunity down the line, but you've got to try and take the opportunity when you can. If you can pick up a 20-run or 22-run over, not only have you potentially won the game, but you've got that guy under real pressure, maybe even taken him out of the attack. And then that forces the opposition to go a different way.'

McCullum's aggression belied the thought that went into his approach, which scotched the myth that T20 was a game of unrefined slogging, lacking any subtlety or strategy. 'There's a lot of preparation goes into how you play the game,' he explained. 'I'll be thinking, right; we are playing at the SCG [Sydney Cricket Ground], the wicket is likely to be on this side of the block, the wind is up today so there's going to be a short boundary on this side, here's their bowling line-up, the wicket might have a little bit of tennis ball bounce, this bowler is going to bowl back of a length, then they've got this bowler who is going to take pace off the ball and their spinners will open up. Where are my boundary options? How am I going to be able to get a big over if I'm behind in the game. What are the dangers on this wicket? What is likely to be a par score and how am I going to be able to make a contribution that's going to be sufficient to assist our team through 20 overs?

'So you're putting all of that in the mix and then when you go out there you've got that in the bank and you know that when you pull the trigger you're a) going to need a lot of luck and b) have to put out all the white noise so you can focus on watching the ball, so you can be in that still position, so you can put the plans into place. A lot of that gets misread. You can't be that aggressive unless you have some level of planning.'

What came so intuitively to McCullum – aggression, risk and daring – was anathema to some batsmen raised on first-class cricket who struggled to abandon the principles that had governed batting all their lives. 'When you try and play aggressive cricket,' said McCullum, 'you need an all-in mentality . . . you're asking guys to go out there and play at a level that may even be slightly uncomfortable for them but it will become more comfortable the more they do it. But initially it will be uncomfortable and what comes with that is a bit of insecurity and a bit of doubt and often a lot of inconsistencies.'

In longer forms of cricket, volume of runs and the average number of runs scored per dismissal was a good gauge of a player's worth. But in T20 it was possible for a batsman to make a large number of runs while harming his team's chances of winning – a phenomenon which became known as a match-losing innings. In T20 volume of runs was still relevant but the rate at which they were scored was far more significant.

In the 2009 T20 World Cup India's Ravindra Jadeja provided a perfect example of such an innings. Chasing England's 153 Jadeja arrived at the crease with India requiring 129 off 98 balls but he scratched his way to 25 off 35 balls, a strike rate of only 71.42. India fell short of the target by just three runs, having only lost five wickets.

Batting in the format is 'high risk, so there's a lot of failure in this format in particular. So it is being brave, sticking to a team plan,' said Kane Williamson, McCullum's successor as New Zealand captain and widely hailed as his country's best-ever Test match batsman. 'You certainly don't want to fear for your wicket. You always want to score and get as many runs as you can, but certainly not at the expense of the team, and there are innings that I think we've all seen in the past where guys have put themselves maybe before the team situation. And then scoring a big score looks really nice but it might have actually been to the detriment of the team. So it certainly is all about the team, and doing your best to move the team forward.'

The struggles in getting batsmen to reconfigure the worth of their own wickets were compounded by the scarcity of meaningful analysis of the T20 format in its earliest years. Not until at least 2008 did data analysis gain any traction in cricket and it wasn't until around 2012 that it started to become more commonplace. As a result traditional barometers of success and failure retained their value, especially among some team owners and coaches who formulated strategies and renewed contracts.

Incentives of players and teams did not always align. What might be best for the team – attacking hard and early in the innings – might not be best for the player, who would rather play himself in before accelerating later on, padding his own statistics and impressing teams who used unsophisticated means of judging players. McCullum recognised these innings when they happened. 'You can actually lose games by not attacking enough. I've witnessed it a fair few times. Guys have missed out in a couple of innings previously and just want to get to 20 off 20 before they pull the trigger.'

As analysis of T20 improved and the format matured, the advantages of aggression became increasingly evident. McCullum, Sehwag, Gayle and the hulking Australian Andrew Symonds led the way, soon followed by A.B. de Villiers, David Warner, Kieron Pollard, Andre Russell and Glenn Maxwell. These were the players who came to dominate the T20 circuit and they were rewarded handsomely with contracts in leagues around the world.

Increased attacking intent had a seismic effect on the way the game was played. In T20's early years batting perhaps experienced more change than at any point in its history, at least comparable to the introduction of helmets in the 1970s or the invention of the leg glance at the turn of the 20th century.

Perhaps the clearest example of the paradigm shift instigated by T20 was the career path of Australia's David Warner. Without a single first-class appearance to his name, Warner made his T20 international debut for Australia in January 2009, thumping 89 from 43 balls against South Africa. Belligerent batting in coloured clothing saw Warner force his way into Australia's Test team despite having made only 11 first-class appearances. He quickly established himself in the Test team with a century in his second match and he would go on to become one of their greatest-ever opening batsmen – adopting a very positive approach to dealing with the new ball, blunting it with aggression rather than stoicism. Warner taught himself the art of defence but his batting was unashamedly founded upon his attacking play. This career path supported the thoughts of Viv Richards that attack, not defence, was the more complex skill. England's Jos Buttler, India's Rishabh Pant and West Indies' Shimron Hetmyer were among those who later followed Warner's lead, with T20 performances laying the foundation for their Test careers.

The 20-over game heralded an age of fearlessness, power and innovation. Those who could not keep up were left behind by batting's very own industrial revolution and the pursuit of power.

***

T20 accelerated and intensified the evolution of batting. 'It has asked guys to play at an even higher speed,' said McCullum. 'It has asked batsmen to develop their game. Players are stronger and more powerful.'

Up until the late 20th century, cricketers were not renowned for their fitness or strength. That began to change with the establishment of the Australian Cricket Academy in Brisbane in 1988. The academy, as well as being the first of its kind, represented the acknowledgement that professional cricket was worthy of rigorous training and scientific preparation. Australia, who lorded over Test and one-day international cricket from 1995 to 2007, belatedly became the first team to hire a specialist fielding coach – the American Mike Young, who transported techniques learned in baseball, which was far ahead of cricket in this area. In the 2003 World Cup, which took place three months before T20 launched, Young was the only fielding coach used by any of the teams.

Before T20 the focus of fitness in cricket had generally been defined by the first-class game, where stamina, endurance and injury prevention were the priority. But the emphasis on boundary hitting in the 20-over game saw attention shift towards muscular power and strength. Within half a decade of T20's arrival, cricketers from the 21st century were unrecognisable to those that came before. Players spent as much time in the gym as they did in the nets – not on treadmills or exercise bikes but lifting weights – transforming themselves from lean and athletic to muscular and powerful. 'T20's been the thing that turned the corner,' said Young, who started working with Australia, in 2000. 'The athletes now are so much better. Seriously it's not even close. It's a different game.'

The most destructive batsmen in T20's earliest years – the likes of Andrew Symonds who bludgeoned a 34-ball hundred for Kent in 2004 or Graham Napier who scored 152 not out off 58 balls for Essex in 2008 – were big, brawny men.

At 5 feet 6 inches McCullum was short but he was immensely strong. Broad-shouldered, barrel-chested and with bulging forearms he cut an imposing figure. As a schoolboy McCullum played rugby for New Zealand's South Island – briefly selected at fly-half ahead of Dan Carter who would become an All Blacks legend.

It was not only the naturally powerful who could clear the ropes; as the players got stronger so too did their equipment. Significant advancements in the quality of cricket bats, made possible by the commercialisation of the industry in the 1990s, empowered even those of a slender build. Mechanisation enabled bat makers to produce far bigger bats that only weighed fractionally more than older models; from 1980 to 2016, the average size of bat edges more than doubled, from 18mm to 40mm. Modern bats performed as if they were turbocharged. It was indicative of their quality that even mishits and edges would sometimes fly for six and when the ball hit anywhere near the middle of the bat, six hitting looked almost effortless.

T20 batsmen would look down in their stance and see a weaponised chunk of wood, often emblazoned with stickers designed to fill the batsman with confidence. Towards the end of McCullum's career he launched his own equipment brand, named after his bloodstock company Vermair Racing. Their logo adorned his bats above the tagline 'never fear the air', because as he explained, 'There are no fielders up there'.

The bat company Mongoose went a step further and produced a bat specifically designed for six hitting. The Mongoose redesigned the traditional shape of the bat with the blade reduced by a third in length but twice as thick. The design ultimately proved impractical but that it ever existed at all was instructive of an age fuelled by power.

Arguably more important than increased strength or bigger bats was simply better attacking batting. Power hitting had traditionally been considered more a product of strength than ability. T20 drove batsmen to think about hitting in a systematic way, giving birth to the specialist hitting coach.

The former first-class batsman Julian Wood worked closely with Gloucestershire and England by focusing on hand speed and maximising good contact. Wood distanced himself from traditional batting coaching by downplaying the role of footwork and instead took learnings from baseball that emphasised the importance of head position and hip drive. His sole focus was helping batsmen hit the ball harder and further.

Wood was not alone in his pioneering approach. The Australian Trent Woodhill, who worked in the IPL and Big Bash League (BBL), also placed maximising good contact at the heart of his methods. Woodhill described himself as an 'organic batting coach' – someone who would enhance natural styles and tendencies rather than teach from a manual. Whatever it was that produced good contact was to be encouraged.

Such methods were augmented by a training routine which encapsulated the T20 era: range hitting. Traditionally cricket training was focused on net practice. But the emphasis on boundaries gave rise to a new training method which involved batsmen going to the middle of the ground, receiving throw-downs from a coach and looking to hit every ball as hard and as far as he could. The benefits to range hitting were twofold: not only did practising six hitting improve the techniques of players but the psychological benefits of batsmen watching the ball sail into the stands emboldened them to attempt similar shots in matches.

T20 encouraged batsmen to hit the ball harder, further and more adventurously. 'T20 has accelerated the process of playing 360 degrees,' said McCullum. Shots such as the reverse sweep and ramp had originated in 50-over cricket as a means of manoeuvring the field but T20 elevated them further still. 'The ramp shot was brought in [in 50-over cricket] to put fine leg back and bring mid-off up so you have an easier shot down the ground. But now the ramp is there because guys think they can hit it for six.'

In November 2018 the extent of batting's revolution was laid bare in an astonishing innings in the T10 League in Sharjah – a ten overs per side tournament launched the year previously. Just as T20 led batsmen to be more aggressive than in ODIs, so T10 led them to be more aggressive than in T20s. Batting first, the Northern Warriors scored a mind-warping total of 183 for 2 from their ten overs against the Punjabi Legends – clubbing 19 sixes and 10 fours. Their run rate of 18.30 runs per over would have seen them score 366 across 20 overs. This was batting of a new age being played by batsmen with hitherto unforeseen range and unimaginable scope.

Forty-three years previously in the opening match of the 1975 World Cup the Indian batsman Sunil Gavaskar essentially refused to attempt to chase England's apparently unattainable total of 332 in 60 overs, preferring instead to use the innings as practice, finishing with an infamous score of 36 not out off 175 balls. Gavaskar's innings at Lord's to that played by the Northern Warriors in Sharjah mapped the arc of modern batting where the impossible had become the mundane and the truth was stranger than fiction.

***

'That's 100 miles per hour!' exclaimed the commentator James Brayshaw. 'A cricket ball does not get bowled faster than that.'

The Australian Shaun Tait was one of the fastest bowlers cricket has ever known. Tait – nicknamed 'Wild Thing' because of his ability to bowl exceptionally fast but with little control – had a slow, lumbering run-up but a powerful, slingy action that hurled the ball towards the batsman at express pace. In a T20 against Pakistan at the Melbourne Cricket Ground in 2010, Tait bowled an over that ranked among the fastest of the modern era with an average speed of 97 mph, with one delivery recorded at 100 mph – only the second time in history a bowler had been recorded at such a speed.

Less than three weeks later Tait was in action again, this time against New Zealand in Christchurch. Tait's first three overs had been excellent – he had taken 2 for 20 on a day when the rest of Australia's attack had been pummelled by a rampant Brendon McCullum. As Tait stood at the top of his run-up, ready to deliver his fourth and final over, McCullum was 100 not out off just 54 balls.

McCullum did not see Tait's pace as a threat to his safety or his wicket. Instead with a short boundary behind him, he saw an opportunity.

'I simply didn't have the power to hit someone bowling full at 150 kph,' recalled McCullum. 'It was all right if he was bowling short because I could cut or pull him. But I didn't have the power to be able to go down the ground.'

As Tait reached the crease to deliver the first ball of the 19th over McCullum made a sudden move across his stumps to get in line with the ball and play the most outrageously daring shot: a ramp, over his head. 'The boundary was short behind me so I recognised that I had to play the shot. If I execute it I'll get a boundary, if I don't then I'll be in trouble. But we need a boundary at this point in time and that was the only way I felt I could get one.'

Tait had seen him coming and fired the ball wider outside off stump, following McCullum. The ball was now heading straight for McCullum's chest, who was squatted down low, legs splayed, holding the bat in his hands like a frying pan – grip rotated, bat face up. Tait's adjustment meant that rather than McCullum just ducking his head out of the way as players typically did with the ramp, he was forced to pull off a remarkable sideways roll, moving his entire body and tumbling away to the off side. Somehow in amongst all this, in a split second moment he had managed to make contact with the ball and such was the pace of the delivery, 150 kph, it flew over the wicketkeeper's head and all the way for six. 'On any other day I could have lost all three sticks,' joked McCullum.

Three balls later he did it again. Tait had not envisaged McCullum attempting an encore; McCullum made a cleaner connection with a ball 5 kph faster and the ball crashed out of the stadium, bouncing into the car park behind. McCullum smirked; Tait could not help but laugh.

No two shots better encapsulated the T20 batting revolution quite like those, not necessarily because of the skill involved – although it was extraordinary – but because of what the shots represented. Less than three weeks previously Tait had bowled one of the quickest overs ever recorded; he was the fastest bowler on the planet. But McCullum saw no threat and had the bravery and the imagination to play the most difficult shot in the game, not just once but twice.

McCullum had made his name way back in 2008 with one of the most significant innings in the history of the game but his impact on T20 went well beyond that heady night in Bangalore. McCullum's commitment to the T20 game – particularly after he retired from international cricket in 2016 – helped enhance the format's sporting integrity in a way that many did not believe was possible. To him T20 cricket was not frivolous entertainment but serious business.

Perhaps no cricketer so embodied the zeitgeist of T20 batting. McCullum's free-spirited approach paved the way for a seminal shift in the nature of batting. The relationship between bowler and batsman had always been more than simply attack versus defence; it was between the hunter and the hunted. Traditionally, big, tall bowlers, charging in off long run-ups were the ones with the upper hand. But in T20 everything was different. When T20 batsmen were said to be 'fearless' it was with reference not to their safety but to losing their wicket. Suddenly it was the hulking batsmen with their huge bats – emboldened by power-hitting techniques, range hitting and the ability to score 360 degrees – that were the ones to be feared. Bowlers were reduced to defensive players with little more than a lump of cork and leather in their hands.

TWO

SELLING THE PRINCE

'Numbers don't lie . . . We've got it down to a science now'
Venky Mysore, chief executive, Kolkata Knight Riders

'Sourav Ganguly?'

On a sweltering day in 2011 at the ITC Royal Gardenia hotel in Bangalore, Richard Madley, the IPL auctioneer, called out Ganguly's name. He was one of India's greatest captains. Perhaps the finest cricketer that West Bengal had ever produced. The Prince of Kolkata.

'That's former Indian captain Sourav Ganguly . . .'

Though he had retired from international cricket, Ganguly was still the captain of the Kolkata Knight Riders. And even if, aged 38, his batting and athleticism had both dwindled, Ganguly had a broader worth: enticing sponsors, selling shirts and, through his razzmatazz, getting more people to watch. In the IPL, commercial and cricketing interests were not easily disentangled. And any sporting benefits to KKR in letting Ganguly go brought risks of a commercial backlash.

'That's Sourav Ganguly, the great Indian batsman . . .'

There were ten tables in the room, each seating a different IPL team. Yet the focus of those in the room and the millions watching on TV lay squarely on one: Kolkata's. To have the chutzpah to let Ganguly go, especially when he was going cheap in the auction, risked being a roadblock to getting 60,000 fans through their gates for seven home games.

'I'm asking for 184 lakh for Sourav Ganguly . . .'

Madley spoke again, an impenetrable auctioneer now given over to sheer confusion about the scene he was presiding over. All he got in return was an eerie silence. It was really true: no one wanted the Prince.

***

A few months earlier, Kolkata had appointed Venky Mysore, an Indian businessman educated in the US, as their new chief executive. Mysore inherited the worst IPL team of the lot. In the first three IPL seasons, KKR had come sixth, eighth and sixth out of eight teams. They were the sole franchise never to reach the play-off stages. These results betrayed a team without a coherent plan.

Mysore came to the conclusion that, for all his pedigree in longer formats of cricket, Ganguly had simply been left behind by T20; like a silent actor in the new age of talkie films, Ganguly was out of place.

'When Sourav went unsold the nation went quiet,' the auctioneer Madley recalled. 'People looked at the Kolkata Knight Riders to say, "How could you?" But that's market forces for you. Nobody picked him. He'd had his day. He was no longer . . . he represented the past of Indian cricket and the IPL is looking for players to represent the future.'

Now, 18,000 international runs and feted national status suddenly counted for less than a player's T20 pedigree, and a strike rate that looked funereal set against those batsmen reared on the new T20 age. Ditching Ganguly represented an embrace of cricketing needs over those of celebrity. Essentially, it was a bet that fans would prefer to watch a winning team than one brimming with ageing glamour. In the trade-off between sporting and commercial goals, KKR had emphatically plumped for sport.

A huge 'No Dada, no KKR' – no Ganguly, no KKR – campaign was launched in Kolkata before the IPL season. Thousands of accompanying leaflets railed against the 'unjust exclusion' of Ganguly, and how 'his glorious career was brought to a sudden halt just because a few businessmen wanted him out.' While calling on fans to boycott matches, it acclaimed that 'people are known by the choices they make'.

'There was a lot of sentiment around it – understandably so because he was such an iconic player,' Mysore recalled. 'There were people who were extremely unhappy. I don't know whether they were already KKR fans or were becoming KKR fans . . . People in the city were extremely upset which was completely understandable.'

In the end a rival IPL team, Pune Warriors, picked up Ganguly as an injury replacement. In 19 games for Pune over two years Ganguly made 318 runs at an average of just 17.67. Worst of all, he made those runs at a strike rate of under 100. Mysore's clinical, unsentimental approach was right. The fan boycott collapsed. Kolkata did not have Ganguly but, for the first time, they had a team who won more games than they lost. That season, KKR came fourth, out of ten sides, and became the first IPL team to record a profit. Ultimately fans wanted to see victories more than they wanted to see Ganguly.

***

Mysore thought of T20 as a new market brimming with basic inefficiencies, believing that notable gains could be made by bringing the same analytical rigour that he had brought to insurance. As a devotee of US sports, he knew the value that shrewd analysis could bring. A study of Major League Baseball analysts by the website FiveThirtyEight found that employing an extra analyst was worth about two extra wins per season to teams. These extra wins would have cost 30 times as much through spending higher salaries on players, showing what a cost-effective way of improving a team analysts can be.

Such thinking informed Mysore's decision not to re-sign Ganguly, as well as release other stars like Chris Gayle and Brendon McCullum; indeed, KKR didn't retain a single player before the 2011 auction. It symbolised a radically different approach to team-building, evoking Pep Guardiola's decision to dispense with star players Deco and Ronaldinho as soon as he took over as Barcelona manager in 2008.

Releasing Ganguly was 'a tough decision to make but it was in the context of a broader strategy. We had to bite the bullet,' Mysore said. 'We said let's go out and build a brand-new team – a new captain, a new team. We basically said that whatever we'd done in the first three years somehow hadn't worked for KKR. It was a shift in focus from thinking about names to thinking about skills, bearing in mind the conditions that we were going to play in. Our entire strategy was about making sure that we got those skills without really bothering about the names that went with it.'

KKR made this decision on a unique table in the auction; every other franchise's table had the team owner on it, but KKR's had only the management, who were entrusted to do what they were paid for without last-minute meddling. And so Mysore was empowered to bring the same cold, unsentimental approach to choosing a cricket team as he had to his career in insurance.

'You grow up understanding that there is risk everywhere,' he explained. 'It's about being able to understand risk, measure risk and then be in a position where you can hopefully make some intelligent decisions on whether to take those risks or not. That was the upbringing in that business. A lot of it applies here, for sure.'

Mysore could also glimpse forerunners of what was possible in cricket. Nathan Leamon, the first-ever full-time team analyst employed by an international cricket team, was already using Monte Carlo simulations to map out probable outcomes in Test matches, playing computerised games with different sets of players and varied tactics to inform England's strategy. Leamon dissected opponents forensically, breaking down the pitch into 20 blocks, of 100cm by 15cm each, and finding the optimal block to target when bowling to each opposing batsman. Famously, he found that Sachin Tendulkar, one of the greatest Test batsmen of all time, rarely scored through the off side at the start of his innings. England nullified Tendulkar's influence by hanging the ball outside off stump, beat India 4–0, and reached the summit of the world Test rankings in 2011.

Though international teams played little T20, data also yielded T20 success. In 2010, England won the T20 World Cup, their first-ever global tournament victory in any format. Leamon and data played a crucial role, notably in encouraging the selection of left-armer Ryan Sidebottom over James Anderson, noting how left-armers were particularly effective in T20. Sidebottom picked up ten wickets in the tournament, including wickets in his first two overs against Australia in the final. A few hours later, England lifted the trophy.

In the early 2000s, as Australia were pushing the boundaries of what was deemed possible, the board enlisted a sports analytics company to study cricket statistics and see if there was a way these could give a fresh edge. The company referred to the sport as 'the Monster', such was the sheer volume of data and variables to process.

In T20, the monster can be tamed. As innings only last 20 overs, it is easier to pre-plan strategy than in the other formats, where scenarios are less predictable. Conditions are also more similar from one T20 game to the next, making comparisons more fertile. Most importantly, as matches are played far more frequently than in the longer forms there is far more data to identify patterns that can lead to a team making better decisions on the pitch. While analysts say that data, for competitions, players or grounds, is superfluous when it is two years out of date, elite T20 players can easily play 50 or more games in that period. And most T20 is played between clubs, rather than countries. Throughout sports history, most leaps in analytics have come from domestic teams.

'It's the market that drives analysis hardest, because of direct and immediate financial pay-offs for improving your valuing of players,' Leamon explained. He considered T20 the format most conducive to using data sagaciously – and T20 leagues particularly well suited to using it. 'A lot of your plans prior to the game go through the game unchanged in T20 cricket.'

Even in the first chaotic years of the IPL there had been glimpses of shrewd thinking being vindicated. Despite having comfortably the smallest playing budget – £1.8 million, when all other teams were at or near the £2.5 million salary cap – Rajasthan Royals won the inaugural IPL, in 2008; a victory for strategy over financial determinism.

'The only thing unanimous about 2008 was that the Royals had the worst team and would come last,' remembered Shane Warne, the legendary Australian bowler who was the Royals captain and coach in 2008. Bollywood owners of other teams resembled over-excited children playing fantasy cricket. Royal Challengers Bangalore assembled a formidable Test team, including Rahul Dravid, Shivnarine Chanderpaul, Jacques Kallis, Mark Boucher, Anil Kumble and Dale Steyn, but found that it was ill-suited to T20, and came second last. Perhaps their attitude to the competition was betrayed by Steyn who, at a Cricket South Africa awards dinner, said that 'the IPL was only four overs a game and it was like a paid holiday; you only had to work hard if you felt like it, which is probably why we finished second last.' Steyn later said he 'was trying to be funny and just ended up being stupid'.

Meanwhile, Rajasthan acted like card counters in a casino. In their XI for each match, teams were only allowed to field four overseas players, so it made little sense to splurge cash on foreigners who might not even play; it was equally illogical to build a team around players who, because of international commitments, would flee before the final stages. And, most of all, they needed to build a team to win T20 matches, not Tests. 'They are two very different games, requiring very different skills,' said Manoj Badale, the co-owner of Rajasthan Royals.

Rajasthan identified their four overseas players – the first of which was Warne, their brilliant captain. 'I was grateful for the opportunity because in the other seven franchises you had Tendulkar, Sehwag, Ganguly, Dravid, Laxman, Kumble and Dhoni, so all the big Indian names, and then there was me, a retired player who hadn't played for 18 months. The other teams had all their coaches too and I was captain and coach as well.'

Warne was joined by fellow Australian Shane Watson, an all-rounder whose skills were ideally suited to T20 yet was among the cheapest overseas players; Sohail Tanvir, an unorthodox left-arm pace bowler from Pakistan; and Graeme Smith, South Africa's captain and opening batsman. This quartet were selected together in almost every game, allowing team cohesion to develop and ensuring each player was clear about their role in the side. This shrewd foreign recruitment was married to signing Indian players far better suited to T20 than other formats – notably Yusuf Pathan, an explosive hitter who ended the season with a strike rate of 179, and Swapnil Asnodkar, an unknown impish opening batsman with no care for the reputations of the opening bowlers he faced.

'Halfway through that tournament we had something special,' recalled Warne. 'Every now and again you get involved with a group of people, whether it is work or sport, and there is just a little bit of magic. You can't quite put your finger on what it is and we just had a bit of magic in our group. Everyone knew their roles and everyone got along.'

The poorest team in the IPL, who played in the most remote area and had the fewest number of overseas players of any side, turned out to be easily the best. In the process they provided a hint of how smart, analytical thinking could overcome the logic of financial determinism in T20 cricket, leaving behind rivals more focused upon Bollywood, cheerleaders and the razzmatazz of the IPL than the actual cricket.

Rajasthan's victory also imbued the IPL with an essential sense of sporting integrity. 'To then go on and win it as we did gave the IPL credibility because everyone loves the underdog story like Leicester with the footy,' remarked Warne. 'The Royals were a great story and you combine that with Brendon McCullum scoring 158 in the first game, suddenly people are thinking, "This IPL is pretty cool!" That first year was something special.'

KKR's tactics had been altogether less enlightened. Yet at least this history of failure liberated Mysore to adopt a radically new approach to the auction, and building the entire team. Gut instincts had failed KKR; instead Mysore embraced numbers.

Mysore empowered A.R. Srikkanth, who was appointed performance and strategies analyst for KKR in 2009, and elevated him to the core of the team's decision-making. These two bespectacled outsiders – united by their rigorous academic training, belief in numbers and their distrust of the sport's tropes and received wisdom – would help transform the sport forever.

***

As chief executive, Mysore sought to bring order to the anarchy of the auction. This was particularly vital as 2011 was a 'big auction' – almost every player would enter the auction, and franchises would have the option of signing them for three years.

The auction is unique across all sport. While there are some similarities with the draft used in US sports leagues, that applies only to young players joining the league, and players are simply paid according to when they are selected in the draft. During IPL 'big auctions', all players are up for sale, barring a few whom teams choose to retain from before. There is no predetermined price; a player's price is only settled when teams have stopped their bidding from the auction floor, and the auctioneer can use his hammer and declare the player sold. Teams can spend what they want on whomever they want, as long as they adhere to the salary cap, which has risen to 80 crore – about £9 million – in 2019.

Those who thrive in this high-octane environment are those who can out-think the competition. Sides are not merely preoccupied with the players they want. They are just as worried about what everyone else wants; if a team overpays for one player, that means less to spend on everyone else, because of the salary caps and opportunities for other sides to sign players for less than they should be worth. It is commonplace for sides to bid for players they don't particularly want, in the hope of starting a bidding war and ramping up the price to leave their rivals less cash to spend elsewhere. With every lot, each team is not merely considering how suitable the player is for their side, they are considering how suitable the player is for the other seven teams too. Every lot subtly changes the power dynamics in the room, and the relationship between what teams want and what they can afford.

Paradoxically, getting the player you most want can be ruinous; if you overspend, it means not enough money to spend elsewhere. The notion of good value is laid to waste as owners – who, in most teams except KKR, generally have the final say – seek to sign their favourite cricketers; Stephen Fleming, the Rising Pune Supergiant coach, resembled a ghost after Pune paid £1.7 million for England all-rounder Ben Stokes in 2017. In the same year, England's Tymal Mills provoked a bidding war after a fine recent run in T20 games; franchises were seduced by recent performances and the allure of a left-arm pace bowler. Mills was sold to Royal Challengers Bangalore for £1.4 million yet played only five games. The next season, no one signed Mills at all. In *Cricket Fever*, a Netflix documentary following the Mumbai Indians in 2018, Mumbai's owner makes it clear that he will not countenance failing to sign Krunal Pandya. Pandya ended up going to Mumbai for £0.92 million, after rivals ratcheted up the price.

'Some just want a player because someone else wants them,' one insider said. The most sought-after players can be affected by the winner's curse: they end up being overpriced, destabilising the rest of their team's auction strategy.

Perhaps nothing is as important as the auction in determining teams' fates. A bad 'big auction' does not merely set a franchise back a season, it can result in years of misery. And a good auction – not outspending the competition, but out-thinking them – can set a team up for years of success. Because domestic T20 leagues are set up to ensure competitive balance between sides, those teams who can find the best answer to a simple question – how do you put a price on a cricketer? – are best-placed to win.

Mysore realised this process was much too important to be left to chance. And so, before his first auction in 2011, KKR outsourced research to a software company based in Chennai. The company established a bidding system based on decision trees, thereby allowing the management to conduct mock auctions and prepare for various scenarios. Auction strategies for other teams were also drawn up, allowing KKR to deduce whom their rivals wanted to buy and whether, if they overspent, it would create bargains for Kolkata in other areas. The decision-making team – typically Mysore, the head and assistant coach, the team manager and Srikkanth, the data analyst and talent scout – conducted mock auctions to prepare for having to make decisions about whether or not to spend millions of dollars on a player in a couple of seconds.

'Randomness isn't under any franchise's control,' Srikkanth explained. 'You just have to plan for every situation and play it by ear.' The process could be as tense as any cricket match and helped determine teams' fortunes for years.

Being as well prepared as possible enabled KKR to be nimble and seize unexpected opportunities on auction day. In the process, they could take advantage of blasé opponents. KKR have what the team call a circuit breaker for every player – an upper price limit they are assigned before the auction, to prevent emotion getting in the way of cold judgement on auction day. Kolkata can go above the circuit breaker, but they need a compelling reason to do so. Ideally, Kolkata only go above a 'circuit breaker' if they have previously got a player for less than their recommended price during the auction.

Mysore's new approach fundamentally deviated from the orthodoxy in the IPL. Unlike other sides, he refrained from targeting players to be captain, avoiding the risk of overpaying. In the 2011 and 2018 big auctions, KKR had no particular name in mind to be captain, only delegating the position after they had assembled their complete squad.

He avoided star players when they were overpriced. While other sides hoarded talent, KKR favoured a lean squad; what was the sense in paying for eight expensive overseas players, when they could only pick four in each starting XI? Under Mysore, KKR routinely had the smallest squad in the IPL; in 2018, they had only seven overseas players and a 19-man squad, when every other team had eight overseas players and a squad stretching the limit of the 25 players permitted. The rationale was that it was more efficient to have fewer, better players, who would all have a realistic chance of making the XI and KKR could invest time in improving.

KKR developed a distinctive on-field style too. With their home pitch at Eden Gardens generally favouring spin, and producing relatively low-scoring games, Kolkata developed a template for how to win games that extended far beyond any individual players. 'It would be safe to say we have always fielded a very strong bowling unit ever since I've been involved from 2011 onwards. That's an important part of the philosophy of the KKR style of cricket,' Mysore explained. This informed the type of cricketers KKR sought to recruit, and then retain. 'So there's a common theme, I think, in how we have always thought which makes it simpler for us.'

At the auction table, KKR consistently prioritised specialist T20 skills over established names. More than any other franchise, they were reliably able to extract value from the bedlam of the auction floor.

In 2012, Sunil Narine, a mystery spinner from Trinidad and Tobago, who could turn the ball both ways, was only a year into his T20 career, and had played just 16 matches. He had played three one-day internationals for the West Indies against India, performing unremarkably. But KKR had observed Narine's mesmerising bowling during the 2011 Champions League, a competition for the world's leading domestic teams, when he took 5 for 18 across eight overs against two IPL sides. The more they perused footage of Narine bowling in domestic games in the Caribbean, the more they were convinced that he was worth a huge investment, especially as Eden Gardens, Kolkata's home ground, was tailored to spin bowling. 'We don't need anyone else,' Gautam Gambhir, KKR's captain, told Mysore. KKR had considered the veteran Australian left-arm wrist spinner Brad Hogg, whose experience seemed to make him less of a risk, but all their research on Narine had told them he was a player with the capacity to transform the franchise's fortunes.

The problem was, Mumbai Indians wanted Narine too. Sitting next to Mysore during the auction, Srikkanth kept imploring Mysore to raise his paddle again and again, even as KKR nudged above their 'circuit breaker' price for Narine. By the time Mysore had raised his paddle for the final time, Narine, with a base price of £31,000, had ended up costing KKR £441,000. The price was based on data, scouting Narine in person and through TV footage and simple 'gut feel', Mysore said.

It seemed an absurd fee for a cricketer just dipping his toes into international cricket. But KKR were vindicated. Narine took 24 wickets in the 2012 IPL and conceded runs at a parsimonious 5.47 an over, a record for any IPL season and the prelude to a magnificent career for Kolkata. While he was player of the tournament, leading Kolkata to their maiden IPL title, Ganguly's Pune Warriors languished in last place.

Glimpsing the potential to gain a competitive advantage through enlightened use of data and forensic planning for the auction encouraged KKR to double down on their approach. 'It's all about enough time being invested in preparation – very rarely are we caught on the wrong foot and have to scramble,' Mysore said.

Before the 2014 auction KKR enlisted SAP, a software company who had been involved in Formula 1 and American sport, to develop a statistical analysis tool designed to assist the management in decision-making during the auction. The tool married player insights with intelligence on the other squads and their remaining funds to predict various scenarios and assist Kolkata in split-second decisions in real time. At each break in the auction, Mysore and the team would scrutinise the software.

'Many different types of businesses that I've been involved in also do a lot of this number-crunching analytics to arrive at good decisions. The environment is so dynamic that it's very important to be prepared,' Mysore said. 'It helps us to become a bit unemotional. And you become emotional when you start thinking in names.'

KKR use a system with around 25 data points to evaluate players before every auction. They pay particular attention to contextualising numbers. So, rather than simply look at a batsman's strike rate, Kolkata look at it in the context of the game situation, preventing them being seduced by players who seem to score quickly, but whose numbers are less impressive given that they play in high-scoring leagues. Scrutinising players in this way allows Kolkata to avoid succumbing to recency bias, and overpaying for players who have just enjoyed an outstanding recent run. As well as standard metrics – strike rate and boundary percentage for batsmen; economy rate in different phases of the game for bowlers, to see how they compare with the competition – KKR use numbers to get a sense of a cricketer's character and temperament too. For bowlers, KKR place special emphasis on seeing how a bowler performs after their first over is hit, or after a poor match. In the cauldron of the IPL, over 14 league matches, no bowler is likely to be immune from punishment; it is how they return from grim bowling figures that separates the best from the rest.

'Numbers don't lie,' said Mysore. 'But numbers are not the be all and end all.'

Kolkata's system divided up potential players in two ways. First, those who are proficient at crucial, yet fairly common, skills – hitting at the death, say, or left-arm orthodox spin. For such players KKR 'have multiple options,' Mysore said. 'You can afford to wait and try and acquire those skills not necessarily at very high costs.'

The other type of player possesses rare skills – as a death bowler or spinner able to bowl in all phases of the game, say. For these players, KKR expect to pay more. 'You can call it a demand and supply situation. There are certain types of skills which are not very easy to get which is where you probably have to be willing to reach into your pocket and spend the money. It's about the auction dynamics, how the marketplace works in that environment and what you're looking for.'

Before every auction, KKR like to reduce the number of options for each position down to under ten, Srikkanth explained. 'And then we would screen them down based on numbers, recent form, recent injury history, what's their attitude been like on and off the field? Have they got a clean record, in terms of being non-controversial?' Players are ranked by preference, and suggested price, allowing Kolkata to be as well prepared as possible, and recognise players who are comparatively underpriced on the market. Before Kolkata signed Chris Lynn in the 2018 auction, other explosive overseas openers – such as Jason Roy, Colin Munro, Quinton de Kock and Chris Gayle – were also on their shortlist.

After implementing their refined auction planning system in 2014, another 'big auction', KKR enjoyed one of the most successful auctions of any franchise in history. Before the 2014 auction, the Jamaican all-rounder Andre Russell had been released by Delhi Daredevils; he had been a peripheral player, featuring in only seven matches over two seasons. Yet as they scoured the market for all-rounders – initially they thought they just needed a back-up to Jacques Kallis – Kolkata recognised how Russell, who had already won one T20 World Cup, had been misused by Delhi. Russell cost only 60 lakhs (£60,000); one season later, he was named as the IPL's Most Valuable Player. In 2016, Russell won five T20 trophies with five different teams, confirming his status as the world's leading T20 player.

At the same time as they signed Russell, KKR also recruited Kuldeep Yadav, even though he had yet to play a professional match in any format.

Srikkanth had stumbled across Kuldeep playing in a Buchi Babu game, a preseason tournament to prepare players for the first-class season, in Chennai the year before. He was wowed less by Kuldeep's numbers – there were scarcely anything to go by – than his potential in cricket's rarest art, left-arm wrist spin. Srikkanth promptly called Trevor Bayliss, who was Kolkata's coach, and texted Mysore to tell them about what he had seen. Further scouting of Kuldeep before the auction backed up Srikkanth's thinking. Within a week of KKR signing him for a budget 40 lakhs (£40,000), the fourth-lowest price available in the auction, Kuldeep took a hat-trick for India U-19s in the World Cup. By the time the year was out, Kuldeep had excelled in the Champions League; three years later, he made a terrific start to his international career.

With both the signings of Russell and Kuldeep, Kolkata exploited one advantage that the IPL auction gave teams. In 'big auctions', players were signed for three-year contracts – but only if the team wanted them to be. The team had all the power; they were free to release a player after one or two years of his deal, or retain him at the same price. This rewarded sides who could think ahead and plan for a whole cycle. Players like Russell and Kuldeep had a huge potential upside, yet their costs, and risks, were minimised. This meant they could be incorporated slowly at first – Russell only played two IPL games in 2014, and Kuldeep none – and then, when established as integral players, still be paid well under what they would have commanded on the open market. Srikkanth and Mysore were like investors spotting stocks that would soar in a couple of years.

Like any good scout, Srikkanth's success was underpinned by sheer hard work; he travelled to leagues all year round and scoured spreadsheets for undervalued players. But KKR's method was not so much to embrace data at the expense of human judgement as to fuse the two.

'We give directives to the scouts as to what to look for and what not to look for and how to identify someone. Once we are satisfied with what we've heard, we'd call the player and go directly ourselves to have a better look,' Srikkanth explained. 'Numbers can be quite misleading as well. You can't purely base your decisions on numbers alone. It's got to be a good mixture of both cricketing intelligence as well as numbers.'

Srikkanth was integral to KKR's rise, helping Mysore and Bayliss identify talent. 'He was very important when it came to the auctions and selecting players that we didn't know much about and doing his homework and research with younger Indian players for example, not just the international players,' Bayliss recalled.

Since Mysore took over, KKR have generally eschewed buying the most high-profile overseas players. As of 2019, KKR's three most-celebrated overseas players were Narine, Chris Lynn and Russell. None had arrived at KKR viewed as among the world's biggest T20 stars; now, all were.

'Venky has given me a cushion and trusted in my decision-making which has helped me go there and look for talent positively and be a little more carefree and willing to take a punt on any player,' Srikkanth said. 'Venky has empowered me to make those decisions and given me a free hand to look at talent and get them down to KKR. Before Venky came it was quite different because everyone was getting used to how franchise cricket would be run. T20 was very new. So the decision-making was not as professional as it is now.

'Just turning up for the tournament and picking random players because you heard those players are good from someone else – it doesn't work that way any more. It has to be through a process and it has to be quality work and quality time put behind every season to pick those players to represent your team.'

After the successes of Russell and Narine – and successfully pushing for KKR to get other players who performed impressively at budget prices, like Bangladesh all-rounder Shakib Al Hasan and Netherlands all-rounder Ryan ten Doeschate, scouted based on his performances in the English T20 competition – Srikkanth became even more ambitious. The best way of all to identify undervalued talent, he figured, was to find players outside the professional system.

One of Srikkanth's other roles was as a performance analyst for the Bijapur Bulls in the Karnataka Premier League, one of the intrastate T20 leagues – smaller copycat versions of the IPL, organised and controlled by state associations in India. Srikkanth recognised that his role allowed him to scout players before others were aware of them. He saw K.C. Cariappa, a leg-spinner with abundant variations, originally honed playing gully cricket with a tennis ball, in the nets and in matches, and was wowed by his promise. Srikkanth organised for Cariappa to bowl to KKR in the nets before the 2014 Champions League, and the team were impressed.

Before the 2015 auction, Madley had never even practised pronouncing Cariappa's name; he did not have a profile page on the exhaustive global cricket website, ESPNcricinfo. 'I was told there was no chance these players would even be presented to the auction. After the event, one is wised.'

Cariappa's lot began at 10 lakh (£10,000). By the time it ended, after a bidding war between KKR and Delhi – whose team mentor, T.A. Sekhar, had been impressed with Cariappa in televised Karnataka Premier League matches – Cariappa had been sold to KKR for 240 lakhs (£240,000).

KKR were pioneers again; it was easily the highest fee paid for any player who had yet to play a professional match in any format. It represented another stage in the maturation of the auction process, as US-style talent ID was embraced. It showed another side of the IPL, too: its ability to transform cricketers' lives in a few seconds of bedlam. 'It is really a dream come true,' Cariappa told *Times of India* after he was drafted. 'My parents have sacrificed a lot for me. With the money I get, I want to buy a house for them.' This was the human side to the IPL's maturation from fantasy cricket to systematic team-building.

Even the shrewdest blackjack players cannot devise a foolproof system – they can simply tilt the odds a little in their favour. Cariappa would only bowl two overs for KKR before, in 2016, moving to a different franchise. He was a gamble that failed; an emblem that no amount of rigorous planning could ever eradicate the essential uncertainty in signing a cricketer. But in 2018, KKR signed Shubman Gill, the vice-captain of India U-19s, on Srikkanth's recommendation; he promptly enjoyed an outstanding debut season. Together with other successful domestic signings – the seam bowlers Shivam Mavi and Prasidh Krishna, who were also in keeping with Kolkata's strategy of signing young players who could blossom over their contracts – it reaffirmed that perhaps no team in world cricket identified undervalued players as consistently as KKR. 'We've got it down to a science now,' Mysore said.

***

For KKR, auction strategy was merely the start of using data. Srikkanth studied their opponents before each game, including compiling a breakdown of each main player, where they scored their runs or took their wickets and how to counter their strengths. He then sat down with Simon Katich – who was appointed assistant coach of KKR in 2015 – to discuss his findings. 'We challenge each other with our thought processes and with the game plan. Once we are convinced of the game plan then we take it to the captain or bowling coach or whoever is part of the think tank.'

Team meetings for batsmen and bowlers entailed sifting through footage and looking at a few vital statistics. These emphasised actionable data to drive KKR to employ better strategies on the field, like bowling a specific bowler to a specific opponent, or setting the field in a way that challenged him and 'put him out of his comfort zone,' Srikkanth said.

Data was central to deciding which team KKR picked for each game. 'We look at match-ups extensively and come up with plans in accordance with the coaching staff and player,' Srikkanth explained. 'We have started to pick bowlers against specific batsmen.'

The moments Srikkanth savoured most are when his insights imprinted themselves on bowlers getting opponents out. When the left-arm wrist spinner Brad Hogg was bowling against Brendon McCullum, a former KKR player, Srikkanth 'noticed that Brendon likes to pull the spinners in the first six overs if it is a little back of a length,' he recounted to Cricbuzz. 'So, Hoggy and I sat down and came up with a plan. We will feed him to pull and we will get him out with the same shot again. So what happened was, Hoggy bowled a slower one, he pulled him for a one-bounce four. Next ball, he left that space open but this time, he bowled a flipper and it skidded through. The idea was to make Brendon do the same thing but the ball skids on from the wicket and gets him lbw. We got him second ball.'

For analysts, these are the moments to be treasured: when all their work trawling through videos and scrutinising the more than 50 data points Srikkanth collects each ball turns them into puppetmasters planning the game before it happens. Another moment Srikkanth savoured was during the title-winning season of 2012. Against Pune Warriors, Yusuf Pathan, a part-time off-spinner, had the former Australian captain Michael Clarke stumped down the leg side. Srikkanth's analysis had found that Clarke was prone to trying to drive through the leg side while lifting his back leg in the air, leading him to tell Pathan to deliberately bowl the ball fuller down the leg side.

Srikkanth considers data analytics more useful for bowlers than batsmen. Studying the numbers can find unexplored nuggets that bowlers can revert to in high-octane situations. Srikkanth studies what opposing batsmen do after failing to score from a couple of balls, and their favoured 'release shot' which they go to in this situation; doing so can help bowlers second-guess what to do and even tweak their field placings accordingly.

Antecedents of this approach were detectable long before T20. In the 1996 World Cup, Bob Woolmer, South Africa's enterprising coach, used video analysis to find that if England's batsman Graeme Hick went several balls without scoring he liked to flick the ball in the air through midwicket. After several dot balls, Hick did exactly as Woolmer envisaged and was caught. But modern cricket analytics brought a new precision to this process; in their sophistication, these were more akin to baseball than what previously existed in cricket. Srikkanth identified the optimal 'comeback ball' for bowlers to specific opposing batsmen – the shrewdest ball to bowl immediately after being hit for four or six, when bowlers are most vulnerable to haemorrhaging runs.

Such insights changed how teams conceptualised the sport. Conventional wisdom had it that bowlers would be mere adjuncts to the salient battle in T20s: which team could thump the ball more reliably. Srikkanth recognised that the comparative ease of hitting boundaries, compared to the difficulty in stopping them, made bowlers crucial and often better value than batsmen in auction. 'Bowlers are equally, if not more important, than batsmen in T20s. Batsmen set up games but bowlers win you games.' Narine's brilliance was central to KKR's title victories in both 2012 and 2014.

'Scoreboard pressure always plays on a team so from a player's point of view they do tend to value wickets in hand a bit more than they should,' Srikkanth said. He believes that he has found a better way: encouraging players to value their wickets less highly, especially early in their innings, so that they play more aggressively. His most radical change was moving Narine to be an opening batsman. This move reinvigorated the idea of a 'pinch-hitter', a tactic of promoting a bowler or all-rounder up the order with the sole intention of attacking and showing no care for his own wicket.

At the start of 2017, Narine had only scored 382 runs in 195 T20 games – fewer than two per match – and had never previously batted in the top four. 'The coaching staff at [Melbourne] Renegades saw me batting in the nets and said, "We could try him opening." That's where it started,' Narine recalled. He was used as an auxiliary opener because of an injury and, initially to target an opposition spinner. In three games opening for the Renegades in 2017, Narine only made 37 runs.

But he made them very quickly, showing a welcome disregard for his own wicket of the sort that specialist batsmen, reared on batting in longer formats, often struggle to do. Srikkanth was at the ground when Narine first opened for Melbourne Renegades, and noted how adept Narine was at clearing the 30-yard circle during the six-over Powerplay.

'The kind of positivity and courage that he had about his own batting – it surprised me. He was striking the ball cleanly in practice games and in the nets. We said, "Let's put him up the order and see what he's got – because if he gets out first ball we're not losing anything." The thinking was that he scored so quickly that he could transform a game in 15 balls,' Srikkanth said. 'If he gets out first ball he gets out. We don't put any pressure on him.'

Narine was deployed like a joker. Playing in such a high-risk way Narine would fail a lot but it didn't matter – he was picked mostly as a bowler, after all. And, because he attacked so brazenly from his first ball, even a brief innings could make an outsized impact. So it was illogical to keep him at number eight or nine, and risk leaving Narine completely unused.

In his first game as an opener for KKR, Narine thumped 37 from 18 balls, showing an unabashed disregard for the concept of playing himself in. 'It's easier batting in T20 because I'm a naturally aggressive person, so I don't have to temper anything,' Narine explained. Srikkanth understood that Narine would fail by conventional metrics, but the upside of him succeeding was huge. In the 2017 IPL Narine was dismissed every ten balls, abominable by standards in longer forms of cricket, and only averaged 17.23, but had a strike rate of 172.3; only two batsmen who scored more runs managed better. The following season, Narine had a ludicrous strike rate of 189.89, more than anyone else who scored as many as his 357 runs.

By reconceptualising what it meant to fail in an innings, Srikkanth turned Narine from a bowler to an all-rounder, discovering new and untapped value in his cricket. And by understanding how hazardous Narine's approach was, Srikkanth ensured that he would be granted an extended run as an opener, even when his style inevitably meant strings of low scores. Narine's transformation allowed KKR to unlock more batting strength – so they could effectively lengthen their batting line-ups without making compromises elsewhere, and were freer to attack from earlier.

Adept at using match-ups to exploit their opponents' weaknesses, Kolkata were also able to conceal their own players' weaknesses. Narine, who was comparatively weak against pace, was paired with the Australian

Chris Lynn, who was brilliant at hitting pace but comparatively ponderous against spin. Opponents liked to bowl spin to Lynn in the early overs, but his partnership with Narine infused this tactic with jeopardy. In their first opening partnership together they broke the world record for the highest Powerplay score of all time, razing 105 in six overs; RCB captain Virat Kohli oscillated between bowling quick bowlers, spinners and back again, spooked by their complementary strengths. The partnership endured: before the start of the 2019 IPL no opening pair in the league's history to have batted more than ten times together had scored their runs faster than Lynn and Narine's 10.57 runs per over, indeed no partnership had scored above ten runs per over. Their partnership was difficult to bowl to and complicated to plan for, forcing fielding captains to adjust their tactics and reconfigure their strategies.

Numbers also informed Srikkanth's belief that wickets had previously been overvalued, leading teams to bat more defensively and in a suboptimal way. At the time of Narine's elevation, the average IPL team lost fewer than six wickets an innings – meaning that, in an average innings, their number eight would not get to bat at all. Over a season, KKR believed, they would make more runs with Narine as opener, so great an impact could he make in those innings when he made a useful score. And when he failed, it was almost irrelevant.

In this way KKR were at the apex of a revolution in the sport. Cricketing orthodoxy has always been that nothing slows down the run rate as effectively as taking wickets. Yet in the major leagues in 2013, the average team batting first in T20 made 154 and lost 6.3 wickets; by 2018, sides batting first made an average of 161 and lost 6.7 wickets. Paradoxically, losing more wickets could even be regarded as a sign of batting teams playing the game more intelligently.

The revolution that Srikkanth embodied is unfinished. 'Data has been around for some time now but the acceptance levels have grown rapidly over the past few years,' Srikkanth said. 'Players and staff accept that data and the use of data is only to enhance their knowledge and not change something fundamental.' In the years ahead 'the use of data would only grow more and more.'

THREE

GAYLESTORM

'Chris Gayle is exhibit A in what's wrong with cricket at the moment'
Telford Vice, South African journalist

After walking out to bat with his opening partner, rather than assuming his position at the batting crease, Chris Gayle sauntered towards the middle of the 22-yard pitch and stood there for a few moments, visualising what was to come and practising his trademark pull shot. He was shadow batting in the cricket ground that had become his playground.

The M. Chinnaswamy Stadium in Bangalore is small and claustrophobic. The tiny boundaries, coupled with a flat pitch and the high altitude, made it a ground of extraordinary feats of batsmanship. Gayle is an enormous man – 6 feet 3 inches tall and 98kg, so broad and muscular that his upper back is hulked under the weight of his strength. As he stood in the middle of the pitch, adorned in the red of the Royal Challengers Bangalore and with the end of his black bandana trailing out of his gold helmet, his presence filled the stadium. The 40,000 people in the stands had already been whipped up into a fervent expectation of what they were about to witness: one of the most powerful batting orders ever assembled plundering runs.

Eden Gardens in Kolkata, steeped in history and with a capacity of 90,000, is Indian cricket's coliseum. The Wankhede Stadium in Mumbai, home to India's great batsmen and demigods Sunil Gavaskar and Sachin Tendulkar, is Indian cricket's cathedral. Bangalore's M. Chinnaswamy Stadium, scene of Brendon McCullum's seminal 158 not out in the inaugural IPL match and home to the batting galacticos of RCB, is Indian cricket's basement nightclub. Eden Gardens and the Wankhede Stadium have more history but if you wanted a good time you'd come to the Chinnaswamy. A good time is what Gayle was about to give the capacity crowd on a sweltering Tuesday afternoon in April 2013.

After one more practice shot in the middle of the pitch Gayle turned around and slowly walked towards the batting crease. Like the tennis legend Rafael Nadal, who would arrange his drink bottles meticulously before taking his position at the back of the court, the game was made to wait for Gayle. He even turned slowing down, the antithesis of all that T20 represented, into a dramatic act.

It took just 8.5 overs for Gayle to reach his hundred. Any delivery from Pune Warriors India's bowlers with a hint of width was flayed through the off side and any ball even fractionally too straight was picked up and whipped through the leg side. Too full and he clobbered it down the ground; too short and he pulled it into the stands. The shot which took him to his century – a straight drive for six off another erroneous full toss – took chunks out of the stadium roof. Shrapnel rained down on to the outfield below as Gayle removed his helmet and sank to his knees in celebration, arms outstretched, as if to say: are you not entertained? It had taken him 30 balls to score 102 runs, the fastest T20 hundred of all time.

Naturally, bedlam engulfed the stands. A few fans took to showing their appreciation in a different way. 'When Gayle bats, fielders become spectators, and spectators become fielders,' proclaimed the home-made sign that one fan had produced during this remarkable innings.

Gayle would go on to score 175 not out off 66 balls, breaking McCullum's record set in 2008 for the highest T20 score. At the end of the 2019 IPL, the record still stood. It was the definitive performance by T20's greatest batsman.

But perhaps more than that innings – an exhibition of brutal power hitting unparalleled in the format's short history – Gayle's true impact was best encapsulated by something else, something which involved him doing nothing at all: the ball bowled so far out of his reach that it caused the umpire to spread his arms out on either side, to signal a wide ball.

One of the hallmarks of sporting giants is making their opponents perform worse. Through the lustre of their greatness, and the awareness that they ruthlessly punish any errors, however infinitesimal, the best athletes enfeeble their opponents.

During Tiger Woods's elite years, his aura was so great that, even though he directly had no effect whatsoever on what his opponents did on the golf course, he made them play worse. The academic Jennifer Brown analysed round-by-round scores from all PGA tournaments between 2002 and 2006, and uncovered a remarkable finding: competitors performed about a stroke per tournament worse when Tiger Woods was also playing. The simple presence of Woods on the same course led his opponents to underperform.

In T20, the ultimate unforced error for a bowler is to bowl a wide or no-ball. This is effectively a donation of runs to the batting side, who also have an extra ball to size up the bowler and exploit weakness. Wides or no-balls are like charity runs given to the batting side, adding to their score without taking anything from their two resources – wickets and balls remaining.

A totem of Gayle's overweening influence upon T20 is that, when he was batting, he received almost twice as many wides as the average batsman: one every 19 balls, rather than one every 35 balls. Bowlers were intimidated by the specimen that awaited them. They knew that any slight erring in line or length was likely to meet the ultimate punishment: a Gayle six. And this knowledge induced them to bowl worse. By the end of 2018 Gayle had garnered 430 runs from opposing bowlers in wides and no-balls, the equivalent of 1.20 runs per match gifted by the opposition bowlers without Gayle having to do anything.

When it came to T20 batting records, Gayle wasn't so much on top of everyone else as hang-gliding way above the clouds. At the end of 2018 Gayle had scored 12,095 runs in T20 – 2,467 more than the next most. He had hit 892 sixes – 340 more than the next most. Despite Gayle's tendency to look to clear the ropes rather than hit the ball along the ground he also held the record for the most fours, 925. A total of 9,052 of his runs had come from fours and sixes. Only McCullum had more runs overall than Gayle had in boundaries alone.

These records were partly a consequence of the sheer volume of T20 that he had played; with 357 matches, only three players had appeared more often. Yet by relative measures Gayle was also absurdly dominant.

Gayle's value lay in his ability to combine a phenomenal scoring rate with exceptional consistency. At the heart of batting exists a trade-off between attack and defence, between intent to score and intent to survive. For most players focusing on one would compromise the other, but Gayle was different.

Among players to have batted at least 50 times in T20 by the end of 2018 only 19 players averaged more balls faced per innings than Gayle's 23.40 and not one of them was even close to matching his strike rate of 148.07 runs per 100 balls. Just 24 players had a higher strike rate than Gayle; most were lower order hitters, and only two, the remarkable A.B. de Villiers and the young Indian tyro Rishabh Pant, were even within 20% of Gayle's average innings length. Gayle spent longer at the crease than almost every other player and while he was there he scored faster than almost every other player.

In Test and ODI cricket the length of the contest afforded batsmen greater scope for large individual scores and the hundred – big enough to be an alluring three figures but not so big that it was unattainable – was a totemic landmark. From 2003 to 2019 in Test cricket the milestone was reached every 19 individual innings and in ODIs it was reached every 34 individual innings. But in T20, the length and nature of the contest made hundreds rare. Attacking at the rate which enabled a batsman to score a hundred involved too much risk for it to be a realistic or regular achievement. On average a T20 hundred was scored every 290 individual innings. Yet by the end of 2018 Gayle had scored 21 T20 hundreds – 14 more than the next most and the same as the next three best players combined. He reached three figures every 17 innings that he played, meaning that a Chris Gayle T20 century was more regular than a Test match century. Nothing better embodied how he mastered the demands of T20 batsmanship.

***

In basketball, three-point shots are those further away from the hoop, so they are riskier and more likely to fail than two-point attempts from closer. That much was well established.

But in recent years analysts in the NBA basketball league have made a startling observation. Although three-pointers are indeed hazardous, they have a higher expected points return than two-pointers from closer. Three-pointers have a 50% greater pay-off, rendering them a shot beloved by analysts – including Houston Rockets general manager, and computer science graduate Daryl Morey. In consecutive seasons in 2016/17 and 2017/18, Houston broke the record for the number of threes in any single NBA season. In 2017/18, 42% of their shots were three-point attempts – comfortably the most for any team in any season. It was also the year in which Houston won more matches than ever before in their history. They were not just playing a better game than their opponents; they were playing a radically different one.

The growth of the six in T20 mirrored the ascent of the three in the NBA, which have more than doubled since 2000. The six, like the three in basketball, has a 50% greater pay-off than the previous highest scoring shot, more than making up for it being harder to execute. Both the six and the three represent the marriage of the athletically spectacular and analytically shrewd.

Increased use of data analysis in cricket has been one of a number of factors – alongside stronger players, bigger bats and power-hitting training – to cause a surge in the rate of six hitting in T20. In 2012 a six was hit every 28 balls. By 2018 that had fallen to one every 20 balls.

Balls per Six in T20 Cricket by Year	
Year	**Balls per Six**
2008	27
2009	28
2010	27
2011	27
2012	27
2013	25
2014	24
2015	23
2016	23
2017	21
2018	20

This is not a normal cyclical shift of the sort common in sport. It speaks of an altogether more fundamental change. From being regarded as the sport's kamikaze shot, the six is now often viewed as its prudent, percentage option – simply the most efficient way to score runs.

The ascent of the six in cricket was a window into how the sports data revolution is not just changing how sports teams prepare and train, but also the essence of how sports are played.

Gayle has never seemed like a cricketer to pay much heed to analytics. This image, so carefully cultivated, concealed his great wisdom. More than any other player of his age, Gayle grasped that boundary hitting would be dominant in T20. And so he developed a unique batting style that revolved almost entirely around hitting fours and, especially, sixes.

In all forms of cricket when batsmen first arrive at the crease they typically take some time to 'play themselves in'. They familiarise themselves with the pace and bounce of the pitch and get used to the opposition bowlers. In Test cricket, with very little time pressure or importance placed on scoring rate, this period can sometimes consume many deliveries. But the shorter the format, the more important scoring rate becomes, and the less significant wicket preservation.

Despite the intense pressure on batsmen in T20 to score quickly, Gayle adopted a method defined by an unusually slow, careful start. Across the first ten balls of his innings, 59% of Gayle's balls faced were dot balls, the highest proportion of any player in the world. In Gayle's first ten balls he played no shot to 11% of deliveries and defended 20%, both well above the global average of 2% and 10%. Yet this caution was carefully calculated: Gayle's extraordinary destructive power meant he could make up for his slow start. Those early periods were essential to Gayle's acceleration. Gayle trusted that his effectiveness in attack was greatly increased by affording himself time to play himself in.

He also eschewed another of the common tropes of T20 thinking: the importance of scoring singles even when playing defensive shots, so as to prevent the total from being bogged down, especially at the outset of an innings. Gayle took a very different view. He regarded sharply run singles as an unnecessary extra risk, and so virtually eliminated the run-out as a form of dismissal. Over his career Gayle has been run out 3% of the time, compared to an average of 10% for all batsmen.

Gayle was able to make up for his slow starts because of his astonishing attacking ability. As a teenager Gayle was slenderly built but imbued with sumptuous natural timing. Early footage of Gayle at the start of his international career showed that, despite a lean frame, his height gave him great presence at the crease, which he capitalised on with long levers and powerful wrists. Even as a young batsman making his way in international cricket he was always a natural boundary hitter – relying not on muscular strength or crisp footwork, just a good eye and scintillating natural timing.

It wasn't until the mid 2000s, when T20 was beginning to boom, that Gayle began to change. Hours in the gym turned Gayle from a rangy kid into a powerhouse. His figure was transformed from lean and athletic to imposing and muscular. What Gayle lost in agility he made up for in power; even mishits often went for a boundary. When playing an attacking shot Gayle scored at a strike rate of 229.42, the fastest attacking strike rate of any player in the world.

Such was Gayle's attacking power, not only was he content to take longer before accelerating than other players but once he got going he continued to adopt markedly different tactics. Gayle recognised that his attacking prowess meant attempting to score through non-boundary attempts was an inefficient approach to run scoring: why run three twos or six ones when he could hit one ball for six for considerably less effort and not risk being run out? Of course, occasionally he could be caught attempting to hit sixes but the pay-off was greater.

Gayle's approach was almost binary: all-out attack or resolute defence, with very little in between. He did not attempt to score off 20% of the balls he faced over his career, the highest proportion of any player in the world. When he did attack, he scored faster than anyone else.

But while Gayle's approach minimised risk for his own innings it carried great risk for his team. By taking so long to get going and by rarely running speedily between the wickets, Gayle increased the potential positive impact of his performance greatly but at a cost of increasing his potential negative impact. If Gayle faced a large number of deliveries but then got out before he could catch up he would have consumed a large proportion of his team's resources to lay the platform for an acceleration that never came.

In the 2012 T20 World Cup final against Sri Lanka, Gayle faced 16 balls. He made just three runs, only playing five attacking shots. The West Indies went on to win but Gayle's innings comprised 13% of his team's deliveries while contributing 2% of their total runs.

Lesser players batting like this would have been disastrous; for Gayle, it was all part of the thrill. His high stakes game inverted the normal rules of T20. 'If Gayle bats six dot balls, then from a bowler's point of view you're thinking, "Crap – he's six balls more into his innings," as opposed to thinking, "Oh good, that's six dots,"' explained Carlos Brathwaite, who has frequently bowled to Gayle in T20 leagues and captained him for the West Indies T20 side.

In May 2015, Gayle arrived for his first game for Somerset, three years after they had originally signed him, only for him to withdraw after a rapprochement with the West Indies. His schedule was so relentless that Gayle had not even had time to have a net in England by the time he arrived on a chilly early summer's evening at Chelmsford, Essex's compact ground, for his debut in county cricket.

A supporting actor cannot afford to play with the crowd's patience. When the lead role does, it only adds to the allure. In pursuit of Essex's 176, the conventional wisdom had it that Somerset needed to exploit the Powerplay – the first six overs, when only two men were allowed outside the 30-yard circle.

With Gayle even leaves assumed a certain theatrical quality. Again and again, he moved his bat exaggeratedly inside the line of the ball, a man not so much leaving the ball alone as trying to get as far away from it as possible. Only off his sixth ball, with a gentle nudge to midwicket, did Gayle score his first run. Yet still he remained almost comatose; after 18 balls, all but two deliveries of the Powerplay, Gayle had just six runs, leaving Somerset scoring at under a run a ball. He continued to defend the ball with ostentatious care and a certain arrogance – a belief that he didn't need to play by the normal rules of the sport and could place a greater value upon his wicket. And he was right, too.

Then it happened: from arch-defender, Gayle was suddenly affronted by the puny size of Chelmsford's boundaries. So he cleared them – and the flats that encircled the ground while he was at it. The foot movement was laconic, the power and timing completely natural. And as the Gaylestorm went from dormant beast to awesome reality, so the Gayle effect made an appearance too. As the margins to avoid being pummelled for six became more minute with each delivery, so Essex wilted: just after Gayle reached 50, they bowled five wides down the leg side – runs that he would get no credit for but had earned. Then a cut to third man – hit hard and low, but straight to the fielder – was spilled. The next three deliveries were thundered for four, four and then six, straight over the scaffolding. By the time he was done, Gayle had scored 86 off his last 41 balls, setting up Somerset's heist.

He had won his team the game, naturally, and hearts and minds to boot. The normally tribal Chelmsford crowd could not resist a standing ovation when he was finally dismissed. Gayle, like a great raconteur, would ensure that all at the ground departed talking about him. He dutifully signed autographs and posed for smiling selfies with the crowd after; he even obliged some who requested a kiss on the cheeks.

'Beautiful,' Gayle declared the occasion. 'It's too cold for me but I stuck it out. I didn't want to make such a slow start and then get out because I know with my capabilities, I knew the runs would come.'

Gayle's entire stint with Somerset in 2015 lasted only three games. He still managed 328 runs – and 29 sixes. In a league that lasted three months, no one managed more.

It seemed to speak of a cricketer with transcendental power.

***

The Gayle lore was built upon being at once an embodiment of cricket's future and a throwback, an antidote to the age of protein shakes and fitness obsession. It is an image that he very deliberately cultivated, publicly detailing his journey from one nightclub to the next and anointing himself the 'Universe Boss'.

Yet Gayle is much less universally adored than he liked to proclaim. The last years of his career have been sullied by several accusations of sexism – most notoriously when he asked a female Australian TV presenter for a drink live on air during a game then told her 'don't blush, baby', comments that permeated the news cycle in Australia, the Caribbean and far beyond. No club in Australia's Big Bash, promoting a family-friendly image, ever signed Gayle up again. Gayle's status within the cricket world was sullied.

The controversies surrounding Gayle, his self-depiction as a nonchalant hedonist, and the show that he created – one IPL insider said that Gayle needed five people just to manage him – obscured his own profound self-understanding about his game, one of the hallmarks of his T20 greatness.

He did not train more than his opponents; instead, he trained smarter than them. Gayle used scenario work – setting particular targets to get – when batting in the nets, and practised by getting specific bowlers to bowl overs to him, rather than different bowlers bowling each ball as is the norm. This is the nearest to the mano-a-mano conflict that T20 represents, and honed Gayle for sizing up and bringing down opponents in a clinical, cold way. He also used range hitting – batting on the wicket in the ground without any nets – to hone his confidence, allowing him to see just how far, and how crisp, his blows were.

These were his general routines. But Gayle also prepared specifically for each game. 'You think about the mix: four or five bowlers, their attributes, how the captain might use those against you, what damage you can lay upon them,' he explained in *Six Machine*, his autobiography. 'You put those things in your mind as early as possible so you can sleep on it and cement ideas into actions. When you wake up, you refresh your mind and go back to the big thoughts. And when you go out there your mind will click back to those images and thoughts, and you will be ready.'

He has also thought deeply about his approach to T20, tailoring an approach designed to marry brutality with consistency. 'You've got to be smart. Wild swinging won't win you games,' Gayle wrote. 'It's not Test cricket, but it's still ball on to sweet spot of bat, and that means having a look – at the pitch, at the bowler, at what the ball is doing . . . I tear attacks to pieces, but I stalk my prey first. You have to calculate. You analyse the bowling attack. "Right, these two, they'll bowl two overs. Occasionally this one, he'll bowl three overs to try to get me out." You work it out, do the maths . . . I analyse every bowler. I analyse the entire game. Who am I up against? How can they hurt me? How can I hurt them more? You learn the game every time you go out there.'

As he amassed more experience of T20, Gayle learned to 'give yourself a little feel, give yourself a couple of balls. You learn what you can do, and how much damage you can do when. So now we're looking at the bigger picture.' He learned, too, that hitting a six is not about aiming to hit the ball as far as you can. 'You trust your bat. Make good contact and that ball is gone . . . Try to muscle it and you will lose your shape. When you're going for maximum power your head is all over the place. Your eyes totally gone off the ball. You'll top-edge it, mishit it or miss it, because there's no actual balance. It's the sound that tells you. The sound tells you it's gone.'

Gayle's image as the six-hitter nonpareil concealed his adaptability. In a 2017 Caribbean Premier League (CPL) game in Florida, for instance, Gayle recognised how a sluggish pitch would only become harder to bat on as the day progressed. Norms were swiftly recalibrated: sixes were mostly resisted, smart placement and sharp running was back in vogue. He batted throughout his side's innings, undefeated on 66 from 55 balls – an innings almost the antithesis of the classic Gayle T20 innings. Twenty-eight of his runs had come from singles, the most of any innings of his career. St Kitts and Nevis, his team, ended up on 132 for 3 from 20 overs – a highly peculiar total, since they lost only three wickets yet ended up with a score that would normally be well under par. But St Kitts won when their opposition's run chase failed to get going on a pitch that became very difficult for batting later in the game, just as Gayle had envisaged. Throughout the entire 2017 CPL season, Gayle, who had been out of form in the lead-up to the tournament and struggling with back injuries, exhibited his batting intelligence, reining in his attacking instincts when prudent; three unbeaten first innings fifties ended up contributing to victories.

Still, for all Gayle's adroit thinking about the art of T20, he was a reluctant bystander of cricket's age of marginal gains. Gayle was not only a unique batsman, he was also unique in his very way of maintaining his game in between matches. Indeed, his core method was so well grooved that he scarcely needed to do any maintaining at all.

'Chris didn't practise last year, very little – just had centre wicket, a few hits every blue moon. Likes his throw-downs before a game, and that's it,' said Jamaica Tallawahs coach Paul Nixon in 2017, after coaching Gayle in previous years and then releasing him before that season. 'He holds it mentally, and he's very good.'

Yet if he batted like a cricketer of 2025, sometimes he could field like a cricketer of 1925.

'In the field, he really struggled, and more people hit and ran to him because he couldn't get down and move very quickly, but you know he's going to make up for it with his runs, and that's the balance that you have,' Nixon observed. 'Fielding-wise? That's his off-cuts, his weakest cut. Because he's worn out. His body's played so much cricket over the years, and he's lifted so many weights to keep strong to hit the ball hard, and all the rest of it. He's feeling the pain now.'

But perhaps the relative lack of interest in marginal gains – the quick single, or the run saved in the field with an athletic dive – was understandable. For Gayle makes tools to gain, or save, a run here or there, look like child's play set against the serious business of adding runs half a dozen at a time. And so he drove opponents to radical approaches to try to nullify his threat. In the 2012 World Twenty20 semi-final, Australia restricted Gayle to facing just 18 balls in the first ten overs, and 41 overall, out of 120, through a concerted attempt to deprive Gayle of the strike. It didn't work. Gayle still had time to plunder six sixes, making 75 not out to set up a crushing West Indies victory.

***

A Premier League footballer can move freely between club teams but only represent one at a time. But, with short leagues played virtually non-stop throughout each year, a T20 franchise player can move from league to league, team to team and back again, in a way that is unparalleled by any other player in any other sport. Just as his batting grasped a simple concept – the worth of the currency of the six in this new game – and took it to its extreme conclusion, so Gayle's career choices did the same. Gayle played for everyone: 25 different teams by the end of 2018, to be exact. No cricketer ever represented so many professional sides.

In an age when the economics of the sport were skewed towards the rich – the West Indies earn £12 million a year from broadcasting rights, while from 2020 England's broadcasting contract is worth £220 million a year, and they also receive more money from the International Cricket Council – the T20 free market allowed Gayle to earn what he was worth, unencumbered by not being from one of cricket's wealthiest nations. Until the IPL Gayle was used to earning £800 per one-day international for the West Indies. Then, he earned £400,000 in his first IPL contract. 'I'm like, "How much?"' Gayle recounted in the documentary *Death of a Gentleman*. 'That can't be real. Then everything just changed just from there.'

And there has been a central irony to his career choices, castigated the most by the same old-world suits in England who, through their backroom machinations, accelerated the growth in cricket's financial imbalance between nations. Gayle's career was not just an expression of his brilliant talents; it was also a reaction to the world that cricket's administrators made, in which any player who had the ill fortune to be born outside Australia, England or India was doomed to third-class earnings from playing international cricket, regardless of how they performed on the pitch. A study from ESPNcricinfo at the end of 2017 found that, across international cricket, the most well-paid cricketers from New Zealand and the West Indies earned only one-sixth as much as the most well-paid from Australia. And while Australia's Steve Smith earned $1.47 million a year playing international cricket, no one outside the sport's economic big three earned over $0.45 million for playing internationals.

So Gayle needed T20 leagues to be treated as an equal to those cricketers from richer nations. And, regardless of whom he played for, leagues needed him. Teams in the IPL, and other leagues, have been able to unlock extra sponsorship with Gayle in their squad. Until recently, the single biggest determinant of viewing numbers for the CPL in India was simply whether Gayle was at the crease. As W.G. Grace – the world's first truly great cricketer – once said after being dismissed: 'They've come to watch me bat, not you bowl.' And so it was for Gayle.

The path that Gayle has embraced is unapologetically transactional and yet also transparent: he depended on the currency of runs, not loyalty accrued over years or being a favoured child of the system. It has been a pioneering path, and one that made him a scapegoat for those who resented cricket's direction of travel.

'Chris Gayle is exhibit A in what's wrong with cricket at the moment,' the journalist Telford Vice wrote for South Africa's *Sunday Times* at the end of 2018. 'What's a mercenary like Gayle to do if the suits keep inventing more of the same ways for him to make money?'

And yet, for all the temptation to attack Gayle as a catch-all for the narcissism and moral failings of the modern T20 player, the image ignored that Gayle had time for 103 Tests in between his T20 gluttony – and managed 15 centuries. Gayle, indeed, is the only holder of a 3-2-1, devised by the cricket writer Jon Hotten, that demonstrated mastery of all forms: Test match triple hundred (two, in fact), one-day international double hundred, T20 international century. His full-throttled embrace of T20 was out of choice, not necessity.

Gayle was almost 29, and over eight years into his international career, by the time of the first IPL. The Gayle effect could actually be felt most strongly among those who followed him, and were born into the world that he and the IPL created. Andre Russell, a strong contender to be the single most valuable T20 player in the world at stages of his career, played just a solitary Test match – one more than Kieron Pollard, the second most prolific six hitter in T20 history. Young cricket careers rapidly acquire their own momentum, one T20 contract leading inexorably on to the next. This is not exactly the path that Gayle took, but it is the world that he helped make. In 2009, when he arrived late from the IPL for a Test series in England, Gayle said that he 'wouldn't be so sad' if Test cricket died out.

***

Gayle's Instagram feed resembled that of an 'influencer', paid to promote nightclubs and alcohol. It was all tailored to giving off a simple message: wherever you were in the world, whatever you were doing, Chris Gayle was having more fun than you.

If only it were that simple. In Gayle's book there is a rather sad admission nestled between the bravado. 'Personally, I can maybe count the loyal people on one hand. One hand. And not even five fingers. That's how it is.'

The freelance cricketer's lifestyle more closely resembled an itinerant film star, forever chasing their next gig, than the traditional sportsman, with their firm attachment to a specific team and place. Dwayne Bravo, Gayle's close friend and another pioneering freelance cricketer, explained: 'I am an individual who plays a team sport, who travels and plays with teams around the world.'

The T20 franchise circuit turned cricket from a team game played by individuals into an individual pursuit. Franchise cricketers are coming to resemble tennis players – they are effectively the chief executive of their own company, responsible for hiring and firing coaches and physios. While freelance players are generally able to make some use of the training facilities at their local first-class teams, they lack permanent access to coaches and trainers. Instead, they must hire their own private coaches and trainers to help maintain their standards – another unwanted stress upon their salaries, meaning that freelance players outside the elite cannot always afford them. And teams are often resentful of players bringing in their own coaches during tournaments, fearing that it will undermine those employed by the side. 'Tennis players are allowed to travel with their own staff – I am not,' said Bravo.

From 2012, Bravo enlisted Zephyrinus Nicholas, a strength and conditioning coach and another freelancer, as his personal trainer, and paid Nicholas for his time out of his own salary. As Trinbago Knight Riders (TKR) captain, Bravo insisted that Nicholas join the coaching staff during the tournament itself. Nicholas sometimes travelled to other competitions too, and would spend the first week of this year's IPL with Bravo, setting out his personal programme for the tournament. 'I can't fly with him everywhere I go,' Bravo said. 'But when I'm home and off season I have my personal team that I work with.'

Whenever Bravo returned from a competition, he returned to Nicholas's private clinic. Nicholas evaluated his physical condition, and puts in place a new gym workout programme designed both to help him recover from his last tournament and prepare for the next one.

'It's all based on what he need[s] at that moment; sometimes it's strictly rehab,' Nicholas explained. 'If he has any injury, he will do therapy then we will do some work on the other part of the body not injured . . . We have a template we work from which includes squats, lunge, hinge, rotation, core, pull and press both vertically and horizontally. Because of his training age he is aware of his body.' This, perhaps, is the logical culmination of the age of franchise cricket: players getting their own private support teams, who will know them far better than the coaching staff during a six-week tournament ever can.

And yet this time is still some way off, so closely do franchises maintain control over players during tournaments. A sportsman tied to one team benefits from interests being aligned; an injury will be equally disadvantageous to both parties. But for an itinerant freelance player, the incentives for player and team are different. Now it is in a team's interests to pressurise a player to get an injection to get through one more game – but doing so may put the player at risk of injuring themselves, and so having to withdraw from future franchise contracts with other teams. 'Understandably the team wants its pound of flesh from the player,' said Tony Irish, the executive chairman of The Federation of International Cricketers' Associations (FICA), the global cricketers' union.

A Netflix documentary following the Mumbai Indians in the 2018 IPL provided a glimpse of the demands placed on players by teams.

After sustaining a wrist injury while fielding in a match the West Indian batsman Evin Lewis missed the next match and was encouraged to have an injection by the team doctor with a view to him returning for the following fixture. But Lewis was clearly not comfortable when batting in the nets and was hesitant to commit fully to his shots. 'You always take a risk when you play on an injury because sometimes, if the injury gets worse, you can be out for months, so you think about your career,' he explained.

In an awkward net session on the eve of the match Lewis appeared to be in some discomfort but Mahela Jayawardene, Mumbai Indians' head coach, was clearly desperate for Lewis to play. With Mumbai struggling in the league, he was under pressure to deliver results.

'I know it is a little bit of pain but you probably have to play with a little bit of pain,' Jayawardene told Lewis, who was visibly disgruntled. 'The way you are batting right now it's as if you don't want to be out there. So that can't happen in the middle if you go out there tomorrow. If the pain is less you should be able to play but your mind has to be right.'

'I can't bat with this,' said Lewis to Jayawardene, gesturing to his wrist.

'This is the best tournament in the world. These guys are going to come hard at you. If you are not prepared to change and evolve you will get found out and then you are just going to be another batsman,' Jayawardene responded. 'Go in again,' he said – nodding towards the nets. 'Grind deep and have a good six to eight balls and see what happens.'

Lewis played the next day and struggled for timing and fluency before being dismissed for a 13-ball ten. 'There is something wrong with his mental state,' remarked Simon Doull on commentary as Lewis trudged back towards the dugout.

Franchises can also be suspicious of freelance coaches, fearing they will undermine the coaching that the team are doing. Flying in a freelance coach – even if they could afford to do so – might be resented, or even outright barred; coaches, themselves insecure, may see their use during tournaments as a threat, or an indictment of their own coaching ability.

'When the private coach loses access then they get replaced with a coach that has an idea of how your player should play,' said Trent Woodhill, a leading T20 batting coach. 'Rarely is there any open two-way communication between coaches.' Instead, players are compelled to build a relationship from scratch with coaches every time they represent a new team. Sometimes, a player's freelance coach works for a rival during a tournament – Woodhill, Shane Watson's batting coach, worked for sides playing against Watson during the Big Bash and IPL.

Yet perhaps the freelancer's greatest challenge of all was staving off the loneliness that a life in hotel rooms and airport departure lounges can bring. Even the swankiest hotel can be like 'a mini-prison,' Gayle once told *The Guardian*. 'You're locked away in your room. You just see the ceiling and the TV. You get lonely sometimes.'

Gayle's singular achievement was to defy these multifarious challenges to establish himself as the Bradman of the first years of T20, a cricketer who has towered above his age. Such figures are often thought of as harbingers for the generation of athletes to follow. Yet while Gayle's propensity to hit sixes, and reliance upon domestic cricket for his income, is of the cricket of tomorrow, in other ways he is best-conceived as a sporting giant of his own time.

FOUR

UP IS DOWN

'In first-class cricket bowlers need to be consistently consistent;
but in T20 bowlers need to be consistently inconsistent'
Australian bowler A.J. Tye

Stuart Broad bowled the ball upon which his great career would be founded. Angling across the left-hander from over the wicket, it pitched on a good length on and around middle stump. In Test cricket, where Broad would go on to take more than 500 wickets for England, it would have been an excellent delivery, invariably met with a respectful defensive shot. But this was a T20 international and everything was different.

The batsman, Yuvraj Singh, seized on the fraction of length offered by Broad, opening his front foot up on to the leg side in preparation to attack. In Test cricket the batsman throwing his hands at a full ball such as this one would be fraught with risk. But – unlike in Test cricket – the white ball used in T20 very rarely swung and pitches were notoriously flat, providing very little seam movement. And, unlike in Test cricket, there was not a phalanx of slips waiting to pounce.

This particular pitch, for the 21st match of the inaugural T20 World Cup, was specifically prepared to produce copious runs.

With two overs left in the first innings, India were well set at 171 for 3 to explode towards the finish. With Yuvraj already having cleared his front leg, he knew that at this point in the innings there would be very little lateral movement to challenge his edge. So in a blur of willow he threw his hands through the line of the ball with almighty force. The ball met the middle of the bat and soared over the midwicket boundary for six. The graphic on the broadcast showed that the shot had travelled 111 metres – the biggest six of the tournament so far.

The next ball was on a similar length, though this time it was a fraction too straight, meaning there was no need for Yuvraj to clear his front leg. Instead he just planted his front foot and flicked the ball over the boundary, helping it on its way for six more runs with effortless timing.

Broad would go on to become England's second highest wicket-taker ever in Test cricket. Over more than a decade he developed a mastery of accuracy and control. With a smooth, repeatable bowling action Broad could hammer away on a good line and length ball after ball after ball. In Test cricket, where the batsmen were defending significantly more often, Broad was almost a consummate seam bowler. Yet, in T20s, consistency was transformed from a strength to a weakness. Broad's first two deliveries were fractionally too full and too straight – but Yuvraj knew where Broad was going to bowl. On a good length and on a tight line was where Broad always bowled.

In a historic moment, Yuvraj would go on to hit all six balls in Broad's over for six, only the third time in any format of the game that such a feat had been achieved. All but one of the six sixes came from good or full length deliveries; the other was an egregious full toss as Broad wilted. Yuvraj reached his fifty off just 12 balls – a record that had not been surpassed by the end of the 2019 IPL. Yuvraj's evisceration of Broad in Durban was in stark contrast with the longer formats of the game, where Broad dismissed Yuvraj four times at an average of 31 runs per wicket.

Broad's mauling at the hands of Yuvraj in that World Cup match carried an essential lesson: effectiveness in longer forms of cricket counted for nothing in the helter-skelter environment of T20. If anything, the skills that elevated bowlers to be so dominant in Test cricket – consistency, control and predictability – were exactly the skills that would be punished in the shortest format.

***

It has often been said of Tests and T20 that they produce such starkly different spectacles that they may as well be different sports entirely. While ostensibly they were the same game, played by 11 players, with two sets of stumps and a 22-yard pitch, T20 inverted the framework of the sport.

Just as T20 triggered a defining shift in the nature of batting, causing the batsman to prioritise attack over defence, it had the opposite effect for the bowler and fielders. 'It's becoming a little bit like baseball,' said the batting coach Trent Woodhill who worked in the IPL and BBL. 'The fielding team is seen as the defence and the batting team is seen as the offence.' This basic but fundamental change totally transformed bowling. And so the essence of what constituted a good ball was altered.

In first-class cricket, when the batsmen were defending the large majority of the time, a good ball was largely universal. This would normally be on a length that was full enough to pull the batsman on to the front foot but not so full that the ball was a half-volley.

'Test cricket is the war of attrition. There's a spot on the pitch six to eight feet in front of the batsman, the size of a tea towel,' explained Jason Gillespie, who took 259 Test wickets and then won the Big Bash as the Adelaide Strikers' head coach. 'Whoever owns that spot is winning the game.'

Occasionally pace bowlers would mix things up with bouncers or fuller, wider tempters or try more unconventional plans to dominant batsmen. But, for all bowlers in first-class cricket, the notion of what a good line and length were was almost universal, and so was the sense that they should try to hit this spot time and again.

In T20, this basic balance between the attacking bowler and the defensive batsman was inverted. And so bowling was turned on its head. Now predictability was an impediment, and unpredictability a boon – especially as batsmen in T20 were more individualistic, meaning that a good ball to one player could be terrible to another.

'Back when we played we placed a lot of effort on consistency and of grouping of deliveries, particularly in Test matches,' said Ian Bishop, a leading fast bowler in the 1990s for the West Indies who has since commentated on T20 around the world. 'Now in T20, while consistency of length is relevant in some stages, it has become less relevant and it is almost second-guessing a batsman and making a batsman guess every two deliveries. There is more pressure being placed on reading the strength of the batsman and then hiding the delivery from that strength.'

Jeremy Snape, an off-spinner from Leicestershire, played an integral role in twin T20 Cup wins in 2004 and 2006 and appeared in the first T20 World Cup. Snape's suitability to the format, although rooted in his skills, was partly a consequence of how quickly and effectively he understood the changed nature of bowling. 'My best ball is not what I was classically trained as,' he recalled of his approach. 'My best ball is the opposite of what the batsman is expecting or what the batsman wants, so that's a change in pace, it is balls under their feet. It is a ball wide of their stance. It is different variations depending on the batsman's skills and strengths.'

Bishop believed that the multifarious demands on bowlers in T20 had led to an evolution of skills. 'The chess match now is so much harder than when we played. I have great admiration for the guys that do it well.'

This change in mindset had a transformative effect on how to measure success and failure of deliveries. 'The paradox of T20 bowling is when you're young you're supposed to bowl a wicket-taking ball or a dot ball. But in T20 you need to educate yourself that you want to give away a single. That is a strange thing,' said Snape. 'So bowling a low full toss on leg stump because you've got two men back protecting that area actually becomes a reasonably safe option because they rotate the strike, the hitter gets down to the non-striker's end and then you get the chance to apply pressure through dot balls on the new batsman that has come in.'

The extent of the change that this shift in focus demanded was well illustrated by the Indian off-spinner Ravichandran Ashwin in a famous interview with ESPNcricinfo in 2016. 'I basically think that six well-constructed bad balls could be the way to go forward in T20 cricket,' he said. This was a remarkable revelation from a bowler regarded as a deep thinker about the game. What he was referring to was the value in remaining unpredictable and of bowling balls that surprise the batsman, especially with a field set for those deliveries. In Test cricket such balls might be considered 'bad' but in T20 if they forced a batsman to settle for a single then they represented a win for the bowler.

The Australian bowler A.J. Tye, one of the world's foremost slower ball bowlers since 2015, neatly encapsulated how T20 changed bowling. 'In first-class cricket bowlers need to be consistently consistent; but in T20 bowlers need to be consistently inconsistent.'

In this respect not only did the batting team and bowling team in T20 become like the batting and the pitching team in baseball in that they shared similar aims, their practitioners became more like one another too.

As well as batsmen and coaches taking learnings from baseball hitters, so too did bowlers from pitchers. The career of English bowler Benny

Howell was transformed after he attended a Major League Baseball game. Howell became fascinated with the battle between the pitcher and the hitter and taught himself the knuckleball using videos of baseball pitchers on YouTube. He was one of a generation of T20 bowlers who became almost entirely concerned with being unpredictable and remaining ahead of the game. These bowlers were obsessed by variation and disguise and were driven by a desire to be as hard to hit as possible.

It wasn't that bowlers were uninterested in taking wickets but they recognised that the balls that took the most wickets – very full or very short lengths – were often the most expensive. By concentrating largely on saving runs bowlers could force the batsmen into mistakes through a build-up of pressure. 'The best way to stop runs is to keep taking wickets but if you stop runs then the batsmen can panic and do something reckless and you might end up with a wicket,' explained Tye. 'It's almost like being an attacking bowler by being defensive.'

What speeds and lengths fast bowlers adopted were largely influenced by the stage of the innings in which they bowled. The earlier a wicket was taken, the more valuable it was to the fielding team. Analysis by CricViz showed that a wicket taken in the first over of the innings typically reduced the total of the batting team by 12 runs but a wicket taken in the last over of the innings only knocked around two runs off their total. Generally this process meant bowlers became increasingly defensive throughout the innings.

The first six Powerplay overs were the only period when consistency of line and length still had some merit. In this period when the ball was hard and new, fast bowlers were tasked with bowling accurate lines and lengths and looking to find any swing in the air or seam off the pitch. With only two fielders permitted outside the circle the batsmen were forced to pierce the infield with classical cricket shots. When the fielding restrictions were lifted and the ball got older, batsmen became increasingly aggressive and fast bowlers were forced to become ever more unpredictable, mixing their lengths and speeds up more often to make life increasingly difficult for the batsmen. By the time the death over phase came around and the batsmen were attacking without care, the emphasis was entirely on unpredictability, with bowlers mixing their lengths regularly from yorkers to bouncers to in between and their speeds from quicker balls to slower balls and back again.

'In the Powerplay [the batsmen] are trying to pierce the field with proper cricket shots but in the middle [and death] overs they are trying to hit you 50 rows back into the crowd because if they do mishit it there's a good chance they'll get caught with five fielders out,' said Tye. 'It is massively different between a Powerplay bowler and someone who bowls through the middle and at the death.'

While all bowlers adopted different tactics and methods there were two clear trends that could be discerned in T20 bowling compared to longer formats. Pace bowlers delivered far fewer of their deliveries on what was considered to be a 'good' length and bowled an appreciably higher proportion of slower balls, opting for variation over consistency.

The change in spin bowling was slightly different but even more profound. T20 spin bowling was also defined by inconsistency and unpredictability but a more general pattern could be identified among most spinners that saw them bowl flatter, faster and shorter overall. They generally spun the ball less but those that could turn it both ways did so more often.

This specific evolution was made necessary because against fuller lengths batsmen could prop on to the front foot and swing through the line of the ball – a so-called 'step and hit'. Instead, the combination of a flatter trajectory, shorter length and faster speed made it harder for the batsmen to get under the ball and forced them on to the back foot. Occasionally a batsman might have been able to play the pull shot, which involved swinging from low to high, but the pace on the ball meant this was a difficult shot to play, requiring nimble footwork from the batsmen to get back in position and have time to play the shot. Instead batsmen often had to settle for cutting the ball out on the off side or punching it down the ground. These two shots were very difficult to hit for boundaries, especially sixes, and normally only brought a single – a clear win for the bowler.

***

Not only did T20 change the art of bowling but it changed the bowlers who had the most success. In both Tests and ODIs pace bowlers were notably more successful than spin bowlers, returning lower averages. Yet in T20 it was spinners who averaged less.

Pace and Spin Bowling Averages by Format		
Format	**Pace Bowlers**	**Spin Bowlers**
Test	30.44	32.80
ODI	31.05	35.09
T20	25.31	24.48

It was for the very reasons that pace bowlers found T20 more difficult that spin bowlers were so effective: speed and movement. The speed that spinners bowled at – around 50 to 70 mph – was significantly slower than the speed of fast bowlers who operated above 60 mph and as high as 95 mph. These slower speeds made spinners harder to hit.

'The batsmen have to create pace on to the ball,' explained the spin bowling coach Carl Crowe who worked in leagues around the world and was a mentor to T20's leading spin wicket-taker Sunil Narine. 'If you're defending against seamers, probably with the pace you're still scoring runs, but with the spinners, obviously you're not.'

It seemed as if the faster it was bowled, the further it went. In T20 cricket spinners had an economy rate of 7.12 runs per over while quicks went at 7.84 runs per over. Across an entire innings that equated to a difference of 15 runs.

The lack of pace on the ball made it easier for spin bowlers to lock down areas of the field as well. Just 24% of runs off spinners were scored behind square compared to 39% for pace bowlers, whose speed opened up scoring areas behind the batsman that were harder to access against spin. Ramp and scoop shots were extremely useful shots against pace bowlers – enabling the batsmen to manoeuvre the field by harnessing the pace on the ball. These shots were essentially useless against spin with batsmen unable to generate enough power. This made setting fields for spinners easier than against quicks who had more boundary areas to defend.

'Spinners take away the easy hitting option,' explained the New Zealand off-spinner Jeetan Patel. 'With a seamer if you're too full you can go over the top, and if you're too short you can be hit square of the wicket so you can't cover all bases. With spin you can cover more of the hitting areas.'

Movement – the ability to spin the ball – was another trait which gave spinners an advantage over pace bowlers. For fast bowlers the ability to move the ball through swing in the air or seam off the pitch, although a skill, was one largely dependent on the type of ball and the nature of the pitch. Pace bowlers could control the direction of the swing – different grips were required for inswing and outswing – but not the direction of seam movement, which was essentially random and was made difficult by the nature of pitches prepared for T20.

For spinners, the motion of imparting spin on the ball caused drift through the air and deviation off the pitch – to a far greater degree than that managed by the quicks and with far greater consistency. Spinners were less reliant on conditions: although some pitches spun more than others, spinners could always extract some movement.

Moving the ball off the straight complicated the process of attacking batting, with the batsmen looking to swing hard and fast through their predicted line of the ball. Once the ball started to move laterally, attacking strokes became harder to execute.

That spinners could control the spin and different types of spinners turned the ball in different ways meant that their captains could choose which batsmen to deploy them against. Batsmen generally preferred the ball spinning into them – towards the arc of their bat swing – rather than away from them. Captains could engineer these basic-level match-ups so that leg-spinners and left-arm orthodox spinners generally bowled to right-handers and that off-spinners and left-arm unorthodox spinners bowled to left-handers.

As analytics within the sport evolved, these match-ups became more specific with fielding captains targeting or avoiding certain batsmen with certain types of bowlers based on their career record against that specific bowler type, rather than just their batting hand. For example, the left-handed New Zealand batsman Colin Munro – who would be expected to struggle against the ball spinning away from him and favour the ball spinning into him – scored at a strike rate of 139 against off spin which turned the ball away, but struggled against leg spin – which turned the ball in – scoring at a strike rate of 121. Match-ups with certain types of pace bowlers did exist – for instance the Australian Ben Dunk averaged 25 against right-arm pace and just 13 against left-arm pace – but these clear gulfs were rarer than against spin. Spin bowling, with its four different techniques and different types of spin, was like a key that could unlock all but the very best batsmen.

The need for tactical precision and the lack of time to react created a more interventionist style of coaching, almost akin to football. 'I get involved from the sidelines,' explained Ricky Ponting who won the IPL as head coach at Mumbai Indians before moving to Delhi in 2018. 'If you can see a bowling change is about to happen, and it's not something that we've talked about or if we feel it's the wrong match-up, we'll try and influence where we can.'

Such a coaching style was more necessary when the captain was inexperienced, as was the case at Delhi where 24-year-old Shreyas Iyer led the team to third place.

'You could map it to the over if you wanted to,' said Ponting. 'As a coach you know, deep down in your heart of hearts, you have to give all the information because if you don't you feel like you're not doing the right thing by the team. We've got a fairly young captain and try to give him as much information as we think is right.

'Every single ball that's bowled in a T20 game is almost like a set play – you're trying to come up with the right match-ups. When you're in the field you want to try and come up with the right match-up bowling-wise to the batsman at the crease. If you can try and manipulate when you're batting what the bowling team can do as well with the way that you stack your batting line-up – little things like that can go a long way to winning you a game as well. Our planning is pretty meticulous and so far the boys have bought into that – and they do a lot of their own individual planning stuff as well.'

Ponting, who had once declared that T20 was 'difficult to play seriously', came to believe that strategy was 'absolutely' more important in T20 than in Test cricket. 'We make sure that when we go into each game that there's nothing that should happen in the game that should take us by surprise.'

Gary Kirsten – who played 101 Tests for South Africa before coaching T20 teams around the world – shared a similar view to Ponting. 'It's very detailed, T20 cricket – much more detailed than Test cricket,' he said on *The Real Science of Sport* podcast. This was an illuminating comment from someone who had experienced both formats close up. 'Test match cricket is the simplest form of the game,' he went on to say. 'You don't actually need that many plans. You are not under pressure as a batsman; you can have a couple of bad overs and you are under no pressure to score runs, whereas T20 cricket is on your case ball by ball.'

***

Batsmen were the headline stars of T20. The format was, after all, designed partly so that they could hit more boundaries, score faster and post bigger totals.

Perhaps most ominously for bowlers, batsmen have an inherent physiological advantage, which they are only properly exploring now, in the uber-professional age. The theory here is very simple: that, because of the strain that bowling puts upon the body, bowlers can only do so much.

'Bowlers will have limited capacity to practise, whereas batsmen can practise almost as much as they like,' explained Timothy Olds from the School of Health Sciences at the University of South Australia. 'You can't have your bowlers practising 300 yorkers, but in theory your batters could practise hitting 300 yorkers,' said Gillespie.

'Batting has really advanced far ahead of bowling,' reflected John Buchanan, the former Australia and Kolkata Knight Riders coach. 'When batters are preparing for a game they'll go to the nets and then the bowlers will go to them for a period of time. Then the bowlers stop. With sports science dominating decision-making around workloads bowlers really don't spend a lot of time training these days, particularly in T20.

'Whereas batters spend a lot of time playing because sports science is not so concerned about their workload, so batters then will move from the nets and say to the coach they need another half hour to work in the nets on specific skills. And then if they're still not happy, and the coach has had enough – they'll go to the bowling machine. And so the batter's skill levels on all the types of deliveries that a bowler might be able to deliver in a game are so far advanced of the bowlers.'

'Bowlers need to train more,' Buchanan remarked. 'They need to have the confidence when they get up to the top of their mark that they have got four or five different deliveries – an Andrew Tye might have eight or nine – that they can call on at any time. At the moment they're just not training enough to be able to land those variations accurately enough, so batters take advantage of that.'

The divide between batting and bowling was exacerbated by T20 encouraging batsmen to attack like never before. The first era of the T20 format was marked by a steady, albeit not spectacular, increase in scoring rates.

T20 provided an immense test, but also a great opportunity, for bowlers. 'Sixty-yard boundaries with guys teeing off from ball one. It's an unbelievable challenge,' remarked England's ODI and T20 captain Eoin Morgan. 'But also it presents a huge opportunity for somebody to be really, really good and make a good living and life around it.' The higher scores got and the better batsmen got, the more valuable bowlers who could restrict and dismiss them became.

'Batsmen are important – of course they are – but I think bowlers are hugely underestimated in T20 cricket,' said Tom Moody, the head coach of Sunrisers Hyderabad from 2013 to 2019. 'Generally the most successful teams are [the ones] that have the ability to bowl their 120 balls most effectively, with the right balance of attackers and defenders within that bowling core.'

The most successful teams in the first era of T20 cricket were those who had strong bowling attacks: Hampshire in England, Kolkata Knight Riders and Sunrisers Hyderabad in the IPL, Peshawar Zalmi in the Pakistan Super League (PSL) and Perth Scorchers in the BBL.

'I'm always a big believer that bowlers win you games in all formats,' said Adam Voges, captain of Perth Scorchers during their years of dominance in the BBL when they reached seven consecutive semi-finals, three times going on to win. 'We've always had a really strong bowling group. That is what our success has been built around. We haven't always scored 180 or 200 runs in a game, but we're the group that can defend 130 or 140 with the bowlers that we've got.'

Taming domestic leagues was one thing. The West Indies, the World Cup champions in 2012 and 2016, had the most economical death bowling of any team across the 2012, 2014 and 2016 tournaments.

Bowling also underpinned Pakistan's remarkable run in international cricket from April 2016. In the following 34 months, Pakistan won 29 of their 33 matches, rising to number one in the T20 rankings.

This brilliant run was founded on a clear and consistent strategy. The foundation of their approach was to win the toss and bat – relying on their defensive strength, with the ball and in the field, to defend even sub-par totals. Across those 33 matches Pakistan won the toss 18 times and chose to bat first 61% of the time in an era when chasing was in vogue. Despite recording a lower average first innings score than India, Australia and England in this period, they successfully defended their score in 18 of the 22 matches when they batted first.

Pakistan had both a strong bowling attack and a deep one. No team averaged less with the ball than their 17.81 runs per wicket, and they had eight bowlers averaging under 23 in this period. This diverse array of bowlers – including three left-arm quicks, two right-arm quicks, two off-spinners, one left-arm spinner and one leg-spinner – enabled Pakistan to tailor their attack to different conditions and tailor match-ups in a way that exploited the weaknesses of opposing batting line-ups.

The bowling attack was supported brilliantly by their fielders – only Australia had a higher catch success percentage and saved more runs in the field per match. They also used home advantage shrewdly. When hosting the world champions West Indies in the United Arab Emirates (UAE) in 2016, they deliberately moved the boundaries out as far as possible, and prepared slow wickets to negate the West Indies' boundary hitting; a series of batsmen were then caught a few yards in from the rope. Pakistan won all 11 games they played in the UAE from April 2016 to February 2019.

In the process they vindicated a philosophy espoused by John Wright, a coach who won the 2013 IPL with Mumbai Indians and had success at Derbyshire by building bowling-heavy teams. 'I've subscribed to the Brian Clough theory that there's no point scoring six if you let in seven. I like the consistency of a good defensive set-up which is your bowling and fielding. Sometimes your batting can be up and down.'

The most fundamental reason for the importance of bowlers was the nature of their usage compared to batsmen. While batsmen could bat for an entire innings and face upwards of 60 balls, in practice the best batsmen were not active for any longer in a match than the best bowlers were. The most prolific T20 batsman ever, Chris Gayle, faced 23 balls an innings – the same number that Sunil Narine, the pre-eminent T20 bowler, bowled. At their best top batsmen can influence much more of a match, but they are a riskier proposition. They can get out first ball, or barely get any time to bat at all. In contrast top bowlers can, and normally will, deliver 24 balls in a match. Batsmen have no second chances; bowlers have 24 chances. On a good day a batsman can define an entire match but a batsman's good day is rarer than a bowler's good day.

Rahul Dravid, a legend of Indian cricket who captained his country and RCB in the IPL before assuming a coaching role at Rajasthan Royals, believed the importance of bowling over batting was most clearly illustrated by the role of the number seven in the team. 'There are enough statistics and data to prove that your number seven, on average, is playing something like eight to ten deliveries per match,' he explained. 'But a bowler at number seven can actually influence the game a lot more because he can bowl 24 balls.'

This basic framework meant that batting was 'strong-link dependent', and bowling was 'weak-link dependent'. This meant that a team's batting would often be as strong as their best one or two players who could in theory bat for the majority of the innings. In the 2016 IPL Virat Kohli and A.B. de Villiers – two of the world's best batsmen – recorded a record T20 partnership of 229 for Royal Challengers Bangalore. Between them they faced 107 of RCB's 120 balls and with almost no help from their teammates they powered their team towards a massive total.

In contrast no bowler can bowl more than 24 balls and at least five bowlers must bowl if the 20 overs are to be completed. This meant that a team's bowling would often only be as strong as their weakest link. In the 2018 IPL final Chennai Super Kings (CSK) chased a target of 179 against Sunrisers Hyderabad despite only scoring 41 runs off the eight overs bowled by Sunrisers' best two bowlers, Rashid Khan and Bhuvneshwar Kumar. Shane Watson, who scored a brilliant match-winning hundred, knew that if he could see off Rashid and Kumar he could capitalise against Sunrisers' weaker options. Watson was on nought after ten balls, opting to simply block against Bhuvneshwar. But later in the innings he made up his lost ground, targeting Sandeep Sharma, Siddharth Kaul, Carlos Brathwaite and Shakib Al Hasan. CSK scored 137 runs off the 10.3 overs bowled by those four bowlers and won the match with nine balls to spare.

In this respect batting, which was strong-link dependent, was like basketball, where a team's best player could single-handedly shape matches. Bowling, which was weak-link dependent, was more like football, where weak players could leave entire teams and systems exposed, as Chris Anderson and David Sally showed in *The Numbers Game*.

Stronger bowling teams were also 'more versatile' than those who were stronger in batting, according to Srinath Bhashyam, head of operations of Delhi Capitals. With a better bowling attack, sides were less encumbered by the result of the toss.

Historically in longer forms of cricket, teams generally preferred to bat first, partly because they could enjoy the best of conditions before the pitch deteriorated and partly because they could avoid the pressure of batting in a run chase. The former Australian captain Ian Chappell once famously said, 'When you win the toss, you bat first nine times out of ten; the tenth time you think about it and bat first anyway.' In the early years of T20 this convention held true with 56% of teams between 2003 and the end of 2012 electing to bat first upon winning the toss.

But as T20 evolved it became increasingly apparent that conditions did not change sufficiently to make batting first preferable. Instead, the onset of dew in the second innings – especially for matches played at night – actually made it harder for bowlers to grip the ball and typically helped the pitch skid on and prove easier for batting, dissuading teams from electing to defend totals. As the scope and range of modern batsmen became clear the pressure of chasing targets was alleviated; increasingly, the clarity of thought provided by a target to chase emboldened batsmen. On the flipside this evolution has made setting an appropriate target trickier.

'The level of skills batsmen have shown, the improvement dealing with levels of risk and finding boundaries means batting units or teams in general are quite comfortable knowing what their target is. The unease of posting a score, or knowing what a good score is, is becoming more and more difficult,' said Morgan. 'Probably over the last three years, having a look at previous results or scores at the ground hasn't been as reliable as in the past. That's made it difficult.'

In addition to the structural benefits to chasing, teams generally preferred to play to their stronger suit in the second half of the match when the parameters of the contest were set. So batting-dominant teams preferred to chase and bowling-dominant teams preferred to defend. Yet the enormity of the challenge facing bowlers in T20 meant there was a relative scarcity of high-quality bowlers in the format. Most teams simply trusted their batsmen more than their bowlers, and were more comfortable chasing.

By 2013 the anarchy of the early years gave way to clarity. Between 2013 and 2018 60% of toss-winning teams elected to chase – responding both to the structure of the format and the relative strengths of their own team which were almost invariably in favour of the batsmen.

Percentage of Toss Winners Electing to Chase	
2003–12	**2013–18**
44%	60%

This imbalance in toss choices provided the best bowling teams with an advantage because the large majority of their opponents wanted to chase. 'If you're a batting team, you're going to want to chase, but if you're a bowling team then the other team will want to chase anyway, so you can actually almost do what you like every game,' explained Moody. 'I think teams that are strong defensively with the ball won't have an issue with defending because they've got bowlers like Sunil Narine, Rashid Khan or Imran Tahir that thrive under scoreboard pressure.'

Batting second also made it easier to plan your bowling innings. Occasionally strategies could be waylaid by a particularly marauding batsman but generally the absence of a target to defend allowed captains to stick to bowling patterns they'd formulated in advance of the match. When a team was bowling second their plans were forced to adapt depending on the circumstances of the match: there would be no sense leaving the final over of the innings to the best bowler if the match was already on its way to being lost. When bowling second, bowlers were more likely to be forced to bowl at a time that did not ideally suit them.

Despite the worth of leading bowlers – and the scarcity of their gifts – bowlers were generally not rewarded as handsomely as batsmen in auctions and drafts. In the 2019 IPL auction bowlers commanded the lowest average salary of all player roles.

Average Salary by Player Role, IPL 2019	
Player Role	**Average Salary**
Wicketkeepers	$577,476
Batsmen	$557,302
All-Rounders	$412,070
Bowlers	$362,701

This discrepancy was the likely product of the prevailing image of T20, which was defined by power-hitting batsmen, not frugal bowlers. It was also a consequence of perspective: a batsman scoring a fifty off 20 balls was far more dramatic than a bowler taking 4 for 20 from his four overs, despite the latter typically being of more value.

Statistical analysis suggested that teams who restricted their opponents to, say, 15 runs under the par score for a ground tended to win more matches than those who scored the same amount over the par score. Paradoxically, saving runs in the field appeared to be more important to teams than scoring runs. This discrepancy could partly be explained by teams seldom losing all ten wickets in an innings. So a team whose batting was relatively weak would still be unlikely to be bowled out, giving them a chance of getting to a good total in spite of losing early wickets, but a team whose bowling was weak would invariably have to chase a large total.

Whether or not bowlers were more important than batsmen, there was broad agreement among analysts that bowlers were, at the very least, undervalued on the T20 market. 'What I think is likely,' observed Joe Harris, a freelance T20 analyst, 'is that the number one ranked bowling attacks cost less to construct than the number one ranked batting line-ups.' Investing in elite bowling was the most proven way to build a formidable T20 team on the cheap.

FIVE

SPIN KINGS

'Opening batsmen typically were not accustomed to facing spin bowlers as much as pace . . . So immediately getting a spinner on up front was a novelty'
Samuel Badree, two-time T20 World Cup winner for the West Indies

A hop, a skip and a jump and Sunil Narine is into his bowling action. The unassuming nature of his approach to the crease belies the wizardry of what is to come. It happens very suddenly. Just as he plants his back leg for delivery, what started as a lackadaisical motion is transformed into a concentration of energy. Power is transferred up through his legs, into his hips and lower back and then like a bolt of electricity it zips through his shoulder, into his arm and finally the ball itself.

Narine's delivery motion, a blur of rotating shoulders, powerful hands and dexterous fingers, imparts an extraordinary number of revolutions on the ball. The scrambled seam gyrates rapidly. The ball is fizzing down the pitch on Narine's notoriously flat and fast trajectory.

Then, for a fraction of a second everything seems to stop as the ball hits the pitch and grips in the turf. This is the moment of truth for the waiting batsman – the left-hander Nicholas Pooran – who will soon know if he's read the direction of the spin correctly. As a fellow Trinidadian Pooran had faced Narine many times before in the nets and in advance of the match he had studied videos and watched the slow-motion replays in an effort to decipher Narine's different deliveries. But here he was batting in a Super Over in the Caribbean Premier League, playing for Trinidad and Tobago Red Steel with Narine representing the Guyana Amazon Warriors, and nothing could prepare him for the real thing. The ball is on a leg stump line and Pooran clears his leg, giving him room to free his arms.

The ball grips in the pitch for what seems like an age before it spits off the turf and spins an almost freakish amount. It is an off break; the delivery that Pooran expected – turning away from him – but he seems stunned by the degree of spin and swings wildly at the ball with almost no expectation of making contact. The wicketkeeper too is shocked and barely gets his hands down in time. One ball into the Super Over, no runs scored.

A Super Over is cricket's equivalent of a penalty shootout in football – used when teams are level on runs after 20 overs. Just as T20 made batsmen more aggressive than in ODIs, a Super Over – with six balls available to three batsmen – had the same effect. The average score in a Super Over was ten; in this particular instance Trinidad and Tobago are chasing 12 to win.

The second ball is on an almost identical line to the first but it is even faster at 62 mph, giving Pooran – who plays the same shot – even less time to respond. The spin is sharp again and this time the bounce is low, scuttling through at shin height. Pooran swings and misses for a second time.

The date is August 2014 and this is Narine at the peak of his powers. The match is being played at the Providence Stadium in Guyana, a venue notorious for its slow, low and dry pitches which make run scoring exceptionally difficult and benefit spinners enormously. No T20 venue in the world has a lower scoring rate – the average score is a meagre 129. Batting in T20 doesn't get tougher than this.

The third ball is a repeat of the second: flat, fast and skidding through. Pooran wildly swings and misses for the third time. The target is now slipping out of reach. Pooran has not yet laid bat on a single delivery in the over.

The stands are a long way from the action at Providence Stadium – the boundaries are enormous – but the vuvuzelas, a trademark of Guyana's loyal fans, erupt in the background. They may be a way away but they are well aware that the world's master spin bowler is casting a spell over Pooran.

The horns hum in the background as Narine gathers for a fourth time. This time he changes the angle by coming tighter on the crease and bowling slightly wider. It is the fastest ball of the over at 64 mph: as fast as some medium-pacers. Narine is still spinning it to an enormous degree and again the ball fizzes off the pitch, getting some extra bounce this time and skipping over the top edge of the bat and into the keeper's gloves. Pooran, who has not even hit a single ball this over, now needs to hit the last two balls of the over for six to win the match.

On the fifth ball Pooran finally makes contact with another ripping off break. He doesn't hit it cleanly though, toe-edging a drive shot high in the air. The long-off fielder steadies himself beneath the ball and takes a comfortable catch well inside the boundary rope. Narine – who until now has remained totally calm – breaks into celebration, punching the air and screaming. With 12 runs needed from one ball the match is won.

The last ball of the Super Over still has to be bowled. The batsman on strike is now the right-handed New Zealander Ross Taylor. The first five balls were all off breaks – spinning away from the left-handed Pooran. For the sixth ball Narine finally unfurls his variation: the carrom ball, which pitches and spins wickedly away from the right-hander, taking it out of the hitting arc once more – a wink from the abyss. Taylor has a wild swing and misses the ball by a foot.

Six balls, five swings and misses, no runs and one wicket. This was perhaps the most remarkable individual display of bowling in the short history of T20. The king – Sunil Narine, in his castle – the Providence Stadium. A wicket maiden in a Super Over.

***

T20 was meant to signal the death of spin bowling. 'We thought they'd be hopeless,' recalled Adam Hollioake, who captained Surrey to the inaugural Twenty20 Cup trophy in 2003. 'When T20 first started everyone thought the spinners would just get smashed,' remembered Shane Warne, cricket's most famous spinner who took over 1,000 international wickets and won the IPL with Rajasthan Royals. 'People thought as soon as the spin comes on, yeah we can whack it.'

The theory was that spinners – who traditionally bowled slowly and tossed the ball up above the batsman's eyeline – would be brutalised by attacking batsmen wielding big bats and looking to club the ball over small boundaries. In contrast, pace bowling was touted as the best option to stem the flow of runs. 'It was a classic fear response – if you're scared, hit somebody harder, be more aggressive, bowl faster,' explained the spin bowler Jeremy Snape.

Yet in T20's first age, no type of player has excelled as consistently and as comprehensively as spin bowlers.

The notion that spinners would struggle in T20 was quickly dispelled. In the early years of England's Twenty20 Cup, Surrey's Nayan Doshi,

Sussex's Mushtaq Ahmed, Leicestershire's Snape, Nottinghamshire's Graeme Swann and Glamorgan's Robert Croft were all among the most successful bowlers. Meanwhile in Pakistan – the third country to establish a T20 league after England and South Africa – spinners were even more effective, making up five of the top six wicket-takers across the first two seasons. Apart from Mushtaq, a leg-spinner and therefore capable of spinning the ball both ways, there was no real magic or X factor to the bowlers who had success in England. Rather, they simply took pace off the ball, were accurate and used their experience to outfox the batsmen.

The First Era of Spin Bowling – Leading Spin Wicket-Takers, 2003–07		
Bowler	**Spin Type**	**Wickets**
Nayan Doshi	Finger Spin	53
Mushtaq Ahmed	Wrist Spin	42
Graeme Swann	Finger Spin	36
Jeremy Snape	Finger Spin	36
Jason Brown	Finger Spin	34
Robert Croft	Finger Spin	33
Thandi Tshabalala	Finger Spin	31
Gareth Breese	Finger Spin	29
James Tredwell	Finger Spin	28
Dinesh Mongia	Finger Spin	28

The man at the forefront of this age was the off-spinner Snape, instrumental in helping Leicestershire reach at least the semi-finals in the first four seasons of the Twenty20 Cup. Snape's most important attribute was his intelligence; already 30 when T20 was introduced, he used this experience to read and second-guess the batsman's intentions. With a wiry frame, balding head and sunglasses, Snape was an unassuming character, but his cricketing intuition, combined with his slow speeds and accuracy, made him immensely difficult to score off.

'We found that taking pace off the ball was a really good way of doing it because it placed the pressure back on the batsman to add pace to the ball and place the ball and do something with it,' he recalled. 'You've got a ring of fielders that are there and there's not much pace on the ball so placement becomes really key for a batsman.'

Snape combined this lack of pace with exceptional control and sheer cunning. 'Where I wasn't getting huge deviation or drift, I could set a field to the line and pace variations which meant I could play with the batsman. And as they got more frustrated I could vary the pace more but still hold my line.'

Together with classical cricketing nous, Snape brought original creative thinking. 'I was innovative and entrepreneurial,' he said. He would walk back to the top of his run-up backwards – never taking his eyes off the batsman. 'The interesting time for the batsman when they are building their strategy and their commitment to their strategy is while I'm walking back in the space between deliveries. So I wanted to catch every clue that I could find in that time so I started to walk backwards past the umpire and watching the batsmen right the way through it and collect the ball at whatever time I needed it because I was building a plan as to what he would do next.

'If a batsman looked to deep midwicket and was eyeing up the stands, I would very quickly shout to my deep midwicket it's coming to you so move a bit squarer, or get a bit taller or whatever it might be. Just by me signalling where the batsman was going to hit it he had to second-guess it and by the time he got confused I was already in my run-up and about to bowl at him. So the confusion and the lack of clarity became a bigger weapon for me than my deviation off the pitch – which was rare in any instance anyway.'

Another innovation driven by Snape was the 'moon ball' – a delivery which saw him approach the crease very quickly and rush through his action before lobbing the ball very high and very slowly in the air. The combination of the speed and the trajectory meant the ball suddenly dropped on the batsman at the last moment and it proved difficult to hit. The loopy nature of the delivery disrupted the batsman's core strength, causing them to lean back on impact rather than into the ball.

In the first era of T20 – before the 2007 T20 World Cup and the launch of the IPL truly globalised the format – conventional finger spinners dominated the T20 circuit, and made up nine of the ten leading spin wicket-takers in that period. There was very little mystery or magic associated with these bowlers. Like Snape, they succeeded by taking pace off the ball, by being accurate and by out-thinking the batsmen. It was a quiet and unassuming start to the transformation of spin bowling.

***

Ostensibly Trinidad and Tobago was an unlikely starting point for a cricketing revolution. With a population of 1.25 million and a GDP outside the world's top 100 it was a country of little political or economic clout. Yet throughout its history these two islands nestled at the bottom of the Caribbean have produced a number of great international players: from Learie Constantine to Larry Gomes to the iconic Brian Lara.

Cricket has formed an intrinsic part of the culture of the country and the rise of T20 provided a format of the game that chimed with the style of cricket the region has always nurtured: free-spirited, powerful and innovative. In the first age of T20 arguably no nation contributed as much to the format, especially spin bowling, as Trinidad and Tobago.

'The style of cricket that West Indians play – it's very instinctive, it's very natural, it's got a lot of flair,' remembered Daren Ganga, who captained the islands between 2001 and 2011 in all three formats. 'A cavalier sort of approach to the game and different formats. The West Indian style fits perfectly with the requirements for T20 cricket because it requires you to be fearless as a cricketer and that's why you see a lot of West Indian, and Trinidad and Tobago players in particular, warm towards this format of the game.'

Trinidad and Tobago was also the Caribbean territory where windball cricket – played with a smaller and lighter ball than a regular cricket ball and with no more than 12 overs per team – was most popular.

The type of players produced by windball cricket was radically different to those produced by the more formalised coaching structures in England and Australia, the game's oldest nations. While in England and Australia cricketers were often more conventional, the windball, beach and street cricket more prevalent in the Caribbean and Asia produced unusual talents with unique skills. Nowhere was this more apparent than in spin bowling where countries with softer balls and fewer coaches produced bowlers with new and distinctive deliveries that spun in unexpected ways.

'There is no coaching out there and what is great – and this is a big lesson for us all in the so-called more modern coaching countries like England and Australia – is that the evidence would seem to be that we stifle the potential talent rather than encourage it,' explained the bowling coach Carl Crowe.

'This is in all sports. In football kids are joining academies at seven and training like a professional player; they should be at the park playing with their mates and playing street football – that's where you learn skills, not in an academy where it is all structured. It's the element of free play that is so important in developing skill in a youngster.

'You very rarely get that creative player where they've been coached since the ages of six and seven because it's coached out of them. You're not encouraging them to have success and failure and trial and error in that environment. Coaches like safety. Safety is not trial and error.'

If Trinidad and Tobago was an unlikely cradle for change, then Samuel Badree and Sunil Narine were even more unlikely agents for that change. But Badree, a PE teacher from the southern, agricultural town of Barrackpore, and Narine, a shy and nervous man from the northern town of Arima, would combine to form a revolutionary spin bowling duo.

Ganga knew both Badree and Narine when they were growing up – captaining Badree at primary and secondary school, before leading the pair at Trinidad and Tobago as well. 'I always knew Badree as "that leg-spinner",' he recalled. Narine meanwhile was 'an introvert, very quiet and kept his emotions to himself, but we recognised the uniqueness of his talent.'

Throughout his professional career Badree combined playing cricket with a job as a PE teacher. 'I'm a full-time professional worker, and a part-time cricketer, I would say. Because as soon as I get back home I'm straight into my work.' Even after winning his second T20 World Cup, Badree's LinkedIn profile read: 'International cricketer/Physical Education Teacher at Barrackpore East Secondary'. It summed up a cricketer who was the antidote to the razzmatazz of the West Indies side. Narine sported earrings, a large gold chain and a spiky Mohican but this showy image belied a reticent personality.

For Narine, more so than for Badree, windball and tennis ball cricket were central to his rise. Narine played with his dad Shaheed – and the ability for him to chuck the ball, rather than just bowl it, encouraged him to learn new deliveries that would have been more difficult to perfect with a conventional cricket ball or a conventional bowling action. 'He is one of the most renowned tennis ball players in Trinidad,' Badree recalled. 'That's where it all started for him and that allowed him to develop that unique grip that he has where he uses his knuckles to deliver the ball.'

'You develop strategies that help you in international cricket inadvertently, and it certainly did for Narine and all players of the past who were really great. They grew up playing tape ball cricket.'

'I had a love for it,' Narine said. 'It helped with my grip and my variations as well. You have different balls that you bowl in windball cricket and I just tried them in hard-ball and they worked out for me, so I just continued developing them.' Naturally windball cricket shaped Narine's bowling action in hard-ball cricket; Ganga remembered that even at the start of his career 'there were concerns surrounding the legality of his bowling action'. These concerns would eventually culminate in Narine being banned from bowling in 2015, while he remodelled his action.

Badree and Narine both featured in a World Cup win in 2012, with Badree winning another in 2016. Both Badree, a leg-spinner, and Narine, an off-spinner, were marked by their ability to turn the ball both ways; Badree with his googly, and Narine with his doosra and carrom ball. Yet their point of difference went beyond simply their direction of spin. Together the Trinidad duo were instrumental in triggering the change that saw spinners bowl flatter, faster and shorter – a seminal shift in the nature of spin bowling that left an indelible mark on their art.

Not only did the pair transform their respective disciplines but they had enormous success as well. In October 2014, in an extraordinary moment for the tiny island of Trinidad, Badree and Narine rose to number one and number two in the ICC T20 bowling rankings. From the parks of Barrackpore and the streets of Arima this unassuming pair of Trinidadians became the best in the world.

***

Although Snape was a spin bowler, very little of his threat actually came from spinning the ball. It wasn't until after the 2007 T20 World Cup and the inaugural season of the IPL that deviation started to be a significant weapon when a group of finger spinners elevated Snape's craft through mystery, innovation and creativity. While Snape and the original finger spinners had relied largely on taking pace off the ball and accuracy, this second wave of bowlers added to these skills big spin in both directions and a flatter trajectory at faster speeds.

Narine did not make his T20 debut until 2011 but he became the figurehead of the second age of spin bowling which spanned from 2008 to 2015. Just four matches after his debut Narine was selected to play for Trinidad and Tobago in the 2011 Champions League after spending the 2009 edition of the tournament unable to break into the team. Over the ensuing weeks a new star was born as Narine snared ten wickets in six matches and maintained an economy rate of just 4.37 runs per over. His mesmerising performances in the tournament, which was competed for by the world's best T20 teams from around the world and played in India, triggered a $700,000 contract with Kolkata Knight Riders in the subsequent IPL auction.

Over the following three years Narine played a central role in two title triumphs for KKR in the IPL and one for the West Indies in the World Cup. His success on the global stage won him contracts in leagues around the world and before long he had followed his teammate Chris Gayle on to the T20 circuit and away from international cricket: a freelance T20 gun for hire.

Windball cricket shaped Narine's effectiveness in T20. The softer, smaller ball allowed him to develop a unique way of spinning the ball with his knuckles which saw him release the ball from the front of his hand while still imparting a huge number of revolutions. This front-on release made Narine exceptionally difficult to read, with almost no discernible change from his off break and the ball that went the other way. This ability to spin the ball in both directions and the difficulty batsmen had in reading which way it would go was the foundation of his success.

Batting against a spinner who could turn the ball both ways was very difficult. 'You've got to pick which way it is going first, which can be tricky in itself,' explained Luke Wright who scored more than 7,000 T20 runs. 'You tend to try and pick up signals from the ball or the pitch – which is even harder. So you need to pick which way it is going and then decide your shot, whereas against seam you are able to just react or decide what shot you are playing but against spin you need to be able to pick it first so it makes your decision-making that much harder.'

'Because he delivers the ball out of the front of his hand, so many batsmen I talk to in and around cricket are saying, "We can't pick him. We don't know which way the ball's going,"' explained Narine's mentor Crowe. 'So you've got very little chance of being able to set yourself up well and have a real clear game plan all the time. You're being very reactive.'

'The uniqueness of his action was a great asset for him,' observed Ganga. 'Everyone was very much used to the conventional off-spinners. Narine – from the way he grips the ball – is very different. Most off-spinners would grip the ball with their index finger and their middle finger but Narine gripped it with his middle finger and his fourth finger and he locked it in. It was very difficult to read him.'

For conventional finger spinners the motion of imparting spin on the ball typically spun the ball up and out of the hand. But Narine's unique grip and front-on release enabled him to impart spin while also pushing the ball out on a notably flatter trajectory. This flight path enabled Narine to bowl short lengths at a good pace, preventing the batsmen from being able to 'step and hit'.

'Coming up in cricket I always used to bowl as tight as possible,' said Narine. 'I was never a big wicket-taker. I always liked the runs as low as possible. So from a young age that is why I have been more effective in white-ball cricket. It started there and I just continued.

'The first thing I do is try and keep down the runs because the batsmen will then try and take a chance and that is how you take wickets.'

Narine may have been the most effective exponent of this new style but he was far from the first. Before Narine's emergence in 2011 the Indians Ravichandran Ashwin and Harbhajan Singh, the Sri Lankans Muttiah Muralitharan and Ajantha Mendis and the Pakistani Saeed Ajmal started to have major success through extracting big spin in both directions and typically on a flatter trajectory.

Wrist spinners were at a natural advantage over finger spinners because for them balls that turned in the opposite direction to their stock ball – known as googlies – were part of the traditional art of wrist spin. For finger spinners getting a delivery to spin the other way was more difficult. The equivalent deliveries for finger spinners, known as doosras or carrom balls, did not emerge until the turn of the century and they were much more complex to bowl than the googly. Yet between around 2008 and 2015 a coterie of finger spinners perfected these mystery deliveries and in doing so ushered in the second wave of T20 spin bowling.

'As a batsman, if you're setting yourself up to hit the ball knowing the ball is going to spin one way, it's not easy, but it's comfortable,' explained Crowe. 'If you've got a guy who spins the ball both ways, [as a batsman] you're very much more reactive rather than proactive, and particularly with the pace off as well.'

As with many developments promoted by T20, the origins of finger spin innovation lie further back in history, before the 20-over format was played at professional level. In the late 1990s and early 2000s the

Pakistani Saqlain Mushtaq brought the doosra to international cricket – a delivery that he had invented when playing rooftop cricket in Lahore with a tennis ball as a young boy. The doosra was swiftly perfected by Muralitharan as well. The word 'doosra' means 'other one' in Hindi and Urdu and the beauty of the delivery wasn't only that it turned the other way to the off break but it spun appreciably, fizzing viciously off the pitch.

The doosra was fiendishly complicated and required an unnatural movement of the arm, pushing the limits of the laws of the game, which banned bowlers from bending their elbow in delivery.

In 2009 the ICC biomechanist Bruce Elliott made a startling claim that his research suggested a lot of bowlers from the subcontinent could bowl the delivery legally but many Caucasian bowlers could not. Shortly after Elliott presented this research, a group of former spin bowlers from Australia decided that they would not teach the doosra to young spinners because it 'offended the laws of the game'. In Asia, where rare talent was more readily promoted, there was less resistance to the delivery.

Muralitharan – born in the hill city of Kandy in the centre of Sri Lanka – founded his career on his mastery of the doosra. However, his brilliance with the delivery was due largely to his extraordinary physicality. He was born with a deformed elbow which meant he could never totally straighten his arm, his wrists were double-jointed and his rapidly rotating shoulder practically dislocated itself every time he bowled. These biomechanical quirks enabled Muralitharan – who imparted spin with his wrist and shoulder as much as his fingers – to become so effective with the doosra.

Muralitharan's career was shrouded in controversy due to his bowling action which pushed the limit of the law: in 1995 he was dramatically called for chucking by the umpire Darrell Hair in a Test match in Australia.

As technology improved so did testing procedures. The ICC soon discovered that all bowlers flexed their elbow in delivery and eventually they permitted spin bowlers 15 degrees of flex in the elbow at delivery, a move that some suspect was partly introduced to accommodate Muralitharan's talents. Continual testing never cleared Muralitharan's action in the eyes of some, but his astounding career ended up with 1,347 international wickets, the highest of all time.

As the T20 circuit boomed in the years after the inaugural IPL, the quality of attacking batting snowballed. For bowlers, necessity was the harbinger of innovation: the doosra became a staple for the off-spinners

Ajmal, Ashwin, Harbhajan and Narine. For these bowlers it was a particularly valuable delivery because it enabled them to take the ball away from right-handed batsman – who faced 71% of deliveries in T20 – taking it out of their hitting arc.

The other option for finger spinners was the carrom ball, a delivery which did not challenge the laws of the game but was arguably even harder to master. Named after the South Asian game 'Carrom' where players flicked disks across a board, the carrom ball required the bowler to flick the ball out of the front of the hand to impart spin.

Tellingly the carrom ball, like Muralitharan, emerged from Sri Lanka, a hotbed of unusual talent and entrepreneurial zest. Mendis came upon the ball when playing indoor tennis-ball cricket. The smaller, softer ball enabled him to grip and flick it in a way that would have been considerably harder with a hard ball. But as the strength in his hands and fingers increased he eventually translated the technique into hard-ball cricket as well. Mendis made a stunning impression at the onset of his international career in 2008, confounding batsmen with his ability to turn the ball both ways with no discernible change in release.

A short, skinny man with large ears and bright wide eyes, Mendis was another unlikely revolutionary. He approached the crease with a neat run-up and his action was very unassuming. It wasn't until the ball pitched that anything about his bowling appeared unusual. It was then that what looked like a floaty half-volley would suddenly stop and grip in the surface before deviating one way or the other – not to a huge degree but enough to beat the inside or outside edge of the bat. In his first year of international cricket Mendis took an astonishing 85 wickets in 24 matches at a scarcely believable average of 11.98 runs per wicket.

Before long Ashwin added the delivery to his repertoire as well. Narine's own version – inspired by Mendis and honed during his days playing windball cricket – also became central to his success. 'When Ajantha Mendis came out my dad said I should try it in softball,' recalled Narine. 'I did it in the nets and Darren Bravo and a guy called Marlon Barclay kept saying I should try it and it was decent enough and in the next game Bravo was in my ear over and over saying, "Bowl the ball, bowl the ball," and it came out that game and I never turned back.'

Naturally the carrom ball required a great amount of strength in the fingers and was exceptionally difficult to control consistently. The smaller and slower spin it produced made it less effective than the doosra, which fizzed and spun sharply off the pitch. Unlike Mendis who largely relied on it, Narine and Ashwin only used the carrom ball as an occasional variation rather than their main weapon.

After his amazing start to his international career Mendis's potency quickly dwindled when he ceased to be such a mystery. His average between 2008 and 2012 was 15.52 but after that point it rose to 31.41. Video analysis allowed batsmen to decipher his different deliveries and gradually batsmen started to play him more off the back foot, giving them time to adjust to the slow and small spin, treating him as a medium-pacer rather than a spinner. Mendis also struggled in the second innings of night matches when heavy dew made his light and delicate grip on the ball problematic. Despite only being 24 when he made his T20 debut Mendis's time at the top of the sport lasted less than five years. Yet his creativity and the carrom ball have endured.

Despite his decline Mendis still had a brilliant career record and between 2008 and 2015 Ajmal, Ashwin, Harbhajan, Mendis, Muralitharan and of course Narine were exceptionally dominant, each taking more than 130 wickets in the format. Only three wrist spinners and just two conventional finger spinners could match their returns in this period.

The Second Era of Spin Bowling – Leading Spin Wicket-Takers, 2008–15		
Bowler	**Spin Type**	**Wickets**
Sunil Narine	Mystery Spin	216
Saeed Ajmal	Mystery Spin	207
Shakib Al Hasan	Finger Spin	195
Shahid Afridi	Wrist Spin	186
Muttiah Muralitharan	Mystery Spin	162
Amit Mishra	Wrist Spin	160
Ravi Ashwin	Mystery Spin	157
Harbhajan Singh	Mystery Spin	154
Piyush Chawla	Wrist Spin	151
Nathan McCullum	Finger Spin	142
Ajantha Mendis	Mystery Spin	134
Pragyan Ojha	Finger Spin	134

Strangely left-arm finger spinners found it harder to adopt these new-age variations with no one able to bowl a doosra and only New Zealand's Mitchell Santner deploying a version of the carrom ball.

Left-arm spinners and off-spinners unable to bowl mystery deliveries were put under a huge amount of pressure. Unable to hide behind the mystery of which way the ball might spin, these bowlers bowled fuller than those who could turn the ball both ways and relied on accuracy, speed changes and intelligence to survive.

'When you don't have a lot of variations you need to be proactive or you need to be a little bit smarter to win certain battles,' explained the Indian off-spinner Washington Sundar. 'Where's he trying to hit me? Where I can bowl where he's not expecting me to bowl? Things like that.'

As attacking batting continued to improve, conventional finger spinners were increasingly used as jokers, selected to exploit certain match-ups and target combinations. For example, in the 2019 IPL, Sunrisers Hyderabad typically picked the off-spinner Mohammad Nabi against left-handed-heavy teams and the left-arm spinner Shakib Al Hasan against right-handed-heavy teams, ensuring in both instances that they had a finger spinner who was turning the ball away from the bat. This intelligent selection helped conventional finger spinners endure but also elevated the value of mystery spinners whose match-ups were not determined by the hand of the batsman.

In late 2014 the game became more onerous for mystery bowlers such as Narine when the ICC initiated a clampdown on bowling actions. Up until then the ICC had turned a blind eye to many of the game's foremost doosra bowlers who always pushed the limit of legal actions. But a change in governance at the ICC prompted a change in policy and with the ICC's showpiece event, the 50-over World Cup, less than a year away the ICC began to suspend bowlers with suspect actions. 'It is arguable that we should've taken this action earlier,' David Richardson, the ICC's chief executive, admitted when asked to explain the sudden change.

Within weeks Ajmal had been banned from bowling in international cricket and Narine was suspended along with a number of other bowlers. Subsequently Narine pulled out of the World Cup to work on remodelling his action but by the end of the year he too had been banned from bowling after his action was found to be illegal.

The ICC's clampdown had a radical effect on the nature of finger spin bowling, reducing the effectiveness of many of the world's leading bowlers who were either forced to remodel their actions and/or bowl fewer doosras to avoid suspension.

Major Off-Spin Bowlers, Before and After ICC Chucking Clampdown		
2008–14		
Bowler	Average	Doosras
Sunil Narine	15.82	46%
Ravi Ashwin	24.15	18%
Saeed Ajmal	16.28	14%
Harbhajan Singh	25.29	5%
2015–18		
Bowler	Average	Doosras
Sunil Narine	24.79	28%
Ravi Ashwin	24.87	10%
Saeed Ajmal	20.85	0%
Harbhajan Singh	27.70	2%

Although finger spinners continued to be effective, they were enfeebled by the ICC's clampdown. They were unable to bowl their doosras as regularly and when they did the delivery lost the bite and fizz that made them so effective. The change in Narine's fortunes was emblematic of finger spinners more generally. Before the end of 2014 Narine effectively combined attack and defence: he took a wicket every 17.4 balls while conceding just 5.45 runs per over. Yet after being suspended in late 2014 and remodelling his action, Narine's strike rate rose to 23.2 and his economy rate to 6.40 runs per over by the end of 2018.

He had a remodelled action that maintained his consistency and accuracy but robbed him of his elan. 'The difference was the speed and the spin. I had to focus more on accuracy because the spin was less,' he explained. Narine was still among the best in the world but was no longer *the* best in the world.

***

As Samuel Badree stood at the top of his run-up before bowling his first ball on T20 debut he had already done something remarkable. Badree was a leg-spinner opening the bowling.

It is an unwritten rule of cricket that pace bowlers should open the bowling. From village cricket up to international level fast bowlers invariably take the new ball. There is logic behind this – the new ball swings and seams more than the old ball which spinners normally find easier to grip. When the ball gets older and softer, batsmen find it harder to create pace on the ball, helping spinners further still. Generally, the spinners operate through the middle before the quicks return at the death.

But in T20 convention has been challenged at almost every turn. Not only has the shortest format proved to be a boon for spin bowlers generally but it has seen them explore hitherto untouched areas of the game and start bowling with the new ball. Before Badree's debut in 2006 a handful of spinners had opened the bowling in T20 – but more as an occasional surprise tactic than a long-term strategy. Across Badree's career he opened the bowling in 160 of his 197 matches.

Leg spin, which involves the bowler imparting spin by rotating their wrist anticlockwise in the way that one might turn a doorknob, is a rare and precious skill. The spin that the wrist imparts is more significant than that applied by finger spinners but the unnatural motion compromises accuracy and control. As a result leg-spinners have long been renowned as bowlers who take wickets but also concede a lot of runs.

On his T20 debut Badree returned the astonishing figures of 3 for 9 from 3.5 overs: the start of a phenomenal career as a Powerplay specialist. Up to the end of 2018 Badree bowled 60% of his overs in the phase, comfortably the most by any spinner in T20 history. He bowled so often in the phase simply because he was so good there, boasting a superb economy rate of 6.08 and a healthy strike rate of 22.9.

Badree's brilliant Powerplay record was founded on a unique, straightforward, method of bowling flat and straight at a good 'Whenever we have a bowling meeting my plan is always th recalled Badree. 'I tried to bowl wicket to wicket on a good l the batsman can't get under the ball. It doesn't matter i hander or a left-hander, I target leg stump on a good le

With only two fielders permitted outside the 30 options were limited. 'In the Powerplay of cours fielders out so I had to be wicket to wicket and there was very little room for experimenting in terms of length.' His method was simple but the basic combination of challenging the stumps and a hint of spin in either direction made attacking him a hazardous task.

'He knows his game and sticks to his plans,' said Phil Simmons who coached the West Indies to the T20 World Cup in 2016. 'I've seen him taken apart but the majority of times he wins the battle. He knows his target, he bowls wicket to wicket with the new ball and it's hard to get him away consistently. He knew exactly what he wanted to do in those three overs and he just came up and he did it. It was unbelievable.'

Spinners who looked to turn the ball a long way often struggled in the Powerplay because gripping the hard new ball and extracting purchase from the pitch was difficult. So, paradoxically, not spinning the ball much was central to Badree's success. With an emphasis on maintaining a tight line so that he could attack the stumps and force the batsmen to hit to his boundary fielders at midwicket and long on, less spin – rather than more spin – was preferable. Badree had four deliveries – the leg break, googly, slider and flipper – but none of them spun far. His primary mode of attack was to push the ball through and get it to skid on. 'He didn't really turn the ball,' remembered Ganga, his Trinidad and Tobago captain. 'The ball skidded on because it was new.'

Badree's role in the Powerplay was enhanced by most opening batsmen being unused to facing spin. Ganga, who first used Badree as an opening bowler in 50-over cricket and then translated that to T20, recognised that 'openers were always expecting two fast bowlers to open the bowling'. Many T20 openers were big, muscular players who relied largely on natural strength rather than the nimble footwork and timing that was required against the slower bowlers. 'Opening batsmen typically were not accustomed to facing spin bowlers as much as pace initially,' said Badree. 'They would have been accustomed to fast bowlers. So immediately getting a spinner on up front was a novelty back then.'

'I've faced seamers most of my life opening the batting,' explained the New Zealand opening batsman Martin Guptill. 'You can't just get into one-pace hitting [against spin]. You've got to keep changing, keep adapting to different bowlers. Over in the Caribbean, it seems that a lot of teams open with a spinner, and it's quite a good tactical ploy.'

Badree's success in the first six overs drove more teams to bowl spin at the start. The proportion of overs bowled by spinners in the Powerplay increased from 6% in 2006 to 25% by 2018.

While many of these overs were bowled by specialists like Badree, the late 2000s also gave rise to a new phenomenon: part-time spin bowlers bowling the very first over of the innings.

The fielding team recognised that opening batsmen very rarely took risks in the opening over of the match and the first over represented an opportunity to squeeze six balls of a lower quality bowler in. It was a trend popularised by Rajasthan Royals in the 2009 IPL when they regularly opened the bowling with Yusuf Pathan's part-time off spin. Other occasional bowlers, like Faf du Plessis at Lancashire and Will Smith at Durham, mimicked the tactic of opening the bowling. These bowlers succeeded by bowling flat, fast and full – firing the ball in at the feet of the batsmen who were unwilling to take a risk. The benefit of this tactic went beyond the frugality of the opening over; it also gave the fielding team wriggle room with their frontline bowlers, enabling them to protect against one of them having a bad day. It was a curious phenomenon that encapsulated the tactical anarchy of T20: the opposition's best batsmen starting their innings against one of the fielding team's weakest bowlers despite only two fielders being permitted outside the circle. This was T20's phoney war.

As opening batsmen became more familiar with facing spin bowlers in the Powerplay, Badree managed to stay ahead of the game by closely analysing opposition batsmen, preparing for games as he might one of his PE lessons.

'I planned, I analysed batsmen using footage. I looked at their strengths and weaknesses. Sometimes with the analyst but sometimes of my own accord. I think that is an important part of the modern game.' Badree's pre-match analysis was made easier by him being able to predict whom he would be bowling to, a benefit not afforded to spinners who operated through the middle overs.

The combination of Badree's erudite perspective and his exceptional skill allowed him to succeed in a fast-evolving game. Bowling in the Powerplay was a treacherous business with only two fielders outside the 30-yard circle and batsmen looking to maximise the benefit of the fielding restrictions. Yet despite these severe challenges he thrived in the role for more than a decade.

Badree mostly bowled three overs in the Powerplay and finished his fourth by the middle of the innings. In this regard Badree assumed the role of a classical fast bowler and in doing so underlined how original thinkers and pioneering players could shape a sport in its nascent years.

Stricter enforcement of throwing laws on doosra bowlers in 2015 ushered in a new age of spin bowling. With finger spinners unable to turn the ball both ways as easily or as often, the spotlight moved on to those that could: the wrist spinners. 'I think it [the chucking clampdown] has helped wrist spinners,' said Badree. 'It has ruled out a few bowlers. Therefore it means there are more opportunities for others.'

Wrist spin had always been a potent bowling style in T20. Mushtaq Ahmed had great success in the early years of the Twenty20 Cup in England before the effervescent Pakistani Shahid Afridi took the international format by storm. The leg-spin masters, the great Australian Shane Warne and Indian Anil Kumble, also enjoyed triumphs in the first few seasons of the IPL. But it was Badree's effectiveness in the Powerplay that heralded a change in the game.

Until Badree leg spin had been viewed almost exclusively as an attacking weapon. He showed that by spinning the ball less, leg-spinners could maintain greater accuracy of their lines and lengths which, coupled with a flatter trajectory and faster speeds, exerted control over batsmen. He lent control to the art of wrist spin that few believed was possible.

Badree was a portent of an era in which, after 2015, leg spin would become the most effective bowling in T20. He was the PE teacher from Arima who tamed the art of wrist spin.

SIX

THE UNICORN

'I could see him reading what I was doing before I did it'
Andrew Tye on bowling to A.B. de Villiers

'I don't overthink it in T20s; my instincts are normally accurate'
A.B. de Villiers

The ball cracks off A.B. de Villiers' bat. There is no real hint of violence; just a marriage of beauty and brutality.

De Villiers' every shot, wondrously crisp and yet flying off his bat with alacrity, feels like a riposte to any who still deride T20 as slogging. The 40,000 at the ground intoxicated by his show are too mesmerised to think of such subtleties.

Welcome to watching A.B. at the M. Chinnaswamy Stadium in Bangalore, an experience that, both on and off the field, feels like the apogee of T20 cricket.

Six follows six, each thundered more emphatically than the last. There are slog sweeps against spin, balls flicked 100 metres over long on like a topspin forehand and drives propelled flat over extra cover. De Villiers seems to have a preternatural sense of where the ball will be delivered and how he will hit it. After each six, the screen flashes up with a reverential sign: 'AB Dynamite' or 'A dmirable B rilliant D azzling'.

The NBA basketball league today is in thrall to its unicorns. Previously the sport had rigid ideas about each position's role. In recent years, these notions have been uprooted by a new breed of players unshackled by the old compromises between tall players and smaller, agile ones. Instead, new-age players like Kevin Durant can do it all, combining the technique of point guards – who run games like deep-lying football midfielders – with the athleticism of power forwards, and so redefine the parameters of their sport.

Batting's unicorn is A.B. de Villiers, capable of playing with dazzling impunity or the self-restraint of an ascetic monk. He has scored the fastest one-day international century of all time, in 31 balls. He has also played with staggering self-denial. In a Test match in Delhi in 2015 he batted for 354 minutes to score 45 off 297 balls – and in Adelaide in 2012, he made 33 from 220 balls to help salvage a draw, the prelude to thumping 169 in the decisive Test a week later. Perhaps no one has done more to show the full range of possibilities in T20 batting. 'A genius' is how Brendon McCullum described him. In the five IPL seasons from 2015 de Villiers averaged 49.74 – the numbers of a great Test batsman, while scoring those runs at a strike rate of 164. No player to average within ten of him had a strike rate of 150.

'You watch Lionel Messi play football and if you love the game you can just see something else in that bloke that other footballers just don't have basically and I think de Villiers is exactly that,' said England's Sam Billings, who played against de Villiers in the IPL. 'That is why he is one of the best players ever to play the game because of that ability to be that versatile.

'It is a tough one to describe. Yeah, fine, someone can score 30 off 20 balls but de Villiers' 30 off 20 balls compared to Player A is just . . . I would pay to watch that.'

The idea of compromise, and trade-offs, is wired into T20 batting. Most batsmen can be thought of as existing somewhere on a continuum, between aiming to hit as many sixes as possible and aiming to score off every ball. Chris Gayle and Virat Kohli – the first an extraordinary six-hitter who allows 50% of his balls to be dots; the second a near-perfect technician who faces just 35% dot balls – embody the two contrasting approaches. Similar trade-offs are detectable in other areas, too. Reliable eviscerators of pace bowling, like Chris Lynn and Brendon McCullum, are comparatively weak against spin. The leading destroyers of spin, like Glenn Maxwell and Shane Watson, can be shackled by pace. Some of the most destructive batsmen in the Powerplay, like Aaron Finch and Alex Hales, can get bogged down afterwards. Those with the most extraordinary strike rates, like Carlos Brathwaite and Kieron Pollard, often sacrifice consistency. Those who are supremely consistent, like Kohli and Shaun Marsh, typically have lower strike rates – particularly at the start of their innings.

The wonder of A.B. de Villiers is that he rejected these trade-offs as false. 'He walks to the wicket and tries to impose himself on the game from ball one,' remarked McCullum. Most players typically would take five or ten balls to get used to the nature of the pitch before focusing on run scoring – Gayle started his innings famously slowly – but de Villiers was different. De Villiers had a preternatural ability to arrive at the batting crease and immediately appear at one with conditions – perfectly attuned to the pace and bounce of the pitch, the dimensions of the ground and the glare of the lights. The apparent comfort of de Villiers at the crease was translated into his performance.

Despite de Villiers often starting his innings in the early middle overs when he was afforded more time to play himself in and run rates were typically lower, he scored significantly faster from the outset than almost every player in the world. In the first ten balls of his innings he scored at a strike rate of 126.72, compared to 107.51 for all players, even while getting out much less frequently.

Quick starts were crucial because they were an efficient use of resources. On the rare occasions when de Villiers was dismissed early he had often still maintained a healthy scoring rate that had made a positive contribution, rather than consuming deliveries with a view to accelerating later in his innings.

Just after the fall of a wicket the pressure was on the batting team but by starting quickly de Villiers was able to flip this around, counter-attacking to put the bowling team under pressure once more. In a Bangladesh Premier League (BPL) match in January 2019 de Villiers arrived at the crease with his team, the Rangpur Riders, 5 for 2 after 1.5 overs chasing 187 to win. De Villiers started his innings in thunderous fashion: six, dot, four, four, dot, six, four, four – 28 off his first eight balls and in a flash the match had been turned on its head. Rangpur ended the Powerplay 63 for 2 with the required run rate back in check and won the match by eight wickets and with ten balls to spare. De Villiers finished 100 not out off 50 balls.

De Villiers' ability to start with alacrity was underpinned by having no obvious weakness against any bowler type. While most players had a clear preference for pace or spin – the skills required for playing one often compromised those required for playing the other – de Villiers was equally strong against both. He scored at a strike rate of 135 against spin and 155 against pace but was dismissed by spin far less often.

One of the first major influences of data analysis on T20 was the rise of 'match-ups' which saw fielding captains target batsmen with specific bowler types based on potential vulnerabilities displayed in the records of the batsman against that bowler type. The issue for fielding captains against de Villiers was that he had no obvious match-up to exploit. All of the six types of bowling produced negative match-ups for the fielding team with de Villiers averaging at least 30, while scoring at a strike rate of over 130 against all of them. He even excelled against what were ordinarily the most effective deliveries: no player scored faster than de Villiers' strike rate of 139 against yorkers, and only three players scored faster than his 189 against slower balls.

Such multifarious strengths allowed de Villiers to be very selective in which bowlers he targeted and when. 'He has the ability to know which bowler he is going to target and when he targets them he takes them massive,' observed McCullum, who played with de Villiers at RCB in the 2018 IPL. 'If he decides to target you then you are in major trouble.'

From Barbados to Bangalore and from Dhaka to Durban, T20 leagues around the world were played in a vast array of differing conditions but de Villiers appeared at home wherever he played. In all five countries where he played at least ten matches – India, South Africa, England, Bangladesh and the Caribbean he averaged at least 30 and scored at a strike rate of at least 130. Different conditions could not quell him.

***

Bowling to de Villiers in T20 could resemble tossing a ball into the mouth of a cannon. Andrew Tye, the Australian T20 international bowler, distilled the experience of bowling to de Villiers: 'I could see him reading what I was doing before I did it.'

Only de Villiers was not really watching the ball. Not for all of the time anyway.

Fewer than 20 yards separate a cricket batsman from the bowler when the ball is delivered. When bowlers reach speeds of 90 miles per hour or more, as Tye and other international bowlers routinely do, that leaves batsmen about 0.6 seconds to ascertain where the ball will pitch, how it will bounce after pitching, whether it will swing in the air before pitching, and whether it will seam off the pitch after it lands. Then, batsmen have to hit the thing, and find gaps between the 11 opponents on the pitch designed to stop them from scoring runs.

When confronted with a 90 mph bowler, 'I'll have a bit of a pre-ball routine. I'll make my mark, and then once I switch on and the bowler's coming in, I try and think of absolutely nothing,' de Villiers explained. 'I want it to be that my mind is a hundred per cent clear. So is my body. So I try not to think about too many things.'

That is sensible, for de Villiers does not have time to watch where the ball lands and how it moves before playing a shot. Even the best athletes need about 200 milliseconds to adjust their shots, depending on the trajectory of the ball, the scientists Michael F. Land and Peter McLeod have found. That means that batsmen must fully commit to their shot 0.2 seconds before the ball reaches them – when the ball still has one-third of its journey from the bowler to the wicket opposite them to go. Whatever the ball does in the last third of its flight it is impossible to adjust. And the margins of failure are infinitesimally small: the batsman must judge the ball's position to within 3cm and the time it reaches them to within three milliseconds if they are to make effective contact.

Human reaction times are simply too slow to 'watch the ball on to the bat', the aphorism endlessly recycled from coaches to players around the globe. Instead, batsmen must use clues from the bowler – their run-up, action in delivery and their own game awareness – to work out where the ball is going to be before it gets there. The best batsmen do not consciously calculate all the variables that determine a ball's trajectory; instead, their subconscious, experience and mastery do it for them.

The research from Land and McLeod showed that elite batsmen only watch the ball for just over half the time after it is released – they watch it after release, then adjust their eyes to where they predict the ball will be at the point it reaches them, and then watch it again as they make contact.

'What I 100% need to do is I don't try and think about too much,' de Villiers explained. 'I try and make sure that I see the ball coming out of the bowler's hands, and then my technique and my body take over.'

De Villiers constructed a template that could easily be transferred across all three formats of the game. This has been underpinned by a purity and simplicity of technique that can withstand the greatest pressures on the field. Whatever the format, the tenets of his method remain the same.

'I've always kept it very simple,' he explained. 'I'm a big believer in the fact that basics stay the same for all the formats. I don't overthink things. I know Test cricket is more about endurance. T20 is more about innovating, creating and the energy at the wicket. And I base my plan on the same fundamentals and the same basics in all three of the formats that I play in. I've never changed that. The only thing that changes is my mindset a little bit at times.'

In the longer formats of the game, a de Villiers hallmark was his adaptability to the situation. In T20, de Villiers is regarded as the opposite: a player who bats as if impervious to the situation – which is meant as a great compliment. The ground conditions; the notion of a par score; who the bowlers are. Such thoughts do not weigh de Villiers down: 'I don't overthink it in T20s; my instincts are normally accurate.'

In any phase of the game, the effect is devastating. But it is particularly potent in the traditional lull after the Powerplay – the nearest T20 has to boring middle overs. Between 2015 and 2019 the average strike rate in overs seven to ten in the IPL was 117.62; for de Villiers, it was 133.33. In the slowest phase of the game, de Villiers was still operating on a different plane.

***

Like football's Premier League, T20 cricket has a tendency to try to monopolise all the sport's recent innovations, presenting all that is good as all that is new and ignoring what came before.

Yet the first intimations of many of the dazzling array of shots that have become standard in T20 came before a professional game in the format. The reverse sweep – in which batsmen play a sweep after switching hands, so that they hit the ball through the off side rather than the leg side – was played in the 1970s by the West Indian Gordon Greenidge and Pakistan's Mushtaq Mohammad, and popularised in the 1990s in one-day cricket. South Africa's Jonty Rhodes took the logic of the reverse sweep further and played the switch hit – hitting the ball as if a left-hander, rather than a right-hander – in an ODI against Australia in 2002.

Perhaps the most remarkable of cricket's shots – the scoop – was first played as far back as 1933 by the West Indian batsman Learie Constantine. 'The ball was as big as a full moon to me that day and I remember I moved out of my crease to meet the ball which Allom was coming up to deliver. He saw me move and tried to send a slow full toss over my approaching form. I spotted it in time. I could not reach it with a textbook shot because there is nothing in the textbook about that situation, so I wrote a new chapter by helping it on over my head and the pavilion.' Constantine was a man well ahead of his time. It wasn't until 2001, when Zimbabwe's Dougie Marillier tried the same thing in an ODI against Australia, that the scoop was played again. A year later the wicketkeeper Ryan Campbell helped it evolve further.

Campbell was sitting in a bowling meeting for a domestic limited overs match in Australia in 2002 when he had an idea. The bowlers kept saying how, towards the end of the innings, they would look to bowl yorkers – balls that bounce right at the batsman's feet and are notoriously difficult to score off.

'I always knew no one ever fielded behind the wicketkeeper,' Campbell said. 'So I thought the theory must be sound: if they're bowling yorkers, and if I get forward and get my bat down, I'm going to get a full toss. And if I get a full toss, it'll just hit the face of my bat and go over my head or my shoulder and it should be runs. That was the theory.'

If only it were that simple. Against fast bowlers, Campbell had three quarters of a second or less to get forward, get down into position – unlike Marillier, Campbell's shot involved going down on one knee to get under the ball – read the line of the ball and execute the shot at just the right moment so that it carried over the wicketkeeper. If he missed the ball he risked serious injury. Being fearful of getting hit – or his teammates mocking him – Campbell had never even practised the shot in the nets before unveiling it in a domestic one-day match, which speaks to cricket's conservatism. The first two times Campbell attempted the shot in a match, he hit the ball for four. With this new shot – the ramp – Campbell had access to all 360 degrees of the pitch with his strokes.

So relatively little of what would become the hallmarks of T20 batting were actually a direct product of the format. What T20 did, though, was popularise such audacious shots like never before. McCullum, who was among the finest players of the ramp and scoop shot, believed 'T20 accelerated the process of playing 360 degrees'. And where once such shots were actively curbed by coaches – Roger Twose, a Warwickshire player in the 1990s, was once expelled from the nets for trying the reverse sweep – T20 led coaches to empower players to expand their possibilities, and play in a more natural and instinctive way.

The intensity of T20 leagues has propelled batsmen to hone their methods against specific types of deliveries – like how to get underneath yorkers and divert them over the wicketkeeper to the boundary, just as Campbell first did. 'The ramp shots were always there but now they're encouraged, they're explored and they're experimented with,' said Trent Woodhill, a long-time batting coach in the IPL. 'Now players aren't afraid of what they look like, they're just concerned now with getting the job done.'

The freedom – indeed, the necessity – to embrace such thinking in T20 led batsmen to innovate further. In the 2009 T20 World Cup the ramp shot was enhanced by the Sri Lankan batsman Tillakaratne Dilshan. While Campbell played his ramp against balls on the full, which had not yet bounced, Dilshan dared to play his shot against balls that had bounced too. This modification – the Dilscoop – required exceptional hand-eye coordination; Campbell had to predict the right line of the ball before making contact, but Dilshan had to respond to the bounce too, before ducking his head out of the way at the last moment.

This was only the next phase of batting's evolution. In the next decade, batsmen like McCullum, England's Jos Buttler, Australia's Glenn Maxwell and de Villiers would push the boundaries further. They would not so much perfect one ramp shot as several, using their wrists to deflect it to the right or left of the wicketkeeper depending on where the fielders were. Even more extraordinarily, de Villiers would perfect a reverse ramp – switching his hands around, so that his right-hand would be on top of the bat, as for a conventional left-handed batsman, and then flicking the ball through third man for four.

During an international career that lasted for 14 years, defying everything from braying Australian crowds to the cauldron of the IPL, de Villiers kept a simple joyful quality to his art. He called this 'the passion', sustained by a training regime that was always evolving, and in which he would experiment ceaselessly with new shots. All of this lent itself to an adventurous spirit and zest for self-improvement which, leaning on his youth as a proficient player of other games, led to the remarkable creativity that defined de Villiers' batting.

'He is just a pure athlete,' Billings observed. 'It combines a lot of different sports . . . I really like that raw ability and raw athleticism in how he plays. A bit uncoached in a way.'

The temerity of his shots earned de Villiers a simple nickname: 'Mr 360'. Most nicknames are mocking; his is reverential, infused with awe at a transcendent talent. De Villiers was equally adept reverse-scooping a yorker over third man for six, or ramping a 90 mph delivery over the wicketkeeper, as he is thrashing a cover drive. 'How many shots should you have? The simple answer is: all of them,' Bob Woolmer, the celebrated cricket coach, wrote in *Bob Woolmer's Art and Science of Cricket*, published posthumously in 2008. De Villiers represented the fulfilment of Woolmer's vision.

Yet Woolmer had also warned of the perils of choosing shots for show, rather than effectiveness: 'Too many batsmen fail because they play all the shots all the time.' While some players with an astounding repertoire of shots can use them ostentatiously, seeming to prioritise extravagance over effectiveness, with de Villiers, it was purely business-like, picking the most efficient way to score the maximum amount of runs from any ball.

As bats have become more imposing, batsmen more athletic and resourceful and boundaries shorter, bowlers clung on to one remaining advantage. At least they knew where the batsman was going to be.

De Villiers recognised this one remaining asset and inverted it. He developed a method in which he could move around with such suppleness, making late, decisive movements – towards the bowler or moving back deeper in his crease; across his stumps to the off side, or backing away to the leg side – that the bowler was deprived of any real clue about where he would be when the ball landed. Often, he would just bluff, shimmying around the crease, disorientating the bowler and yet actually meeting the ball in an orthodox position.

Like no other batsman in history, de Villiers weaponised his batting stance, turning it into another tool to enfeeble bowlers. 'The era of batsmen reacting to bowlers is over. From here on, bowlers react to batsmen,' the South African author Tom Eaton wrote of de Villiers for the *Cricket Monthly*.

'You get guys who are good, then you get guys who are excellent, then you get A.B. de Villiers,' his long-time South African teammate Dale Steyn once gushed, calling de Villiers 'limitless'. Steyn has not only learned this over 14 years bowling to de Villiers in the nets, and watching him in international games. He has also learned from his own tussles with de Villiers in the IPL, and two clashes that transcended the normal humdrum of IPL group matches.

The first time, in 2012, Steyn came on to bowl defending 39 from 18 balls. The first ball was dropped a little short outside off stump, and de Villiers pulled it over midwicket for six. The second was a yorker speared into leg stump, which de Villiers still flicked for two. The third, on a full length outside off stump, was smeared through midwicket as de Villiers went down on one knee. To the fourth, a yorker on middle stump, de Villiers backed away, exposing all three of his stumps – and thumped the ball over extra cover for six. To Steyn's fifth ball, pushed outside off stump to prevent a repeat, now de Villiers moved the other way – going so far to the off side, that he exposed all three stumps again. Down on one knee, de Villiers scooped a 90 mph delivery over fine leg for four. All that was left was to take a single off the final ball, taking it to 23 off the over and ensuring that de Villiers would be on strike for the next over to finish the job.

The next time the two met at a decisive juncture in an IPL match, in 2014, Steyn returned to bowl defending 28 from 12 balls, sensing the chance of revenge. He began with an off-cutter that moved into de Villiers: six, over square leg. Then a full ball outside off stump: another six, this time straight. A leg bye followed, before a single to return the strike to de Villiers, with 14 more to win from eight balls. Steyn tried a leg-cutter: de Villiers eviscerated it through long off for four. Then, the best of the lot: Steyn tried a yorker outside off stump. De Villiers went down on one knee, and scooped the ball over fine leg and into the second tier of the stands. De Villiers had scored 23 from a Steyn over again, though this time he did so from only five balls. All that Steyn could do was clap.

For de Villiers, these overs were the moments when the full scope of his talent came into view – the moments when he realised just what he could do. Reflecting on those takedowns of Steyn, he said: 'I've started really loving those kinds of situations where you need 12 or 13 an over and the best bowler in the world's bowling and how can you create something from nothing? Where it puts him under so much pressure that he starts making mistakes. And then that's where I started creating those types of shots, just sort of trying to stay a step or two ahead of the bowler, and putting him under pressure.

'It's not really a technical thing, but a mental switch, where you start believing and start having confidence that you can pull anything off from any situation. And once you cross the line once or twice like that, you really start believing that you can do it more often.'

***

In the 1950s, the English football manager Charles Reep became the first man to systematically record statistics on matches. He came to a startling conclusion: most goals came from moves of three passes or fewer. From this fact came an entire theory of how to play the game: booting the ball up the field, and adhering to Reep's mantra – 'not more than three passes'. The trouble was, Reep's research had a fatal flaw. While most goals indeed came from passes of three or fewer, this was because football is a game in which possession is turned over very quickly. He was oblivious to two findings that would only emerge decades later, and invalidated the long-ball theory. First, passes closer to goal had much more chance of leading to a goal than punts from within a team's own half. And second, while long-passing moves led to fewer goals, this was because they were rarer; a move actually gained a higher chance of leading to a goal as it grew longer.

The lessons of Reep remain as important as ever: using data smartly in sport is never easy, and being too fixated on data can leave teams worse off than if they ignored it altogether.

The onset of big data in sport has made most teams far shrewder. But it has also led to some overreacting to small sample sizes, driving them to make suboptimal decisions. Perhaps this is the best reason for the curious case of de Villiers' T20 international career, which yielded an average of 26.12 and strike rate of 135.16 across 78 games; still useful enough, especially considering he would often come in late in the innings, but meagre set against his record in the IPL where he scored 4,395 runs at an average of 43.08 and a strike rate of 151.23 until the end of 2019.

In the semi-finals of the T20 World Cup in 2014, South Africa were batting first against India. De Villiers did not arrive at the crease until the last ball of the 14th over. So one of the finest T20 batsmen in the world was reduced to being used as a finisher, a player to apply pizzazz at the death rather than shape an innings. Data was to blame.

After South Africa's defeat, head coach Russell Domingo justified why the team had held de Villiers back, both against India and earlier in the tournament. 'A.B. has batted at three a few times and has had limited success. It's not the number he bats, it's the situation of the game when he comes in,' Domingo explained. De Villiers' batting position, Domingo said, had been based on statistics showing that he was far more effective coming in after the tenth over. South Africa planned to send de Villiers out only when the first wicket fell in the second half of the innings.

This theory was endorsed by numbers. The trouble was, the sample size was tiny. When Domingo said de Villiers thrived coming in late in an innings, he was referring to eight innings played over eight years. South Africa overinterpreted the findings of a small amount of data. In doing so, they ignored how players – especially those as great as de Villiers – evolve. Many analysts consider data that is over two years old obsolete, so swiftly is T20 evolving.

De Villiers' struggles in international T20 cricket also reflected the curious position occupied by the international game in T20. Apart from the T20 World Cup, much international cricket entails substandard teams – with many leading players rested – playing games that are no more than friendlies. After the 2014 WT20, de Villiers went 15 months until his next T20 international, denied the intensive period of concentrating on the format and his role within a side that he is afforded during the IPL. Throughout his international career he only played in 41 matches outside the T20 World Cup – a puny four matches a year – partly because he was often rested.

'I haven't really found a rhythm yet in T20,' he said in 2013. 'I'm still finding my way . . . exactly where I'm going to bat, whether I'm a finisher, in the middle order or in the top three, maybe.'

South Africa spent his whole T20 international career trying to work out the answer, even as de Villiers evolved into the most prized wicket in the IPL. During his entire international career, de Villiers never batted more than six matches in the same position.

'We decided on A.B. at the top a while ago, and to change that would be a sign of panic,' declared captain Faf du Plessis before the 2016 T20 World Cup. But two games after a 29-ball 71 opening against England, de Villiers was shunted to a roving brief in the middle order. For all his staggering achievements in both Test and one-day international cricket, de Villiers was wasted by South Africa in T20.

Because de Villiers' gifts were so effervescent, sides were tempted to use him as an elite-level utility player, reasoning that he was capable of concealing any weakness in their batting order. It was not until 2015, when he was already 31, that de Villiers began to lord over T20 with quite the same regal air as he did Tests and ODI cricket. What changed was not his game – he had also been a batsman of staggering repertoire and chutzpah – but how he was able to declutter his approach.

That was because of being given role clarity. After years of oscillating between positions, de Villiers now had a settled role. Between the end of the 2016 World Cup and the end of 2018, de Villiers batted in 64 innings; in all but one he batted at three or four. Finally he was empowered to make full use of his gifts, rather than try to cover up the frailties of others. The years ahead were marked by de Villiers managing the audacious feat of scoring both ever more quickly and ever more consistently, exploring the outer limits of batting's possibilities. In this period at number three and four de Villiers scored 2,414 runs at an average of 46.45 and an astonishing run rate of 9.82 runs per over, passing 50 a scarcely believable 23 times. More than one in five of the balls he faced went for a boundary, but less than one in three was a dot ball.

Compared to bowling even at Gayle, 'A.B. is far tougher,' said a figure who was involved in strategy for several IPL teams. 'He is great against both pace and spin, but relatively better against pace.' The best method, the strategist suggested, was to try to bowl left-arm spin to de Villiers at the start of his innings. If de Villiers survived that, he said, 'Then you can only pray.'

All the while, de Villiers provided affirmation that, for all the moves to specialism, six-hitting training and players bulking up, what T20 rewards more than everything is brilliant batsmanship, just refined for a new age. Batsmanship will continue to evolve, but de Villiers has done more than anyone else to map its trajectory.

***

Naturally, de Villiers inspired a legion of followers to try to imitate his style in T20. None have been more successful than England's Jos Buttler, who ostentatiously tries to learn from de Villiers' method.

'For me he's one of the best ever to play the game – and the most complete batsman across all the formats,' Buttler said. 'It's natural to just look at guys like him and try and watch what they do, the shots they can play and the decisions they make at certain times. He's a natural guy to look at as a great example for everyone who's trying to improve as a player.

'It's the range of shots at his disposal which makes him so hard to bowl at. You play against him and you watch him on TV and he seems to know what the bowler's going to bowl all the time – reads the game incredibly well. It's having lots of options and also the selection of when to use which option and choosing the right balls, which seems to be second to none.'

The similarities between Buttler and de Villiers extend way beyond their actual batsmanship. Both had elder brothers – one in Buttler's case and two in de Villiers' – and were both the youngest children. Having older siblings significantly increases the chances of an athlete making it to the top, in cricket and beyond, because it builds a child's resilience, gets them used to playing with more physically developed opponents, and means they are more likely to have unstructured play at a younger age. 'On a very primal level you're always running to keep up,' explained Raph Brandon, the ECB's head of science, medicine and innovation. De Villiers would later recall that his brothers 'would try to intimidate me'.

Younger siblings are generally less likely to accept things as they are, and more likely to challenge conventions. A remarkable finding, recounted in Adam Grant's book *Originals*, is that younger brothers are ten times more likely than their older brothers to attempt to steal a base in baseball. Perhaps something of this spirit, and this freedom to challenge the status quo, can be found in the dazzling creativity of de Villiers and Buttler.

As children, both Buttler and de Villiers benefited from multisport upbringings. For all the tendency of parents to encourage their children to specialise in one sport alone – so-called 'tiger parenting', inspired by the notion that reaching the pinnacle of sport requires 10,000 hours of purposeful practice – research has shown that most children are better off playing a range of sports until deep into their teens. Doing so aids children's motor development, allows them to retain the basic joy of playing sport, reduces the risk of physical and mental fatigue, and helps them unconsciously take skills learned in one game into another.

'It's invaluable, the kind of experience I picked up there, about how to handle pressure and how to manage my own space in preparing for the tournament,' de Villiers said of his extensive time spent playing golf, rugby and especially tennis in his youth. For hours at a time, he used to hit a tennis ball against a wall at home. 'I often speak about tennis being one of the most important sports when I was growing up, for my hand-eye coordination and quick feet.' The de Villiers flick for six over long on evokes the topspin forehands that he used as a child to defeat Kevin Anderson, who would later be ranked number five in the world.

Buttler extensively played other sports as a child too, above all hockey – which encouraged him to develop his ramp shot – and squash. To see him whip the ball through point is to see a hint of the squash that Buttler played proficiently. After hitting a remarkable 150 in a one-day international in the Caribbean in February 2019, when he needed just 34 balls to vault from 45 to 150, Buttler said that the way he strikes the ball 'does feel like a golf swing in the way you time it'.

***

Engraved in black pen at the top of Buttler's bat are two words: 'f*** it'. They act as a reminder to Buttler – whatever the format and whatever the colour of the ball – to play as he wants to, not as someone else's idea of what a batsman should do.

While Buttler's overall output across cricket's three international formats remains far off de Villiers', despite a highly encouraging return to Test cricket in 2018, in T20 he has, in some senses, evolved batting even from de Villiers. Buttler's audacity to change his technique and stance after every ball surpasses even that of de Villiers.

At the very start of his innings – including from his first ball – Buttler likes to use his feet to charge down the wicket to seam bowlers. 'I feel walking at the bowler just gets me going a bit and gets me into the contest.' Buttler finds this can negate opponents' plans to dismiss him. 'I know guys a lot of the time will try and get me out by nicking me off outside off stump and sometimes they put a slip in and take that guy from midwicket.'

The intent at the start of his innings sets the template for how Buttler uses his feet and batting stance as a weapon, to open up new parts of the field and disorientate the bowlers. 'You try and put bowlers under pressure as much as you can. I like to move around the crease as much as possible to create angles – if someone sets a wide yorker field, for me it doesn't really make sense to stand in front of your stumps. You may as well move over there. If someone then bowls at your stumps, then fair play to the bowler for being brave enough to do it but I think if you then move into that position you then give a bowler a decision to make while he's running up or at the point of delivery. Hopefully then as a batter you put them under more pressure which makes it harder for them to execute.

'If someone is bowling wide yorkers – to me it just makes sense to step into the line a bit. And then if they do come straight I try and back myself to hit it and get off strike.'

There is an essential intrepid spirit to Buttler, a cricketer completely unencumbered by batting conventions: 'That's a real fun part of the game – trying things and having that mentality of just playing around.' His training methods – 'exploration stuff in the nets, just trying to work out how can I get a ball in different areas' – are tailored towards constantly increasing the options he has to any given ball. One development in his game has been his ease changing his grip from ball to ball, moving around his hands subtly in a way that is particularly well equipped to deal with a certain delivery.

'A lot of the time for me especially, always closing the face of the bat – sometimes you can hit the inside half a lot. Why don't I just change my grip and open the blade up which would hopefully keep it on plane for longer? And if you want to access the off side more, opening that same swing – the ball will deviate in a different direction. Same if I close the bat face down, so they're the fun bits of the game. Just playing around and seeing what does and doesn't work.'

The impact of such audacity has been particularly stunning against yorkers, the most effective delivery for seamers at the end of an innings. In ODIs and T20s Buttler scores at a strike rate of 130 against yorkers; well above the global average of 94.

'The big thing about those shots is trying to pick up a length as quickly as you can,' said Buttler. 'So when you are batting your best the biggest thing I notice is that in the first yard of the release I feel like I'm picking up the length better.'

Buttler gave great thought to combating the yorker – knowing that, if he does so, it can give the bowler nowhere to go. As well as hanging back in his crease – thereby turning a yorker into a half-volley, which he can club away reliably – Buttler tweaks his grip when he expects the bowler to revert to a yorker. 'If someone is bowling yorkers really well I'll then think about, 'Okay, well he's getting them in, I will change my grip because that may help me slice a yorker out or something like that.' Ball by ball I'm quite happy to play around with that.'

At his best, Buttler is like a puppetmaster, manipulating the field and then hitting the ball into gaps he has created earlier in his innings. His best innings fuse dazzling skill with meticulous planning.

'Having options both in front and behind the wicket allows you to feel like you've got options and put some bowlers under pressure to set a field,' he explained. Careful preparation, and studying video footage and data analysis of the opposition bowlers, liberates Buttler to be spontaneous in high-octane situations. 'I like to know what variations they've got, what ball they go to under pressure, what ball they follow up a boundary with.

'Those kind of statistics are really good but you don't get too caught up in them – you've still got to be out in the middle reacting to what happens. Statistics are an average of what's happened – so on any given day a certain delivery they might bowl differently because of the conditions. So as much information as you can get is good but then to use it in the right way and still be trusting your instincts and reacting to whatever is going on in the game at that certain time.'

The research by scientists Michael F. Land and Peter McLeod highlighted how little time batsmen have to adjust to the ball. These margins are even smaller when playing shots like the ramp, which involves moving the entire body around. Buttler is one of the most adept in the world at playing a ramp shot – or even a reverse ramp, switching his hands to hit the ball as if he were a left-hander. 'Shots like the ramp shot are 100% premeditated but you still adjust throughout the shot.

'That's when you improvise and use your natural talent and instinct to relax. Other times you might be targeting certain areas of the ground but you're still then trying to be more reactive to what comes down and not put all your eggs in one basket of this is the exact shot I'm going to play to this ball. Because, as much as you can, I think now in T20, like you would do in the longer formats, you practise certain shots and try and be in a clear state of mind and react to what comes down.'

Rather than seeing it as an indulgence, Buttler embraces the ramp as a pragmatic option. 'There's never a fielder behind the wicketkeeper so it just made sense to me that between fine leg and third man is one of the biggest gaps in the field, so why not try and utilise it? And it just developed over time.'

The first time that Buttler remembers playing a ramp in a professional game was against Sussex at Hove against the medium pace of Robin Martin-Jenkins. Buttler was 19, and playing only his second professional T20 match.

'I felt like he brought fine leg up but I still felt he was going to bowl into the wicket. So to go down and do it wouldn't work. To stay up – that's how the thought process went. I wasn't really brave enough to keep my head in the way either so it just developed from there.' Now, Buttler has a range of ramp shots, each subtly different from the last, so that he can exploit any vacancy in the field.

But as Buttler matured he realised that, sometimes, he was best advised to leave the ramp alone completely and instead hit the ball straight, with the full face of the bat. 'Some days you just get a feel of something's working, some days it just feels a bit off.' His 150 in an ODI against the West Indies in 2019 – the second-fastest 150 in ODI history, after one from de Villiers four years earlier – contained only two ramp shots.

The brutality of his strokes is underpinned by timing more than raw power. Both players used bats that weighed no more than average – Buttler's bat weighed 2lb 9½oz, de Villiers' was 2lb 8oz – to make his contact as smooth as possible.

He honed a slightly idiosyncratic method of hitting sixes: by hitting the ball unusually flat and low, which gives a better chance of making a clean connection with the ball. 'Sometimes on those slower wickets if you're looking to hit up that would actually end up going higher than I wanted to and then my weight would be back. So the actual mindset of hitting a ball flat means I have to come back into the ball and actually even on slower wickets it might end up going a bit higher anyway. So I'd rather that way than it goes straight up.'

Buttler reached this stage by focusing on what a shot achieves, not on how it looks. 'My way of practice is to think of the outcome first and then work back from that. So if I want to hit the ball flat, pretty naturally your body gets into position. As opposed to "right, I'm going to get my weight forward".'

Like de Villiers, a fundamental simplicity underpinned the range of Buttler's batting. 'I actually like to nail the really basic stuff as well, so I feel like if I'm hitting on drives I'll just get someone to throw from the hand if possible. For me to play that shot I have to be getting in the best positions I can that suit my game.'

In the same way as de Villiers, Buttler has at times suffered from his adaptability, for it means that he has been shuffled around the order to cover up his team's failings, rather than be empowered to bat where it suited him best. Up until the 2018 IPL Buttler was used largely in the middle order, where he averaged 27 at a strike rate of 141. On the rare occasions when he opened the batting he was even more effective, increasing his average to 35 and strike rate to 147.

On 2 May 2018, Buttler arrived in Delhi for an IPL match with Rajasthan Royals. He had been playing in the middle order, and only contributing middling returns. Then, it rained. In their desperation at requiring 151 from only 12 overs, Rajasthan elevated Buttler to open; he promptly smote 67 from 26 balls. So began a record-equalling run of five consecutive fifties in the IPL, which ended with 95 not out and 94 not out: on both occasions, Buttler hit the winning runs in triumphant run chases.

Here he was enacting the lessons he had learned when given his first proper run opening in T20 the previous IPL season, with Mumbai Indians. 'That was a big moment for me actually – opening the batting for Mumbai. It went okay. It could have gone really well. But having the confidence of Mahela saying I think you'll be a really good opener – that was good. It actually gave me a new lease of life; being 27 and learning a new position, actually it was really invigorating,' he recalled. 'The exciting bit for me was knowing that I'd played a lot of middle order cricket and batting at the end. If I could marry up the two – the Powerplay and the end – it could have really good effects.'

The ambiguity over where best to bat Buttler in T20 was no more. He had only opened once for England before 2018, making 73 not out from 49 balls, but was now entrusted to the role permanently, making 60s in his first two innings as full-time international opener. All told he made 13 fifties in 28 innings as opener from the start of the 2018 IPL to the end of the 2019 season.

It all added to the sense of a cricketer whose clean hitting, range of shots and sheer chutzpah channelled the spirit of A.B. 'Buttler is an incredible prototype of a T20 cricketer,' said John Buchanan, the former Australia coach. In 2018, Buttler scored 1,119 runs, averaging more than 60 and scoring at an astonishing strike rate of 165.

Alfonso Thomas, who played with Buttler at Somerset, drew an unprompted comparison between his former teammate and de Villiers. 'I had the privilege of playing at the Titans in South Africa when de Villiers came into the side and A.B. had a very strong belief which was not arrogance at all – but he knew where he was going and I saw that same characteristic in Jos when I first came across him,' remembered Thomas. 'People laughed at me when I said this kid could be as good as de Villiers. He was fantastic. People said 'no chance' but look now – he's not far off.'

As he reaffirmed in the 2019 World Cup, Buttler is an extraordinary cricketer in an extraordinary phase, not just elevating his own game, but the art of batting itself. Like de Villiers, he approached batting as if he were an explorer trying to uncover hidden lands.

'T20 skills, with the invention of the game and natural evolution of people trying to improve – people are just getting better and better at these things and more consistent,' Buttler said. The world he embodies, and is shaping, is best summarised by one shift. Once, 'the practice would have been forward defence all the time. Now, people are practising hitting sixes all the time.'

SEVEN

THE IMPOSSIBLE JOB

*'You could bowl six good balls and go for six boundaries.
That's how much it has changed'*
Jade Dernbach

Jade Dernbach had just bowled the over from hell: two no-balls, one wide, nine balls and 26 runs. 'I still remember it like it was yesterday,' he recalled more than five years later of a night that had been burned into his memory. 'A.B. de Villiers single-handedly ended my international career.'

The date was 29 March 2014 and the venue was Chittagong, a major port city nestled in the Bay of Bengal in south-eastern Bangladesh. England were playing South Africa in a must-win match in the T20 World Cup.

'The conditions out there were as tough as I've ever had. The dew factor, how hot it was, the humidity. Everything that I had never faced back in England.

'It was honestly like bowling with a bar of soap. In order to bowl a yorker you've got to have full confidence that you can just chuck it up there because one mistake, you get your warning and you're taken out of the attack. Then you throw into the mix the batsman is A.B. de Villiers who is probably the world's greatest T20 batsman, plus I wasn't in great form. It was a perfect storm.'

After 17 overs of South Africa's innings they had 141 runs on the board and England were hopeful of restricting them to a manageable run chase on a good batting pitch. It was then time for Dernbach to assume his designated job as death bowler and close out the innings.

This was a role that Dernbach was familiar with. The majority of his overs in T20 were bowled either in the Powerplay or at the death – the two phases of the innings where the batsmen attacked hardest and scoring rates were highest. Only fourteen bowlers in T20 history bowled a greater proportion of their overs at either end of the innings than Dernbach's 87%.

The intensity of the role forced bowlers to take risks in order to survive. Dernbach had been selected for the role because he was prepared to take those risks and because he was good at taking them: his slower balls, yorkers and decent pace were ideally suited to countering marauding batsmen. Dernbach was prepared to try, and able to execute, skills that very few bowlers in the world – and certainly none in England – could.

The nature of this role was highly volatile. T20 was designed to produce close finishes and because Dernbach would invariably bowl at the death he was often bowling when the match was seemingly won or lost, even if events earlier in the day were just as significant. Dernbach was either the hero or the villain, and in a weak England team it was often the latter. Dernbach accepted as much. But this time was different.

'I remember thinking at that time – and it's not been often that it's happened in my career – I was running up to bowl and I felt like there is nothing I can do to stop this guy. It was ridiculous.'

'Some of the shots . . . I'd bring third man up and he reverse swept me. I dropped everyone back leg side and he got back and swept me over short fine leg. I missed my length and he banged me back over my head. Everywhere I seemed to put the ball it was disappearing.'

Not only was Dernbach's bowling – littered with trick balls – flashy, but his appearance was as well. With slicked back hair, earrings, tattoos and a penchant for sledging batsmen, Dernbach was an ostentatious cricketer. The combination of his role at the death, the high-risk nature of his bowling and his flamboyant guise made him a popular target for criticism.

Bowling in T20 was exceptionally difficult, bowling pace in T20 was even harder and bowling pace at the death was as hard as it got. But if this wasn't enough, life was only made more complicated by the intense scrutiny of the media and wider public – something Dernbach found himself regularly subjected to.

As de Villiers tore into Dernbach, shredding England's World Cup hopes, social media was ablaze. 'Imagine if Dernbach spent less time in the tattoo parlour and more time practising in the nets. He'd still be shit but maybe less so', tweeted one user. 'Hopefully that is the last we see of Jade Dernbach in an England cricket shirt – again he turns a promising position into likely defeat', fumed another. 'So Jade Dernbach's slower ball bouncer/full toss/yorker tactics help yet again. Surely time to stop the experiment and pick a bowler?' raged a fan.

Dernbach's over cost 26 runs and turned the match on its head, shifting the momentum irrevocably in South Africa's favour. From that point the match spiralled out of control. Fifty-five runs came from the final three overs and South Africa finished with a final score of 196 – a total which proved too many for England who were eliminated from the tournament with the finger of blame pointed at Dernbach.

'It almost looked like to everyone else that it was a complete and utter capitulation,' he said. 'It's difficult to really put into words. To feel completely helpless out on that stage at a World Cup and in front of all these people but you feel completely helpless because someone is that good. It's quite a tough place.'

'That one over by Dernbach is the reason England lost the game. England fans must have hard time seeing Dernbach in their team #EngvSA #wt20', tweeted one man after the match. 'The reason England lost in the Cricket today in 2 words, Jade Dernbach! That guy is a fkn club cricketer at best', ranted another.

'I first started playing for England when Twitter was just coming to the forefront and it was great because I was doing well,' recalled Dernbach. 'You're getting a load of followers, people are sending you a load of love on there and you think this is a great platform and you're loving this.

'Then, when stuff wasn't going so well and you still find yourself there because it was new and I searched through looking for something positive to pick you up . . . You think let's find a bit of love out there. And inevitably there isn't. You're just getting completely slated. It felt relentless.

'Stuff on social media started escalating and getting worse and worse and worse. After that World Cup defeat I remember the worst message received was after that MH370 flight went down and someone sent me a message saying I wish you were on that flight.

'This is a game of cricket where someone has been better than you – nobody deserves to be sent that. And I remember coming home and thinking I don't want to leave my house. It was that bad. I didn't want to leave because any time you did you felt like people were looking at you and talking about you. That's paranoia. Everybody has a bad day in their job but it is amplified at this level.'

For Dernbach with England, that night in Chittagong was the end. He was dropped for the last match of the tournament – a dead rubber against the Netherlands two days later – and never played international cricket again. He bowed out of the game with the joint highest T20 international economy rate of all time – a reflection as much on when he bowled his overs as it was on his ability.

'If you are going to play T20 and bowl in those situations you have got to accept that batters are so good that you will get dealt with sometimes. That's how good they are. So it is how you react to it. It's about adjusting your mindset when it comes to bowling at those times.'

In many ways, Dernbach embodied what it was to be a fast bowler in T20. For all his bag of tricks and willingness to bowl in the tough periods, his career was marked by the immensity of his task. Fast bowling in T20 was the impossible job.

'It is a tough world out there for fast bowlers. But the thing you have got to remind yourself of is that people don't pay to come and watch a bowling masterclass and them score 120 runs. That's not what puts bums on seats. So we've got to understand that we are in the entertainment business after all.'

It may have been an entertainment business and bowlers may well have been the support cast but that did not mean that they would not fight back. To try to keep pace with increasingly powerful and aggressive batsmen, bowlers had to continue to evolve and master a wide range of often contradictory skills: accuracy in the Powerplay, variation outside it; slower balls, yorkers and bouncers at the death. Even all that would rarely be enough.

'Bowlers have had to accept that things are stacked up against you,' Dernbach added, 'but you have got to find a way. That's the beauty of T20.'

***

The role for which Dernbach became renowned – for better or for worse – was as a death bowler. But before he would assume those unenviable responsibilities at the end of the innings he would more often than not start a match by bowling two overs in the Powerplay.

Bowling with the new ball in the Powerplay was unlike bowling in any other phase of a T20 innings. For the majority of the time in T20 the primary focus of the bowler was on run preservation rather than taking wickets. But for fast bowlers in the Powerplay both wickets and control were in demand. The death over phase may well have been more difficult, with the batsmen focused purely on hitting rather than having to protect their wicket, but at least then the objective was straightforward. In the Powerplay bowlers had to focus on competing demands – and do it while just two fielders were allowed outside the 30-yard circle. No other phase of the innings asked as much of them.

Statistics played an increasingly prominent role in T20 but among players and teams no number was more regularly referenced than the simple fact that if you took three wickets in the Powerplay you won 69% of the time. This was a statistic that encouraged bowlers to look for wickets in the first six overs. Bowlers who could make early inroads were potential match-winners.

Dernbach was one bowler heavily influenced by this perspective. 'You have to go for wickets early on,' he said. 'The stats back it up. If you take three wickets in the first six overs then your chance of winning goes up to around 70%. That's a huge stat. That suggests you should go all out.' The challenge for fast bowlers tasked with taking early wickets was to find

T20 Win Percentage by Wickets Taken in the Powerplay	
Wickets Taken	**Win Percentage**
0	32%
1	41%
2	55%
3	69%
4	82%
5	90%

the tiny amount of movement that the new ball or the fresh pitch might provide and ensure that if and when that movement arrived the ball was in the right area to find the edge or challenge the stumps. The balls used in T20 swung so little and for such a short period that sometimes the bowler might only get one or two balls where they would find enough movement to challenge the batsmen but if the ball was fractionally too short or fractionally too wide it would be wasted.

Yet while wickets were precious commodities, the Powerplay fielding restrictions meant the first six overs of the game were a dangerous period for the fielding side. The lack of fielders protecting the boundary meant captains often deployed the fielders in the circle in run-saving positions rather than in catching positions in the slips where they might take catches off any edges the bowler may find. Sometimes fielding captains might only leave a slip in position for one or two deliveries – when the ball was at its freshest – before withdrawing them.

The conflict between attack and defence was a complex one and different bowlers in different teams opted for different approaches. Dernbach chased wickets.

'At the top of my run-up I'm thinking wickets. That might mean that I am a bit more expensive but I will be willing to gamble on certain deliveries in the hope of getting a wicket in the Powerplay because I think it sets up the game.'

While Dernbach would opt for aggressive full or short lengths, tempting the batsman to take his own risks, the most consistent Powerplay bowlers were those that combined attack and defence. The success of these bowlers was underpinned by their length: full enough to tempt the drive but neither so full that it was a half-volley nor so short that the batsman could cut or pull. This length was called a 'good' length, largely because in first-class cricket – whatever the match situation, it was just that: a good length to bowl. In T20, though, such consistency was only appropriate in the Powerplay, after which unpredictability trumped accuracy.

This explained why the first excellent generation of Powerplay bowlers were great Test match bowlers: the Sri Lankan Chaminda Vaas, the South African Shaun Pollock and the Pakistani Mohammad Asif were brilliant exponents of control and incision, and all masters in the red-ball format. As the format matured, T20 Powerplay specialists emerged but those who had success in the Powerplay were bowlers of a similar mould. Modern champions included the Australian Jason Behrendorff, the Englishman David Willey and the Jamaican Sheldon Cottrell. All bowled a classic Test match length, and all took wickets at a regular rate but without compromising control.

All three were also left-armers. The angle posed by left-arm bowlers, going across right-handed batsmen – who made up 72% of top three batsmen – from over the wicket, meant that even when the ball wasn't swinging they were challenging the outside edge, bringing the wicketkeeper and any slips into play. Left-armers also had the option to change that angle entirely and go round the wicket, angling the ball into the pads of right-handers, something that right-arm bowlers couldn't do so easily.

In the 2010 T20 World Cup England selected the left-arm quick Ryan Sidebottom after analysis suggested that left-arm bowlers were more effective in T20 – particularly in the Powerplay. Sidebottom took ten wickets and England won the tournament.

'T20 has changed how left-armers are viewed. You look around the world and most teams have a left-armer,' said Sidebottom. 'Left-armers give variety of going over or round the wicket – taking it away from the right-handers so they can only hit on the off side, then coming round the wicket and digging it into the pads.'

The value of left-arm quicks, and their relative scarcity, made them very popular in drafts and auctions. Sometimes left-armers with inferior records were preferred over right-armers. Two of the three most expensive bowlers sold in IPL auctions have both been left-arm quicks: the Englishman Tymal Mills for £1.4 million in 2017 and the Indian Jaydev Unadkat for £1.25 million in 2018. Both were fine bowlers, yet their value was multiplied by the rarity of the left-arm angle.

To bypass the lack of movement on offer some bowlers sought other advantages. The Pakistani Sohail Tanvir – also a left-armer – found success with an unusual bowling action that saw him deliver the ball off the wrong foot, the Englishman Dimitri Mascarenhas consistently bowled off-cutters and leg-cutters – subtly deviating the ball off the pitch. Both Tanvir and Mascarenhas found a home at the Rajasthan Royals in the IPL – one of the first teams to encourage and promote unusual talent.

Height could also be a benefit. The Pakistani giant Mohammad Irfan who was 2.18 metres tall, and Australian Billy Stanlake who was 2.04 metres tall, used their height to extract steep bounce. In the 2018 Caribbean Premier League Irfan bowled the most economical four-over spell in T20 history, not conceding a single run until his final delivery. The wickets of Chris Gayle and Evin Lewis made Irfan's spell a Powerplay bowler's dream: both openers dismissed and just a single run conceded.

Yet, as well as all being defined by their control and movement, the most successful Powerplay bowlers were also marked by their comparative struggle to succeed in other phases of the innings. Behrendorff, Irfan and Stanlake regularly bowled three consecutive overs in the Powerplay and would complete their quota by the end of the middle overs. Their biggest weapon in the Powerplay, their consistency, became their biggest enemy elsewhere, particularly at the death.

***

Dernbach was one of the few bowlers who combined effective Powerplay bowling where attacking skills were most important, with effective post-Powerplay bowling where defensive skills were most important.

Outside the Powerplay the game changed. Any hint of movement that the new ball might have offered through the air or off the pitch had gone. With five fielders permitted outside the 30-yard circle, ones and twos were readily available and hitting boundaries required less precision and more power. This transformed the nature of the contest.

'At the death it's a real baseball thing,' said the batsman Brad Hodge. 'It's either going to be a yorker, a slower ball, a length ball or a bouncer. They are the only four options that death bowlers can go to.'

After the Powerplay, sameness was the enemy for the bowler – regular changes in delivery type complicated the batsman's attacking process. Slower balls were at the forefront of this zeitgeist, with bowlers seeking to disrupt attacking batsmen through changes in speed that left batsmen far too early on their shots and confounded by the difference in reaction time.

Not only were slower balls hard to pick but they were hard to play as well. The most fundamental reason for the dominance of spinners in T20 was that they forced batsmen to generate their own pace on the ball. Slower balls – normally between 60 and 75 miles per hour – had exactly the same effect. Around 21% of balls from fast bowlers in T20 were slower balls compared to 13% in 50-over cricket and 3% in first-class cricket. T20 was a boon for those who sought to take pace off the ball with T20 encouraging a coterie of such bowlers.

Taking pace off the ball was only part of the challenge; the more difficult part was concealing those balls that did so – and it was here that Dernbach excelled. By releasing his slower ball from the back of his hand Dernbach could take pace off the ball while maintaining an upright seam position as if released from the front of the hand, giving the impression of a conventional delivery before it would suddenly drop late on the unsuspecting batsman. Dernbach flummoxed some of the world's very best batsmen with the delivery: M.S. Dhoni, whose big backlift often saw him beaten in the flight by the slower ball, was dismissed six times in 14 meetings in international cricket against Dernbach.

Slower balls were viewed with suspicion by many within the game because they represented a break with traditional coaching structures. Taking pace off the ball and concealing it demanded innovation in grips and release from bowlers that challenged conventional teachings.

Dernbach – who was born in South Africa to an Italian mother and didn't move to England until he was 13 – learned his slower ball not from a coaching manual or an academy, but from a junior player at Surrey. 'I actually saw a kid I played with at Guildford and at Surrey – a guy called Will Sabey – who had this back of the hand slower ball that he was bowling on a Saturday and getting old guys to duck into it left, right and centre. I was watching this thinking I've got to try this,' remembered Dernbach. 'It was probably two or three years in the making of trial and error hitting the side of the net, the top of the net.'

Not only did the ball arise from outside coaching systems but those within the system actively discouraged it. 'I remember during Under-17 games my coach Mickey Powell saying if I bowled another one of those he would kick me somewhere where it might hurt. So there was a lot of work that went into these deliveries so by the time people came to see it, it was four, five years in the making. I really worked hard to identify that. But that's how it is. You see someone do something and you want to capture what they are capable of doing.' By the age of 25 Dernbach had earned an England debut in 2011 largely thanks to his back of the hand slower ball.

Andrew Tye, like Dernbach, also learned his slower ball – a knuckleball – from a teammate in club cricket, rather than from within the professional coaching system. Tye warned of the dangers of over-coaching stifling such innovation. 'There is a concern now that coaches over-coach,' Tye reflected. 'If you're over-coached from a young age you might start to do something that isn't natural. And yes, coaches need to be there to imply the basics but at the same time the players need to have their sense of ownership and adventure to be able to experiment and try different things and do things differently because if we are all producing the same sort of bowler then the game isn't going to grow. You've got to set yourself apart from other bowlers so you can actually have an impact on the game.'

The father of the slower ball was Franklyn Stephenson who played county cricket in the late 1980s and early 1990s. Stephenson was a pace bowler at professional level but occasionally bowled spin when playing league cricket in Lancashire to ease the burden on his body. When bowling spin Stephenson experimented with occasional quicker deliveries with no discernible change in action, a method he inverted when bowling pace. In the late 80s with Nottinghamshire and the early 90s with Sussex, Stephenson's changes of pace caused havoc in county cricket. Stephenson claimed that 25 of his 125 championship wickets in 1988 were taken using his slower ball.

Word quickly spread of Stephenson's new variation. By the late 1990s it became a potent weapon at all levels of the game and all round the world. The growth of limited overs and then T20 – with bowlers seeking to confound attacking batsmen – accelerated its rise. Two of its early masters were Adam Hollioake at Surrey and Ian Harvey at Gloucestershire, who both proved instrumental in periods of dominance for their counties in limited overs cricket in the late 1990s and early 2000s.

As the benefits of slower balls became ever greater, variations of it emerged which were harder to read and behaved differently through the air and off the pitch. Stephenson's original slower ball was an off-cutter delivery which involved the bowler running their hand down the side of the ball, taking pace off but also imparting spin which helped it grip and stick in the surface. But for a batsman aware of this ball being in a bowler's armoury this was fairly easy to spot – both out of the hand and through the air.

The Australian all-rounder Steve Waugh, whose bowling was a key factor in Australia winning the 1987 50-over World Cup, was the first to experiment with a slower ball released from the back of his hand – later perfected by Dernbach – which was not only harder to read but dipped in the air, bounced more than the off-cutter and forced more miscued shots. Other variations included a split finger slower ball which appeared to float out of the hand; a deep in the fingers slower ball which was released later and perhaps the most difficult to master but the hardest to face: the knuckleball, inherited from baseball and combining a floaty release with unpredictable movements through the air and skiddy bounce off the pitch.

The Indian fast bowler Zaheer Khan was one of the first exponents of the knuckleball, which – contrary to what its name suggested – did not involve the bowler gripping the ball with his knuckles but saw the ball lodged in the hand by the fingernails which meant the ball was not only released significantly slower but with almost no spin imparted. The lack of spin reduced the magnus effect on the ball and caused it to move unpredictably through the air and often dip on the batsman. 'It's a tricky ball to hold in the first place,' explained England's Chris Woakes, 'let alone land it in the place you want to.'

Mastery of the knuckleball was very difficult but the first two to do so were Bhuvneshwar Kumar and Tye. With a coterie of other variations Tye emerged from the cricketing wilderness, without a professional contract aged 26, and established himself as one of the leading T20 bowlers within three years. In 2018 the only bowler to take more wickets than Tye's 75 was Rashid Khan.

The rise of the slower ball bred a range of new and unusual bowlers. Gloucestershire's Benny Howell became hugely successful by bowling almost exclusively slower balls. With a top speed in the low 80s Howell's threat came not from the change down in speed but the variety of movement – both in the air and off the pitch – of his different deliveries. His reliance on movement rather than speed change saw Howell describe himself as 'more of a spinner' than a pace bowler.

Bangladesh's Mustafizur Rahman was an inverse version of Howell, a left-armer who bowled with slower ball grips, primarily the off-cutter, but still released them at high speeds. 'My flick and rotation of the wrist is different to most bowlers and I can bowl fast cutters as well as slow ones,' he explained. Mustafizur was a fascinating bowler from the rural town of Satkhira in Bangladesh, who in 2018 travelled to the IPL with a translator, paid for by his team Mumbai Indians, because he could speak almost no English.

The trouble for bowlers such as Dernbach, Tye and Mustafizur who relied upon the mystery of their slower balls was that familiarity bred understanding among batsmen who would became increasingly adept at identifying variations. This was enhanced by video analysis which enabled batsmen to study bowlers in super-slow motion in an effort to detect clues. After initial periods of success Dernbach, Tye and Mustafizur experienced palpable downturns in their fortunes as batsmen became better at reading and playing their various different deliveries.

This placed an emphasis on bowlers continuing to evolve. 'Tye did not become a bad bowler overnight,' commented Dernbach. 'He just found that people understand how he bowls more and now he has to find a different way to do things. I can certainly relate to that. When I first came on to the scene I was probably one of the only people to bowl the back of the hand slower ball. It worked for a long period of time but then people found that out.'

Tye recognised the same challenge. 'I don't want to just fizzle out and people say, yeah, he had a really good period he really mastered the knuckleball but then everyone started bowling the knuckleball and he had nothing else after.'

Bowlers were constantly fighting to survive. 'It's about staying relevant and having an impact in a batsman's game of being an effective bowler,' Tye reflected.

'There are many other facets of the game that you can add to,' said Dernbach. 'Your yorker then has to become better. Can you be on the money with your bouncer? You can be smarter with your field placings. As a bowler you've got to keep developing. If you just get chucked on the heap because you're not deceiving people and looking amazing then all of a sudden people think you're not good enough. And I don't think that's the case.'

The one slower ball specialist who most effectively withstood the test of time was the West Indian Dwayne Bravo. By the end of 2018 he had taken 460 wickets: more than any other bowler in T20. Bravo was a fantastically skilled bowler with a skiddy bouncer and several brilliant variations, including wickedly dipping slower balls. Yet perhaps more important than his skills was how and when he deployed them. Intelligence was essential for a pace bowler, particularly in the death overs when the batsmen were looking to hit every ball for six.

'He has played so much cricket – all the information is stored in his memory bank,' said Simon Katich who coached Bravo at Trinbago Knight Riders. 'Dwayne is a very clever bowler, he sets his fields and bowls to them very well. He can change from wider yorkers to around-the-wicket leg-stump yorkers to keep the batsman guessing what line he is trying to achieve.'

At the death in particular there was an emphasis on the bowler to second-guess the batsman's intentions as they moved around the crease and looked to target the unprotected areas of the ground. Bravo's vast experience made him well suited to this. 'You try to watch a batsman as long as possible . . . try to always be ahead,' said Bravo. 'If you see a batsman try to go down on to his knees to try to lap you, you might have [had] intentions to bowl a yorker or faster ball, but because he moved earlier, you then can change your delivery – bowl a slower ball or vice versa.'

Death over bowlers were in high demand on the T20 circuit. Although dominant Powerplay bowlers were statistically more valuable due to their ability to take early wickets, they were notably rare and often dependent on conditions being in their favour. Their skills were also less versatile than death bowlers who could operate in defensive roles throughout the innings while the 'pitch it up' swing and seam bowlers were largely ineffective outside the first six overs.

Rising run rates around the world and in all phases of the innings also placed greater emphasis on death bowlers' defensive skills. With batsmen attacking more and becoming better at doing so, bowlers who could limit the damage were essential.

For death over specialists at least one good slower ball – cleverly disguised and mischievous through the air or off the pitch – was essential. Yet a slower ball alone was rarely enough. The slower ball was one indispensable weapon; the other was the yorker.

***

It must have looked inconspicuous at first. Just as Somerset's net sessions were winding down Alfonso Thomas and Jos Buttler would wander away from the rest of the group and take a net to themselves. In this net, for around 15 minutes, Thomas would bowl yorkers to Buttler. Every two or three balls the pair would meet in the middle of the pitch and Thomas would point to where his fielders would be before returning to the top of his mark and bowling again.

Yet it would quickly become apparent to anyone watching that this was anything but inconspicuous. This was a meeting of two astonishing talents practising the skills that defined them. Thomas was one of the world's finest T20 fast bowlers – he would play over 200 T20 matches and take 263 wickets, a career built upon his brilliant yorker. Buttler would become one of T20's most spectacular batsmen and among the most effective hitters of yorkers.

Their expertise at bowling and hitting yorkers was honed in these unassuming net sessions, where Thomas elevated the delivery and Buttler learned how to destroy it. This was the coalface of T20 evolution.

'I used to practise a lot,' Thomas said of his yorker prowess. 'I used to put myself under pressure. After normal practice I would take Buttler down to the nets and I would bowl yorkers at him and tell him I am only bowling yorkers for the next 24 balls. And this is my field. After two or three balls the two of us would have a chat and see what works.'

No ball better encapsulated the plight of fast bowlers in T20 than the yorker. It was simultaneously the riskiest but the most effective delivery in the game and one defined by an ongoing conversation between batsman and bowler, each pushing the other to improve and evolve in their playing and bowling of it.

A yorker was a ball that bounced in the small area around the batsman's feet, typically on or around the crease line. Most batsmen, unable to get underneath the ball, were restricted to jamming their bat down and squeezing it out while trying to protect their toes from being crushed.

Get it right and it was fiendishly difficult to hit, let alone score off; but get it even fractionally wrong and it was cannon fodder – too full and it was a full toss, too short and it was a half-volley. 'The margin for error is so small,' Dernbach bemoaned. 'When you are trying to land that ball you are trying to land it in such a small space. When people talk about stepping and hitting if you miss your yorker that's generally where you bowl it – that or a low full toss.'

'The yorker can be a bit of a lottery,' explained Woakes. 'If you miss your length it is going fifteen rows back.' Woakes's England teammate

Tom Curran agreed. 'The margins are obviously so small; you miss it by a foot and it is the difference between getting a wicket and a six.'

Analysis from CricViz showed that balls landing on a yorker length – between one and three metres from the batsman's stumps – concede runs at 6.53 runs per over but balls two metres too full cost 9.94 runs per over and balls two metres too short cost 9.91 runs per over. In a game where the bowlers are constantly under attack the yorker is their greatest weapon but also their greatest enemy.

Thomas attributed his brilliance with the delivery to his willingness to not only practise it regularly but to put himself under pressure when doing so. By bowling to Buttler, Thomas honed his method against one of the most destructive players in the world. Buttler's ability to scoop and ramp and his rapid hand speed were perfectly suited to taking on yorkers which made Thomas's margin for error even smaller. And it rendered bowling during matches comparatively easy.

Despite the huge risks involved the yorker was the go-to delivery of most of the world's fast bowlers – even those less effective than Thomas – and particularly in the death overs when the batsmen were attacking every ball.

Woakes estimated that only about 50% of attempted yorkers were successful and ball-tracking analysis supported this with CricViz suggesting the figure to be around 52%. That was only fractionally better than a coin toss.

'I banked on them missing,' said Brad Hodge whose role was to bat at the death. 'If you face six balls from a yorker bowler the likelihood of him nailing six balls is slim. He's probably going to get three. So my mindset was that I am going to get three opportunities that he misses and I have to hit at least one of them out of the park and I'll back myself to do it.'

It was illustrative of the ongoing battle between bat and ball that while Thomas was developing his method by bowling to Buttler, Buttler was doing the very same thing against Thomas. Paradoxically Thomas's practice made him better at landing his yorker while at the same time stimulating changes that would make the target area he had to hit smaller.

Developments in technique, led by de Villiers and Buttler, made the margin for error against the best players shrink smaller still. These were changes accelerated by the T20 format as fast bowlers increasingly turned to the delivery under pressure and batsmen were forced to find ways to counter it. Buttler's net sessions with Thomas were at the forefront of this change.

'Today if you miss your yorker with the bats and the boundary sizes it's going to go miles,' said Tye. 'Whereas you look 20 years ago and if a bloke missed his yorker you might not get punished as much. That's the evolution of the game and how much it has progressed in the last 20 years.'

'The issue with bowling yorkers is the margin of error is really small,' observed Steffan Jones, a fast bowling consultant for Hobart Hurricanes and Rajasthan Royals. 'Combine that with an increase in the physical and technical capacity of the batters to clear the ropes, there is now a greater scope for things to go wrong at the end of the innings.'

Before the revolution of the bat industry in the early 21st century a big reason for the effectiveness of yorkers was that the toe-ends of bats were very thin and had almost no power. This meant even when batsmen managed to lay a bat on a yorker the best chance of actually scoring any runs was if a bottom edge flew past the wicketkeeper and away for four. But as bats became bigger and more powerful the lower part and toe-end of the bat was weaponised, turning all but the most inch-perfect yorkers into potential scoring opportunities. Some players who batted in the death overs had bats specifically made with unusually low middles to respond to yorkers more effectively. This development was enhanced by the strength of modern-day players with powerful wrists and forearms generating rapid hand speed through the ball.

Advances in technique also reduced the effectiveness of yorkers, enabling batsmen to not only survive them but smash them. Buttler and Dhoni were at the apex of batsmen developing lower backlifts, tailored to hitting yorkers and any delivery that fractionally missed the spot. The evolution of ramp and scoop shots dissuaded bowlers from full lengths for fear of conceding runs behind square, with batsmen deflecting the ball adroitly past the close fielders. Batsmen's dexterity moving around their crease and coming down the pitch meant bowlers were often aiming for a moving target with their lines and lengths upset by the quicksilver footwork of the increasingly confident batsmen. 'Now even if you get it 100% right,' said Dernbach, 'you have got guys who are lapping it.'

As batsmen fought back against the yorker, mastery of length was no longer enough: bowlers were forced to bowl precise lines as well. In the

2009 T20 World Cup the England bowler Stuart Broad experimented by bowling around the wicket to right-handers and bowling wide yorkers way outside off stump, as close to the tramlines that signified a wide as possible. This wider line took the ball out of the hitting arc of the batsmen who were becoming increasingly adept at punishing fractional errors in length against straighter yorkers. After the 2009 T20 World Cup, the wide yorker became increasingly common, increasing from 14% of all yorkers before the tournament to 21% after. 'The wide yorker has now come into play,' Dernbach explained, 'especially guys who set up and try to stay quite still and hit you to mid-on and midwicket.'

Even the laws of the game complicated life for bowlers. The fielding restrictions made it harder for bowlers to disguise their intentions. Having only five boundary riders meant the fielding team could never defend all boundary areas and the field setting would often telegraph their intentions. For instance, if long on and long off were on the boundary the next ball was unlikely to be short because short lengths are typically hit square rather than straight; if third man was back then a wide yorker was more likely than a straight yorker and if fine leg was back and third man was up then it was the other way around.

'If I am bowling a yorker I have to set my field back on the leg side which means I have to bring my fine leg up,' said Dernbach. 'So almost by setting your field you are giving the batter a telltale of what you are going to do and there are so many guys who lap and are not afraid of getting down on one knee and popping you over the keeper's head.'

Batsmen were acutely aware of these giveaways. As the bowler was walking back to his mark the batsmen could often be seen surveying the field, counting the boundary riders, weighing up the options. This kept them a step ahead of the game and in a position to premeditate shots based on where they expected the bowler to bowl. The most audacious bowlers would have the chutzpah to bluff with their field settings, deploying a field to suggest one delivery but bowling another – even though, with the field they had set, this meant an infinitesimal margin of error.

'It's something that Alfonso Thomas at Somerset was fantastic at – bowling the wrong ball for the field he would set, trying to bluff batsmen and bring fine leg and third man up and then bowl a fast bouncer and stuff like that,' Buttler explained of his old teammate. 'Against someone like a de Villiers they are the things you have to try because he's so good at picking up signs and signals from your field.'

Strict rules regarding bouncers also enfeebled bowlers. Until 1991 bowlers were allowed to bowl an unlimited number of bouncers per over in Test cricket, meaning that the bouncer was integral to the yorker's threat. Fast bowlers like the West Indian Joel Garner pushed batsmen back in their crease with a barrage of bouncers before deploying a surprise yorker. But in T20 bowlers were only permitted one bouncer above shoulder height per over. Not only did this reduce the potency of the yorker but, like the field settings, it had the effect of telegraphing the bowler's intentions. If the bowler used his bouncer early in the over it provided the batsman with an advantage of being able to set themselves for fuller deliveries in the knowledge that another short ball would be unlikely because it ran the risk of being called a no-ball if it bounced over shoulder height. Bowlers typically opted to use their one short ball around the middle of the over: too early and the rest of the over was predictable, too late and the bouncer was predictable.

It took an exceptional bowler to master an exceptional delivery. Although Thomas was superb, the undisputed king of the yorker was the Sri Lankan bowler Lasith Malinga. Malinga mastered yorkers playing tennis ball cricket on the beaches of Galle as a teenager, where the lack of bounce on the sand made full lengths a necessity. His effectiveness with the delivery was based on a unique round-arm action that saw him release the ball with his arm at a 45-degree angle, rather than nearer 90-degrees as was the case for most players, earning him the nickname 'Slinger Malinga'. Across his career he landed an astonishing 63% of his yorkers, the highest proportion of all players. His effectiveness was heightened by bowling at speeds of around 90 mph.

Malinga's dominance was no coincidence. Hours and hours of practice with a set of shoes placed on the batting crease grooved his method. But more than anything else his bowling action gave him an advantage. 'Bowlers with slingy actions bowl yorkers better due to their low arm, and there is less possibility of getting it wrong due to their flatter trajectory,' Jones explained. Chris Jordan and Wahab Riaz – both bowlers who had lower than normal release points – also had terrific records with their yorkers.

Malinga's was particularly effective because his arm was so low that the ball was released with the seam almost horizontal to the pitch which meant he could swing the ball down into the pitch – a phenomenal skill which gave the appearance of the ball suddenly dropping and dipping on the batsman like a Cristiano Ronaldo free kick. This effect and the difficulties in picking up the ball from such a low angle, also made Malinga's full toss harder to hit. This rendered his margin for error on the yorker appreciably larger and encouraged him to attempt more of them. Typically full tosses cost ten runs per over and took a wicket every 20 balls; Malinga's full tosses had an economy rate of 7.75 runs per over and took a wicket every 13 balls.

The effectiveness of low-arm actions such as Malinga's was accentuated by the advantage it gave them when bowling bouncers as well. The low release generated skiddy bounce which helped bowlers reliably bowl short lengths that challenged the upper body and neck of the batsman without flouting the rule permitting only one bouncer above shoulder height per over. The skills required to bowl bouncers and yorkers enhanced one another, just like the deliveries themselves.

Yet for most bowlers the yorker remained a source of immense frustration. In contrast, skills such as slower balls which were also popularised by T20 had far greater margin for error.

'Unlike a slower ball, the yorker can only be bowled perfectly into the blockhole,' said Ian Pont, a fast-bowling coach. 'If the bowler misses his spot it can get hit for six – whereas the slower ball can be bowled "poorly" but still be effective.'

So the skills needed for a yorker were more precise – and, Pont believed, it was simply more difficult to bowl well. 'Bowlers are less skilled in yorker bowling than they are slower balls and change-ups of speed. It is far easier to slip in a cutter or roller of the fingers than to master the discipline of hitting a yorker length.'

Yorkers were not the only skill that fast bowlers needed to practise. 'As well as yorkers I've also got to practise bowling my length balls, slower balls, inswingers, outswingers, wide of the crease, tight on the crease, so I've got a load of things I need to concentrate on,' observed Dernbach. 'Whereas if a guy is specialising in coming in in the middle order or back end of the innings and all he has to do is focus on clearing the rope then it makes his job a hell of a lot easier because he just practises that one skill.'

It was telling that both Thomas and Malinga, two of the most effective yorker bowlers, established their predominance with the delivery in unusual circumstances: Thomas's experience training with Buttler and Malinga's on the beach with his unique round-arm action were not easily repeatable methods. For all but the very best bowlers, the idea of the yorker remained far better than the reality.

***

Fast bowling in T20 asked more of bowlers than any other role in the game. They were forced to attack and to defend, to be consistent and to be inconsistent, to swing and seam the ball and to control the ball, to bowl fast and to bowl slow, to bowl full and to bowl short. And all the while they were being asked to do this in the two toughest phases of the match with an unresponsive ball, on flat pitches and against batsmen who were relentlessly attacking with big bats and looking to clear tiny boundaries.

It was indicative of the enormity of the challenge facing fast bowlers that so few players managed to sustain long careers at the top of the game – perhaps only Malinga and Bravo could lay claim to having done so. Dernbach, like Tye and Mustafizur, embodied how bowlers needed to constantly replenish their catalogues to keep pace with batsmen.

'Batting has evolved faster than bowling because bowling can only go to a certain point,' said Dernbach. 'There's only so much you can do as a bowler. I'm bowling 24 balls in a game. That's all I can do to showcase my skills – 24 balls and generally it is to combat a situation. Whereas a batter goes out there and he has got the freedom of the whole innings to show off. He might face 50 or 60 balls so you have a greater window in order to showcase your skill set.'

Nothing quite encapsulated the size of their task greater than the fact that at times bowlers could do exactly what their captains and coaches wanted them to do – bowl precisely to the field that had been set – and still be punished. 'You could bowl six good balls and go for six boundaries,' said Dernbach. 'That's how much it has changed.

'If I run up and say I want to bowl a back of the hand slower ball, turning away from off stump to hit the top of the stumps. That's the skill I want to produce. I run up and do that and I get carted over midwicket for six. Technically speaking I have performed my skill. That is exactly what I wanted to produce, same as if I bowl a perfect yorker and Jos

Buttler gets down and laps me over the keeper. I've put the ball exactly where I want to but it has gone for six.

'The game has changed in that sense. Now people are seeing how talented batsmen are and how good they are and actually as a bowler there's not a hell of a lot you can do. You just have to accept sometimes that guys are that good. It's a matter of how can I limit the damage? If I can limit that damage to an acceptable amount then we have more chance of winning.'

This was a remarkable mindset for a professional sportsman to adopt but it was emblematic of the balance of power in the format. Fast bowlers in T20 had little choice.

EIGHT

SINK OR SWIM

'Batting like in a Test match in Twenty20
cricket is not really going to work'
Kane Williamson

He was already well on his way to being hailed as his country's finest ever batsman and, at 27, was international captain and in his prime. Yet there was a growing feeling that, in Twenty20, his multifarious gifts did not translate into being an asset for his country.

'If Kane Williamson doesn't open in T20, he shouldn't be playing,' declared the former New Zealand player turned commentator Simon Doull in February 2018. 'His record opening is very good – at three and four, it's not that great. But he shouldn't be in the T20 side.'

Doull's concerns were not misguided. In his previous two T20 innings, Williamson had scored 9 off 14 balls and 8 off 21, injuring his side in two ways: not scoring many runs and, just as importantly, chewing up a lot of balls.

Even as Williamson was well established among the leading three cross-format international batsmen of his generation, along with Virat Kohli and Steve Smith, there was a gnawing sense that the demands of T20 were outgrowing his classical batsmanship. In the previous year's Caribbean Premier League, Williamson mustered 172 runs at an average of 17.20 – and a strike rate of just 89. Williamson was used both as an opener and a number four, but with equally dire results. As he painfully tried to muscle boundaries, he resembled an opera singer struggling to sing pop.

Williamson's fate spoke to broader changes in the game: the vastly divergent skills required in T20 and Test cricket. For those like Williamson who were brilliant Test and ODI players, the schedule did not allow them as much space to play T20 as short-format specialists. And T20, with its emphasis on muscularity and power, simply seemed to have no need for what orthodox Test batsmen could do, even when they were as fantastic as Williamson.

Then, a funny thing happened. In his very next game after Doull's comments, Williamson – batting at number three, just as Doull said that he should not – crafted 72 from 46 balls, winning man of the match in New Zealand's victory over England. In the 2018 Indian Premier League, which began two months later, Williamson enjoyed the third most prolific seasons of any batsman in IPL history, scoring 735 runs at an average of 52.50 – but, most importantly, with an excellent strike rate of 142. Williamson captained Sunrisers Hyderabad to the top of the IPL league stages – they would eventually be losing finalists. In the process he suggested that reports of the death of classical batsmen in T20 had been exaggerated.

***

The debate around the value of classical batsmen such as Williamson in T20 spoke to wider conflicts between old and new, defence and attack and style and substance.

T20 heralded a shift in the nature of batting, emphasising aggression, power and boundary-hitting. Players like Andrew Symonds, Virender Sehwag, Brendon McCullum, Chris Gayle, Kieron Pollard and MS Dhoni, and later AB de Villiers, David Warner, Aaron Finch, Jos Buttler, Andre Russell, Glenn Maxwell and Hardik Pandya, embodied this approach.

The evolution ran contrary to the most prized batting skills in Tests and ODIs – wicket preservation and strike rotation. And so it led to some of the world's leading batsmen – who played long innings, but often fell short in terms of scoring rate – being evaluated in a different way. 'Batting like in a Test match in Twenty20 cricket is not really going to work,' said Williamson.

The very notion of some of the world's best Test and ODI cricketers being ill-suited to T20 illustrated how radically T20 differed from its older siblings. That it was classical batsmen who were squeezed by the shortest format was particularly pertinent because this resonated with the concerns of traditionalists about the future of the game – that ultimately T20 was a simplified game, morally and intellectually inferior. There was a profound sense that traditional cricket lovers wanted classical batsmen to succeed in T20 – and that acceptance of the sporting merits of the format partly hinged on them doing so.

'Mahela Jayawardene shows beauty can thrive in game of beastly hitters,' wrote a headline in The Guardian during the 2010 T20 World Cup, when Sri Lanka's Jayawardene was top-scorer. 'This may well be seen as a tournament for the musclemen, those powerhouses who can clear the front leg out of the way and force the ball vast distances beyond the boundary,' The Guardian's esteemed chief cricket correspondent, Mike Selvey, wrote in his article. 'Jayawardene represents the antithesis to this, a slender presence, but one whose wrists are of tungsten and whose technique is a thing of beauty.' Similarly, ESPNCricinfo gushed that 'Jayawardene is showing the world that an orthodox approach can be wildly successful in Twenty20.' The implication was that this notion made T20 an altogether more satisfying game for those reared on the longer formats.

After the 2017 IPL – when Hashim Amla, another orthodox Test great thrived – Sunil Gavaskar, one of India's greatest Test batsmen, launched a staunch defence of a more conservative approach. 'T20 is not about sixes . . . T20 is about making sure that there are no dot balls and both these batsmen have made sure that there are very few dot balls,' Gavaskar said. The comment did not stand up analytically: in T20, the number of boundaries that a team hits is a far better predictor of whether they will win than the number of dot balls they allow. But Gavaskar's comments distilled the desperation for T20 to find a place for archetypal Test batsmen.

The world's best batsmen in Test and ODI cricket were in many ways considered the sport's finest artisans – very elegant players, with supreme technical proficiency in attack and defence. In the 1990s and 2000s Sachin Tendulkar became the sport's first global mega-star and was one of a coterie of modern batting greats alongside Brian Lara, Ricky Ponting, Jacques Kallis and the Sri Lankan pair of Jayawardene and Kumar Sangakkara. In the 2010s the torches were passed to India's

Virat Kohli, Australia's Smith, New Zealand's Williamson and England's Joe Root. These players appeared to find a sweet-spot between many of batting's trade-offs: wicket preservation and scoring rate; strike rotation and boundary hitting; strength against pace and strength against spin.

In the early years of T20 many teams blithely assumed that the very best Test players would simply be good 20-over players. Royal Challengers Bangalore's batting order in the inaugural IPL was a perfect example of this misunderstanding. Bangalore signed the great Test batsman Rahul Dravid as an 'icon' player and then proceeded to build an entire batting order of similarly orthodox players at the auction: Kallis, Shivnarine Chanderpaul, Mark Boucher and Wasim Jaffer, as well as the 18-year-old prodigy Kohli. This batting order was quickly exposed as lacking the requisite power: no team in the 2008 IPL hit fewer boundaries or scored at a slower rate.

As understanding of the realignment between attack and defence in T20 grew, batsmen became more adept at power-hitting. And so teams began to realise that having a batting order with more than one or two classicists was inappropriate for the demands of the modern game.

'At the start of T20 you'd have one or two hitters,' recalled Luke Wright, who played more than 300 T20 matches in a career that started in 2004. 'So in terms of setting a score you had to have one or two players really sit in an anchor role. And you don't really see that anymore: it is mainly hitters.'

This evolution was turbulent. Understanding, particularly among traditionalists, was complicated by batting's primary statistical measure: the batting average. In longer formats, this was an effective measure of success or failure for batsmen. But in T20 batsmen could make a large number of runs while harming their team's chances of winning. This was a particularly acute problem for classical batsmen who were very comfortable playing long innings but who struggled to do so at a fast rate.

In the 2016 T20 World Cup semi-final, Ajinkya Rahane provided a perfect example of the danger of orthodox batsmen in T20 when he played a classic 'match-losing innings'. Rahane was a very elegant player – strong off the front and back foot, adept against pace and spin and a natural timer of the ball – and built a fine Test career. But he was also exactly the kind T20 was leaving behind.

Batting first at the Wankhede Stadium, a venue known for high scores, Rahane scored 40 off 35 balls – an excellent strike rate even in ODIs, but pedestrian for a T20 on a high-scoring ground – while quick scoring from the rest of India's top order saw them post 192 for 2 from their 20 overs. Rahane had faced 29% of India's deliveries and only scored 20% of their runs. He had scored at 6.84 runs per over while the rest of his teammates had scored at 10.08 runs per over. Rahane's long innings also prevented powerful lower order batsmen Hardik and Suresh Raina from even batting. West Indies chased India's target down with seven wickets and two balls to spare.

According to the traditional batting average Rahane's 40 runs was a significant contribution – the highest batting average in T20 history for anyone with 1000 runs by June 2020 was 43.01 by Babar Azam. But Rahane's innings was totally out of sync with the match around it.

Perhaps it was revealing that Rahane's innings came in such a high-octane match. When the stakes were highest – in knock-out matches – teams could have a tendency to play more defensively. But such fear of failure meant they embraced suboptimal tactics: any team who prioritised minimising the risks of a collapse was liable to score too slowly.

It wasn't until around 2012 that meaningful data analysis started to become commonplace and not until nearer the end of the decade that such measures became publicly available. One such measure was CricViz's match impact, which sought to quantify the impact – positive or negative – of players on the scorecard. By this measure, Rahane's innings in Mumbai cost India eight runs compared to an average player batting in the same situation – comfortably the worst contribution in India's innings despite it being the second highest individual score.

As awareness of the downsides of innings such as Rahane's grew, so too did the concept of 'roles' in a T20 side. No role was more pivotal than that of the orthodox batsman. While an entire batting order of classicists was inappropriate there could, in certain situations, be value to one – or possibly two – such players, depending on the balance of the rest of their batting line-up.

The growth and rise of power-hitters meant teams were increasingly stocked with aggressive batsmen. These players were capable of scoring rates well out of reach of players like Williamson and Rahane but their attacking approach made them less secure at the crease and so prone to playing shorter innings on average. An entire batting order of aggressive hitters could, if several fired together, score huge totals but their one-dimensional nature meant they were also prone to collapse and could flounder in tougher batting conditions. In the 2019/20 Big Bash, Brisbane Heat scored 209 for 3, 109 all out and 212 for 3 in consecutive matches, a run that embodied the boom or bust nature of their approach.

The proliferation of big hitters lent justification for the presence of a counter-balance, a batsman or two who scored slightly more slowly but could do so more consistently. It was here that the skills of orthodox batsmen came to the fore.

Such players like Williamson lent stability to their teams. Their exemplary techniques and general robustness against both pace and spin meant that they could succeed in a range of situations and a multitude of conditions. In this respect these classical players resembled all-court players in tennis, who could succeed on a variety of different surfaces. Many of T20's new-age players, like McCullum and Maxwell, were particularly destructive in good batting conditions – which were commonplace on the T20 circuit. But on slower, lower pitches or on pitches that gripped and turned, their aggressive, swing-through-the-line approach was far less effective.

So, among most teams a very specific role emerged for the orthodox batsmen – the 'anchor'. These batsmen were tasked with holding the team's innings together and enabling the more aggressive players to bat around them. Anchors were generally deployed either as an opener or a number three; either way, they sought to bat for a significant period of the innings to provide stability. For players of such technical quality this part of the job was not a problem. Babar, for example, averaged 35 balls per dismissal – almost one-third of an entire innings.

The bigger and more pressing challenge was scoring quickly enough. As T20 run rates rose, they dragged the lower limits of what was acceptable from orthodox players with them. In the first half of the 2010s, strike rates of around 120 were passable and strength against pace was sufficient – Australia's Michael Klinger, who played for the great Perth Scorchers dynasty was the archetypal early anchor. But as the game changed that floor was lifted up towards strike rates of 130, which in turn required improvement against spin, and then in higher scoring leagues sometimes strike rates in excess of 140 were demanded from anchors.

This shift quickly placed pressure on players of Klinger's ilk, amplifying the difficulty of the role. Kohli's evolution encapsulated the changing demands on anchors; he lifted his strike rate from 125 from 2008-2015 to 143 from 2016 to June 2020.

It was generally accepted that anchors would score more slowly than the innings run rate – but if they did so by much, they could become a drag on their team. These pressures were further accentuated by the belief among many analysts that wickets were overvalued in T20 and teams should bat with more aggression.

Yet, for all the scientific thinking applied to T20, elements to the anchor role were much harder to quantify. The most effective anchors – who maintained healthy scoring rates while not compromising wicket preservation – gave batsmen around them freedom to bat aggressively, because they were not fearful that their team could collapse. The benefits of the anchor's ability to rotate strike reliably, particularly scoring singles to ensure a more dominant batsman could move on strike, was also difficult to measure; such batsmen could ensure their most destructive players could face the most balls possible and, if need be, protect unreliable hitters from the opponent's best bowler. Perhaps most significantly, the very best anchor players brought versatility on a variety of pitches and against different types of bowlers and were savvy enough to adjust their games depending on the match situation.

These various benefits meant that an anchor could play an innings that could be seen – or even calculated – to have a slight negative impact, yet helped their team by empowering more destructive players. The best anchors were the ultimate role players.

At times, the role required forgoing their wicket for the greater good of the team. This acceptance was crucial because failure to do so could result in match losing innings such as Rahane's in Mumbai.

Williamson was one anchor who recognised the role demanded selflessness. 'I believe T20 cricket is, out of all the formats, the most 'team' format of cricket,' he said. 'There are innings that I think we've all seen in the past where guys have put themselves maybe before the team situation. And then scoring a big score looks really nice but it might have actually been to the detriment of the team.'

Anchor batsmen were best seen as facilitating players, akin to playmakers in football: players whose contribution could be unobtrusive and sometimes hard to quantify, but who set up the game for their teammates.

Ultimately, the deployment of one or two anchor batsmen in a T20 line-up amounted to what behavioural economists described as 'defensive decision-making.' This is the idea that in medicine, the stock market and beyond, humans don't make decisions that are optimal. Instead, they make decisions to 'cover their ass', as Gerd Gigerenzer argues in *Risk Savvy*. These decisions don't necessarily maximise the chance of success – but they do minimise the chances of failure, a subtle but significant difference. Essentially, the selection of an anchor batsman often lower a batting side's ceiling – but it also raised their floor, and their susceptibility to humiliating collapses.

The higher the standard of cricket the more valuable anchor batsmen generally became. Anchor batsmen were particularly adept at dealing with the world's best bowlers and enabling batting sides to effectively navigate through tricky overs. And so a batsman like Williamson was better suited to the IPL, for example, than the T20 Blast in England where the lower standard meant less technically gifted players who batted more aggressively could thrive. In higher quality matches the class of elite anchor batsmen came to the fore. The best anchors were like all-court tennis players who could succeed in all conditions, observed Nathan Leamon, England's white-ball analyst. 'A large part of their value is insurance against difficult pitches and protection against the best bowlers.'

Whether a team embraces the anchor role is a window into their broader approach.

Broadly speaking, the more a team focuses on batting in assembling their side, and the better a team's core set of batsmen are, the less need for a classicist. When ESPNcricinfo selected a T20 all-time XI in 2020, Kohli did not find a spot. 'If we needed someone to bat through the innings, that sort of traditional player that franchises love, who can handle the best opposition spinner and take the innings deep, then Kohli is perfect for that,' explained Jarrod Kimber who worked as an analyst for a number of teams. 'The thing is that is not an 'all-time' position because of the guys we have around him.' Essentially in a fantasy team the need to guard against the failure of the batting line-up is less pertinent.

England's T20 team between 2018 and 2020 was perhaps the closest example to such depth. With a potential top six of Jason Roy, Jos Buttler,

Jonny Bairstow, Alex Hales, Eoin Morgan and Ben Stokes, England could not always find a place for Joe Root in the side. Although they lacked an anchor, the top six so effectively combined fast scoring and consistency that Root's skills were rendered less valuable. England also had depth below the top six, with even most of their bowlers capable of useful innings, rendering the reliability of an anchor player less attractive.

England's decision to move away from Root was enabled by the quality of their batting but was also tied to their bowling. Leaving Root out was an acknowledgement that they might at times need to score slightly over-par to win matches due to their comparatively weaker bowling, so had to stock their batting accordingly.

At the very same time, a similar debate was going on in Australia who took the opposing path of selecting an anchor, picking Steve Smith ahead of more explosive batsmen D'Arcy Short and Chris Lynn. Australia were emboldened to do this largely because their bowling attack was particularly potent. Where England recognised they needed to score above par to win matches, Australia felt more confident defending lower totals, making an anchor like Smith more attractive.

A similar theme could also be discerned with regards to chasing and setting totals. Deploying an anchor when a team was setting a target raised the chance of a competitive total, ensuring that the bowlers had something to bowl at. Whereas chasing with an anchor reduced the team's risk of low totals but probably lowered their chance when chasing larger totals.

So the extent of a team's embrace of an anchor often illuminated a side's philosophy. The more bowling-orientated the team, the more likely they were to feel comfortable deploying an anchor. Any anchor's fate was tied to the style and resources of their team; Root would have improved many fine T20 teams – but, England's batting meant that they came to believe that he did not improve theirs.

***

Williamson has shown how the best classical batsmen can evolve. He has kept the essential tenets of the game that have made him a phenomenal Test and ODI player, while adding tweaks to make his game better-suited to T20. While Williamson will never have the raw power of some new-age batsmen, he has developed a lap sweep shot against pace bowling that adapts his essential skills – his brilliant hand-eye coordination and timing – to the demands of T20.

He has also become more-willing to embrace risk. In a T20 run chase against India in January 2020, New Zealand needed 43 off four overs, two of which would be bowled by Jasprit Bumrah, the best quick bowler in the world. Rather than accept ones and twos against Bumrah, and target the other bowlers, Williamson, who was well-set- dared to try and take down Bumrah. Across eight deliveries from Bumrah in the 17th and 19th overs, Williamson hit four boundaries – including two whips through the leg side – to leave New Zealand needing just two from the final four balls before he was dismissed for 95. Somehow, India salvaged a Super Over. In the Super Over, Williamson again used his paddle sweep against Bumrah, hitting him for a six, before India chased down 18. The misfortunate end could not conceal how Williamson had given a brilliant distillation of how his batsmanship could thrive in T20.

And yet in the 2019 IPL, when Warner returned from his ban, Williamson could no longer command an automatic place in Sunrisers's XI. It emphasised how demanding the anchor role was, how it demanded players to constantly refine their games and how vulnerable anchors could be to changes in strategy – in 2019, Sunrisers played on better batting wickets, targeting higher scores. Deeper batting orders, improved power-hitting techniques and evermore aggressive approaches are increasing the pressure on anchors to adapt or die.

In 2019, ultimately Sunrisers preferred Warner and Bairstow over Williamson. Through one lens, this could be seen as preferring two aggressive top-order batsmen over an anchor. But perhaps it was better seen as a glimpse of the future of anchors. At their best, Warner and Bairstow were two players in one, matching Williamson's capacity to consistently bat for 30 balls or more with a greater range of boundary-hitting options. And, like Williamson, Warner and Bairstow were adept at minimising dot balls and scampering between the wickets. Warner, in particular, essentially combined all the virtues of anchor players with a higher strike rate; from 2015-2019, he was top scorer in three IPL seasons out of the four he participated in, and second only to Virat Kohli's record 973 runs in the other.

By 2020, Warner could boast an IPL average of 43 and a strike rate of 142 – so his average innings was 43 from 30 balls, simultaneously anchoring and providing early impetus. It was a snapshot, perhaps, of what could be within reach for modern batting's elite: the consistency of the very best anchors, but without the trade-off of slower scoring.

NINE

FROM WAR OF THE WORLDS
TO KINGS OF THE WORLD

'Every decision in T20 cricket should be an aggressive decision. It should be to try and get a hundred, it should be to try and take a wicket . . . It goes against human reactions. We have a safe nature. When you peg back you feel safe. But you should go the other way'
England captain Eoin Morgan

Every year in early April, two photographs were invariably spotted in the sports pages of English newspapers. One would show a county cricket match played in front of thousands of empty plastic seats and under dark, leaden skies. In the foreground there would normally be one or two spectators – old men wrapped up in winter clothing and a blanket, perhaps with a dog or a picnic hamper at their side, a flask in their lap and a newspaper crossword in their hands. The other photograph would be of an IPL match, but rarely the cricket. Instead it would show scantily clad cheerleaders, leaping in the air in celebration, pom-poms in hand, their perfectly made-up faces beaming at the camera, flames, smoke and confetti licking the side of the frame. Behind them would be thousands of rapt fans.

The comparison was so regularly rolled out that it quickly became hackneyed. But it struck at the heart of a schism that would gnaw away at English cricket: a collision of the old world and the new.

The IPL allowed players to earn more in six weeks than many had earned in their entire careers. The average IPL salary for international players in 2008 was £213,000 and the biggest was worth £750,000; many contracts vastly outstripped even the largest international alternatives at the time, estimated to be worth around £500,000. Happily for players of almost all nationalities, the IPL, played in April and May, came at a time of year when their schedules were generally quiet.

There were two major international teams where this wasn't the case. Most severely afflicted were the West Indies, where international contracts were worth relatively little and player relations with the board were often terrible. Many players regularly chose club over country, rejecting central contracts from the board, and remained in India while weakened teams took to the field in home internationals or on tours of England. Paradoxically, the very strength of West Indies in T20 meant that their Test team was particularly depleted by the format.

But the clash was starkest with England. The start of England's home season clashed directly with the IPL. Each year, while the IPL got under way in India, several thousand miles away in England the traditional first-class season – played by the 18 counties, with origins in the 19th century – began. It was the ultimate contrast between the past and the future.

As the IPL season reached its climax, England's international summer would begin, typically with a series against one of international cricket's smaller, poorer teams – New Zealand in 2008 and 2013, West Indies in 2009 and 2012, Bangladesh in 2010 and Sri Lanka in 2011 and 2014. These sides often arrived in England with depleted squads. Their leading players would only land in the country a couple of days before the Test series began: in 2008 five New Zealand players missed warm-up matches in England to play in the IPL instead. Sometimes players would even be absent for the Tests completely.

English cricket's opposition to the IPL ran deeper than it cared to admit. The IPL represented more than simply a challenge to the start of England's traditional season; it amounted to an assault on the notion that English cricket, and what were considered its values and traditions, somehow still represented the pinnacle of the sport.

For half a decade Kevin Pietersen, England's best and brashest cricketer, feuded with England over whether he would be allowed to embrace the IPL. 'To me it's an English cricket problem,' wrote Pietersen in his book. 'A problem about India. A problem about money.'

***

Cricket had originated in England and was spread to disparate parts of the globe on the vessels of the British Empire. For the large majority of the 20th century England remained the sport's focal point: its financial and political force, even if England were seldom among the best international teams. Until 1993, England and Australia, the two old-world powers, both retained the power of veto in the body that became the ICC. England 'has not got over the Raj hangover,' said I.S. Bindra, then president of the BCCI at a famously tempestuous meeting at Lord's in 1993. 'We in the subcontinent want to prove to the rest of the world that whatever they can do, we can do better.'

In the years that followed, power in world cricket shifted irrevocably east. The Asian bloc shared the hosting of World Cups in 1996 – a seminal moment in the commercialisation of cricket – and then 2011. Bangladesh became the tenth Full Member of the ICC in 2000, adding to the bloc's clout. In 2005, the ICC moved their offices from Lord's, where the organisation had resided since its formation in 1909, to the desert of Dubai so they could take advantage of more lenient taxation. The symbolism was unavoidable: cricket was no longer a sport run by the Lord's suits.

All the while, the Indian economy and satellite TV boomed in unison. For Indian cricket, demography was destiny. Other countries were kept afloat by the cash earned from incoming tours by India, so knew to vote with India in ICC board meetings. 'Things have changed since the old imperial days,' wrote Pietersen in his autobiography. 'Big style.'

Before the IPL, as rich and powerful as the BCCI had become, one crucial fact remained: India needed someone to play against. While political differences prevented regular meetings against Pakistan, matches against England remained the most lucrative. Dominance off the pitch was one thing but there was still something to be said for victory on it as well. So although the BCCI was wealthier than it had ever been, it still needed English cricket and more broadly the international game to provide competition and relevance.

The IPL marked the Americanification of Indian cricket: sport as an international event, with the best players from the world over, but with an Indian team always winning. The single most significant consequence of the league was how it redefined cricket's economy from one that was entirely reliant on international competition to one that seemingly had the potential to survive without it. The Indian broadcasting rights to the first ten years of the IPL were sold to Sony for $908 million. Now, India did not need the rest of the world to get rich from playing cricket.

'For football the money comes from Europe and the popularity comes from Africa and South America and the players come from everywhere,' observed Sanjog Gupta, the executive vice-president of Star TV Network. 'That's not true for cricket. The money comes from India – the Indian subcontinent – the players come from India, the popularity comes from India.

'In the Indian fans' eyes the IPL is not a domestic tournament because it actually has the best in the world playing in it,' Gupta explained. 'We don't believe that fans watch IPL and think they're watching domestic cricket. Yes they're watching a lot of Indian players but they're watching IPL because they believe they're getting the best T20 cricket possible.'

The IPL presented an economically and socially liberalised India to the world. The author Aravind Adiga described in an interview with *The Guardian* how the IPL had inverted cricket's power structure. 'This game that in some ways began in England and was . . . an aristocratic backlash against emergent industrial capitalism – that game has become the spearhead of the new Indian capitalism. There has been a democratisation of cricket . . . cricket has spread both away from the big cities and down the social hierarchy.'

In James Astill's book *The Great Tamasha*, published in 2013, the then-BCCI vice-president Niranjan Shah gave a glimpse of the BCCI's imagined future. 'Like in baseball, America is not worried about whether any other country is playing or not,' Shah declared in a statement that caused consternation around the cricket world. Whether or not the BCCI would – or even could – break away from international cricket was moot; the very threat that they might was enough. India now ruled cricket; England, like everyone else, were merely acquiescent.

England's fractious relationship with the IPL was exacerbated by the inevitable comparisons with county cricket. The county game was an anachronism seemingly out of place in this new world, but an institution with roots deep in the soil of English cricket. County cricket was unglamorous and attracted modest crowds but it fostered 18 first-class teams which remained central to nurturing the game in England and had a rich history dating back more than 150 years. Many cricket fans in England resented anything that threatened to undermine county cricket. With its cheerleaders, city-based teams and blaring music the IPL was everything that county cricket was not.

Writing in *The Spectator* magazine in 2018 the writer Geoffrey Wheatcroft embodied the attitude of English traditionalists towards the game's direction of travel in a withering diatribe. 'Sixty years ago there were 18 cricket matches – real cricket, first-class matches, played over several days, with two innings a side – at Lord's during June and July. Thirty years ago that had shrunk to five. This year there's just one, Middlesex playing Warwickshire in what's left of the county championship at the end of July,' he wrote. 'Otherwise it's a monotonous diet of one-day matches and "T20 Blast", the infantilised game of Twenty20Trash, a parody of cricket and a perfect parable of our age, with a subtle and elegant game sexed up and dumbed down.'

The English media perpetuated distrust of the IPL. In the early years of the league, coverage of the cricket itself barely existed in England. The first two seasons were televised on the subscription channel Setanta Sports, tucked well away from the eyes of all but the most ardent sports fans. When ITV acquired the rights – and broadcast every match on the free-to-air channel ITV4, the first cricket on terrestrial television in England in half a decade – broader media coverage remained threadbare, even though viewing figures sometimes exceeded half a million, vaulting past ITV's expectations. It wasn't so much that the English media couldn't see the IPL; it was more that they didn't want to. The little coverage that existed mostly belittled the league; like the ECB themselves, English cricket's media gave the impression of being offended and threatened by the IPL.

'What's really changed cricket isn't so much T20T [sic] itself as its supreme incarnation in the Indian Premier League, which now completely dominates, and dictates to, the whole game,' wrote Wheatcroft. In response, he advocated 'a Campaign for Real Cricket'.

County cricket, previously largely ignored, was suddenly held up as a paragon of virtue in comparison to the seedy private ownership of the IPL. Not only did the IPL and T20 threaten the county game; some believed it threatened the entire edifice of the sport.

'Everything worthwhile about it is being destroyed,' wrote the former editor of the *Wisden Cricketers' Almanack* Matthew Engel in *The Guardian* in 2017. 'Its culture that the umpire's decision is final; the delicate balance between bat and ball as the game degenerates into a six-hitting contest; and that even more delicate balance between individual and team.'

Perhaps most of all, the IPL frightened English cricket. It was, after all, the ECB who had created the T20 format back in 2003. Much like with the creation of one-day cricket in the 1960s, English cricket had again been at the forefront of change in the sport. Yet T20 had huge unintended consequences for cricket's global balance of power, restructuring the sport's economy and entrenching India's hegemony. Thanks to T20, 'cricket is now more known as a vibrant Asian sport than a traditional English sport,' reflected Jon Long, the ICC's former head of strategy.

England's place in this new world was alarmingly uncertain. 'Despite having created and developed the Twenty20 format. England failed to see its potential and the fact is, they are gutted that India has got a hold of the strongest tournament in world cricket,' wrote Pietersen. 'The ECB have been trying to get the genie back in the bottle ever since.'

The IPL triggered copycat leagues in Bangladesh, Sri Lanka, Pakistan and the Caribbean with private ownership and city-based teams, while Australia and South Africa overhauled their T20 competitions to make them more appealing to broadcasters. For England, modernisation was more complicated: the ECB tried rebranding their existing T20 competition to broaden its appeal, but it remained an 18-county competition. Central to the popularity of the IPL was that the eight-team system was perfect for television with no two matches played simultaneously, allowing every match to be televised as a stand-alone event. This simple structure helped teams establish identities and let narratives take hold, particularly among more casual fans unable to or uninterested in keeping track of many more teams and hundreds of players.

England's 18 first-class counties gave the game roots around the country but they did not lend themselves to blanket broadcasting coverage. The couch was the new grandstand. In 2010 England's T20 competition featured 151 matches of which 135 were played simultaneously and just 35 were televised. The problem for the ECB was that the 18 counties held the votes required to force change and a two-thirds majority was required to establish a more streamlined competition featuring fewer teams. Plans to create an English Premier League, based at what was then nine Test match venues, collapsed in 2008 – to the great frustration of Eoin Morgan, according to his then Middlesex teammate Ed Smith. 'On the morning of a Middlesex T20 match, Morgan saw a newspaper report saying the EPL was not going to happen after all. He was not impressed,' Smith later wrote.

As the world transformed, English cricket was gripped by existential angst. 'We are in a war of ideas and we are not confident about our allies,' wrote ESPNcricinfo's UK editor David Hopps. 'Whether we know it or not, when we watch the IPL, it is our fears about our own future that trouble us . . . It is entirely natural that even those of us in England who quite like the IPL resent it at the same time.

'The glamour of the IPL is a reminder of our weakening economic power, of the sense that we are a nation in decline. While the IPL parades its power, England gets a glimpse of how we used to be.'

Despite the lack of warmth and more general suspicion from the wider media, between 2015 and 2018 viewing figures for the IPL in the UK rose 40%. By the 2019 season even the BBC carried live commentary of every IPL match – a recognition that the IPL could no longer be ignored.

***

Initially it seemed as if the ECB could navigate this new terrain. No England players signed up to the first IPL auction, with the league likely to clash directly with international commitments. Even after the auction both Pietersen and Andrew Flintoff, the two England players most likely to attract the interest of franchises, pledged their immediate futures to the national team.

The league's impresario Lalit Modi accepted a first season impasse, even while making it clear that the IPL was coming for England's players. Weeks later, Hampshire all-rounder Dimitri Mascarenhas became the first English player to join the league when he was picked up in the second mini auction by Rajasthan Royals. Although Mascarenhas occasionally featured in England's ODI and T20 teams, he was not a centrally contracted England player and therefore the power to let him play rested with his county, Hampshire. Even they provided 'a lot of resistance', Mascarenhas recalled; Hampshire only allowed him to go for two weeks, to miss as little county cricket as possible. Mascarenhas played a solitary match in the 2008 season but he was the lone English player to do so. He became a quiet revolutionary.

Mascarenhas' experience that April and May, shifting between county cricket and the IPL, distilled the shift under way in cricket. 'The IPL was totally different – 50,000 Indians, who are just more passionate than any nation you can imagine about cricket, just screaming and shouting the whole time. The noise was just relentless. It was a proper atmosphere,' he recalled. 'I always called for more English players playing straightaway. They could only benefit from that experience.'

As the inaugural season sparked into life, England's players, even from afar, observed what a paradigm shift the IPL represented. Pietersen was the first player to request that England adjust their schedule to allow players to feature in the league. Within weeks stories surfaced that Pietersen was already close to agreeing a deal for the following season – even though, in theory, no franchise could bid for him until the auction.

Tensions between the players and the board bubbled beneath the surface. Ravi Bopara and Luke Wright, two players on the fringe of England's white-ball teams, were dissuaded from playing in the IPL after the ECB warned them that doing so would not be viewed favourably and could harm their England careers.

The ECB were deeply suspicious of the IPL and well aware of the threat that it posed. This much was made apparent by their astonishing liaison with the Texan billionaire Allen Stanford.

In 2006 Stanford, who had ostensibly made millions dealing in real estate in the US and later established a bank, became a significant benefactor to West Indian cricket. He promised to reinvigorate sport in the region with a $28 million investment and launched a T20 competition among the Caribbean islands. Stanford quickly eyed bigger prizes. In 2008, he approached both the Indian and South African boards with an offer to play an annual $20 million winner-takes-all match against a Caribbean XI, featuring the region's best players as selected by him. Both India and South Africa rejected Stanford's offer. The ECB, aware of the opportunity such a match posed to ameliorate players who had missed out on IPL cash, had no such qualms.

Two months after the IPL began, the ECB chairman Giles Clarke welcomed Stanford and his Stanford-emblazoned helicopter – it was actually rented, and just had his company logo painted on – on to the outfield at Lord's. Then, in front of a perspex box seemingly filled with $20 million in $50 bills, Stanford, flanked by Clarke and ECB chief executive David Collier, unveiled English cricket's brave new world.

The match itself, played on 1 November 2008, turned out to be a late Halloween surprise for England. They were eviscerated: bowled out for 99, and their total overhauled by the Stanford Superstars in just 12.4

overs. England left the Caribbean humiliated, and with none of the money intended to douse the IPL flames. Three months later, Stanford was found guilty of an enormous Ponzi scheme and sentenced to 110 years' imprisonment for fraud in the US. Some West Indies players never got their winnings: they reinvested them in Stanford's businesses, and then lost everything when Stanford was exposed.

England's players were reportedly not averse to playing politics either. Following the Mumbai terror attacks in November 2008, England's Test series in India, scheduled for early December, was in jeopardy. Yet despite security concerns England's players remained keen to travel. When the tour went ahead there were whispers that the allure of the IPL rupee and an urge to appeal to Indian markets and the IPL was a factor in their act of sporting diplomacy.

The collapse of the Stanford deal left the ECB with no choice but to relax their IPL policy. In January 2009 England's centrally contracted players agreed a deal permitting them three weeks in the league, a compromise position between Modi's demand for four weeks and the ECB's desire for two. The agreement meant England's Test players would play no first-class cricket before their first Test series of the summer, enraging traditionalists. But 'the alternative was for England to be the only country that forced its players to choose between playing for country and IPL, and that was a dangerous place to go,' warned Sean Morris, the Professional Cricketers' Association chairman.

At the 2009 auction less than a month later, Flintoff and Pietersen became the league's most expensive signings, earning contracts worth £750,000 at Chennai Super Kings and Royal Challengers Bangalore. Three more England players – Paul Collingwood, Owais Shah and Ravi Bopara – also earned deals. The auction took place while England, with Flintoff, Pietersen and Collingwood in the side, were playing a Test against the West Indies in Jamaica; England collapsed to 51 all out in their second innings to lose spectacularly.

Despite the agreement, the truce between the ECB and the players remained uneasy. Clarke had explained: 'What would be said if a centrally contracted player was allowed to go to the IPL, then got injured and couldn't play in the Ashes?'

Clarke's prophecy proved correct. Two Tests into the home Ashes, Pietersen was injured, and his Achilles problem in part blamed on his IPL involvement. Flintoff was also injured during the IPL and retired from Test cricket at the end of the Ashes series. He never played for England in any format ever again.

The terms of the accord also precluded England players from being embraced by IPL franchises quite as they had hoped. As the IPL matured, franchises' recruitment became more rigorous and teams started valuing continuity. Signing England players for a mere few weeks, and having them miss the tournament play-offs, became less attractive. Rules regarding players reimbursing their counties often forced them to enter the auction at a high price, further dissuading suitors.

The bargain also became less advantageous for the ECB: while they had the financial heft to keep their international players onside, the IPL relegated the first Test series of England's summer to a B-list event, with the IPL either depriving their best opponents of practice time in English conditions, or increasingly leading to star visiting players missing the series altogether. Naturally it was Pietersen who exposed these fissures, in the summer of 2012.

***

The clash between Pietersen and the ECB had long been forewarned. Pietersen, born in South Africa to an English mother and a South African father, only moved to England aged 20 to further a stalling career. His rare batting talents quickly became evident to everyone – no one more than himself. As brilliant as he was on the pitch, he was equally disruptive off it. Pietersen was not encumbered by the English system nor was he afraid to challenge the structures that supported it. It took someone from the outside to force change.

As a young player, Pietersen's loud haircuts, tattoos, celebrity girlfriends and cocky swagger antagonised many within the traditionally conservative environment of the England hierarchy. Pietersen's brief stint as England captain ended in January 2009 when he demanded that England sack their coach Peter Moores. In the event, both lost their jobs.

The IPL's rise accentuated tensions between Pietersen and the board, no longer his sole paymasters. Every IPL team would have welcomed Pietersen; after being dumped as England captain, the IPL became even more appealing to him, and he captained Royal Challengers Bangalore in his debut season in 2009. A very uneasy truce continued: England now allowed their best players to play in the IPL – but, unlike players from every other country, they were never able to play a full season because of England's home fixtures.

In 2012, a dressing room split, involving Pietersen bad-mouthing his captain, Andrew Strauss, to their opponents South Africa by text culminated in Pietersen being left out of the team. While the coverage focused on the minutiae of player relationships, the IPL was at the heart of the whole affair. Pietersen was furious at head coach Andy Flower's refusal to countenance his full involvement in the league, and had retired from international limited overs cricket in protest. When Pietersen clashed with Strauss during the second Test of the series, Strauss felt, 'It was almost as if he was trying to engineer an excuse to turn his back on the team,' he later wrote in his autobiography *Driving Ambition*.

The financial appeal of the IPL was obvious to Pietersen and he was not ashamed to admit it. 'You only play this game for a short while,' he said in the film *Death of a Gentleman*, 'you've got to make the most of your opportunities.' But for Pietersen, a natural showman, there was more to the IPL than just money. Unlike his increasingly fractured international career the IPL offered Pietersen the adoration that he craved. 'The IPL had an audience of a billion people in India alone,' he wrote in his autobiography. 'Every time you walk out on to the field there are at least forty thousand people watching you from the stands. Under the floodlights, no matter where you are, the place buzzes and crackles with electricity and excitement.'

There was also a cricket benefit to playing in the IPL, as Pietersen trumpeted to the ECB. For six weeks the IPL brought the best players and coaches in the world together in an environment where knowledge was shared between players from different countries, allowing players from different cultures to learn from each other. 'The IPL has become a great global tournament,' wrote Pietersen. 'Look at the guys they would be playing with. You can only get better by playing against the best.'

After the fallout of the summer of 2012 Pietersen was 'reintegrated' into the England team and played for England for another year. It proved another uneasy truce. A harrowing 5–0 whitewash in the 2013/14 Ashes opened up old wounds between Pietersen and the rest of the team. Despite Flower's resignation as head coach, this time Pietersen's relationships with his teammates, particularly senior figures Alastair Cook and Matt Prior, had seemingly broken down beyond repair. In February 2014 Pietersen's England career was ended by the ECB who sought to rebuild the team without him. Personal differences had ended Pietersen's England career, but, it was the conflict over the IPL that caused these to flare up.

If the tensions caused by the IPL, and T20 generally, were most fervent in England, they were not confined to here. After becoming the first Australian to opt to become a freelance player when still in his 20s, despite his first-class record leading to suggestions he could play in Tests, Chris Lynn forged a fine career as a T20 specialist.

'I guess just the other formats, the longer format, wasn't for me,' Lynn explained. 'It's frowned upon in Australia, as every little kid's dream is to wear the baggy green – and I think whilst that's an amazing achievement, there's more to life than wearing that baggy green. And do I get judged as a different person because I have one or not? Or my interests are with the shorter format?

'But I think they're coming around to it. I just think they'll fall behind if they don't embrace what the player wants. We've seen it in other countries.'

Lynn crafted a Sheffield Shield double century over eight hours and slammed a Big Bash century in an hour. The T20 hundred was 'absolutely' more fun. 'And I can have a beer that night, and then the next day I might be a bit sore, but I get to do it all again in two, three days' time. So it's just something that excites me. And I love that go-hard-and-go-home attitude.'

'I don't have to stand in the sun for a couple of days and then get my opportunity to bat. I could play three times a week and try to smack the ball out of the park. And obviously the entertainment factor is something that I really enjoy.'

Pietersen found something similar when, in the year after being sacked by England, he appeared for five different teams in five different leagues: the Melbourne Stars in the Big Bash League, St Lucia Zouks in the Caribbean Premier League, the Dolphins in the RAM Slam T20 Challenge, the Quetta Gladiators in the Pakistan Super League and Rising Pune Supergiant in the IPL. Pietersen's globetrotting reflected the sport's direction of travel. For the first time since the 19th century, the best players did not need to be playing international cricket to be in the top earners in the sport.

***

England's performance in the 2015 World Cup was like a compendium of their greatest hits of limited overs incompetence. It was not merely that England were trounced by Australia, New Zealand and Sri Lanka, and then were defeated by Bangladesh to fail to qualify for the quarter-finals. It was also that their way of playing ODI cricket was exposed as anachronistic, overly cautious and rigid, completely oblivious to how big hitting – and T20 – had reshaped the game.

'What's really happened in this tournament which has come home to me is the crossover between T20 and 50-over cricket now. It's immense,' Paul Downton, the managing director of English cricket, told the ECB website, seeming shocked at how rapidly T20 had changed the norms in ODI. 'It is a fact that not many of our players play much T20 cricket full stop, whether that be abroad or at home. That to me is the biggest lesson coming out of this tournament: how much T20 is influencing one-day cricket now.'

The 2015 World Cup was not an isolated instance of English ignominy in the tournament. From 1996 to 2015, England played 26 games against Test-playing opposition in the World Cup, and won only seven of them – including losing every single time they played any of Australia, India or New Zealand. Across the three World Cups from 2007 to 2015, Ireland defeated more Test nations than England in the World Cup.

Within two months of England's exit, Downton and Peter Moores, the coach, had both been sacked. Andrew Strauss, Downton's successor, identified improving England's abject form in both ODIs and T20s – where England had stumbled upon a side to win the T20 World Cup in 2010, but they had swiftly regressed to their normal struggles, failing to reach the knockout stages in both 2012 and 2014, when they lost to the Netherlands – as a priority.

Strauss was not an obvious figure to be at the vanguard of England's white-ball revolution. Educated at Radley – one of England's most exclusive private schools – he was viewed as the embodiment of English cricketing conservatism. The Test team Strauss captained reached the top of the world rankings through an attritional style of play, and he was never as effective – as either a batsman or captain – in white-ball cricket.

He was also one of Pietersen's major opponents on being able to play in the IPL more extensively; in Pietersen's autobiography he compared talking to Strauss about the IPL in 2012 to 'speaking to the vicar about gangster rap'. Yet, after he took over as director of England cricket in May 2015, Strauss embraced Pietersen's view of the IPL, changing the ECB's stance on the competition decisively.

In 2014 Strauss was invited to the IPL final in Bangalore. He was taken aback by what he saw. 'I think the IPL is a brilliant thing to have happened to cricket,' he told the IPL's official website. 'You look at the calibre of the players who are playing here and it is really taking the game of cricket forward. It's really difficult to say anything negative about this tournament. It's been a fantastic addition to the game. To sample it in the flesh is the best way to figure out how good it is . . . It's a bit tricky with the English season clashing with the IPL. But I think it would be great if players from England could participate as it would benefit them a lot.'

Strauss's U-turn came too late for Pietersen but it was also vindication for his tireless crusade. It is tempting to label Pietersen as being ahead of his time; in reality the rest of English cricket was simply lagging behind.

'Clearly there were other pressures brought to bear around that time. There was a decision not to make players from the UK available to IPL in the early stages. In retrospect that might have been out of a misunderstanding of what IPL was all about,' said Tom Harrison, who became chief executive of the ECB in 2015. 'There were some real growing pains around how T20 was going. You've got to understand the context of how confusing times were then and the kind of pressures that might have been around.'

After Strauss was appointed director of cricket, he resolved that England should appoint a head coach based largely on their pedigree in limited overs cricket, for the first time ever. Strauss recruited Trevor Bayliss, who had coached Sri Lanka to the final of the 50-over World Cup, and twice won the IPL with Kolkata Knight Riders. In his contract, Bayliss was given a healthy bonus for winning the 2019 World Cup, which England were hosting and the ECB identified as a crucial opportunity to reinvigorate the sport in the country. Strauss was also decisive in retaining Eoin Morgan, who had only been appointed ODI captain two months before the World Cup – the ultimate hospital pass – and empowering him to shape England's white-ball revolution.

In England's first match after the 2015 World Cup, captain Morgan was 5,000 miles away, playing for Sunrisers Hyderabad in the IPL. Such was Strauss's determination that English players should get more IPL exposure.

'There has been a sea change,' Strauss told ESPNcricinfo later that year. 'These leagues are a melting pot of different ideas around white-ball cricket. Look at the 2015 World Cup, look at the semi-finalists. I think 38 out of 44 players had played in the IPL. You're going to get great experiences of playing under pressure. Over the last decade or so we've been behind a lot of teams in white-ball cricket. It seems an opportunity that we cannot afford to turn down.'

In the following auction only three England players were sold, but in 2017 that number rose to ten. In 2018, 13 appeared, including those picked up as injury replacements. Once a curiosity, now English players in the IPL were seen as essential both for the teams and by the England national side.

'The IPL experience is an invaluable one to learn and play against the best players in the world in those situations,' explained Jos Buttler, whose international career was reinvigorated by the IPL. 'I've learned a lot about myself and how to get the best out of myself.'

Playing in the IPL was also instrumental in Morgan's development. 'I got to play with Anil Kumble, Rahul Dravid was in the same team; Jacques Kallis, Mark Boucher, Dale Steyn, Kevin Pietersen,' he said. 'Watching how these guys went about the new format was really interesting because they were very experienced, skilful cricketers but they were throwing themselves into it like kids.'

A little like Pietersen, though without antagonising his teammates in the process, Morgan was ahead of his time in embracing the IPL. In 2013, Morgan played in the IPL after being dropped from the Test team, against the wishes of the head coach. 'Andy Flower called me and said, "If you want to get back in the Test team, you have to come back,"' Morgan later told the *Cricket Monthly*. 'And I argued, "No, I'm learning more here for the last two seasons and this season, even if I'm not playing well, than I've learned in four years of county cricket. So with all due respect I'm going to take this opportunity."'

For Morgan, the benefits of the IPL were psychological as well, and extended beyond simply the player involved. 'When you have the biggest tournament in the world, demanding the best players in the world, when there are players go for large sums of money, it's a compliment to them as a player to start with but it also brings added pressure,' he observed. 'When our top players go and perform there under massive pressure and one of them becomes the MVP [most valuable player, as Stokes did in 2017] and the others are the talk of the town it does bring confidence to our squad and reinforce that the skill level we are constantly producing and competing against each other in the team is actually moving forward. It's as good as anything else in the world so for the young guys coming through it actually makes the IPL a lot closer than it used to be because we only had a couple of players that ever went and it was seen as a bit of a taboo place to go.'

On occasion, IPL experience appeared to be more impediment than benefit. In 2017 Jason Roy went to the IPL as England's potential tournament winner in the Champions Trophy, played in England soon after. He left the IPL having played three games out of a possible 14, including one batting, incongruously, at six rather than as an opener. His form disintegrated, and he was dropped during the Champions Trophy.

Still, even this chastening experience did nothing to deter England from embracing the IPL with ever more gusto. The new Future Tours Programme, from 2020, was planned to minimise England's internationals in May – thereby making England's players available for the entirety of the tournament, and hence far more attractive to franchises. Counties – even Surrey, who generated so much cash from home T20s that they were by far the wealthiest – no longer tried to prevent their players joining the IPL, even as replacements in the final days before the county season began. County cricket in April and May soon became, in effect, played only by those not deemed good enough to win an IPL deal.

In 2016, Sam Billings entered the auction at Strauss's encouragement but received such a low fee – Rs 30 lakhs (approximately £31,000) – that, when taking into account reimbursing his county Kent, Billings was losing money from his IPL experience. Strauss used the ECB's coffers to reimburse Billings. Where once the ECB dissuaded their players from taking part in the IPL, now it actively paid them to do so, such was the haste with which England's attitudes towards the competition were transformed.

Billings had initially entered at the lowest possible auction price for an overseas player. Unaware that the ECB would reimburse him, he was content to make an overall loss from his contract if it meant being part of the IPL – even if he wouldn't get a chance to play. 'So the technicality

Surrey won the inaugural Twenty20 Cup in 2003 with their captain Adam Hollioake appearing ahead of his time – identifying that sixes were the format's most valuable currency. *Getty Images*

Australia and New Zealand's players pose for a photo ahead of the inaugural T20 international. New Zealand's players wore retro kit and wigs, treating the game as a bit of fun. Man of the Match Ricky Ponting said afterwards, 'I think it's difficult to play seriously.' *Getty Images*

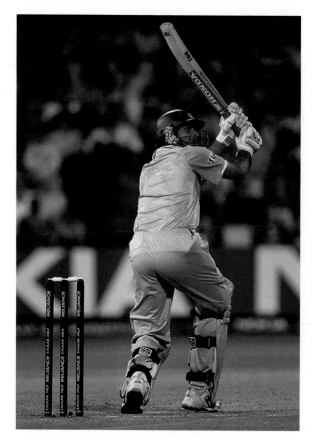

Yuvraj Singh hits the second of his six sixes in an over off England's Stuart Broad. Yuvraj's feat lit the touchpaper of three weeks that would transform India's relationship with T20 cricket. *ESPN Cricinfo*

India celebrate winning the 2007 T20 World Cup – a result that laid the platform for the transformative success of the inaugural IPL season. Pakistan's Misbah Ul-Haq is pictured in the background, despairing after his fateful scoop shot was caught by Sreesanth. *ESPN Cricinfo*

The IPL's impresario, Lalit Modi, watches the opening ceremony of the tournament in 2008. Modi's cult of personality was integral to the phenomenal early success of the tournament. *ESPN Cricinfo*

Sourav Ganguly (right) congratulates Brendon McCullum (left) during McCullum's century in the inaugural IPL match in Bangalore in 2008. McCullum's 158 not out was a landmark moment in cricket history. *ESPN Cricinfo*

Rajasthan Royals captain, Shane Warne, lifts the IPL trophy in 2008. Despite spending the least money and being the least glamorous franchise, Rajasthan won the tournament thanks to Warne's leadership, smart recruitment and innovative tactics. *ESPN Cricinfo*

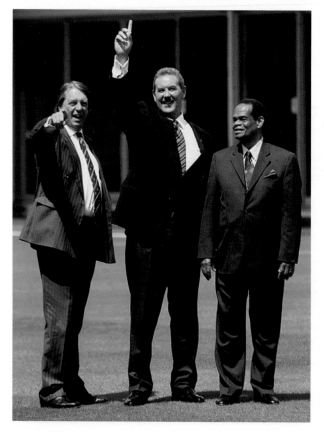

Giles Clarke (left) welcomes Allen Stanford (centre) to Lord's, alongside the president of the West Indies Cricket Board, Julian Hunte (right), ahead of launching the Stanford 20/20 tournament. Less than a year later Stanford was sentenced to a life imprisonment for a ponzi scheme. *ESPN Cricinfo*

Chris Gayle is the iconic player of the first era of T20 and the format's most prolific batsman with more than 12,000 runs and 21 hundreds. His 175 not out, pictured, remains the highest score in T20 history. *ESPN Cricinfo*

The businessman, Venky Mysore (right), transformed Kolkata Knight Riders from one of the weakest IPL teams to pioneers, revolutionising their strategy on and off the pitch. One of his first moves was to sign Gautam Gambhir (left) as captain in the 2011 auction. *ESPN Cricinfo*

Kolkata Knight Riders lift the IPL trophy in 2014 – the second of their two titles in three years. KKR's fortunes were transformed by the arrival of Venky Mysore as Managing Director who embraced analytics and with Gautam Gambhir as captain built a spin-heavy team with Sunil Narine at the centre of their attack. *ESPN Cricinfo*

Jade Dernbach despairs as AB de Villiers tears him apart in Chittagong in 2014. Dernbach bowled a nine ball over which cost 26 runs and ultimately his international career. Fast bowling in T20 cricket was the impossible job. *ESPN Cricinfo*

Brad Hodge was a bridge between the old-school finishers, who scored in unusual areas, and the new-age power-hitters, who were defined by strength as much as touch-play. *ESPN Cricinfo*

Lasith 'Slinga' Malinga is arguably T20 cricket's greatest bowler. His unique round-arm action enabled him to bowl yorkers consistently. *Getty Images*

Kieron Pollard announced his talents to the world in the 2009 Champions League – in the tournament a number of the T and T players sported loud haircuts to help attract attention of IPL teams. *ESPN Cricinfo*

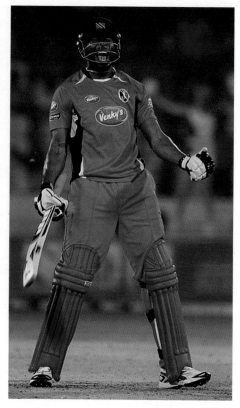

Trinidad and Tobago's Samuel Badree transformed wrist spin bowling by bowling flatter, faster and straighter, bringing unusual accuracy to the art. Badree was a pioneering spinner who took the new ball and bowled primarily in the Powerplay. *ESPN Cricinfo*

Pollard roars into the night's sky after completing one of the most significant innings in T20 history – his 18 ball 54 not out completed a stunning heist for Trinidad and Tobago and transformed power-hitting. *ESPN Cricinfo*

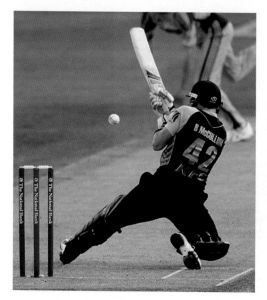

Brendon McCullum's 158* propelled cricket into its new age that few came to embody as much as him – his fearless approach to batting encapsulated the format. Left, he scoops the world's fastest bowler, Shaun Tait, for six in Christchurch, 2010. *ESPN Cricinfo*

Sunil Narine celebrates after bowling a maiden in a Super Over for Guyana Amazon Warriors against Trinidad and Tobago Red Steel in the 2014 Caribbean Premier League. *ESPN Cricinfo*

AB de Villiers is the most complete batsman to have played T20 cricket. He combined raw power and natural timing with 360 degree scoring. *ESPN Cricinfo*

Norman Mungaroo (centre) – founder of a hugely popular windball league in Trinidad and Tobago
– is flanked by Kieron Pollard (far left), Rayad Emrit (left), Sunil Narine (right) and Lendl Simmons
(far right) – all of whom played in Norman's league and represented the West Indies.

Kevin Pietersen's career was defined
by his clashes with the ECB regarding
making England players available
for the IPL. Pietersen recognised
the enormous benefits of the league
to players but it wasn't until after
Pietersen had retired that the ECB
relaxed their policy on the league.
ESPN Cricinfo

Jasprit Bumrah (right) learnt from Lasith Malinga (left) at Mumbai Indians. Despite very different bowling actions both men mastered the yorker delivery and were a lethal pairing at the death. *ESPN Cricinfo*

Royal Challengers Bangalore owner Vijay Mallya was a hugely influential figure in the early years of the franchise, exercising a veto on selections and sitting in on team meetings. *ESPN Cricinfo*

Chennai Team Principal Gurunath Meiyappan is swarmed by the media during the 2015 IPL spot-fixing scandal that ultimately saw CSK and Rajasthan Royals suspended for two seasons. *ESPN Cricinfo*

De Villiers inspired a generation of players to score 360 degrees and no one was more effective at doing so than England's Jos Buttler who broke new ground by unfurling such shots in the Powerplay phase when the field was up. *ESPN Cricinfo*

RCB captain, Virat Kohli, gives a team-talk in the 2019 IPL. As Indian captain, Kohli was one of the most powerful individuals in the game and his captaincy was rarely questioned publicly, but in private many believed he didn't understand the nuances of the format. *ESPN Cricinfo*

One year after KKR owners, Red Chillies Entertainment, purchased the Trinidad and Tobago Red Steel in 2015, the Trinbago Knight Riders won three CPL titles in four years. The Knight Riders were the first multi-team brand in global T20 cricket and shared many coaching and backroom staff and some players. *ESPN Cricinfo*

West Indies embark on a lap of honour after their 2016 T20 World Cup victory. The West Indies style of T20 cricket was defined by their muscular power-hitting from the likes of Andre Russell (left) and Darren Sammy (centre). *ESPN Cricinfo*

Carlos Brathwaite celebrates after hitting his fourth six in as many balls to propel the West Indies across the finish line against England in the 2016 T20 World Cup final – one of the greatest T20 matches of all time. *ESPN Cricinfo*

On January 1st 2017 the Melbourne Renegades asked Sunil Narine to open the batting to target the spinner Michael Beer – Narine scored 21 off 13 balls, the start of his radical transformation into a pinch-hitter. *ESPN Cricinfo*

Chennai Super Kings' captain, Mahendra Singh Dhoni, is one of the defining figures of the first era of T20 cricket. Dhoni's calm captaincy, tactical acumen and ice-cool batting was integral to CSK's decade of dominance. *ESPN Cricinfo*

Thirty-six-year-old Shane Watson celebrates his hundred in the 2018 IPL Final. Watson was 0 not out off 10 balls but caught up later against weaker bowlers, displaying experience and calm that defined CSK's victorious campaign. *ESPN Cricinfo*

The Jamaican Andre Russell was the prototypical T20 player, contributing with bat, ball and in the field. His 2019 IPL represented the most advanced iteration of modern power-hitting. *ESPN Cricinfo*

Nepalese leg spinner Sandeep Lamichhane followed in the footsteps of Afghanistan's Rashid Khan in breaking into the major leagues from a non-major cricket nation. *ESPN Cricinfo*

was I was on very much the lowest base price for a capped player but because of the current payments I had to pay back to Kent I think I made probably £7,500 those two years so I was essentially going for free compared to everyone else,' Billings said. 'I just thought it was a priceless opportunity and I think a lot of the time people just see the dollar signs of going to the IPL and actually it is far more than that.'

It wasn't only the IPL that England embraced. The English season may have clashed with the IPL but it didn't clash with any other southern hemisphere leagues and quickly English players became regular features in the leagues around the world as well, notably Australia's Big Bash and the Pakistan Super League.

England's acceptance of foreign T20 leagues had been driven by Strauss's desire to improve results on the field. Yet the shift in policy represented a tacit acknowledgement of the balance of power off it as well. Blocking or discouraging English players from appearing in leagues, particularly those who weren't centrally contracted by England – and therefore on considerably smaller county contracts – was no longer viable. If counties refused permission to players appearing in foreign leagues they risked losing them to counties who would not block their participation. It was the free market in action.

After Strauss's appointment, the number of English players in major T20 leagues snowballed. Before 2015, an average of 12 English players per year appeared in major T20 leagues; since 2015, an average of 35 have. This reflected a new virtuous cycle for England's white-ball cricket. As more England players got picked in the IPL, so England's limited overs cricket improved; and as England's limited overs cricket improved, so more England players got picked in the IPL.

The extent of the transformation in attitudes towards short-format cricket was distilled by England announcing a new eight-team city-based competition in April 2018. After years of machinations with the counties the ECB finally forced through change, opting not for a new T20 competition but a new 100-ball per innings game with the first season to be played in the year 2020. In a saturated market, it amounted to an ostentatious attempt to seek a point of difference, rather than devise another competition that would inevitably be seen as an IPL-lite. Once they had railed against the IPL and what it represented. Now, England created a competition that sought to extend the logic of the IPL – the brevity of games, the concentration of talent, and the fusing of sport and entertainment – even further.

***

The noise rose from the pavilion like a rising tide before engulfing the ground in a flood. It started in the Long Room of the pavilion where the members turned to see Ben Stokes and Jos Buttler walking out to bat for the Super Over. As they emerged on to the steps and into the light the noise spread to the Allen and Warner Stands to the left and right of the pavilion, down the Grand Stand on one side and through the Tavern and Mound Stands on the other. A cacophony of fervour greeted England's batsmen as they marched out into the evening sun once more.

It had been the most remarkable day of cricket that the world's oldest ground – or perhaps even any ground – had ever seen. The 2019 50-over World Cup final between hosts England and New Zealand had been tied; nothing could separate the teams across 100 overs of cricket. The result would be decided by a Super Over – cricket's equivalent of a penalty shootout and the first of its kind to decide a 50-over match.

There was a dreamlike quality to events on that July day. A mid-morning shower had seen puddles collect around the Mound Stand which stood at the bottom of the iconic Lord's slope. By 7.00 p.m., after nine hours of enthralling cricket, those puddles had long since evaporated in the haze of a golden summer afternoon.

England's path to this moment began when Strauss, Bayliss and Morgan resolved to treat ODIs less like short Test matches, and more like elongated T20s. In their first multi-match series after the 2015 World Cup, against Brendon McCullum's New Zealand – who had just reached the World Cup final with a buccaneering approach that inspired Morgan – England packed their team with T20 hitters such as Jason Roy, Alex Hales, Ben Stokes, Buttler and Morgan and attacking bowlers such as Chris Jordan and Adil Rashid.

In the first match of the series England posted their highest ever total – 408 for 9 – and racked up three more scores of over 300 to win the series. This was a radically new approach.

'A lot of it was trying to do something different,' recalled Morgan. 'Everything we'd been a part of for the previous four years was so dated and it actually wasn't that fun to play that brand of cricket. It was very much correlated with Test match cricket at the time and batting long and cashing in at the end. Which was great but we'd get to a score where the opposition would easily chase it down and we wouldn't have enough on the board.

'We didn't ask too much of the players. We said we were going to give them a longer period of time selected in the team even if they made mistakes; as long as they bought into what we were trying to do they would continue to be selected so that reinforced trust when it happened and that created a nice feel around the group.

'When the guys posted 408 in the first game against New Zealand the feeling surrounding that innings that we put together was incredible. And the guys can always relate back to that and it was a nice benchmark to have.'

The combination of England's open-border policy to foreign leagues, the renewed emphasis on white-ball cricket and aggressive selection policy produced dramatic results. In 2016 England reached the T20 World Cup final, only losing to West Indies in an extraordinary final over; in 2017 England appeared on track to win the Champions Trophy only to suffer a shock defeat to Pakistan in the semi-finals. Between March 2017 and the 2019 World Cup England's only defeat in an ODI series was in a one-off game against Scotland. In May 2018 they reached the summit of the ODI rankings.

The contours of England's approach were shaped by T20: their bowlers attacked and looked for wickets, while their batsmen were infused with a spirit of audacity. In 44 years of ODI cricket up until the end of the 2015 World Cup, England scored more than 300 34 times; in the four years after the 2015 World Cup they did so an astonishing 44 times – including scaling 400 four times, which they had never done before. Their highest total of 481 for 6 against Australia in 2018 broke their own world record of 444 for 3 against Pakistan set two years before. Ten of England's fastest 11 ODI hundreds of all time came after the end of the 2015 World Cup with Buttler's 360-degree scoring matched by the power of Hales, Roy, Morgan and Jonny Bairstow.

'T20 has allowed you to accept that eight or nine an over is okay to be able to chase it down as a run rate. So the impact that has had in 50-over cricket is massive,' Morgan observed. 'It's changed the mindset in batting in particular because you can now chase any score in any format.'

Once England – unfairly in the view of their white-ball analyst Nathan Leamon – had been derided for their use of data. After the 2015 World Cup debacle, Strauss commissioned Leamon to research how previous World Cups had been won. He found that victorious sides tended to be very experienced – which encouraged England to identify players at the start of the World Cup cycle and sticking with them. On the field, batting strike rate – how quickly teams scored – was the single biggest factor that separated winners from other sides. Leamon said this work 'strongly buttressed' the ideas of Morgan and Bayliss.

The rule changes after the 2015 World Cup – with only four men outside the circle from the 11th to the 40th over, but five for the last ten – 'perfectly suited' attacking with the bat early as Morgan envisaged, rather than the backdated approach England had previously favoured. 'You had a 50-over innings where the best and easiest time to score was the first ten overs, then the next 30 and then the last ten was structurally the hardest time to score quickly,' Leamon explained.

Rather than being inhibited by data, Morgan found it liberating, and an aid to the buccaneering style of cricket he wanted England to play, in both ODI and T20 cricket. 'Guys have become better at taking risks,' Morgan observed. 'There is stuff you think as captain that might work but you might not pull the trigger on it unless it is backed up either with another opinion or some data and data has helped that decision-making process massively because if it backs that up then you are less hesitant to go to it.' Before the 2016 T20 World Cup final, Leamon uncovered Chris Gayle's relative weakness against off spin, encouraging Morgan to get Joe Root to bowl the second over; Root took two wickets, including Gayle's, in his first three balls.

From football teams who are behind in matches not making attacking substitutions early enough, to ice hockey teams who are losing not pulling the goalkeeper early enough, sports sides have routinely played in a more conservative, risk-averse way than data suggests is optimal. Paradoxically, given the previous image of data in cricket as stultifying the team, Morgan used data to embolden his side.

'People talk about taking risks all the time and T20 cricket being so risky. And naturally you don't take as high a risk as you should and as data tells you to,' Morgan explained. 'Every decision in T20 cricket should be an aggressive decision. It should be to try and get a hundred, it should be to try and take a wicket.

'It goes against human reactions. We have a safe nature. When you peg back you feel safe. But you should go the other way. That's where data is really good.'

Morgan also used data to provide clarity in high-octane situations in matches. 'One of the main challenges in T20 is being able to make a clear-cut decision very quickly,' he said. 'I actually think one of the hardest jobs is trying to juggle your bowlers and identifying which is the moment to try and bowl them.

'Where it has evolved for me probably more as captain, is identifying pressure times in the game that I might not have done in the past. So keeping an eye on the par score, bowling out your main bowlers by the 16th over so you are still in the game, trusting your [other] guys to bowl at the lower order. As a batsman, learning to trust the data. If somebody bowls wide yorkers and that's their go-to the whole time, you trust it and you account for that whereas in the past you might have needed two balls to see if he was going to bowl wide yorkers. I think it has evolved massively.'

England's approach to data was to use Leamon and then Morgan as filters, only relaying to other players a few of the most pertinent findings that they could use in matches. 'There's no point giving guys information if it's not going to impact their performance,' Morgan said. 'We don't sit in long meetings and go through everything. That's down to myself, the coach and the analyst. And we do a lot of work on it.'

England also used a 'wins above replacement' model developed by Leamon as a tool to aid their selection. In T20s and ODIs, this tool allowed England to substitute one player for another, run thousands of simulations of the game and find out which XI would give England a better chance of victory according to the model. This was particularly useful when gauging whether to make a change that wasn't like-for-like – replacing a specialist batsman with an all-rounder, say – and would change the balance of the side. 'Over a period of time you can see if your opinion on a player is actually backed up,' Morgan explained. 'Does he get runs in big games? Does he get runs when wickets are down early? Does he get runs against the opposition's best bowlers? When you are coming to World Cup selection you need to know what guys can produce against better teams so it's not a bad model.'

To Bayliss, T20 provided the impetus for the 50-over side to bat with a level of consistent belligerence that was unparalleled in ODI history.

'Fifty-over cricket influenced Test cricket years ago when it first came in: the scoring rates went up, the fielding standards rose. I think T20 cricket has taken the 50-over game to another level as well as we've seen recently with the number of big scores.'

For the World Cup, the final benefit to England's team that T20 brought lay in a brilliant fast bowler named Jofra Archer. Archer, born in Barbados to an English mother, only fulfilled his qualification period in May 2019. He had only played 14 50-over games in professional cricket before his call-up. But England's selectors placed faith in Archer's consistent success on the T20 circuit where his pace, bounce and a pinpoint yorker had dominated in the IPL and beyond.

Although slow pitches in the tournament complicated England's path to the final, their aggressive batting was at the forefront of their campaign. England plundered 397 against Afghanistan in the group stage with Morgan hitting an ODI record 17 sixes in a single innings. Attacking stroke play from Roy and Bairstow was instrumental in crucial victories against India and New Zealand in the group stage and a thumping victory over Australia in the semi-final. In that game Rashid took three middle order wickets with his leg spin; though no English leg-spinner had previously taken more than five wickets in ODIs, Morgan identified Rashid as integral to England's ODI and T20 plans after the 2015 World Cup.

After seven weeks, a white-ball revolution with T20 cricket at its heart culminated in the most distilled format possible: a Super Over. Where previously Strauss had cited that 38 of the 44 semi-finalists in the 2015 World Cup had played in the IPL, now nine of England's XI for the 2019 final also had IPL experience, and so did two of their four non-playing squad members. All of England's 15-man squad had played in a major overseas T20 league, compared with just six in the 2015 squad.

England's two most successful T20 exports were Stokes and Buttler. In the 2017 IPL auction, Stokes was sold to Rajasthan Royals for £1.7 million. The following year he was joined at the Royals by Buttler – signed for £490,000 – who had previously been with Mumbai.

In the final, Stokes and Buttler hauled England back into the match with a 110-run partnership, before returning to face the Super Over together. Thanks to T20, Buttler had first-hand experiences of Super Overs: he had batted in one for England against Pakistan in 2015 and for Mumbai Indians against Gujarat Lions in 2017. On both occasions Buttler finished on the winning team.

While Lord's creaked under the burden of expectation, Buttler and Stokes retained their equipoise. In the Super Over both men each hit perfectly placed boundaries, laid a bat on every delivery and scampered desperately between the wickets to take England to 15 from their six balls.

After two of England's IPL stars helped them to become favourites, now Morgan turned to the side's third proven IPL performer to finish the job. Archer was the youngest and least experienced member of the team – 24, and just 73 days into his international career. But while Archer was a relative newcomer to the international stage he had played more BBL and IPL matches than all but three of the 22 players in the match.

When a marginal first-ball wide was followed by a high-risk knuckle ball dispatched into the crowd by Jimmy Neesham, New Zealand required seven from the last four balls. But two yorkers and one slower ball bouncer left New Zealand requiring two from the last delivery.

The ball from Archer was full and angled into the pads. Martin Guptill squeezed it out on to the leg side and set off for two. Fielding, which had played such a prominent role in the frantic last half an hour, was once again under the spotlight. Roy charged in from midwicket and made a perfect clean pick-up – only two balls previously his fumble had turned one into two. Roy's throw was wayward but Buttler had the presence of mind to collect the ball and break the stumps in one clean and glorious motion. Guptill's desperate dive left him metres short of the crease.

Astoundingly, for the second time in the day New Zealand had tied with England: both teams were level on 15 runs apiece from the Super Over. England only won because of the controversial tiebreaker: they had scored 26 boundaries to New Zealand's 17. Yet, however unfathomable these fraught final moments, it was entirely in keeping with England's revolution that, even in a scrappy, low-scoring game, their ultimate triumph should come after scoring more boundaries than their opponents.

TEN

SURVIVAL OF THE FITTEST

'India watches Indian cricketers. India doesn't watch cricket'
Sanjog Gupta, executive vice-president, Star TV Network

At the Bvlgari Hotel London, a five-star hotel on the edge of Hyde Park, in June 2017, Brendon McCullum declared, 'All of us are unashamed T20 mercenaries now.'

McCullum, who had retired from a brilliant international career the previous year, was exactly the sort of player coveted by T20 leagues around the world. Signing him, along with a raft of other elite players, was seen as a harbinger of good times to come for South Africa's brand-new T20 franchise tournament. Having the launch in London was designed to affirm that this competition was the Global T20 League, as its name declared. It was envisaged that combining many of the best players in the world with several Indian owners, who would drive interest in India, would create a league with global appeal.

Four months later, these illusions were scotched. The first season of the Global T20 League was cancelled after failing to secure sufficient broadcasting revenue and sponsorship income. The debacle ended up losing Cricket South Africa an estimated £11 million – about half their total cash reserves – and the job of their chief executive, Haroon Lorgat. A year later, another league was cancelled before its first ball: the UAE T20x, a T20 franchise tournament in the UAE. In August 2019, a third league – the Euro T20 Slam, a competition featuring sides from Ireland,

Scotland and the Netherlands – was also cancelled before its first season. All the while, most T20 leagues around the world were consistently posting financial losses.

All of this shattered the myth that T20 tournaments guarantee profit. Instead, creating a T20 league is more like starting a Silicon Valley company: the few that are most successful make gargantuan amounts of cash, while most of their rivals haemorrhage cash.

***

Traditionally, international cricket subsidised domestic matches. These fixtures – between counties, states or regions – could justifiably operate at a loss because these matches were the nurseries of international cricketers.

The status of international cricket was instantly transformed with the inception of the Indian Premier League in 2008. The elite of the game – in terms of fan interest, quality of play and player remuneration – was no longer confined to international matches.

Many leading players now had a better-paid alternative to the international game. India, who did more than anyone else to create this new ecosystem, were the one country completely immune from these forces, because of the sums their players earned from playing international cricket. Since its creation, the IPL has not merely got stronger; it has also made international cricket weaker, by destroying the international game's near-monopoly over the sport's best players.

Before the IPL, only around 2% of the Indian board's total broadcasting rights came from domestic cricket. Today, thanks to a $2.55 billion contract for the IPL rights from 2018 to 2023, 71% of India's broadcasting revenue comes from the IPL, while only 29% comes from home internationals.

Even if Indian internationals remained worth slightly more on a per game basis, the metamorphosis of the value of domestic cricket spoke to how T20 has recalibrated the economics of cricket.

For the first time, cricket has a domestic league that is a serious player in the global sports broadcasting landscape. Broadcasting rights for the IPL are worth $8.5 million per game – four times what each NBA match is worth, and two-thirds what each English Premier League game costs, although the IPL has a significantly shorter season.

From its first game, the IPL has been so utterly out of kilter with all that domestic cricket was before that it induced jealousy in other cricket boards. Naturally, they sought to create their own versions.

'Matches include fashion shows, after-match parties and entertainment,' wrote Yorkshire chief executive Stewart Regan in an email to other county executives in 2010. 'They have launched the word "CRICKETAINMENT" which I think is really innovative.'

There were certainly broader lessons from the IPL, though not necessarily those Regan proclaimed. Unlike in England's T20 Blast, every IPL game was televised, enabling an easily understandable narrative to develop around the competition.

Perhaps most pertinent was the importance of competitive balance, an idea the IPL had embraced from US sports. Through salary caps that stopped teams stockpiling all the best players, the IPL protected the fundamental uncertainty of who would win any game: a crucial point of difference in an age of more predictable international cricket, marked by the growing divergence in financial resources between countries and the increasing salience of home advantage.

Even so, anyone studying the IPL could not ignore that the competition was unique. Ultimately this was not a reflection on the failings or lack of imagination of other administrators. It spoke to a simple truth: the IPL was built on India's enormous population, growing wealth and profound love of both cricket and celebrity, a cocktail that no other country could ever replicate.

This did not stop them from trying. Since the Indian Premier League was formed, the Big Bash League, Caribbean Premier League, Pakistan Super League, Bangladesh Premier League, and the new English franchise competition have all been launched. Barring Bangladesh, these nations all had T20 leagues before the IPL. But now they hoped to channel the glitz – and wealth – of India's competition.

Several leagues also made very obvious attempts to woo India. Teams in England and the Caribbean established tie-ups with IPL franchises. The Caribbean Premier League, whose time difference was unconducive to gaining a foothold in India, even experimented with playing matches early on weekday mornings to suit Indian viewers: it did nothing for Indian audiences while alienating local fans.

South Africa's stillborn league made a big show of two of its teams having Indian owners, deluding themselves that this alone would be sufficient to entice millions of Indian fans to watch. The Indian market is 'something you should factor in when developing your league,' Lorgat declared while developing the Global T20 League.

No league could have challenged the IPL anyway. Still, the Board of Control for Cricket in India made sure of as much by banning all Indian players from taking part in foreign T20 leagues, despite other leagues imploring them to relax the stance. This was disastrous for the commercial viability of other leagues because 'India watches Indian cricketers. India doesn't watch cricket,' said Sanjog Gupta, the executive vice-president of Star TV Network.

The BCCI barring its players from playing abroad would have been vulnerable to either a legal challenge, or Indian players abandoning their contracts for free agency, but the BCCI had the financial clout to dissuade them from doing so. For as long as this position holds, it will act as a roadblock to another league gaining serious traction in India.

'A lot of the success or failure of leagues will be determined by whether they are able to get Indian players to participate or not. That for me is a huge inflexion point,' Gupta observed. 'If any of these leagues are able to do that, then it will potentially change the value of the stocks for the league.'

Instead, other T20 leagues will be dependent upon their home markets to make themselves financially viable, in keeping with the norm for all sports leagues worldwide. 'Most sporting events raise the vast majority of their revenue from their home TV market,' explained Paul Smith, a sports media expert from De Montfort University. Similar dynamics are at work in T20 leagues: the CPL, a league with a small domestic economy, raises only 35% of its broadcasting and commercial income from beyond the Caribbean. The biggest source of revenue in the CPL, like most leagues beyond Australia, England and India, is ticket revenue.

The financial accounts of leagues and teams are completely out of sync with the common perception of T20 leagues as facile money-making machines. In the early years of T20 franchise leagues, making losses has been the norm. In Pakistan, the board has made a profit of over £1.5 million a year from the Super League's first year, but the teams themselves lost around £750,000 in each of the first three years; only in the fourth did most franchises enter the black. It took the Caribbean Premier League until its sixth season to turn a profit for the first time. In Bangladesh teams absorbed losses because most are owned by rich industrialists who viewed running a franchise as 'part of our CSR [corporate social responsibility],' explained Obeid Nizam, the chief executive of Dhaka Dynamites.

Many investors – national boards and private backers alike – did not seem to grasp how long was needed to turn a profit. Even many IPL franchises took until 2018, the first year of the bumper new broadcasting contract, to start recording a consistent profit.

The Big Bash League made a £17.5 million loss over its first five years. The league viewed these sums as an investment – and it was vindicated by a bumper new commercial deal, which began from 2018/19. But that it took an admired league in cricket's third-biggest economy so long to make cash embodied the wider economic challenges of T20 franchise cricket. As of 2019, insiders only considered the IPL, Big Bash and Pakistan Super League safe vehicles for both the competitions themselves, and the teams participating, to make money.

While McCullum was speaking in London, investors in South Africa's Global T20 League were working out how they could justify spending around £5.3 million a year each on their new teams. They soon concluded that they could not. These costs were simply too much for private investors to absorb without a clear road to profit. 'This venture had to undergo the same process and be tested against our standard investment criteria as all other investment proposals,' explained the chief executive of Brimstone Investment Corporation Limited, when the company withdrew from running the proposed new Stellenbosch franchise. It was a red flag for leagues the world over.

Most T20 competitions – Australia's Big Bash and England's county competition are notable exceptions – follow the IPL's model of privately owned teams, which may encourage innovation but also exacerbates the risk of short-termism. And when owners can't see where the money is coming from, they are prone to fleeing.

***

On 2 January 2016, 80,883 cricket fans crammed into the Melbourne Cricket Ground. They were there watching two teams who had not even existed five years earlier: the Melbourne Stars and Melbourne Renegades, who were playing in the new Melbourne derby. The game vaulted past the previous record crowd for any domestic match in Australia by an absurd 28,000. It was a seminal moment in the league, and franchise T20 cricket.

With scorching weather forecast the organisers were expecting a large crowd but they were totally unprepared for the eventual number. Thousands more fans abandoned going to the game because the queues for tickets were so large. The stadium ran out of food and drink to sell halfway through the match.

The man of the match was Stars' opening batsman Luke Wright, who scored a second-innings century. Wright won the T20 World Cup with England but he considered the century the proudest individual moment of his career.

'I think during the first half of the match there were about 50,000 or so in and as we were coming off [at the change of innings] you could see people streaming in,' said Wright. 'When I came out to bat with Bobby Quiney we were just looking out and going, oh my God, this is just nuts.

'You sort of knew that the crowd were there – there was a constant hum – but every time you hit a boundary there was a roar of noise.'

The impact of that derby fixture was particularly outsized because of the juxtaposition with international cricket, which was enduring one of its most underwhelming summers for years in Australia. A week earlier, just 127,069 – an average of 32,000 a day, under half the number who had turned up for the Melbourne T20 derby – had attended the four days of the Australia-West Indies Test, which began on Boxing Day. It was the smallest Melbourne Test crowd in two decades.

'Everything felt it was absolutely at its peak,' said Wright. 'We knew at that time that everyone was looking at the BBL with envious eyes. It was run like international cricket but it was domestic cricket. We were getting bigger crowds than Australia were getting playing at home and everyone was getting swept up in it.'

That fewer fans wanted to attend the Test, or watch on TV, was partly the fault of the BBL. During the tepid Australia-West Indies Test series, six West Indies players, including five with Test experience, were instead playing in the BBL, where they could earn more cash.

'The Big Bash League has changed the dynamic a lot, and let's be open: all over the country it has cannibalised the demand for international cricket,' the then-chief executive of Cricket Australia, James Sutherland, acknowledged at the time. It was a microcosm of a much broader question: how could the international game, and the rapacious growth of T20 leagues, peacefully co-exist?

Since England's T20 Blast launched in 2003, leagues have popped up on the whims of national administrators, opportunistically slotted in whenever there is a brief gap in the calendar. Without broad agreement among administrators worldwide about what the overall schedule should look like, leagues have jostled for territory.

T20 has created a new 'club versus country conflict,' reflected Tony Irish, the head of FICA, the sport's players' association. 'Due to lack of coherent global scheduling, players are often forced to choose between the two.' For many players this was really no choice at all. The time-wage ratio of playing was inverted in T20 leagues, with players paid much more to be on the field much less.

By 2019, only the two months given over to the 50-over men's World Cup and preparations for it lacked a T20 league. In August and September three leagues with official status – England's T20 Blast, the Caribbean Premier League and the new Euro T20 Slam – were scheduled for the same time. It was the first time ever there had been such a three-way clash – or, at least, it would have been had the Euro T20 not been cancelled at two weeks' notice.

The strife extends to international cricket, which is facing unprecedented pressure thanks to T20 leagues. It is, as Sutherland said, at risk of being cannibalised.

Club cricket has several salient advantages over the international game. Urbanisation throughout the world, with a growing proportion of people living in major centres, has made club vs club games a more appealing way of organising fixtures. The impatience of the modern world is another boon: the notion of waiting four years for A.B. de Villiers or Chris Gayle to return for their next games in India, as they would have done before the IPL, seems quaint.

For administrators, T20 leagues have another crucial advantage over the international game: they do not rely on the cooperation of any other country. Relations between national boards have frequently been poisonous, with tours planned late and curtailed at minimal notice; when India reduced their tour to South Africa in 2013/14, it cost South Africa an estimated £15 million. Prioritising domestic T20 cricket is prudent risk management by boards, allowing them to reduce their dependence upon other countries touring. When the Pakistan Cricket Board – who have lost an estimated £150 million from rarely playing at home since 2009 – launched the Pakistan Super League in 2016, they declared that within five years it 'will be the most exciting event of the year, far more exciting than any FTP [Future Tours Programme event] could ever be.'

The rise of T20 leagues has meant that the biggest countries generate a lower proportion of their overall revenue from the international game, they have become less dependent upon it and so are less inclined to play fixtures that aren't lucrative. And, with so much T20 action to watch, fans are becoming less enamoured with the international game – at least, when matches are not marquee.

The upshot has been to exacerbate divisions in wealth within international cricket. Dwindling interest in India for India's away matches against mid-ranking international teams – really, all opponents bar Australia, England and Pakistan – means that those boards aren't able to raise as much in broadcasting rights when they host India, intensifying the financial chasm within the international game. Players from smaller markets could often earn more playing domestic T20 than playing internationals. This has driven premature retirements from international cricket, either in one format or across all three. Star quality confined to T20 leagues alone diminished the appeal of international cricket.

T20 leagues, with each season building up to an overall winner, have highlighted the failings of international cricket, which has lacked any coherent structure. 'The lack of clarity and consistency in scheduling and formats is causing bilateral cricket to rapidly lose its appeal to broadcasters, fans and players,' FICA noted in a report in 2016. The unflattering contrast with T20 leagues, expressed in the preferences of viewers and broadcasters, was an influence in the ICC introducing new league structures in Test and one-day international cricket, beginning in 2019.

Administrators agree that the unprecedented pressures on international cricket are a major problem; devising a solution has proved rather more onerous. One of the biggest challenges facing the sport, observed Andrew Wildblood, a former executive vice-president at International Management Group (IMG) who was instrumental in launching the IPL, is 'dealing with the short-sighted petty provincial politics that continues to blight many cricket administrations through aligning stakeholders behind a collective strategic approach embracing all formats both domestically and internationally.'

The ICC has often discussed making distinct windows for T20 leagues – limiting all leagues to, say, six months a year, thereby providing a free chunk of the calendar for international cricket. Yet every new T20 league that is created makes this change ever more unworkable. More controversially, the ICC has also mooted limiting players to appearing in a total of three leagues a year – forcing players to choose between leagues, rather than between leagues and international cricket. Such a policy would be unlikely to survive a legal challenge.

The contours of cricket's near future – really, its present – are increasingly discernible. In its structure cricket is likely to resemble football, with the majority of revenue derived from the club game, and internationals focused around tournament play.

'That change will continue – it has to happen,' said Gupta. 'At a fundamental level the only way that you can significantly augment the supply of the game and thus continue to grow the game is by going down the path of moving away from nation v nation.' He envisaged a future in which 'franchise-based cricket occupies 50% of the calendar and you have major global tournaments, typically multilateral, that occupy the rest of the calendar.'

T20 would also occupy a greater share of the global calendar. 'T20 is the format of the future both at international level and league level. Both have to grow in volume significantly. There has to be some level of replacement of cricket days in the calendar of Test and ODI days with T20 internationals, especially multilateral T20 internationals. The volume of T20 cricket will go up, leagues will continue to take up more calendar space, and multilateral T20 tournaments will become more frequent.'

Over the coming years, Irish predicted, 'the game will continue to trend towards T20, and continue towards a more club-based model for cricket, as more and more money, players and fans shift that way.' These are the two overarching trends of this age of cricket: a sport simultaneously being reoriented around T20 and the club game. The question is not about the direction of travel in the sport but how big a stage will be left for the international game and longer formats.

'The evolution of T20 has been a great positive for the game, but we advocate for an appropriate balance between the traditional and international cricket market and the rapidly growing domestic T20 market,' Irish said. 'If that doesn't happen then I think the future of the other international formats, especially Test cricket, is in real danger.'

***

'The winner takes it all,' Abba once sang. These were prescient words about the future of the global economy in sport and beyond. In the 21st century, globalisation and technological change have allowed industry leaders to gain larger shares of their markets, and so become more successful and richer than those which came before them. This has made the margins between success and failure more brutal – and also entrenched the elite.

As the T20 calendar has become more saturated so leagues are also increasingly in competition with each other, not just international cricket, for viewers' eyeballs and broadcasters' cash.

'What will happen in these leagues is they will continue to go on because there's enough local interest to continue to sustain themselves but growth for them will be a major problem,' said Gupta. When the Mzansi Super League, a scaled-back version of South Africa's original plans for a franchise T20 league, launched at the end of 2018, its domestic broadcast rights were reportedly given away for free.

In the years ahead, the gap between different leagues is likely to grow further. The IPL's next broadcasting contract, beginning in 2023, is widely expected to set new records – and leave every other league even further behind. This is also likely to usher in a bigger IPL, too. The competition is better placed to sustain more sides than when it trialled having nine and ten teams, rather than eight, at times between 2011 and 2013.

'The Indian team can only play so many days in a year,' Gupta explained. 'If you were a leader or a CEO and had a product that was working and wanted to significantly increase its consumption then the only way you can do it is by increasing the supply, especially if the demand seems to be fully met.'

So the future of the IPL seems certain to involve more teams, more games and a longer tournament, exacerbating the pressures the competition creates both for international cricket and other T20 leagues.

'I think two more teams for sure,' Gupta said. 'There can't be a better time for the IPL to expand for the good of Indian cricket, for maximising value and for fans. It's the best time for it. You can't find more of a tailwind than you do currently. It's absolutely the right time for the IPL to expand.'

Pune and Rajkot, who both had IPL franchises in the past, are prime candidates to host teams once again. Staging sides in the states of Uttar Pradesh and Madhya Pradesh would also be attractive for the IPL. Ten teams may well be one part of the competition's expansion, not the end.

'Over a ten-year period maybe 12 teams, in fact,' Gupta envisaged. 'With ten teams it should expand by at least two and a half weeks. Two and a half, three weeks is what one would expect it to grow by. With 12 teams potentially a month extra or maybe more than a month – a two-month tournament becomes a three, three and a half-month tournament.' The new normal could be that the IPL runs from February to late May.

As well as growing in teams, fixtures and season length, the IPL is also likely to expand geographically. Matches have been played abroad before, but owing to clashes with elections, not any concerted strategy.

'Preseason or All-Star games could definitely be looked at as showpiece events abroad to grow the popularity of IPL,' said Gupta. This would follow on from leagues like Major League Baseball, the National Basketball Association and National Football League, who all staged regular season matches in London in 2019. As the popularity of women's cricket grows, IPL franchises are becoming more supportive of the idea of a women's IPL, which is likely to launch at some point in the early 2020s. IPL teams are also considering launching either a youth league – played by, say, under-23 players – or a B-League staged in cities that currently lack IPL teams.

The upshot will be to intensify pressures on cricket outside the IPL even further. Cricket West Indies – who have produced many of the most coveted IPL players, even while their board has been penurious and dysfunctional – have argued that, in return for the release of international players and the effective halting of all top-tier international cricket for two months a year, the IPL should better compensate other countries. The league's release fee to national boards for each player they sign – 10% of the value of the player's contract, which is matched by the Indian board – scarcely makes up for the money that national boards lose from broadcasting and sponsorship when they cannot stage international matches involving their best talent.

It is, former Canadian prime minister Pierre Trudeau once said of being next to the United States, not comfortable being a mouse lying next to an elephant. 'No matter how friendly or even-tempered is the beast . . . one is affected by every twitch and grunt.' So it is – and will continue to be – with the IPL's impact on the rest of the cricket world.

Belatedly, from 2020 the IPL will effectively get its own window in the calendar, free of any clashes with major internationals. No other league gets this privilege. This amounts to tacit acceptance that, when international cricket goes up against the IPL, it is international cricket that appears diminished.

***

There may be a deep market for T20 leagues around the world. Yet the broadcasting pot of cash is simply not great enough to sustain a multitude of leagues competing for A-list talent.

'T20 leagues outside India need to be funded by domestic broadcasters in the host country first and foremost. Countries with weak domestic broadcast and media markets will struggle,' said Wildblood. 'Only the strong will survive; it will be sustainable if the metrics for successful modern sporting events – entertaining, audience attracting and therefore commercially viable – are met. Events need first to be sustainable on a local level.'

Even in some of the most popular leagues, the identikit nature of the squads from one competition to the next means that teams can struggle to create a compelling reason for international fans to watch, admitted Pete Russell, the chief operating officer of the Caribbean Premier League. 'I look at the number of international players we have in the CPL and actually, I'm thinking yes, it's good for the tournament, gives it the right profile, they're great to have around but actually are there too many of them? Because they're just the same faces that pop up in all the leagues so there's no differentiation between a player playing in PSL, IPL, for us and what will be the Hundred.

'Almost the easy bits have been done – setting up these leagues. Now it's how people sustain them – that's going to be the challenge.' Russell said that the ecosystem of T20 leagues has 'got to give somewhere'.

'People get the IPL because of what it started as. But do people really make an appointment to view PSL or CPL or any of these other leagues unless you're from that region? That's the challenge – how do you keep the international interest?'

One possibility is that T20 leagues may resemble football and basketball around the world. In these sports, there are undisputed industry leaders: Europe's big five football leagues; and the NBA in the US. For cricket, the NBA is the better comparison, because the US's economic clout in basketball is similarly overwhelming to India's position in cricket. The IPL, like the NBA, effectively has a monopoly on the best talent in the sport, and both leagues view other leagues as breeding grounds for future talent. The salient difference is that, because the IPL is a two-month league rather than a nine-month league it also allows leading players, at least as long as they're not Indian, to play elsewhere.

While there are unlikely to be fewer T20 leagues in the future, there will be a distinct hierarchy of leagues. The IPL will continue to occupy the top tier. A small coterie of others – the Big Bash, Pakistan Super League, Bangladesh Premier League, Caribbean Premier League and England's new Hundred competition – will vie to cement their position in the second tier. 'IPL is going nowhere – it's just going to get bigger and better,' Russell said. 'I can see there being two or three super leagues and then the also-rans if that's the right expression.'

Tom Harrison, the chief executive of the England and Wales Cricket Board, envisaged a similar future. 'There'll be a tiering of leagues – there'll be a top tier which continue to dominate and control the window they operate in. And then the second tier which will have much less choice on player availability, they can probably operate in different times of the year but they won't be able to compete with the big leagues.'

Other leagues may be akin to feeder leagues. The most viable future for incipient leagues in smaller markets would be as development vehicles for glitzier leagues – a little like how Dutch football's Eredivisie has found a role for itself in the shadow of the big five football leagues.

'For the younger players now you almost have a pyramid where you play in these other leagues so you get recognised and get the experience,' Russell explained. 'But it's all about IPL. That's the lottery ticket for them.'

Even leagues established in the tier below the IPL will have to adapt to remain relevant. The Caribbean Premier League has long been attracted by the possibility of teams in Canada or the US, thereby becoming an American League. 'In my dream league I'd have teams in the Caribbean, teams in the US, maybe a couple of teams in Canada,' Russell said, saying that such a proposition – with a total of somewhere between eight and twelve teams, up from six now – could be viable anytime from 2021.

Perhaps the most likely outcome is for a rationalisation – with the biggest leagues expanding, and others merging, across nations. Cross-nation leagues are common in other sports – rugby union now has South African domestic teams playing in European domestic competition – and might soon do so in T20 too.

A pan-nation Asian league – featuring a series of countries, though not India, who would have no need for such a venture – would be an attractive concept, Gupta explained. 'Commercial viability will force nations to collaborate more. If nations don't collaborate they will start struggling with the viability of the leagues.'

For leagues to become more commercially viable, one solution is an old one: the Champions League, which was scrapped after its sixth edition in 2014. 'The fates of some of these leagues are intertwined with that of the Champions League,' Gupta observed.

Yet the reason that the Champions League was abandoned is emblematic of the broader problem facing T20 leagues beyond India: there was simply limited interest in India to watch matches not involving Indian sides, leading to the competition being culled midway through its broadcasting contract. This speaks to the broader imbalance in cricket's economy. While football's Champions League has established itself as the pinnacle of the club game, cricket's version was, in terms of eyeballs and cash it attracted, little more than an IPL-lite.

In its desperation to appeal to Indian fans – which could be best done by ensuring that as many Indian sides as possible were involved for as long as possible – the Champions League also shed any vestiges of sporting probity. While non-Indian teams were restricted to two overseas players, IPL teams were permitted four. In 2011, after injuries to Indian players, Mumbai Indians were allowed to field a fifth overseas player 'to ensure the integrity of the tournament'.

The Champions League's failure affirmed a wider truth, often poorly understood by delusional administrators in other countries. In India in 2018, virtually as many people watched the Tamil Nadu Premier League, an intrastate T20 competition, as Australia's Big Bash. 'It doesn't say much for the BBL's following here,' said Gupta.

Any reintroduction of the Champions League would also need to be accompanied by concerted attempts to grow the brand of the non-Indian teams. If it is to return, the Champions League 'needs a certain context which is unique,' Gupta explained. 'For example if it was Champions League T20 happening many years down the line when relations between India and Pakistan were better and Pakistan teams were participating, Champions League T20 could have more prominence.'

After a certain point the tussle between T20 leagues threatens to become a zero-sum game: for one to grow, another will need to weaken. The supply of elite cricketers, and the amount that fans will watch, is limited. Most importantly, broadcasting cash is finite.

'We'll see a few leagues going down the tube and not sustaining a footprint in the world and other ones that will continue to grow,' Harrison said. 'There are very few that are commercially successful – that's the reality. Most of them are effectively losing money. Inevitably players will migrate to the tournaments where they feel it makes the most sense for them to hone their skills.'

So the road to T20's new ecosystem will be Darwinian. For some leagues to surge to new heights, others may have to flounder – or even completely cease to exist in their current guise.

***

In 2013, City Football Group, the umbrella company who own Manchester City, bought a majority stake in a new football team in New York. It presaged a radical new approach. By May 2019, City Football Group had stakes in seven teams around the world – in England, China, the US, Australia, Spain, Uruguay and Japan.

The project – having a network of interconnected clubs in different continents – was unprecedented in its scale or ambition, across football or any other sport. City Football Group executives believed that each club could also help each other on the pitch, and that the cross-continental scale of their operation would give them advantages, even if others believed that the idea was driven by finding ways for Man City to circumvent Financial Fair Play laws.

Like McDonald's stores around the world, each team in the group subtly promotes the others. 'We are part of a global organisation that brings incredible benefit, but we operate locally,' Scott Munn, Melbourne City's chief executive, explained at Melbourne's training ground, where even the changing rooms were explicitly modelled on Man City's.

For Venky Mysore, Man City's model provided a template of what was possible for Kolkata Knight Riders. For all the enormous popularity of the IPL, its teams suffer from a simple problem: the league is very short. Each team only plays a guaranteed 14 games a season. In 2019, the entire season only lasted 50 days.

That leaves IPL teams with ten months a year when they aren't actually playing. 'In the discussions with our owners, one of the questions we were trying to address was: how do we grow? The IPL and other leagues are fantastic but they happen over such a short period of time,' Mysore explained. 'The question always was how do you keep your brand alive for the rest of the year? How do you grow your business and increase your revenues, grow your fan base and grow your brand?'

And so Mysore stumbled upon a plan. Red Chillies Entertainment – the parent company of KKR, where he was chief executive – would become like City Football Group, operating teams around the globe. 'What we landed on was to figure out a way to potentially own multiple franchises – or assets, as we call them – and in an ideal world we said that if we have three or four or five assets then it becomes a year-round activity. That was the thought process.' The idea, Mysore believed, would also help KKR reduce their reliance upon Shah Rukh Khan, their Bollywood owner, and help people conceive of KKR more as a sporting brand and less as an entertainment one.

The Rajasthan Royals were the first IPL team to attempt to become an international brand, acquiring a stake in teams in foreign leagues and changing their nicknames to Royals. 'Our plan was to create a global network of like-minded franchises,' explained Manoj Badale, the co-owner of the franchise. The idea was scrapped, he said, because 'with all players bought through the auction, the benefits of these link-ups are primarily marketing related.'

Mysore brought the same systematic planning that he applied to IPL auctions to which teams would be a suitable fit to pair with KKR. In 2014, he began conversations with the Caribbean Premier League about purchasing a team in the league. A year later, the CPL told Mysore about an opportunity to buy Trinidad and Tobago Red Steel – particularly appealing for Red Chillies Entertainment because of the large Indian diaspora in Trinidad and Tobago. 'Of all the owners I know, he has the most vision,' said Pete Russell from the CPL, who was involved in the negotiations. 'Their whole thing is about building a global brand.'

Russell believed that the KKR model would become more common in the years ahead. 'If you're building a sports team and you have the opportunity to run it all year round then it makes perfect sense for commercial partners, staff and players. There's a huge amount of upside to it.'

After their first season owning the team, Red Chillies Entertainment changed the team name, to Trinbago Knight Riders, solidifying the link with KKR. In the four years after being bought by Red Chillies Entertainment, Trinidad and Tobago won three titles.

This was a 'hub and spoke model', Mysore said, with India the hub. 'From an operational perspective, we try to bring in all the efficiencies by looking at the team that's in India and the ways it can support what we do in Trinidad and Tobago.'

KKR's decision to partner with TKR – and, briefly, a team from Cape Town in South Africa's aborted T20 franchise league in 2018 – was driven by a belief that this would make the side more attractive for sponsors. 'We are able to provide a lot more value for brand and opportunities for them to activate throughout the year,' Mysore explained.

Franchises abroad also gave fans another way of staying involved in the team. 'The two pillars on which you build a sports franchise are your brand and fan base. Through what we're doing you build your brand and extend your fan base quite significantly.'

Merchandising only accounted for around 5% of all KKR's revenue, as of 2018; by a Knight Riders team playing more, albeit in the Caribbean, Mysore hoped that figure would increase.

Yet for commercial possibilities to open up as KKR envisaged, the Indian board would need to allow Indian players to play T20 leagues abroad.

The lack of Indian players abroad helps explain why other IPL franchises have not yet emulated the Knight Riders in buying a team overseas. Indian fans don't watch cricket; they watch Indian cricketers.

Still, owning TKR brought natural synergies, with KKR able to use their expertise to build a new brand and, by transferring staff and methods honed in India, keep costs down. 'The intention is to bring best practices to each of these businesses and leagues around the world,' Mysore said. 'That will financially make it very efficient for us – we don't have to recreate the teams in those other countries and franchises.'

While commercial logic drove the links between KKR and TKR, KKR soon recognised that the partnership could bring on-field benefits too.

Coaches and trainers were contracted to both teams, rather than just one, with Simon Katich, the former Australian player and KKR assistant coach, given head coaching experience with TKR. This allowed staff to work together across different teams and leagues to develop their expertise and range of experiences.

'We want to replicate the culture of the Knight Riders organisation,' Mysore said. 'We try to keep the core of our support staff the same.' The continuities beyond the franchises, Katich observed, are particularly beneficial at the start of a T20 league. While most rivals are trying to assemble their new teams, for the Knight Riders 'it feels like business as usual'.

Although the IPL and CPL operated completely different contracting systems, meaning players could not simply be contracted to both Knight Riders franchises, strong links in personnel developed between the different sides. A.R. Srikkanth worked as an analyst for both teams. He used his involvement with TKR to scout emerging talent, from the Caribbean and elsewhere, and develop knowledge which could then aid KKR – either helping to inform whom to sign, or simply giving more knowledge of players whom they would subsequently encounter in the IPL.

As an analyst from TKR, Srikkanth faced many players who represent Kolkata, giving him first-hand experience of how opponents look at these players. With Kolkata, Srikkanth then helps the players second-guess what IPL opponents might have planned for them. 'We've done that quite a few times. We've given information to the players about what the opposition, especially the coaches, might think about them. And give them a heads-up as to what to expect in the game.' The opener Chris Lynn regularly played against Trinbago, before later signing with them, so Srikkanth knew that Kolkata's opponents would be likely to focus on bowling either to Lynn's hips or slower and fuller.

The City Football Group model is predicated on playing the same style of football at all their teams around the world, abetting the transfer of players, coaches and ideas between teams. Increasingly, tactics used at one Knight Riders franchise are being transferred to the other. 'If you look at the way we play in the CPL, as well as at KKR, it's pretty similar,' explained Srikkanth. 'We go hard at the top and it doesn't matter if we lose wickets in a cluster because we've got the batting in the team to take responsibility and get the team to a decent score.' In 2018, Sunil Narine opened with the Australian Chris Lynn both for Kolkata and Trinbago.

Having a team in the Caribbean, which has comfortably produced more elite T20 talent in the world per head of population than any other region, helped Kolkata remain at the cutting edge of T20 thinking. And it provided opportunities for experimentation: tactics could be trialled in the Caribbean and then, if successful, mimicked in the IPL. At the CPL auction, Mysore himself could be observed personally selecting TKR's squad. By maintaining a year-round Knight Riders operation, he could also ensure that Kolkata's needs were attended to outside of the IPL season itself: in 2018 the physio Zeph Nicholas was flown from Trinidad to Antigua by the Knight Riders just to work with their star all-rounder Andre Russell, who would begin the next IPL season in astounding form.

This was one example of how, in pursuit of competitive advantage, Kolkata were trying to move from being a team who merely played the IPL every year into a 12-months-a-year operation. After 2018, KKR built an academy in Kolkata. Any players could come there, anytime. The idea was that, whenever they were free, domestic players would come to Kolkata, where their skills could be honed, and physios could ensure they were in prime shape when the squad reassembled at the start of each season.

'This is now clearly a round-the-year activity for us,' Mysore said. 'We're genuinely saying if we can help them improve as players in skills and fitness and they do well in domestic cricket, they perform, then you're suddenly going to start seeing a different kind of dynamics within the team, because the conversation will be taking place throughout the year. It turns it into a very different environment. It makes it richer and we're seeing already that players are becoming more confident and getting better. That is going to help KKR too in the end.'

In early 2019, City Football Group announced that they had bought a team in China, the seventh club to be part of their network. If KKR remain a long way beyond in their collection of sides, this does not owe to any lack of ambition.

'The whole global strategy of expanding the Knight Riders brand into other leagues is a well-thought-out plan,' Mysore explained. 'We keep fine-tuning this model but it has reached a certain level of stability and we're quite happy with the model that we've built. The intent is to take this model and, like all global companies do, replicate this model in different geographies and hopefully get some good positive results. We have certainly outperformed in the Caribbean. Three championships in four years is an amazing job.'

As City Football Group already have done, so Mysore and the Knight Riders hope to expand into the United States. 'We're always looking at markets. I know there's a lot going on in the Emirates, and people are talking about North America.

'We've passed on a couple of opportunities as well but at the same time whenever we think it's a good fit and we can build our brand, expand our brand and expand our fan base in different geographies and if the business model makes sense then we're always ready. We've gained a lot of experience in how to manage from a distance so from that perspective I'd have to say we're way ahead of the curve.

'Whenever there's a new league that's being contemplated, invariably the first proposal lands up on our desk,' Mysore said. 'Where we're able to tick all the boxes, we'll invariably be there.'

For the Knight Riders – and, perhaps, other imitators – the ultimate ambition extends well beyond merely thriving in the IPL. It is to develop a global network of teams that will reshape the sport.

ELEVEN

THE THRILL OF THE CHASE

*'Do you want to be remembered as a legend or do you
want to be remembered as a mercenary?'*
West Indies Cricket Board administrator to Kieron Pollard in 2010

'Kieron Pollard, in my opinion, is not a cricketer'
Former West Indies bowler Michael Holding

As Kieron Pollard crouched in his stance his bat looked like a toothpick in his hands. This was not because the bat was small – in the hands of a normal man it would look like a railway sleeper – but because Pollard, clad from head to toe in Trinidad and Tobago red, was a giant. Standing six feet, four inches tall and weighing 98kg, he was built more like a heavyweight boxer than a cricketer. As the bowler ran in, Pollard tapped his bat delicately on the ground – perhaps he feared he might break it if he exerted any more force – and looked up.

Pollard had just arrived at the crease in Hyderabad in a group stage match of the 2009 Champions League T20. Pollard was playing for his native Trinidad and Tobago against New South Wales. It was the 14th over of the match and he was about to play an innings that would transform not only his life, but T20 cricket.

'That innings changed everything for me personally,' remembered Pollard. 'I played international cricket beforehand, but that innings changed the way everyone looked at me as a cricketer.'

With 24 balls remaining Trinidad and Tobago required an improbable 51 runs to win – New South Wales, one of the strongest T20 teams in the world, had never conceded that many in the final four overs of an innings. A victory for Trinidad and Tobago would virtually guarantee their progression to the semi-finals of the inaugural Champions League – the most expensive tournament in cricket history, sold to the Indian broadcaster ESPN Star Sports for $1 billion earlier that year and competed for by the world's strongest T20 clubs.

The trouble facing Pollard and his partner at the crease, Sherwin Ganga, was that 12 of the remaining 24 balls would be bowled by Brett Lee – one of the best and fastest bowlers in the world. Lee's first two overs that evening had cost just nine runs and had taken one wicket. Plausibly, Trinidad and Tobago could hope for 16 runs off Lee's 12 balls which would leave 35 to get off the remaining 12 deliveries.

The New South Wales captain, Simon Katich, could have given the ball to the off-spinner Nathan Hauritz or the leg-spinner Steve Smith – but bowling spin at the death was always considered risky. Katich's other frontline quick bowler, the left-armer Doug Bollinger, had already finished his four overs which left the medium-pacer Moises Henriques as his only option.

Henriques was exactly the kind of bowler that Pollard liked to face: not fast enough to push him back with a short ball nor accurate enough to consistently nail his yorker. But recognising the opportunity was the easy part; it was another thing actually taking it.

Pollard was still only 22, yet already bigger and stronger than most players in the world. 'He was always a very big fellow,' recalled Daren Ganga, Pollard's captain at Trinidad and Tobago. 'Even as a teenager he carried the same sort of size so it was very easy to identify him.'

Three years previously Pollard announced himself to the Caribbean as a T20 player of great potential when, aged just 19, he bludgeoned 83 off just 38 balls against St Kitts and Nevis in the semi-final of the Stanford T20. 'That was a significant innings for me,' said Pollard. 'That brought me on the map as well in terms of my ability to hit long balls.'

Since then he had played a number of brutal cameos – the most recent of which came in Trinidad and Tobago's previous Champions League match against the IPL's Deccan Chargers. Pollard's 14-ball 31 included four sixes and was instrumental in toppling a heavily favoured IPL team.

'The moment that defined us is when we played that game against Deccan Chargers in Hyderabad and we won against an IPL team,' said Pollard. But what he was about to do against New South Wales would leave an indelible mark on his own career.

The first ball of the 17th over was a wide; the fifth was a dot ball. The other five balls were all smashed to the boundary. In a remarkable assault Pollard plundered three sixes and two fours from Henriques' over. 'It was just a matter of trying to clear the boundary every delivery,' said Pollard. The bowling was poor – two full balls right in the slot, one short slower ball, and a full toss – but the power of Pollard's hitting was magnificent. Bad balls or not they still had to be dealt with. The sixes didn't just clear the ropes, they sailed far into the stands as if jet-powered. In the space of just six balls, Pollard had scored 27 runs and had turned the match on its head.

'I was focused and I was determined,' recalled Pollard. 'When it comes to these sorts of big games and you're playing against these big players there's some fire inside me that actually comes out even more in these sorts of situations.'

To Pollard and to many of the players that day there was more meaning to that match than simply the result. Two IPL seasons had already been played and the Champions League T20 – played in India and in front of a global television audience – represented a shop window for players to attract IPL interest.

'I remember clearly when we arrived in India to play the first edition of the Champions League there was a lot of fanfare behind the tournament,' said Ganga. 'The IPL had already taken off and the microscope and the focus and the buzz around T20 tournaments and this tournament in particular got a little bit to the heads of my players. You had all these different guys doing different funky hairstyles, trying to define themselves and to be recognised because they understood the opportunities which were before them in terms of getting an IPL contract and having good performances and how that will impact them and their careers.'

Pollard was at the forefront of this urge to be recognised and had '20-20' shaved on the side of his head and sported large diamond earrings. Brazenly, Pollard also asked Ganga if he could bat at number three – where he had scored his 83 against St Kitts and Nevis three years previously but had only batted twice in his career. He normally batted at five, six or seven.

'I had a young guy like Pollard who was trying to upset the apple cart in terms of trying to bat higher on the premise of him really wanting to do well and progress his career,' said Ganga. 'Those were challenges that

I faced as a captain – especially with the young players who were eager to do so well.'

Pollard batted at number seven that day, but the 27-run over had bent the game to his will, leaving Trinidad and Tobago only requiring 24 from the last three overs. Pollard's enormous strength allowed him to find the boundary even when he mistimed or edged the ball. Indeed, from the fourth ball of Lee's next over, Pollard's thick edge brought a boundary and took Trinidad and Tobago to the brink of victory with only 16 required from 12 balls.

Despite his mauling in the 16th over Henriques returned for the 18th. The first ball was a low full toss and Pollard hammered it back down the ground for four; the second was another low full toss and this time Pollard dispatched it back over the bowler's head for six. 'It was see ball, hit ball. I was in a zone where I didn't think I would mistime anything. And it worked.'

Henriques landed the third delivery but by now Pollard was into his groove: 'I was seeing the ball big and just wanted to finish it.' Pollard took a small stride forward and bludgeoned the ball hard, flat and over long off for six. The boundary, his eighth in nine balls against Henriques, brought up both his own fifty – off just 18 balls and the victory, with an absurd nine balls to spare. As the final six soared into the stands Pollard bent back with his bat in one hand and let out an almighty roar. His entire body shook as he released the nervous energy of the run chase and bellowed into the Hyderabad night sky.

Pollard's innings was momentous. It gave rise to a new T20 megastar, and redefined what people thought was possible in run chases. Teams had scored more runs in the last four overs of a match before but no team had ever scored so fast. Trinidad and Tobago had razed 51 runs in 15 balls – a run rate of 20.40 runs per over. Hitting of such brutal efficiency had rarely been seen in cricket and never on such a big occasion. It was a transformative moment in the evolution of T20 batting. Quite suddenly – in less than half an hour of crazy hitting – no total was safe, no target was out of reach and no asking rate was too steep.

Three months and three days after the Hyderabad heist, Pollard found himself the subject of a fierce bidding war in the IPL auction between Chennai Super Kings, Kolkata Knight Riders, Royal Challengers Bangalore and the Mumbai Indians, to whom he was eventually sold for

$750,000. This made him the joint most expensive player at the auction, despite only averaging 17.50 in T20 internationals and 13.50 in ODIs.

'I was overwhelmed, seeing that sort of price. Straightaway the pressure got to you but then you realise it was an opportunity for you to go out and showcase your talent and show that you're really worth every penny of it.'

***

As a young boy Pollard never dreamed of being a millionaire cricketer. T20 was not played at professional level until he was 16 years old and the IPL did not exist until he was 20. 'I never even thought you'd have another version of cricket,' he remembered. 'I always grew up watching Test cricket and 50-over cricket and aiming to represent Trinidad and Tobago and then the West Indies. That was the goal.'

Pollard grew up a long way from the riches of the IPL, and the global T20 circuit on a housing estate of 20 prefabricated flats called Maloney Gardens, located on the East-West Corridor of Trinidad – a half-hour drive from the capital, Port of Spain. The area was marked by pastel-coloured flats with boarded windows and draped with drying washing. The flats were punctuated by overgrown fields. It was here that Pollard spent his formative years.

Pollard was raised alongside two younger sisters by his single mother in tough circumstances. They were not a wealthy family and Maloney Gardens was synonymous with drugs, gang violence and gun crime.

'Where I grew up it has a stigma for violence and drugs,' said Pollard, 'but there was also a lot of sport.' And it was sport that gave Pollard's life meaning and direction. 'It was all about "play" as we would say.

'Cricket would be six months of the year and then football and then athletics. We would move with the tide. Say for instance if it was an Olympic year, everyone would come outside and go and run. And you'd be Maurice Greene. If there was a football World Cup you'd be Ronaldinho, Ronaldo, whoever. Then cricket came back around. Brian Lara scores runs, today you're Lara. Curtly Ambrose takes wickets, you're Ambrose. Courtney Walsh takes wickets, you're Walsh. That's how it used to be.'

Sport offered Pollard a retreat from the toil of life in Maloney Gardens as well as the tantalising prospect of an escape. 'In 2000 one of my friends who I used to play with made the Trinidad and Tobago Under-17 football team. And that was a big achievement for us. Him coming from there and playing for Trinidad and Tobago.'

Pollard was always big for his age which put him at an advantage playing sport. 'Growing up I was always a bit taller,' he said. 'I was a bit skinnier than I am now. But big enough.' In particular his size made him well suited to boundary hitting. 'I had a natural ability to hit sixes.'

At secondary school Pollard's power quickly attracted attention. In 2006, Pollard played for West Indies Under-19s. Later that year he would play the first professional T20 match of his career: for Trinidad and Tobago against the Cayman Islands in the Stanford T20. Pollard did not bat but he bowled and took a wicket. The match was also the debut for leg-spinner Samuel Badree, another player who would change T20 cricket.

It didn't take long for Pollard to make the step up: in 2007 he made his ODI debut at the World Cup. But while Pollard was breaking through in the Caribbean, the sport's tectonic plates were shifting. In September 2007 India won the T20 World Cup; months later the first IPL auction was held, exposing players to untold wealth. Only England, who established their fateful relationship with Sir Allen Stanford in the Caribbean, blocked their players from participating. There had never been a better time to be a cricketer, and in particular a West Indian T20 cricketer: uniquely, they had the opportunity to play in both the IPL and Stanford's million-dollar match.

These two events changed Pollard's life. First came the Stanford match in November 2008. Pollard took three wickets in the game, helping rout England for 99 before the Stanford Superstars razed the target with 7.2 overs to spare. 'The first pay cheque when I got huge amounts of money would have been the World Cup but the 2008 Stanford game was a different level.' Each player on the winning team took home one million dollars. 'So then life was comfortable and all I had to do was work hard.'

Less than a year later Pollard shot to global acclaim with his brutal fifty in Hyderabad; shortly after he landed an IPL contract with Mumbai Indians worth $750,000. Pollard's price tag had a profound impact on his attitude towards the game.

'Going into the IPL, where all the megastars were, as a big-priced player was very satisfying to me,' said Pollard. 'That sort of changed my mentality towards cricket – you have to go out there and be that ultimate professional. I think I've really, really done that especially in the IPL.'

Being in demand on the T20 circuit set Pollard on a collision course with the West Indies Cricket Board (WICB). The WICB found themselves vying for Pollard's attention with T20 leagues around the world who could pay him better money, for less time. Pollard wanted to play for the West Indies but he also wanted to play in T20 leagues; being contracted by the WICB meant he had to be available to play for the West Indies at all times and left his availability for domestic leagues controlled by the WICB.

In 2010 Pollard took the widely vilified decision to refuse the offer of a central contract from West Indies after they requested that he made himself available for an A tour of England rather than fulfil his contract with Somerset. 'It's a decision that I never took lightly,' he recalled. 'It's something that I sat and thought about.

'I was in and out of the West Indies team for a bit and I had a decision to make: am I going to back myself to play and go around the world, back my performances, take that chance? Or am I just going to sit back in the Caribbean, wait and see what they are going to do with me and when they are going to do it?'

Both options were lined with risk. The West Indies contract offered far more certainty – locking him in for 12 months, but at $80,000 per year it was worth a lot less. On the other hand, the freelance T20 route was far less secure, with contracts lasting only six weeks and determined at drafts and auctions where vagaries of form and fitness play a large role in selection. But the potential rewards were far greater.

The T20 circuit was still viewed with great scepticism by administrators and many former players, whereas the international circuit was regarded as the arena where reputations were forged. In 2010 the former West Indies fast bowler and commentator Michael Holding, a staunch critic of T20, attacked Pollard because he had not played Test cricket. 'Kieron Pollard, in my opinion, is not a cricketer,' he said.

Holding's view embodied that of many 'purists' who valued Test cricket above all else. 'All these people motivated me quietly without people knowing and understanding the situation,' said Pollard. 'You would never understand the situation until you are in the situation.'

One West Indies administrator pointedly asked Pollard: 'Do you want to be remembered as a legend or do you want to be remembered as someone who is a mercenary?' 'I said at this point in time I'll take my chances and I'll go around the world, I'll back myself and I'll back my ability.'

Pollard continued to play for the West Indies when selected and appeared in more than 100 ODIs and more than 50 T20Is over his career. But he refused his central contract and set himself on a path as a T20 freelancer.

Absent from the large majority of West Indies' international cricket, Pollard was a case study in what might drive cricketers of the T20 age without the motivation of representing their nation.

'I think the key for me is three things,' said Pollard. 'One is family. Cricket is a way to provide that comfortable life for your family. I had my first kid, Kaiden, when I was young. Everything happened at a young age. The responsibility was always there and the responsibility was on myself. So that in itself keeps me going, knowing that there are other people depending on me to go well in order for them to have a comfortable life and see different things.

'Secondly is knowing that being a sportsman you can only play cricket for a certain amount of time. You wanna maximise every opportunity that you get. So knowing that now I am 31, 32, it is not going to be as long as when I was 21. So that keeps me in check and wanting to stay fit and wanting to learn and to improve.'

At the heart of Pollard's choice there was also a universal truth: professional sportsmen wanted to excel and they wanted to win, whichever team they were playing for.

'The third thing is you always want to do well and be at the top of your game,' he said. 'The game is changing. Everything is changing. And you want to change along with it and you want to challenge yourself alongside the younger guys as well. You want to maintain that sort of standard for yourself and have that personal pride in your performance. No matter what team you play for, what competition you play in, you have that willpower to win in anything you are doing. So for me it is about the team and it is about winning.'

By May 2019 Pollard had played for 14 different T20 teams in eight different countries. The boy from Maloney Gardens had become a pioneering, gallivanting T20 cricketer.

'I got a lot of backlash for it from the media all over the world. I took a lot of licks, I took a lot of punches, I took a lot of different things, but I have lived to see the day where cricketers are leaving international cricket to play T20 around the world when they still have a lot of international cricket left in them. But in order for it to happen someone needed to take the initiative and make the change.'

Across a career spanning more than 450 T20 matches, Pollard had plundered more than 8,000 runs, more than 600 sixes and more than 600 fours, and he had taken more than 250 wickets and 250 catches. Only one man – Chris Gayle – had scored more runs than Pollard and he was seven years his senior, and Pollard had scored his from the lower middle order, where he faced fewer balls and was asked to bat in more varied situations.

Although Pollard was too modest to admit it, T20 had not only made him very rich, but also a legend of the format. Pollard had once been presented with a choice between becoming a legend or a mercenary. He had done both.

'T20 cricket has given me a lot and that I appreciate daily. To the guys who have belittled T20 cricket and said what they said about T20, it is for them to look now and see what it has become.'

***

The Sawai Mansingh Stadium in Jaipur is a cacophony of noise and a kaleidoscope of colour. Horns sound, drums beat, people scream, music blares. Vendors selling popcorn, sweets, chicken and local delicacies squeeze their way through the throngs of people – the ground is at its 30,000 capacity on a sweltering April night. The air is heavy and thick as yet another IPL league stage match lurches towards a frenetic conclusion. The IPL show rolls on.

Four enormous floodlight towers reach high into the night sky, illuminating the insects that buzz in the air and throwing bright light on to the playing area below. It is so loud inside the stadium that there is no use in the fielding captain shouting to move his fielders; instead he waves his arms frantically to capture their attention as if conducting an invisible orchestra.

At the centre of it all and standing at the striker's end is Brad Hodge, the 37-year-old Australian batsman and Rajasthan Royals' designated finisher. From the distance of the stands Hodge is just a blue speck – a man in the eye of a storm. The big screen shows him close up: his bat is on his shoulder, his blue shirt – tight against his muscular body – is covered in sponsors. Sweat drips from the peak of his helmet. 'When you actually walk to the crease you need 12 runs an over. There's no good feeling,' said Hodge. 'There's nothing good about it at all. You are under pressure. Your stress levels are high and basically it is all up to you.'

If Hodge is stressed then his eyes aren't showing it: they are alert, darting from fielder to fielder as he surveys the field, but they are at the same time calm: he has been in this situation many times before. Hodge was one of a generation of exceptionally talented Australian batsmen and although he struggled to establish himself in Australia's teams he carved out a very successful career at domestic level in the T20 format. He is repeating a process that has become second nature to him.

The role of the 'finisher' in limited overs cricket was originally defined as much by psychology as by power. In ODI cricket in the 1990s run rates in the last ten overs of the innings hovered around a run a ball. Asking rates such as these were most effectively scaled by batsmen carefully managing risk. As complicated as the skills of batting themselves was knowing when to execute them and against which bowlers. Pakistan's Javed Miandad in the 80s and 90s and Australia's Michael Bevan in the 90s and 2000s carved out great ODI careers through their judgement, placement and mental strength more than their boundary-hitting prowess: Bevan, who played from 1994 to 2004, hit just 21 sixes in 9,320 balls in his ODI career, one every 443 balls he faced.

In this era the South African all-rounder Lance Klusener had an unparalleled ability to pummel opposition bowling attacks at the death: he produced a series of extraordinary performances in the 1999 World Cup, when he scored 281 runs for only twice dismissed, and scored at over 70% more than the average during the last ten overs of an innings.

The origin story of Klusener's astounding tournament lay in an ankle injury he received a year earlier, rendering him unable to bowl and forcing him to return home from a tour of England. This meant that, rather than split his practice time between batting and bowling, Klusener could divert himself entirely to one skill. And, rather than train his batting as normal, Klusener trained for the very specific challenges of batting at the death in a way no player had done before.

Klusener set the bowling machine to bowl in 'the slot': either low full tosses or half-volleys, the deliveries that he faced at the end of the innings, when fast bowlers attempted yorkers and erred fractionally. Then Klusener would hit them – again and again and again. 'It was 500, 600 balls a day in that area, and just hitting them as hard as I could and as straight as possible,' he recalled. Klusener was also among the first to embrace range hitting: practising hitting sixes from the middle, so he knew exactly what he needed to do to clear the ropes.

'It's not just about going and hoping to hit sixes. You have to be clever about how you're going to do it.' His method was 'a combination of power and technique – using your body as much as possible, trying to get your whole body into a shot instead of just hitting with your arms. I worked out that – pretty much like a golf swing – it takes your hips and your core and your shoulders and arms all working at the same time. And that was kind of my theory: if I could hit the ball as I would a golf drive, then that would be the optimum, instead of just hitting with your hands. Hitting a six is, I always say, for me it's a brutal thing. It's not a pretty thing. And that was something that I tried to do, hit that ball with my whole body.'

It was a harbinger of what was possible with systematic focus on how to hit sixes and embracing new training methods.

Klusener was also a bowler and fulfilled the role of an all-rounder for South Africa. Finishers being all-rounders was a common theme in the world game – something that perhaps emboldened them with the bat. Assuming two roles for the team meant players were less concerned about losing their wicket and inoculated them from fear that they would be dropped after a couple of low scores, meaning they attacked harder with bat in hand. Of the ten players with the highest strike rate in T20 seven were all-rounders and one was a wicketkeeper.

Although T20 intensified the demands on batsmen and asked them to elevate their boundary hitting, batting at the end of the innings in the early years of the format remained as much about the mind as it was about skill.

T20 exacerbated the psychological challenge faced by the finisher. The shots may have looked spectacular but what was going on inside the minds of those batsmen was also remarkable. 'It is all about calculation,' said Hodge. In mere seconds batsmen batting at the death would compute a dazzling array of considerations that enabled them to then play the shots they did with such confidence. 'Making good decisions under pressure separates the standout finishers from the batters who win you the odd game,' said Ryan ten Doeschate, who excelled in the role for the Netherlands, Kolkata Knight Riders and Essex. 'I get excited by the challenge and the chance to find a solution to the equation at hand . . . It's a bit about managing risk, so if Rashid Khan or Jasprit Bumrah had one over left you might accept a low-risk seven off that over.'

At the centre of these calculations was of course the basic runs and balls equation. It was from this that everything followed. While a team may require, say 40 off 24 balls, a single batsmen will never face all 24 of those deliveries. So the first challenge was breaking it down by batsman.

'I worked on how many balls I thought I could face,' said Hodge. 'If you went in with four overs to go and there's access to 24 balls, the likelihood is that you're only going to face 12 or somewhere around that figure and it is about working out how much impact you can have in that period.'

Then it was about breaking those balls down according to which bowler might bowl them and who represented a weak link. 'Which bowlers of those 12 balls could you actually target a lot harder than someone else? So a more specific match-up that gives you the likelihood that you'll actually get success more than others.'

For Hodge this was based on self-assessment and understanding his opponents. 'It was an educated calculation about which bowler I would take down. So when you're looking at Jasprit Bumrah and Mitchell McClenaghan finishing off the innings and you've got 24 balls from those two, the likelihood of taking down Bumrah is slim. So you go a lot harder against McClenaghan.'

As data analysis played an increasingly prominent role in the game, these match-ups would be informed and guided by team analysts and the management. Rajasthan Royals specifically deployed Hodge as a pace power hitter after analysis in 2012 showed he scored at a strike rate of 157 against the quicker bowlers and just 115 against spin. 'I actually could have gone harder against spinners but in my own calculations I thought the risk was higher,' said Hodge, who backed himself to make up ground against the quicks.

Beyond these macro-considerations, batsmen calculated how to manage risk and execute their skills within specific overs and against certain bowlers. Central to this was reading the field and interpreting where it meant the bowler would bowl. With only five fielders permitted outside the 30-yard circle, the location of these boundary riders represented major giveaways as to what lengths and lines the bowler would target. These clues might take young players time to process but for someone such as Hodge it was hardwired. 'You've computed it a number of times. That's where experience comes into it a little bit and reading the play.'

Batsmen also considered boundary sizes: Northamptonshire, who reached three finals in England's T20 Blast in four years from 2013 to 2016 despite having one of the lowest budgets in county cricket, bought a measuring wheel from local builders, which they used to measure boundary dimensions at grounds, informing which sides of the ground their batsmen targeted. Generally targeting the leg side boundary when it was shorter was considered optimal – ideally, when hitting with the breeze too.

Managing the strike and reading the field was important when the batsman was partnered with a weak lower order player. 'Having a peripheral sense of where exactly the fielders are is important, mainly for running between the wickets when you don't get a boundary,' said ten Doeschate. 'I'll pick areas for every type of ball I'm expecting – like hitting hard behind square if he bounces me, hit inside third man if he gives me width. So it's very important to know where fielders are and where the better fielders are.'

Specific bowler analysis would also enhance the batsman's position. For Hodge this would be focused on the skills he knew he would be facing at the death. 'What does his yorker look like? What's his slower ball?' said Hodge. 'The slower ball was the most important of the two because I wanted to calculate what that looked like and what I could maximise off it.'

All these factors represented a vast amount of information for players to compute. The challenge was intensified by the pressure of the match itself and the noise and fervour in the stadium.

'You have to learn to deal with chaos,' said Jos Buttler, who performed a finishing role for England and in the IPL before moving up the order later in his career. 'A lot of the time it is making sure you show that externally you are cool even if you're not on the inside. That is really important. You need to trust in your ability and trust in your preparation that allows you then to let your subconscious take over in the middle. People talk about the zone. How do you access that and be consistent in that? Does that stand up to high-pressure situations?'

'It is about managing your emotions through experience. I think trying to break situations down and know what's required from this over, this next ball is the clearest place you can get to. It's very cliché to say "one ball at a time" but it is important to bring it back to being that simple – managing what you need to do right now, rather than anything in the future.'

After calculating the equation, targeting the bowler, reading the field and anticipating their delivery – all in a matter of seconds, the batsman then had to actually face and play the ball. And for that they had even less time.

***

For players such as Hodge – who relied on their game awareness more than belligerence – asking rates of around ten runs per over were eminently manageable. It was when rates began to climb beyond this point that they would start to flounder. 'Whenever the asking rate was 10s – you're comfortable because really in 12 balls you only have to find the boundary twice,' said Hodge. 'When it gets to 12 that increases so you have got to find the boundary probably three times in 12 balls. So the pressure mounts, scoreboard pressure, psychological pressure.'

Pollard, and his match-winning 54 against New South Wales, changed everything. 'What he did by that particular performance is he gave belief and hope that any equation was possible,' remembered Ganga. 'Even if you look at that Champions League final that we played against the same opposition, we were in a similar situation and we still had belief that we could win that final despite our run rate going sky-high. Pollard, his style of play, his power as a player, always gave you that belief.'

The rise of Pollard signified a decisive shift in T20. Where previously asking rates of around ten were considered the ceiling, suddenly no asking rate seemed too steep. 'The goalposts have shifted a little bit,' said Hodge. 'With the power hitters now – Pollard, Andre Russell, Carlos Brathwaite and all these huge West Indians, it's hard to keep up with these superhumans.'

This not only altered the nature of the death over phase of the innings but allowed teams to revise how they built their innings prior to the final few furious overs. 'We played according to the resources we had in our team,' explained Trinidad and Tobago captain Ganga. 'We had Lendl Simmons, Adrian Barath and William Perkins at the top of the innings being flamboyant and flashy but managing risk. Then we played with myself and Denesh Ramdin being more consolidators in the middle overs to set things up for our power players: Dwayne Bravo and Pollard.'

While a player like Hodge was a pure batsman – he started his T20 career as an opener for Leicestershire – Pollard was the first player to move the foundation of the role irrevocably towards power hitting. Hodge was powerful but could not rely entirely on that side of his game. Instead, he was also forced to score in unusual areas, pick gaps and run hard. Pollard was the first of a generation of players whose batting was defined by six hitting – typically in an arc between midwicket and long off.

'Power. That's what distinguished Pollard from the rest,' said Hodge. 'His mishits still went over the fence which was unlike most people. He is of the opinion that no ground is big enough. I think he was the first who was ever seen. No one else had really tested that strength or power.' By the end of the 2019 IPL Pollard had hit 607 sixes and 600 fours making him one of only two players – Russell was the other – to have hit more than 200 sixes and have hit more sixes than fours.

Pollard had technique and skill to match his brawn. Attacking batsmen would often be found swinging across the line of the ball, looking to hit the ball towards midwicket. While swinging in this direction was a natural motion it was one that compromised contact by closing the bat face on the ball. In contrast Pollard's batting was marked by the straightness of his hitting.

At secondary school Pollard played a variation of indoor cricket designed to encourage better techniques: batsmen would get out if they hit the ball in the air on the leg side. Pollard developed a technique that saw him hit hard, flat and straight. 'So front foot drives, straight drives, those things were always part of my forte because of the restrictions and it never left me. So that was something that I learned as a kid.'

Evidence of this technique endured; he brought a consistency to his hitting at professional level that was founded on this method. 'Putting my big left foot down the track and hitting the ball straight back over the bowler's head.'

'If you look at him he will always be trying to hit the ball straight down the ground,' said Ganga. 'The times when he hits the ball to leg it is because it has made contact with the inside part of the bat. His intention was always to hit the ball down the ground. It's very rare that you see him open up to hit through the off side. It's very rare you see him cut the ball behind point. His power is go straight down the ground.'

Pollard's technique was built for six hitting. 'For me it's about having a stable base,' he said. 'I just try and stand still and pick my areas. The strength comes naturally – with a little bit of gym work now. It's just a matter of trying to time the ball. When I try to hit the ball too hard is when I miscue. It's about having that stable base and backing my strengths to clear any boundary in the world.'

The game evolved in waves. In the early years after Pollard's ascent he could rely overwhelmingly on his power. But as the game progressed and power hitters proliferated, bowlers and fielding captains learned how to counter these players with specific bowlers and tailored plans. For batsmen the challenge became psychological and strategic once more.

'When I first came out it was more of a hitting gig,' remembered Pollard. 'You'd just go out and try and be aggressive. But over the years it has evolved into more of a thinking sort of game – with different match-ups and winning certain periods, the opposition keeping their best bowlers for you. It has evolved from just coming in and trying to be aggressive from ball one. You have to be smart about it.

'I tend to play the situation. Whichever situation I walk into you watch the scoreboard – if you're chasing a total according to what the run rate is and if you have time; if not you just have to target a particular bowler – you back yourself and have to play to your strengths. For me now it's more playing the situation rather than just walking in and trying to be aggressive.'

Pollard's greater scope for destructive batting meant he could be even more selective in whom he targeted. By the end of the 2019 IPL Pollard had played more T20 matches than anyone and this vast bank of experience enabled him to read the game adroitly. He honed this approach by utilising 'scenario training' in the nets – placing himself in predefined situations against specific bowlers and with specific field settings.

Klusener, one of the first great power hitters, recognised how the role had become more arduous as bowling evolved. 'I think that was a little less complicated back in the 90s . . . I think nowadays with slower balls and slower ball bouncers and the skill of the bowlers I think finishing is a lot harder than it used to be in the past.'

The master of combining power and intelligence was the legendary Indian batsman M.S. Dhoni. Smaller than Pollard but bigger than Hodge,

Dhoni was a strong man and wielded his huge, bottom-heavy bat with rapid hand speed. He developed a distinctive, and sometimes perplexing, approach to finishing off matches: Dhoni often seemed to delight in taking the game to the last over, and then sealing victory with a theatrical flourish. He was often highly selective in which bowlers he attacked, using the experience acquired in over 500 international matches for India.

Dhoni's method bore similarities with Chris Gayle's where he would start slowly before accelerating rapidly. Of course, the stage of the innings afforded Gayle longer to play himself in, making Dhoni's approach even riskier. In the first ten balls of his innings Dhoni only scored at a strike rate of 114.88 but in ten-ball intervals that quickly rose to 143.11, then to 163.74, then to 197.83 and finally to 281.81. This crescendo method brought great success: in winning run chases Dhoni averaged 54 runs per dismissal.

Between 2008 and 2018 the death overs of T20 were transformed by power hitting. Pollard was at the vanguard of that change. In 2008 the average run rate in the last four overs of the innings was 8.77 runs per over, and a six was hit every 17 balls. By 2018 the average run rate in the last four overs of the innings had risen to 9.51 runs per over, and a six was hit every 13 balls. The type of players who thrived in the role changed from hybrid hitters such as Hodge to muscular, power-orientated players such as Pollard. Even in the 2019 IPL – with Pollard in his tenth year at Mumbai Indians – he continued to put in spectacular performances. In one match against Kings XI Punjab his 83 off 31 balls helped Mumbai chase 133 off their last ten overs.

Just as Pollard's seminal innings against New South Wales initiated a sea change in the way the finishers batted, the performances of Andre Russell in the 2019 IPL initiated the next step in the evolution of T20's most unforgiving batting role.

'I remember having a conversation years ago with some friends at home,' recalled Pollard in early 2019 after Russell's astounding start to that year's IPL. 'And we were comparing Bravo, Russell and me and I told them that Russell – if he wants to realise his true potential – he can be better than both of us.'

Between 2015 and 2017 Russell matched the feats of his fellow West Indian, combining power hitting, versatile bowling and athletic fielding in a thrilling package. In 2016 Russell played for title-winning teams in the BBL, PSL, T20 Blast, CPL and BPL. Russell's all-round role for five champion teams established his reputation as one of the most valuable players on the T20 circuit.

In January 2017 Russell's career was dealt a setback when he was banned for 12 months for a whereabouts clause violation by an independent anti-doping panel in Kingston. The ban took Russell away from the game and what he loved for a year but it triggered a shift in his approach to the game.

'When I look at Cristiano Ronaldo and LeBron James, I watch their progress. They work hard and that's why they're so successful,' said Russell in an interview with ESPNcricinfo. 'I changed my mentality since I got banned. [Before] I was slacking off. I was big. I was lazy. I wasn't practising hard. Then when I got the ban, I came back stronger, leaner, more muscle.'

It wasn't until the 2019 IPL that the effect of Russell's training became clear. As destructive as Pollard was, the one thing he had struggled to do was maintain consistency. The aggressive nature of his role meant his form was prone to oscillating wildly. It was thought that it was essentially impossible to contribute reliably with such an attacking approach. That theory was scotched by Russell who in an outlandish IPL season scored 510 runs at a strike rate of 204.81 and average of 56.66: a sequence the likes of which cricket had never seen before. Russell unfurled scores of: 49 not out, 48, 62, 48 not out, 50 not out, 45, 10, 65, 15, 14, 80 not out, 24 and 0. Across these 13 innings he clubbed 52 sixes, the second most in an IPL season after Chris Gayle, who hit seven more from 206 more deliveries in 2013. Russell was the first batsman in IPL history to score 500 runs at a strike rate of more than 200. The previous record was held by Glenn Maxwell when he scored 552 runs in 2013 at a strike rate of 187.75.

'He has worked on his game and he has taken it to a different level now,' said Pollard. 'To be consistent in that role takes a lot of practice, a lot of courage and a lot of hard work. Gone are the days where 15 runs an over is impossible.'

'With my batting – it's just a gift. I work hard at it as well,' explained Russell to ESPNcricinfo, 'because you might get a gift – like Steph Curry is good at shooting three-pointers, but if he takes a week away from the gym and doesn't shoot any ball, he's going to become rusty. That's how I'm consistent. I make sure I keep batting, keep bowling, do something.'

Central to Russell's success was opening up scoring zones through extra cover that previously had remained off limits for power hitters who had targeted midwicket round to long off. In the 2019 IPL season he hit an IPL record 14 sixes over mid-off and extra cover.

'If you look at Pollard's wagon wheels he doesn't really hit it from anywhere from point through to third man and nothing behind square,' remarked Hodge. 'It's easier to plan for as a fielding captain.'

By bringing extra cover into play Russell made the margin for error in terms of line even smaller for bowlers. Suddenly wide lines outside off stump no longer took balls out of the hitting arc and were instead balls that gave Russell room to free his arms and hit over the off side. 'He has opened up a whole different area of the ground in terms of power hitting,' said Pollard.

In the same IPL season India's Hardik Pandya, a far smaller man than Russell, also pushed hitting technique forward. Standing deeper in his crease and more across to the off side, Hardik's stance was set up to hit. He opened up his front side to create a base, rather than moving into the ball once it was bowled, compromising his stability and power.

Russell's greater range made it nigh-on impossible to stop him once he got going. All that stood between Russell and destruction was either an inch-perfect yorker or pure bad luck.

In one league stage match Jasprit Bumrah – arguably the league's best fast bowler – bowled a wide ball way outside off stump, millimetres inside the tramlines. It would have been a superb defensive delivery to almost every player in the world; but not to Russell. Just as Bumrah released the ball, Russell had made a small movement to the leg side, clearing his front leg to open up the leg side. But as soon as he spotted the wider line his initial movement towards the leg side allowed him to throw himself back into the line ball, transferring the weight off his front foot and into his back leg which was firmly planted deep in his crease.

It was then that Russell's rapid hand speed and absurd strength kicked in. Russell threw his hands at the ball with such force that as he made contact with it his hands and bat whipped up towards and then round his head like a rapier. As the ball flew hard, flat and fast off the bat, Russell's front leg flicked up off the ground. With the ball soaring towards the rope like an Exocet missile Russell hopped on his back leg to retain his balance. He was the world's most destructive ballerina.

'As in everything else,' mused Pollard, 'the world is changing, technology is changing, T20 cricket is changing, scoring a lot of runs at the back end of the innings is changing.' This was the future of T20 hitting: Pollard's power and intelligence, with added dynamism.

TWELVE

CHEATING TO WIN; CHEATING TO LOSE

'Some of these owners are dodgy as fuck'
International cricketer who appeared in multiple T20 World Cups

In January 2018, video footage of the Ajman All Stars League, a pop-up T20 league in the UAE mostly featuring semi-professional players, went viral. The reason was not belligerent six hitting, acrobatic fielding or pinpoint yorkers.

Instead, it was because of the Sharjah Warriors' batting – if it could be called that – against the Dubai Stars at the Ajman Oval. The Sharjah Warriors were bundled out for 46, thanks to a series of fantastical dismissals.

Players repeatedly ran down the wicket, scarcely feigning an interest in hitting the ball, and were stumped. Other players ran anaemically between the wickets and were run out. When a ball was misfielded, the batsmen stopped in response, and ran so slowly – decelerating as he got closer to completing a run – that the run-out could still be completed.

'Absolute comedy going on,' exclaimed the commentator on the live feed. He said later: 'I'm really finding it hard to explain what I'm seeing . . .'

But there was a very simple explanation. It was all a fix, no more real than WWE wrestling.

The Ajman All Stars League was an unofficial T20 league which had not been sanctioned by the Emirates Cricket Board, the governing body in the UAE. Yet although the crowds were virtually non-existent for the matches, the games were still televised, including in India. And as they were televised, this meant that the matches could be bet on. The ICC believe that the games were completely corrupt; as the matches were not sanctioned, its Anti-Corruption Unit (ACU) could not sanction the players involved, though it could bar them from getting involved in any official matches in the future.

The league 'was set up purely for fixing,' said one insider in the fight against corruption. 'It was rigged from start to finish.' The economics of the crime, he explained, appeared to be to make '500 rupees 20 million times': that is, getting a huge number of small bets in India which would add up to making the fix worthwhile.

It was a window into cricket's susceptibility to fixing in the T20 age. Any league, anywhere, could be a vehicle for corruptors. If you could bet on it somewhere in the world, then you could probably fix it.

***

'It never occurred to me that one man could start to play with the faith of fifty million people – with the single-mindedness of a burglar blowing a safe,' Nick Carraway says in F. Scott Fitzgerald's *The Great Gatsby*, disbelieving of how the 1919 World Series was fixed.

In the late 1990s, cricket was 'exceedingly naive – naive, blind and short-sighted' to the threat of corruption, said Ehsan Mani, who was president of the International Cricket Council from 2003 to 2006. Such illusions were shattered when a series of fixing scandals broke around the turn of the century, with South Africa's captain Hansie Cronje, and a series of prominent Pakistani players, among those affected.

During the mid 1990s, regarded as the modern golden age for cricket fixers, virtually all betting in cricket was concentrated on matches involving the nine nations who were permitted to play Test cricket. The simple reason was that very few other matches were televised internationally – and, without broadcasting coverage, there was a lack of funds in the betting markets. Without enough liquidity in the betting markets, corruptors couldn't make enough cash for it to be worth their while getting players to fix.

T20 changed this equation. It meant that the number of games with enough money bet on them to be worth fixing went from in the region of 150 a year, the total number of top-tier international fixtures each year in the late 1990s, to five times as many. In 2018, there were 719 T20 fixtures played worldwide. And the potential pool of players of interest to corruptors – barely into three figures in the late 1990s – was now 2,119, the number of cricketers who played any official T20 games in 2018. So there were about 15 times more players worth corrupting than 20 years earlier.

Simple mathematics explained the burgeoning threat to cricket. 'The amount of cricket being played now is phenomenal,' the anti-corruption insider explained. 'It's the amount of opportunities that people have got.' While the surge in interest in domestic cricket begat by T20 was celebrated, criminal gangs recognised the trend as a new business opportunity.

The years ahead would show that domestic T20 matches did not merely share the same vulnerabilities that international games had long possessed. Instead, domestic T20 was even more susceptible to corruption. The historic lack of interest in domestic games meant that authorities were initially blasé to the threat of fixing – so matches were not policed as rigorously as the international game, which itself remained vulnerable. Player education about corruption was also less thorough at domestic level, with a solitary brief PowerPoint presentation at the start of seasons generally considered sufficient; players who arrived late often did not even have that. As the matches included players who were paid far less than in international games, getting players in on a fix was less expensive. Low-paid and insecure players, unsure of whether they would even get another contract, appearing with or against international players earning millions a year could also foment jealousy. It was not uncommon for players earning only a couple of thousand for a league season to play alongside players earning hundreds as much for the same work.

And so for players who fix, taking money to underperform could be entirely rational, as the sports economist Stefan Szymanski wrote. 'On the "selling" side, the players must balance the reward from fixing against the potential cost of being caught. This cost is the probability of being caught multiplied by the penalty for fixing.'

***

The first great fixing scandal to be exposed that was caused by the new T20 ecosystem allegedly began in a hotel room. In 2008, the former New Zealand international cricketer Lou Vincent was playing in the Indian Cricket League, a T20 league in the country that was launched before the

IPL, but was never approved by the Indian board. Vincent would later claim that he received a phone call from someone claiming to be a cricket equipment manufacturer, inviting him to a hotel room. He went to the room, but found no equipment. The man offered a prostitute as 'a gift' – along with a huge wad of American dollars.

This, Vincent would say, was the start of his involvement in match-fixing. In return for promises of US$50,000 per game, Vincent deliberately started underperforming. In the ICL, it was not uncommon for teams to move from odds of evens – suggesting a 50% chance of winning – to near 3/1 on (or 1/3) – suggesting a 75% chance – on betting exchanges for no apparent reason, suggesting a high degree of fixing.

'I probably had a chip on my shoulder over my career. I left New Zealand pretty heartbroken and a bit angry at the system,' Vincent later told New Zealand's TV3. 'And as the match-fixing world opened up to me . . . I thought, "Yeah, I'm going to make some big money now, so stuff the world."'

Until his career ended in 2013, Vincent was a fixer. The next year, he admitted to 18 charges of fixing and was banned for life. A teammate he claimed had encouraged him to fix – Chris Cairns, the captain of the Indian Cricket League franchise Vincent was playing for in 2008 – was acquitted after a bruising trial in London in 2015. Indeed, the lack of criminal convictions for fixing, partly explained by the difficulty of explaining the mechanics of fixing to a jury who do not understand the game, may heighten incentives to fix if players deduce that there is scant chance of being caught.

Vincent's claim that he initially thought that he was simply meeting a cricket equipment manufacturer was typical of how many corruption cases begin. Corruptors often approach players by befriending them in a manner that Ronnie Flanagan, the long-time chairman of the ICC's Anti-Corruption Unit, has likened to grooming. Players are approached by those claiming to be businessmen in bars or even over WhatsApp, and cultivated for several weeks.

This can be done in a subtle way: for instance, by pretending to offer a clothing contract. Mohammad Ashraful, the former Bangladesh captain who was subsequently found guilty of fixing in the Bangladesh Premier League in 2013, originally got gifts to celebrate his successes. Fixers can befriend players – then feigning personal financial debts, they will ask a player to underperform in a one-off way as a favour. If the player agrees, corruptors can threaten to reveal their corruption if they do not oblige in future. Sometimes, criminal gangs use honeytraps; a player can then be blackmailed – with the gang threatening, say, to release images to his family – to be persuaded to fix. 'They tend to hunt the bars for you,' Chris Gayle wrote in *Six Machine*. 'You've got to be careful out there.'

When he began fixing, Vincent played for the Chandigarh Lions, and then the ICL World XI, in the Indian Cricket League, an unofficial T20 tournament which was not sanctioned by the Indian cricket board. With pop-up teams created in new leagues, there was no semblance of player loyalty. While players had shown themselves willing to fix international cricket too, temptations were sharpened in franchise cricket. Players regularly appeared for five or more teams a year; the whole relationship between a player and their side could easily be reduced to the transactional.

'It's a very strange environment when you turn up a day or so before the first game – play, golf, play, occasional beers and then at the end you leave 12 hours later,' said Jim Allenby, who played for Peshawar Zalmi in the Pakistan Super League in 2016. He said that such a dynamic had 'no real team aspect or build-up so it's hard to encourage guys to play as a team', and this could make it 'easier to convince [players] to fix'.

'There are so many more people around the team and around the hotel,' said Allenby, who noticed a notable change when he played in the 2016 PSL, his first T20 franchise league aged 33. 'It's very hard to protect players in those environments. It's hard to say for sure but some strange guys will come up to you in the bar late and start chatting and asking questions but we would just try and move away so it never went further.' Younger players may not have found it as easy to close down what may have started out as a harmless chat.

For corruptors, the beauty of the fix is that getting one player, once, is enough to get them forever. A player who has fixed once can then be blackmailed: should they refuse to be involved in fixes again, then the gang say they will leak details of the fix, or threaten the player more directly. 'Some of it starts very young . . . If I get you as a 19-year-old I've hooked you up,' said the anti-corruption insider. 'If I've recruited you I'm going to use you whenever I can.'

One-time fixers could effectively be trapped in perpetuity. Ruthless gangs moved to target players ever-younger, including in U-19 tournaments. A fix in one of these tournaments, which might have seemed relatively innocuous – a player could be enlisted to bowl a single no-ball, not for the fixers to make money off but simply as a way of blackmailing the player subsequently – could put the player on to the path of fixing for life.

Fixers using youth competitions as a way of recruiting players highlighted the importance of player education. But standards of education varied hugely around the world, meaning that gangs could pick off teams who offered the greatest likelihood of succumbing when their players were young. Such historic differences in player education are one reason for amnesties, such as for those in Sri Lankan cricket in 2019 – which allowed personnel to report their involvement in corruption without being reprimanded – could help protect the sport from future corruption.

Corruptors did not need to fix a match to enrich themselves; instead, they often merely needed to corrupt one player to make a profit. By knowing that one player was going to underperform in a certain way – either that a bowler would concede a large number of runs, or that a batsman would get out early or score much slower than required (preferably both) – corruptors could bet against this particular team before the period of deliberate underperformance. Then they could bet on the team after their period of deliberate underperformance, meaning that they traded themselves into a position when they could make money on the match market regardless of the actual final result. So players could be paid to fix, but their team would still be able to win without affecting corruptors' profits.

On Indian websites, so-called 'white label' sites offer a way for gamblers to bet, including on run brackets. Here, gamblers can bet on how many runs will be scored in segments of a T20 game – typically the six-over Powerplay, the seventh to the tenth overs, the eleventh to the fifteenth overs, and then the final five overs. As such, overs at the end of a 'bracket' are regarded as the most susceptible to fixing – as a bowler bowling, say, the tenth over would be able to determine whether the runs scored in the bracket from the seventh to tenth overs reached a certain number, if necessary by bowling wides and no-balls or bowling poor balls that can be easily hit for boundaries. Bringing fine leg up, and then bowling on a batsman's leg stump, meaning a batsmen can easily guide the ball past the fielder, is regarded as a classic way of ensuring a batsman scores the runs required by the fix. Batsmen, conversely, can bat slowly to ensure that their team scores under a certain amount in a bracket.

Signals that are known to be used include batsmen changing gloves, taking their helmets off and putting them back on or retaking their guard. For bowlers, aborting their run-up or starting their over with a wide are both known to act as signals. 'Spotters' in the ground then contact the gamblers to confirm that a fix is on.

Yet the vast majority of liquidity in most betting markets remains concentrated on the most common bets. Who will win a match accounts for 96% of betting on T20 games on Betfair, a leading online betting exchange.

But corruptors might only need one player to make a profit. Vincent, for instance, would often score deliberately slowly at the start of his innings. So those who had paid him could back against his team before he began his innings, and then watch their odds lengthen, due to Vincent's slow scoring. The fixers could then back Vincent's team to win at longer odds, meaning they had manipulated themselves into a position where they were guaranteed a profit, regardless of who actually won. In this way, the internet was a boon for fixers the world over, enabling them to manipulate the odds in a way that could make thousands in a few minutes – an altogether easier process than fixing in the pre-internet age, when fixers might need to buy off most of a team to be sure of making a profit. This changing dynamic also created the image of fixing as a victimless crime. An opening batsman, say, could agree to play out a maiden in the first over of an innings – which would mean their side's odds would lengthen significantly – but still score a century and help his team win.

***

Gurunath Meiyappan was rather endearingly viewed as akin to a lucky mascot for Chennai Super Kings. The son-in-law of N. Srinivasan, the owner of the team and president of the BCCI at the time, and a cricket fanatic, Meiyappan was appointed as team principal. It was essentially an invented role of the ilk that became common in the IPL, designed to give those who were powerful enough a legitimate reason to be involved with the team.

As team principal, Meiyappan had the right to go to team meetings, and access to some of the most sensitive information about the inner workings of the team, like injuries and team selection. Meiyappan even had 'team owner' credentials, allowing him full access to IPL venues, and to attend IPL auctions on Chennai's table. He was living every fan's dream.

Only, Meiyappan was not just a fan. He was also a gambler. In 2013, the Mumbai police arrested Meiyappan on account of gambling on matches involving Chennai, benefiting from information he was privy to in his role as team principal. He was also found to have passed on sensitive information to illegal bookmakers.

Meiyappan would be banned for life from cricket. So, at exactly the same time was Rajasthan Royals' part-owner Raj Kundra, who also bet on matches involving his team. As a result, Chennai and Rajasthan were suspended for two years from the IPL, missing the 2016 and 2017 seasons.

These affairs were a window into how, for corruptors, players were just one of their potential partners. In franchise T20 leagues, corruptors could go right to the very top. Indeed, sometimes those at the top were the corruptors. The structure of T20 leagues more broadly may embolden such nefarious behaviour: with no promotion and relegation, teams in leagues are insulated from being punished for underperformance.

Senior officials in teams could abuse their positions to enrich themselves at the expense of their team. In 2014, the managing director of the Dhaka Gladiators was found to have attempted to fix a match.

Insiders believed that some owners bought teams in T20 leagues simply as a vehicle to make money through corruption. By getting a team to underperform – through poor recruitment and team selection, simply bribing their own players to lose, or saying that they needed to underperform in a solitary game to regain their contracts for the next season – owners could gamble against their own sides, and make money that far exceeded the extra prize money they missed out on by losing.

There was also scope for owners to use privileged information – like if a star player was injured – to be able to bet against their team and then, when news of the injury was revealed, back their team, meaning they had manipulated the market in a way that guaranteed a profit.

The appeal of such malfeasance could be explained by the economic situation in leagues. The IPL's $510 million a year TV deal, which began from the 2018 season, moved teams decisively into profitability, meaning those running the franchises had no need to make up the shortfall in alternative ways.

But in most leagues, it was commonplace for teams to lose money. Owners thus had to recoup their investment any way they could, nefarious or otherwise. This created the incentive for them to want to fix. And the nature of anti-corruption work in leagues, which did not have an equivalent of English football's fit-and-proper-person test for owners, created opportunity.

'Some of these owners are dodgy as fuck,' observed one player who played in multiple T20 World Cups.

The economics of leagues also impacted on players' incentives to fix. In several leagues – notably the early years of the Bangladesh Premier League – players were routinely paid extremely late. Aggrieved and with a financial shortfall, players in such situations could be more vulnerable to fixing.

While Mumbai police were charging Meiyappan, they were also investigating Asad Rauf, a widely respected umpire who was a member of the ICC Elite Umpire Panel. In 2016, Rauf was banned for five years by the Indian board on charges of corruption and misconduct. During his stint in the Indian Premier League, Rauf allegedly received gifts from corruptors, for which he is alleged to have passed on information, like about the pitch or ground conditions.

Ample scope existed for match officials to impact results in return for cash. Most T20 leagues were slow to embrace the Decision Review System, which meant that umpires had scope to influence results. Even if DRS was used, teams were only allowed one review per innings each, and borderline calls stayed with the on-field umpire after review. Match referees, who imposed disciplinary bans on players, could also be of interest to corruptors. If they knew that a star player was about to be banned for a period, that would impact the match and tournament odds.

***

While greater attention is being placed on policing the pinnacle of the sport, the fear is that the threat may merely have been displaced. Even T20 leagues regarded as second tier now attract far more cash on betting markets than Test matches. On the UK betting exchange Betfair in 2018, an average of £6.5 million was matched for each Test, compared with £52 million for each IPL game. Even more strikingly, £34.8 million was matched on each Afghan Premier League game – two-thirds as much as each IPL match, and over five times as much as each Test. In some matches in the Tamil Nadu Premier League, a regional T20 league in India, which doesn't even have official T20 status, over £30 million would be matched on Betfair alone.

Such figures are only a small proportion – reckoned to be under 5% – of the total amount bet on each game, meaning that some Afghan Premier League matches could be expected to have over £600 million matched on them worldwide, largely through illegal bookmakers based in India and east Asia. Only a tiny proportion of this £600 million could be traced reliably. Fixing in the Afghan Premier League (APL) was 'rife', said one prominent figure in Afghan cricket in 2019.

The onset of new leagues – in T20, and the incipient T10 format – were 'clearly a key integrity risk for the game,' said Tony Irish, the head of FICA, the global players' union. He suggested that fixing was 'perhaps becoming an even greater risk with the exponential increase of new events and new stakeholders which aren't subject to consistent minimum standards, including in the area of anti-corruption.'

Such concerns were shared by a prominent betting trader, who was a regular source of intelligence for the ICC's Anti-Corruption Unit. 'I don't trade the Afghan Premier League or Canada League. Those tournaments are only set up by owners to fix.'

Another prominent trader said that 'in franchise cricket, my belief is that fixing mostly occurs as a vehicle for manipulating closer finishes – for the image of the league, keeping viewers interested, television etc – particularly in the PSL and IPL.' He asserted that: 'In general though, there is a habit in the IPL of making games closer than necessary,' which raised suspicions.

Instead of the biggest international markets, corruptors increasingly came to target domestic T20 leagues. Here, the cocktail of relatively low-paid players with insecure futures – often enviously playing alongside millionaires – and uneven quality of anti-corruption education and monitoring between different leagues created ample opportunities for fixers.

'In some leagues the anti-corruption measures are good and in others they aren't,' said Irish. 'There are no enforced minimum standards and there are no minimum player education requirements. There are many T20 league players moving around the world from league to league without any proper centralised monitoring of the standard of anti-corruption education they are receiving, or even whether they are receiving any appropriate education.'

Between leagues, the quality of anti-corruption officials, and how well resourced these bodies were, varied dramatically. Generally boards do their own anti-corruption monitoring for their own domestic T20 leagues, enlisting their own national anti-corruption units, rather than the ICC's. The ICC ACU attended tournaments when they were invited by the home boards, but many home boards decided not to invite the ICC. This created the possibility that, if corruption went all the way to the top of the administration of cricket in a particular country, there would be no one who was genuinely focused on catching the corruptors; those nominally employed by the board to police matches would have different motives.

For Associate teams – those outside the 12 Full Members – the only mandatory anti-corruption training they received was a 30-minute PowerPoint presentation run by the ICC ACU before the start of ICC qualifying events, ESPNcricinfo journalist Peter Della Penna reported in 2018. Home boards, who invariably lacked cash, are responsible for providing supplementary education.

This meant that, by the time that players got their brief education from the ICC, it could already be too late. In 2018, two Hong Kong players were charged for breaching the anti-corruption code during the 2016 Men's T20 World Cup.

T20 leagues from the IPL to South Africa's Ram Slam League, the Pakistan Super League and Bangladesh Premier League have all suffered proven cases of players match-fixing. Pretty much every other league has been the subject of dark rumours. In 2018, Betfair withdrew their markets from the Karnataka Premier League, another regional T20 league in India, after what appeared to be suspicious betting behaviour.

***

Corruptors have shown themselves to be endlessly adaptable. Hassan Cheema, the manager of Islamabad United, a Pakistan Super League team who had two players banned for corruption in 2017, explained: 'The Pakistan Cricket Board had this thing that players had an early curfew so that they wouldn't get into the world which becomes like quicksand . . . But even if you have a curfew what's stopping you from meeting during the day, or even in the hotel lobby?'

And while fixers tended to lure their targets in through elaborate means, they could resort to violence too. 'When you don't agree to them it's not you – it's the threats against your family,' said the anti-corruption insider, referring to what he has observed in south Asia especially. Across sport, fixers are so sophisticated that the UN Office on Drugs and Crime has noted the involvement of organised crime syndicates to rig games.

For the ACU, following the money was too often impossible. Worldwide, only about 15% of sports betting is legal and fully visible to regulators, according to the International Centre for Sport Security. About 35% is under-regulated and partially visible; and fully half is illegal and invisible to regulators, largely in Asia. Here – including, most significantly in India – gambling is mostly illegal, rendering it nearly impossible to follow betting patterns, and thus trace suspicious bets in the underground betting economy. This was a boon for fixers. Given where cricket's strongholds are, it is likely that even less than 15% of all betting on the sport is legal. Gambling being illegal in so much of the world was perhaps the single biggest obstacle to keeping cricket clean.

Even while gambling is illegal in most countries, match-fixing itself is not – perhaps because to legislate on match-fixing would amount to tacit acknowledgement that betting goes on. But this serves to limit the ACU's powers. The ACU has the right to demand mobile phones, phone bills and bank account details – only, it cannot be sure that a suspect handing in their phone uses another strictly for fixing purposes, or that one showing their bank details has another Swiss bank account to receive their payments from fixing. If the suspect is hiding a bank account or mobile phone, the ACU must be able to prove that the suspect is failing to comply before being able to charge them for non-compliance.

So while the ACU has become more activist, and successful in its cases, in recent years, the body remains hampered. To be truly empowered, and as effective as possible, the ACU would need the same powers of law enforcement.

All of this highlighted a simple truth, as the anti-corruption insider noted. For corruptors, the age of T20 meant 'there's more opportunities than ever before . . . Logic tells you a lot of games are fixed because of the amount of games being played.'

***

Over the 1990s, the physique of baseball players in the US was transformed. Players, including those who had been professional for years, became fitter, stronger, and able to hit the ball further and harder. Burly arms moved from being the exception to the rule. All of this was heralded as a triumph for uber-professionalism, sports science and players' sheer determination to gain every possible advantage on the field.

Undoubtedly, it owed to all these things. But it also owed to something else: performance-enhancing drugs.

Even as rumours swirled over certain players taking drugs, baseball fans, and the authorities, consoled themselves with a simple thought: baseball was a skill-based game, so cheats couldn't prosper. Unlike other games, the sport was too skill-based and too subtle for drug cheats to benefit. The illusion was maintained even as records for home runs were broken.

This comfort blanket ignored that, if two hitters are equally skilful, one who is able to hit the ball further will be far more effective. The need for huge skill in hitters, then, did not prevent them being able to accrue an advantage by taking performance-enhancing drugs to bulk up. Besides pure strength, steroid use brought wider benefits – notably to a player's recovery time, so they would miss fewer games, which would increase their output and make them more valuable to teams.

Baseball was 'head in the sand' about the drug threat, George Vecsey wrote in *Baseball: A History of America's Favorite Game*. It had never had a problem before, so why should one emerge?

In 2005, this unthinking faith was shattered. Soon, baseball was grappling with a steroids epidemic. Barry Bonds, one of the greatest sluggers in history, was forever discredited by allegations that he had taken performance-enhancing drugs. Congressional hearings uncovered rampant doping; insiders commonly estimated that at least a quarter of players – many more, some claimed – doped.

The parallels between cricket and baseball are often noted. They extend to the benefits for players of using performance-enhancing drugs, too. 'We know the ICC and World Anti-Doping Agency [WADA] view that the power-based skill set required in T20 makes it a sport that fits within a similar profile to baseball,' said Irish. 'It would be naive to think that it's not an integrity threat to any elite sport.'

The surge in six hitting in recent years mirrors the rise in home runs hit during the steroids era. While there are a myriad of reasons for the splurge in sixes, notably batsmen being trained specifically for T20 and being trained to value their wickets less, the six-hitting boom has distilled what could be gained from using performance-enhancing drugs to hit the ball further and more reliably.

Balls per Six in T20 Cricket by Year	
Year	**Balls per Six**
2008	27
2009	28
2010	27
2011	27
2012	27
2013	25
2014	24
2015	23
2016	23
2017	21
2018	20

'In the risk profile of sport, cricket is generally designated as a low-risk sport. But I believe that T20 cricket has changed the nature of the game – in that format at least. It is now probably, and this is an exaggeration, approaching a form of baseball,' said Dr Shuaib Ismail Manjra, chairman of the Cricket South Africa medical committee and a board member of the South African Institute for Drug-Free Sport. 'The risk of doping should be higher in T20 cricket and the risk profile should be amended accordingly.'

Being physically bigger and stronger brought a far greater advantage in T20 than the sport's longer formats. The early years of T20 have seen players bulk up as the sport professionalises – a revolution that remains unfinished. 'The physique of players is changing massively,' said England's T20 captain Eoin Morgan. 'Eventually everyone is going to be big and strong. Bowlers might not change that much in terms of physique but batters certainly are.' Only in recent years, with the professionalism of players elevated to a new level, has cricket reached the stage where training regimes are sufficiently rigorous for players to even benefit from doping.

'T20 cricket is about power, force and strength, in addition to the other skills required,' Dr Manjra explained. 'There's tremendous intensity in 20 overs of batting. Furthermore, many of these tournaments consist of back-to-back games which require quick recovery. So there is a greater potential for doping.'

The salience of physique has created a greater incentive to dope. 'T20, being a more athletic and dynamic version of cricket, places increased demands on players' bodies and power outputs,' explained Andrea Petroczi, a specialist in sports drugs from Kingston University in London. 'This makes the sport more prone to drugs, relative to the more traditional, 'leisurely' first-class form, as T20 demands better fitness levels, higher levels of strength, speed, agility and reaction time.' Petroczi cited anabolic steroids, such as testosterone, and other anabolic agents – like clenbuterol and selective androgen receptor modulators – as being particularly attractive to those looking to hit the ball further, because they can promote the development of muscle and, therefore, power. Doping to aid power hitting feels very much like a sin of its time.

For bowlers the advantages of doping are less immediately obvious. Yet, as Petroczi explained, just as with pitchers in baseball, drugs like anabolic steroid hormone, which increases the level of testosterone in the body, could help bowlers recover from injury at a dramatically faster rate, or become less susceptible to injuries. With players' earning power tied to their availability, returning to play earlier could have appreciable financial benefits for T20 players – who could therefore earn more cash by playing a fuller part in T20 leagues. Doping could even help fast bowlers bowl quicker. Indeed, there are periodic murmurings on the T20 circuit about fast bowlers who have acquired new pace at a suspicious rate.

Instead of multi-year contracts, that were the norm in domestic cricket competitions in first-class and one-day cricket, T20 contracts are often only a single year, and salaries are tied to a player's fitness and form. So even missing a few matches brings a notable financial cost. In the IPL, for instance, overseas players' fees are on a per-match basis, with players earning only 50% of their allocated match fee if they are unavailable for a game, and 80% if they are available but not selected. A player signed for $1.4 million would get $100,000 for playing in each of the 14 group matches, and lose $50,000 if they were injured for a game.

The economist Gary Becker was once late for an appointment. He chose to park on the street illegally, calculating that the low chance of being caught was worth the risk. He didn't get a ticket, and declared that 'criminal behaviour is rational' – those who break laws often weigh up the risks of an action against the rewards. Seeing performance-enhancing drugs through this prism, the incentives for taking performance-enhancing drugs are compelling for some players.

For older cricketers, who may already be planning for their life after cricket, the risk-reward calculation of doping – a big hitter using steroids to bulk up, say – is particularly attractive. Getting caught would merely end a career nearing the end of its natural course; using drugs to perform well enough to survive for a couple of extra years on the T20 circuit could easily be worth a seven-figure amount.

So if the explosion of money in cricket reduced incentives for players to deliberately underperform, at least at the top level, it may have had the opposite impact on would-be dopers. If the sport's financial boom has made the cost-benefit analysis of cheating to lose less advantageous, it has made the cost-benefit analysis of cheating to win – doping to gain an unfair advantage – more favourable.

This attraction is compounded by the insecurity of the T20 circuit. Freelance T20 players have both the most job insecurity and, because all they play is T20, the most to gain from bulking up, or making sure they are fit to play in more tournaments.

Many of the same underlying problems with how cricket is structured encourages both match-fixing and doping alike. In both cases, the risks are exacerbated by 'transient workplaces and high-performance environments, combined with a lack of globally coordinated, enforceable or accessible minimum gold standard education across the entire approved cricket framework,' said Irish from the global players' union.

The insecurity inherent in T20 life may make the rewards of cheating to win, or to lose, more appealing. In 2018, FICA found that 55% of players felt insecure or very insecure about their employment situation, and 66% of cricketers worldwide lacked any contract of longer than a year. Most revealingly, 88% said they favoured a long-term secure contract rather than the benefits of being able to move freely and flexibly.

In the case of doping, the ICC was not oblivious to this threat. The ICC began drug-testing at its events in 2002, became a signatory of the WADA code in 2006 and approved WADA's whereabouts rule in 2010. Most significantly, in 2017 the ICC introduced blood testing, and athletic biological passports, at its events. This was driven by a belief that EPO [Erythropoietin Stimulation Agents] and HGH [Human Growth Hormone], which are not covered under the standard urine analysis and can only be detected through blood analysis, were at risk of being used by cricketers. The ICC's integrity app, launched in 2017, means players should be completely aware of which substances are banned. From 2019, samples collected at ICC will be subject to long-term storage for ten years, belatedly catching up with what has been standard policy in many other sports for years. Samples will now be able to be retested for prohibited substances for which there is currently no reliable test for detection.

But, even within ICC events themselves, considered to have the most robust anti-doping procedures in cricket, testing figures remain notably lower than in other sports. One player who appeared in five ICC global events, including multiple recent editions of the T20 World Cup, said he had only been tested once during these events.

The real concern is that the ICC's remit on doping remains very limited, creating a fragmented anti-doping structure. While the ICC conducts out-of-competition testing on cricketers who have played, or been a substitute, in international matches in the previous two years, players who have not played international cricket in this period, or have retired from the international game, are not subject to ICC testing.

Strikingly, the ICC's whereabouts rules for cricketers only affects players ranked in the top eight one-day international countries, criteria which excluded the West Indies, the T20 World Cup champions, for several years. Indeed, there are just 88 players eligible for whereabouts out-of-competition drugs testing by the ICC at any one time. Under ICC rules, only the top five ranked batsmen and bowlers, and leading wicketkeeper, for the top eight ODI countries are liable to be tested by the ICC's whereabouts out-of-competition programme, though the ICC still does out-of-competition testing for countries from outside the top eight.

'The thought that the rules on anti-doping aren't the same for every country in world cricket is bizarre – frankly it amazes me,' said the senior medical official from a leading nation. 'The fact that only the top eight are subject to that is a huge surprise.' This means that when countries from outside this eight compete with ones ranked higher up in the World Cup, 'they're not playing by the same rules'. With many T20 leagues and national governing bodies doing few tests, that leaves many players dependent upon their national anti-doping organisations. Yet national anti-doping organisations focus upon Olympic sports; most seldom, if ever, Test cricketers.

Such policies seem designed for an era in which international cricket was still indisputably king. Yet now it looks archaic that some leading players in the IPL, Big Bash and other T20 leagues – players including Shane Watson, Brendon McCullum, Kieron Pollard and Kevin Pietersen in recent years – spent years not liable for drug testing by the ICC, after their international careers were over, while comparatively obscure, and far worse paid, players still playing international cricket were.

'It is ridiculous really – hopeless,' said Ivan Waddington, an anti-doping specialist from the University of Chester. 'If you're going to have a whereabouts rule you have to have one properly. Every player beyond a given level has to know they may be eligible to be tested by an out-of-competition test at any one time.'

Out of competition testing is the bedrock of successful testing programmes, Waddington said. 'Anyone who fails in competition testing has to be pretty stupid or pretty incompetent because you know when the date of competition is.

'If cricketers are using performance-enhancing drugs then I'd have thought that they'd be unlikely to be picked up by a system which is full of holes.'

Freelance players not being eligible for any out-of-competition testing by the ICC was a particular concern. This meant that, unless their national anti-doping organisations do out-of-competition tests – which is rare for cricket – such players wouldn't be subject to any out-of-competition testing whatsoever.

'Other drugs which are used during training periods, such as anabolic steroids, are better detected in out-of-competition testing when athletes are training at home,' Petroczi explained. Athletes using performance-enhancing drugs cut down on their usage as their next tournament nears; if they doped in between T20 leagues and were tested during these leagues, their doping may well pass undetected.

'It's the guys who decide to cut their ties with their national federation and not play any cricket nationally that will be able to wander around the world,' said David Howman, the former director-general of WADA. 'So you could go from league to league and never be tested.'

As the ICC is only responsible for testing in international cricket it is up to leagues themselves to organise testing in domestic competitions.

As with anti-corruption, the attention given to doping varies markedly between leagues. There are around 80 tests in the Indian Premier League each season. Yet in the Bangladesh Premier League, considered the second-best paying league in the world at the time, there were no drugs tests at all in the first three years. In the next three seasons – in 2016, 2017 and early 2019 – there were only between eight and 12 tests each year.

The Caribbean Premier League conducted only two tests per team in their first two seasons – players could not be tested if two of their teammates had already been tested during the tournament, unless they reached the final when there was an extra test per team. Since 2015, the league has enlisted the ICC to conduct their tests, but said that it was unaware of the numbers. In the Pakistan Super League, the number of tests conducted each season rose from between 14 and 18, in the first three seasons, to 30 in 2019, an improvement but still a very modest number. Largely for reasons of budget, the Hong Kong Blitz tournament, which attracted a high calibre of overseas players, and was a vehicle to get picked up in a more high-profile league, did not do any drugs testing at all in its first three seasons.

'Inconsistency would not be surprising given the lack of enforceable global minimum standards across the sanctioned cricket framework under current regulations,' Irish explained. Australia and England, which both considered themselves among the leaders for drug testing in cricket, refused to divulge official figures for the number of tests they conducted in their T20 leagues. In total, 262 tests were conducted by the England and Wales Cricket Board in 2018, across all levels of the sport at men's and women's level. Cricket Australia said they conducted an average of over 500 tests a year in total from 2014 to 2019 across the men's and women's game.

The small but growing number of private T20 leagues might be particularly susceptible to doping. In 2018, the Global T20 Canada League attracted players including Chris Gayle, David Warner, Steve Smith and Lasith Malinga – yet did not do any drug tests at all.

'It's a concern for the world of cricket when they've got these private leagues,' Howman said. 'The fact that these leagues are privately owned and privately run means that they are outside of the normal anti-doping programmes unless the players are members of their national federations. If they don't have any doping clause in the contracts then there's nothing to scrutinise.

'Any player who is freelance will not be in any testing pool, and is therefore unable to be tested by the ICC out of competition. The player free agency trend in cricket does emphasise the need to ensure that there are coordinated player education programmes around the world.' In New Zealand, for instance, players who appeared in any competition in a country signed up to the World Anti-Doping Code could be tested in theory. But the national anti-doping organisation in New Zealand prioritised 'current and emerging [age-group] national sport representatives for our out-of-competition testing,' a spokesperson for Drug Free Sport New Zealand explained.

The lack of standardised testing in T20 leagues means that the risk-reward calculation for would-be dopers in Bangladesh's T20 league, say, is a lot more favourable than for those in Australia's. There is a worrying divergence between anti-doping policies in different countries – including in their T20 leagues – with the frequency and quality of drug testing varying widely. As such, Irish viewed 'the risks [of doping] lying more across the T20 leagues landscape where there is no consistent regulatory framework and no consistent education of players.'

Most national anti-doping organisations budget for little, or any, testing at all in cricket, because it has historically been viewed as low risk, and these bodies prioritise Olympic sports. This means that domestic tests are normally funded by the national governing bodies for cricket in a particular country – where the funds and inclination to test vary hugely between nations.

The upshot of such an inconsistent and fragmented anti-doping structure is that the true scale of doping is hard to gauge. 'You'd like to see more consistent testing,' said one senior medical official for a Full Member nation. 'The big question that we don't know the answer to is how big a problem is this? Clearly if cricket isn't doing as much testing as other sports it probably comes from a position that assumes that doping isn't as prevalent. It's a dangerous assumption.'

Even the biggest league in the world was far from implementing best practice on doping. 'If the IPL wanted to show that they were world leaders then they would run a programme which would be overseen by the ICC and monitored by WADA. That would give them a seal of approval,' said Howman, the former director-general of WADA.

***

A comparison with baseball illustrated how tepid cricket's anti-drugs policies were. In 2018 baseball conducted around 27,000 tests at Major and Minor League level in the US. In cricket worldwide in 2018, there were just 1,434 drugs tests done, according to the ICC. So there were 19 times more tests in baseball in the US alone than all of cricket.

In Major League Baseball, each player was tested an average of ten times during the season. But in T20 cricket in 2018 there were just 978 domestic drugs tests, amounting to 0.47 tests per player. Even including ICC tests, there were just 0.68 drugs tests per T20 player worldwide in 2018. Both these figures were actually slightly inflated: the figures included tests on female cricketers too, though the vast majority were in the men's game.

Drug Testing and Violations in Cricket (Figures from ICC, covering men's and women's cricket – NB all violations to date in the men's game)				
Year	ICC Testing	ICC Violations	Domestic Testing	Domestic Violations
2014	456	0	728	2
2015	385	0	559	1
2016	447	1	547	2
2017	387	1	759	3
2018	456	0	978	6

In practice this meant that T20 players, especially those retired from international duty, could go years without any testing. Hundreds of players would know that, for large windows of the year, they had only a minuscule risk of being tested. As such, players could dope at periods when their chances of being tested were negligible; the drugs would then have washed out of their system by the time that they played in one of the few leagues with even a reasonably thorough doping programme. If players doped in such a strategic way and were then tested during these leagues, the players would not test positive.

Steroids, for instance, typically take a few weeks to pass out of an athlete's system, creating scope for players to use them between major competitions. Before a season, a batsman could use a course of steroids to 'build up the shoulders and muscles in the arms' and would not need to take the drug when they returned to play to benefit from it, said Ivan Waddington, an anti-doping specialist from the University of Chester.

'With doping it's presumed that in-competition testing is only scratching the surface,' explained a medical official from a leading nation. 'At a minimum you need really good out-of-competition testing. Certainly there's a washout period for everything so you can get a lot of advantage out of competition.'

The rise in free agency made the need to coordinate player education programmes throughout the world particularly pressing. The new T20 landscape, with players more transient and based in their home countries less frequently, renders educating players consistently more difficult. 'A comprehensive, accessible and minimum gold standard global education programme' was needed to reduce the discrepancies in doping education between countries, Irish said. 'We think the entire anti-doping framework needs to be looked at moving forward.'

Worldwide, 'there should be greater surveillance and requirements of the independent tournaments,' said Dr Manjra, chairman of Cricket South Africa's medical committee. 'With the rise of high-profile, money-spinning leagues it could become a problem. Now we have players like A.B. de Villiers and Chris Gayle who jump from T20 to T20 tournament – professional T20 players. There will be more in the future as the nature of the game changes – where players will essentially be free agents and not contracted. So we need to flag it as a risk.'

The paucity of drug testing in cricket may also have encouraged a culture of recreational drug use. In 2019, just before the 50-over World Cup, England's batsman Alex Hales was dropped from the national squad after twice failing tests for recreational drugs.

Even for international players, there may also be stark differences in how often those from different countries are tested, outside ICC-run events. One medical official working inside cricket suggested that countries not always accompanied by a team doctor – all those apart from Australia, England, South Africa and New Zealand – might be especially vulnerable to doping. 'One of the roles of the doctor is to check WADA compliance for any medications or substances that each player is considering taking, and teams which don't consider medical input to be important are clearly not going to be doing compliance checks to nearly the same extent. You'd tend to think that if doctors don't have a presence around a team that there won't be much checking of WADA compliance.' In 2017, according to WADA, the West Indies Cricket Board only conducted 12 drugs tests for steroids. The BCCI only conducted ten – and the Bangladesh Cricket Board just one.

Players could pass tests even if they were doping: Lance Armstrong passed 250 drugs tests without failing one, largely because he was warned before testers would come. An anonymous survey at the World Athletics Championships in 2011 found that one-third of athletes admitted to taking banned substances, yet under 2% fail a doping test each year. And so while higher numbers of drugs tests ostensibly indicates that a league or national board takes the threat of doping seriously, the tests that really count are targeted tests driven by investigative work, which cost tens of times more to do than routine ad hoc testing.

Across sport, 'we're spending a lot of money running a testing programme where other parts of our society would probably be told to shut it down because it's not producing the results we might expect from our investment,' Howman said. 'There doesn't seem to me to be too much worry about that.

'Testing is one thing, numbers is one thing, the quality and efficiency of testing is another. You and I could go out today and test 50 cricketers and say we've tested 50 cricketers and none of them were positive. You've got to have a programme which is proactive and not randomly select people. That's the only chance you've got of getting an effective programme – otherwise the science isn't up to it.'

Without such testing, doping may be alluring, especially for players in less policed T20 leagues.

'You then have to worry about their agents and other members of their entourage who have to ensure they make money as well. That's a common factor in other team sports, particularly at a lower level – so those who are trying to break into it are often tempted to be doing things they shouldn't be doing,' Howman reflected. 'In lower levels of tennis it goes on because there's less scrutiny and less risk of being caught. So that happens in cricket as well, I'm sure.'

Yet if the lesson from other sports is that only testing based on rigorous investigative work is likely to yield results, the degree to which it has been absorbed by different leagues is unclear. And so too often, for T20 players – especially freelancers – the deterrents to doping are weak. According to insiders, only a tiny proportion of drugs tests in cricket are on the basis of rigorous intelligence work of the sort that is much more likely to catch cheats.

'I don't know how you can pretend that elite athletes, including cricketers, are in any way worried about being caught if they decide to cheat,' said Renee Anne Shirley, the well-respected former head of the Jamaica Anti-Doping Commission. 'Bottom line, if cricketers take care and dope in the off season, it is doubtful that testing them in the margins of international competition in their hotel rooms or training facilities that their doping will be caught.'

Shirley said that cricket's vulnerability to doping was best viewed as a microcosm of the wider vulnerabilities in the sports ecosystem. '[The] global anti-doping model is not working and needs a radical overhaul.'

***

Even when players contravened anti-doping rules, rulings often haven't been enforced with much severity. Afghanistan's Mohammad Shahzad, once ranked the seventh-best T20 batsman in the world, was banned in 2017 after testing positive for clenbuterol, an anabolic agent which was once popular in East Germany, in an out-of-competition test. Shahzad received a 12-month ban for his positive test – but, remarkably, this was backdated to when he failed the test, not to when he actually stopped playing. In between failing the test and stopping playing, Shahzad played another 17 internationals; Afghanistan received no reprimand for selecting him in this period.

Andre Russell, among the world's leading T20 players, was also banned in 2017. Russell was banned for a year for failing to file his whereabouts three times in a year with the Jamaica Anti-Doping Commission, who accused Russell of 'gross negligence'. Yet, after news broke of his missed tests early in 2016, Russell played on for 11 months – winning a raft of trophies, including the T20 World Cup, in the period, and earning in the region of £1 million. His treatment 'does seem unusual compared to how athletes in other sports have been treated,' said Paul Dimeo, a specialist in performance-enhancing drugs in sport. That such a high-profile player could play on for nearly a year after contravening WADA requirements – and with his missed tests seldom remarked upon – suggested a sport oblivious to the threat of drugs. The apparent lack of interest from the media in cricket doping is not merely a semantic point; many successful investigations into doping in sport have been abetted by the media, as in *The Sunday Times* journalist David Walsh's 15-year pursuit of Lance Armstrong.

But in recent years the trickle of doping cases in cricket has grown. In each year from 2014 to 2018, there were two, one, three, four and then six violations of the doping code detected either by the ICC or, most often, by domestic authorities. These results appeared to suggest that the risks of doping are growing.

'You can look at cricket in the same way as golf in some ways because they're modelled on spurious spirit and values and so on. There's been this feeling that people will not cheat by doping in cricket and golf. That's long past – you can't utter that any longer. People take shortcuts where there's money to be made, no matter what sport,' Howman reflected. 'The money that is now available in cricket is pretty formidable to what it was ten years ago. So you're going to have temptation there. And if you look at the way that some cricketers have been tempted by those who groom players to engage in spot-fixing or match manipulation then the same sort of grooming can of course occur with doping.' Just as with match-fixing, criminals could be enriched by doping – though this time to provide the drugs to help cricketers win, rather than pushing them to lose deliberately.

And – far more so than with match-fixing – would-be dopers have been abetted by the relative lack of scrutiny paid to the subject. 'I don't think it's a world that has been explored properly,' Howman said. Even when players would not actually benefit from a particular drug, they could easily be attracted to taking it by mistakenly thinking it brought physiological benefits. 'My concern nowadays is not medical or physical, it's psychological – people think by taking a pill they're going to get better.'

While there is little reason to believe that doping is anything like as systematic as in sports like cycling, the fear is that the lack of cases uncovered, as was true of match-fixing until the late 1990s, says less about how clean the sport really is than about the lack of attention paid to doping.

'I'd put my house on there being substantially more cricketers using drugs than you'd think from those figures,' said Waddington. 'The pressures are all in one direction, which is greater pressure for players to use drugs.

'There is not a single sport in which the number of violations is an adequate indication of the number of players using drugs. In every single sport the drug-testing programme is really quite ineffective. The one thing you can be absolutely certain of is that those six violations will be a small proportion of the total number of players using performance-enhancing drugs.'

Indeed, the comparative neglect of doping, compared to match-fixing, reflects an underlying point: cheating to win seems far more forgivable than cheating to lose. One irony is that, as the economics of the game have been transformed, incentives to throw matches at the very top levels have been reduced because it is much harder to buy a player out. Yet if the explosion of money in cricket may have helped mitigate one form of corruption, it has also incentivised another.

THIRTEEN

WHY CSK WIN AND WHY RCB LOSE

'Just because you are owned by a big businessman or a film star they don't know cricket. You don't teach them how to run a business. Cricket should be run by cricketing professionals'
Former RCB bowler Murali Kartik

You have £8.5 million to build a T20 team. You really shouldn't end up with Corey Anderson bowling your death overs. But at Royal Challengers Bangalore in the 2018 IPL, that is exactly what happened: not just once, but in three different matches.

RCB had only signed Anderson as a replacement player for the injured Nathan Coulter-Nile, who was expected to be their primary death bowler. When Coulter-Nile was ruled out weeks before the season, RCB's squad was already loaded with powerful overseas batsmen. But rather than replace Coulter-Nile with another bowler, RCB plumped for Anderson instead. 'Corey plays a bold game and has incredible potential,' explained RCB's head coach Daniel Vettori. The statement had corporate fingerprints all over it: that season Bangalore's official hashtag was #PlayBold.

Anderson had played 100 T20 matches but he was a batting all-rounder who had only ever delivered 26 overs in the last phase of the innings. He had an eye-watering economy rate of 10.26 runs per over when doing so.

A month later the sagacity of RCB's decision was about to be tested. Anderson had already bowled three overs in previous matches at the death that season and haemorrhaged 41 runs. But with Chennai Super Kings requiring 71 runs off 30 balls to chase down RCB's imposing score of 205 at the M. Chinnaswamy Stadium, Anderson stood at the top of his run-up once again.

***

RCB's captain Virat Kohli turned to Anderson at the death, despite his poor record, because his team was conspicuously lacking in alternatives. Umesh Yadav was RCB's attack leader but he was a Powerplay specialist. The core of RCB's attack was made up of spinners Yuzvendra Chahal, Pawan Negi and Washington Sundar, who all typically operated in the Powerplay or through the middle. That left just Anderson and the inexperienced Indian Mohammad Siraj to bowl with the match in the balance.

Earlier in the evening Umesh, Chahal and Negi had reduced CSK to 74 for 4 after nine overs to put RCB on top. Bangalore's problem was that the fourth wicket brought Chennai's captain, and one of the greatest T20 chasers, Mahendra Singh Dhoni to the crease.

Dhoni had a penchant for taking chases deep, choosing his target carefully and capitalising clinically. So when RCB's best bowler Chahal returned for his final over, the 13th of the innings, Dhoni was content to play him cautiously and take no risks – settling for six runs from the over despite the asking rate nudging above 14. CSK had never scored that fast to win a match but Dhoni knew RCB's weakness and was coiled to exploit it.

With seven overs remaining, the last threat was posed by left-arm spinner Negi. Turning the ball away from the bat, Negi represented a challenge for both Dhoni and his right-handed partner Ambati Rayudu. Against Negi, unlike against Chahal, Dhoni was prepared to take a risk. Dhoni knew if he could attack Negi's third over he could hit him out of the attack, leaving RCB's death over options exposed and Kohli with nowhere to turn.

A calculated attack, which included consecutive sixes from Dhoni down the ground, took 19 from Negi's third over – meaning that Kohli would be loath to risk bowling him again. Dhoni had navigated his way through the middle overs. Just Siraj and Anderson stood in his way with five overs remaining.

***

Facing Anderson was facile for a batsman of Dhoni's quality, especially at the death. When he entered the attack, with five overs left to bowl, his first over was plundered for 16 runs; Anderson's second was bludgeoned for 15. The left-arm angle from over the wicket delivered the ball right into Dhoni's hitting arc, where his rapid hand speed and astonishing eye combined stunningly.

At the other end Siraj was exposed too, conceding ten from the 17th over and 14 from the 19th. In that penultimate over he was so determined to keep the ball away from Dhoni's arc he delivered three consecutive wides in what became a nine-ball over.

Dhoni's assault had reduced the equation, but with six balls remaining CSK still required 16. Kohli didn't want to risk Washington's off spin into the right-handed Dhoni or Negi's left-arm spin after the earlier onslaught. Despite conceding 31 from his first two overs Anderson returned for his third consecutive over in an attempt to close out the match. It took CSK four balls to end it, Dhoni sealing a remarkable win with a seventh thunderous six. By the end of the season, Anderson had bowled 8.4 overs – and conceded 115 runs.

'Coulter-Nile got injured and they replaced him with Corey Anderson,' reflected Rahul Dravid a legendary Indian captain who played for three seasons for RCB between 2008 and 2010. 'Corey Anderson bowling at the death . . . that's not going to win you many matches.'

CSK's heist propelled them to the top of the IPL table; defeat saw RCB rooted in the bottom half, from which they would not return. The result embodied the different traits of the two teams.

Chennai were the IPL's most successful side – that season they would seal a record-equalling third IPL crown and in 2019 continued their perfect record of reaching the play-offs in every season. They were renowned for pulling off comeback victories like the win at the Chinnaswamy.

For RCB, the defeat was an all too familiar experience. After their fearsome batting order posting 205, their bowling was 'just not acceptable', as Kohli lamented after the defeat. Batting might and bowling weakness were RCB's leitmotif: despite signing a coterie of the world's most destructive batsmen, they had never lifted the IPL trophy.

The IPL, with its salary cap and resetting auction process, was designed to produce competitive balance. Yet after 12 seasons CSK had won 61% of their matches; RCB had won just 45%.

Their contrasting fortunes were a window into the strategic currents that shaped the T20 format.

***

'The fight is won or lost far away from witnesses – behind the lines, in the gym, and out there on the road, long before I dance under those lights,' Muhammad Ali once said of boxing. And so it was in the IPL: in many ways the league was not won or lost on the field of play but in the air-conditioned function rooms of glitzy hotels where the annual player auction would be held.

The divergent fortunes of CSK and RCB started at the very first auction in 2008. Unbeknown at the time were how the rules on player retention would evolve, which allowed teams to maintain the core of their squad across a number of seasons. This placed a disproportionate influence on the first auctions, in which franchises formed the nucleus of their team which they then tweaked over the coming years. In contrast, franchises who misjudged their strategy in early auctions were left scrabbling around for the remaining quality players, and forced to take more risks.

Dravid believed that Chennai's owners gave them an advantage in the early years. 'CSK's owners India Cements have had a culture of cricket and cricket teams for 30 to 35 years. They've run club teams, they have a company team and they have always had people in the system,' he explained.

'When they got into the IPL, Chennai probably had an advantage over a lot of other franchises because they [India Cements] were already in the business of running cricket teams. CSK was just the most high-profile team that they ran. So in a sense they've always had people on the ground and their scouting system was probably better right at the start than any other team and I think that helped.'

The sagacity of India Cements contrasted with RCB's owners. The United Breweries Group, headed by the multi-millionaire businessman Vijay Mallya, had no prior cricket experience. Despite Mallya's naivety, he commanded great authority over RCB's team and its selections. 'Mallya used to sit in the meetings and had a veto on what could be done,' explained Murali Kartik who played for four IPL teams, including RCB.

'In the IPL the owners believe that they know cricket,' said Kartik. 'It doesn't happen that way. It has to be left to the professionals. Just because you are owned by a big businessman or a film star they don't know cricket. You don't teach them how to run a business. Cricket should be run by cricketing professionals.

'The CSK team is handled by professionals. By that I mean when it comes to the marketing and logistical side of things there are different sets of people who don't stick their toes into the cricket.' It was upon these contrasting foundations that both teams were built.

Arguably the most significant auction signing in IPL history was Chennai's acquisition of Dhoni in 2008. Just months earlier Dhoni had led India to the inaugural T20 World Cup. He was the perfect cricketer for the T20 age: an explosive batsman, sharp wicketkeeper and very astute captain. Chennai paid £750,000 for Dhoni, making the 26-year-old the most expensive player in the first auction.

Alongside Dhoni, Chennai formed a strong Indian core, recognising the importance of local players who knew the conditions and whose availability would go unchallenged by clashes with international cricket or intrusive foreign boards. In the first auction CSK signed the dynamic batsman Suresh Raina and an upcoming off-spinner Ravichandran Ashwin, both of whom would have notable careers for India. CSK also targeted less-heralded players who played their state cricket in Chennai: the fast bowler Lakshmipathy Balaji and the batsman Subramaniam Badrinath were the two most prominent examples. In 2012, CSK completed the nucleus of their team when they signed the left-arm spinning all-rounder Ravindra Jadeja, another Indian international. The Indian quintet of Raina, Dhoni, Ashwin, Badrinath and Jadeja would all play more than 100 matches for CSK by the end of the 2019 IPL.

'Right from the word go CSK focused on having the best possible Indian players,' observed the Australian batsman Mike Hussey, who played for Chennai in three stints between 2008 and 2015 before returning as a coach in 2018. 'Obviously you might have the odd standout overseas player here or there but generally speaking over the course of a season the overseas players cancel each other out but the teams that are consistently good are the teams that have a really strong Indian contingent in their squads. And we've been quite lucky since the inception of the IPL in that we've had a really good core of top-quality Indian players.'

Targeting the best Indian players really amounted to shrewd economic logic: focusing on where the supply of elite talent was scarcest. 'It's a case of market resources,' explained Dravid. 'There a lot of foreign players available for four slots. But there are a limited number of quality Indian players available, and the fact that CSK have been able to get some of the best guys has meant that they have always had that core.'

Chennai supplemented this Indian core with overseas players in roles harder to fill with Indian players. In 2008 the powerful opening batsmen Matthew Hayden and Stephen Fleming and the middle order batsman Hussey were joined by the lower order aggressor Albie Morkel. Unlike the stable Indian core, the overseas players changed slightly over the years: Faf du Plessis, Shane Watson, Dwayne Bravo and Imran Tahir later became regulars. But while the characters evolved their place within the broader system did not. Overseas players were important but they were not defining, such was the strength of CSK's Indians.

Chennai Super Kings: Players with 50 Caps or More (2008–19)	
Player	**Matches**
Suresh Raina	188
Mahendra Singh Dhoni	184
Ravichandran Ashwin	121
Ravindra Jadeja	116
Subramaniam Badrinath	114
Dwayne Bravo	103
Albie Morkel	92
Murali Vijay	86
Faf du Plessis	71
Mike Hussey	64
Mohit Sharma	58
Shadab Jakati	55

'The biggest reason we did well was our approach to the auction,' Morkel told *Cricket Monthly*. 'CSK invested heavily in our Indian players and made sure we had the best. Other teams went the other way, spending big money on one or two overseas players and then filling the team with lesser-known Indian guys. That didn't work out so well because you just can't rely on the big-name players to win you a competition like the IPL. It's just too long and intense.'

This same local-heavy structure was later replicated by the only IPL team to win more titles than Chennai, although they were less consistent: Mumbai Indians, who built a squad around an Indian spine and added their overseas players around this.

The emphasis on a strong domestic core was a common strand of successful teams in other leagues too. In Australia, Perth Scorchers, who reached five finals in six years from 2012 to 2017, adopted a similar approach to squad building: in the 2017/18 BBL season they only filled one, rather than two, of their overseas spots, and still topped the group stage. In the Pakistan Super League, Islamabad United, champions in 2016 and 2018, also recognised the critical importance of strong local players. In the 2019 PSL draft, nine of the ten players retained by Islamabad were from Pakistan.

Bangalore's approach to squad building was the antithesis of Chennai's: they struggled to form a stable Indian core back in the early seasons and relied heavily on overseas players instead. By the end of the 2019 IPL, CSK had five Indian players with over 100 caps and eight with more than 50; RCB had just one Indian player with over 100 caps and five with more than 50.

This could partly be attributed to the original auction where RCB's two most expensive Indian players – Dravid and Anil Kumble – were already approaching the end of their careers and retired soon after. At that auction Bangalore spent the majority of their purse on overseas players rather than Indian talent.

RCB had scope to change tack. Yet in the 2011 mega auction, when teams were forced to release the majority of their squads at the end of the first contract cycle, Bangalore doubled down on their previous folly. Instead of focusing on quality Indian players, RCB splurged money on overseas stars such as A.B. de Villiers, Tillakaratne Dilshan and Chris Gayle. These were all terrific batsmen – but, when the amount spent on them was added together, they did not create a balanced and well-rounded side.

Gaurav Sundararaman, who worked as an analyst for CSK and RCB, believed that auction shortcomings were at the root of Bangalore's struggles. 'RCB's problem comes more at the auction than on the day of the game because I've seen them make numerous mistakes in the auction. Every year we can pinpoint numerous mistakes. Every single season it is the same thing. The kind of money they spend is very disproportionate.'

Dravid – who played for RCB for three seasons before joining Rajasthan Royals – saw similar failings. 'Bangalore have never balanced their team very well. I think they've been very poor with selections and auctions.'

The difficulty facing RCB was that most star Indian players were continually retained by rival teams. Yet the examples of Mumbai Indians and Kolkata Knight Riders, who both recovered from similarly tumultuous early seasons, showed that it was possible to build an Indian core by focusing on intelligent scouting to identify good T20 players who had not yet been noticed by rival teams. These teams were both pioneers in establishing extensive scouting networks that worked all year round, forming the bedrock of their success across the next half a decade.

Royal Challengers Bangalore: Players with 50 Caps or More (2008–19)	
Player	**Matches**
Virat Kohli	192
A.B. de Villiers	127
Chris Gayle	91
Yuzvendra Chahal	83
R. Vinay Kumar	70
Rahul Dravid	52
Anil Kumble	51

At least in the IPL teams existed on a level financial playing field. In England, Northamptonshire reached three finals in four years from 2013 to 2016, winning two, despite being among the five poorest of the 18 counties. They illustrated how meticulous planning, with pre-match dossiers of up to 25 pages, shrewd recruitment – Northants specialised in finding undervalued players, often finding players who were comparatively undervalued because of unathletic looking physiques – and an open-minded approach could overcome the logic of finantial determinism in sport.

It was hard to detect such a systematic approach to recruitment at Bangalore. For instance, in the 2011 auction Bangalore spent £990,000 on Saurabh Tiwary – a 21-year-old Indian batsman who had shown promise but who had only played 31 T20 matches. The fee made Tiwary the most expensive player at the auction who had not played international cricket. After three underwhelming seasons, in which he made just one 50 in 31 innings, Tiwary was released.

RCB also developed an unfortunate penchant for releasing players who then excelled at other teams. Before the 2018 season, Bangalore released the dashing Indian batsman Lokesh Rahul and Gayle, whose returns had been dwindling. Both players were reunited at the top of the order for Kings XI Punjab and plundered a combined 1,027 runs. Watson was also released by RCB that year and excelled for CSK, proving much more effective at the top of the order than in the middle order where RCB had deployed him. The following season, Sarfaraz Khan and Quinton de Kock were both released by Bangalore and proceeded to have the best IPL seasons of their careers at their new clubs.

The case of Sarfaraz was particularly interesting because it showcased Bangalore's mismanagement. An RCB insider, speaking anonymously, recalled how bowling coach Ashish Nehra shot down Sarfaraz in a way that dented his confidence. 'Sarfaraz got 90 off 30 balls in a warm-up game on an absolutely horrible wicket against our full-strength bowling attack – he smashed it.' After others had praised him, 'Nehra pulled him aside and absolutely gave it to him.'

Another auction trick that Bangalore struggled to exploit was utilising local state players as Chennai did. While Ashwin, Badrinath and Vijay all made more than 75 appearances for CSK, not a single Karnataka player did so for RCB. In 2018 Bangalore were ruled out of play-off contention when they lost against a Rajasthan Royals team powered by figures of 4 for 16 from Shreyas Gopal and cameos with bat and ball from Krishnappa Gowtham – two young players who represented Karnataka in state cricket but had been snapped up by another franchise. It was a humiliating result for RCB that underlined their failure to utilise their state network.

For all the complexities inherent in the auction, Bangalore's travails made them figures of fun. In 2017 Bangalore were bowled out for 49 by a Kolkata bowling attack comprising Chris Woakes, Nathan Coulter-Nile, Umesh Yadav and Colin de Grandhomme. Next year, RCB promptly signed all four players at the auction. Although this wasn't a predetermined plan, it could be considered a classic example of what psychologists term the availability bias, with decision-makers drawn to who came to mind most readily – the bowlers who had flummoxed Bangalore the year before – rather than evaluating everyone fairly. And it rather encapsulated what Bangalore had become. If you can't beat them, sign them.

***

Do teams win because they pick the same team or do teams pick the same team because they are winning? It is not an easy question to answer but over a decade CSK and RCB provided two fascinating case studies.

Bangalore finished in the top four in two of the first three IPL seasons but without a title retained just one player, Virat Kohli, before the 2011 mega auction. At the auction itself, they only bought back four players. CSK – who had reached three play-offs and had one title to their name – retained four players and bought back seven, foreshadowing the approach they would adopt at the 2014 and 2018 mega auctions. The success of Kolkata Knight Riders proved that radical squad overhauls could be effective but they required planning and thought that RCB didn't appear to apply.

'The group is pretty much the same every year,' said Sam Billings who played for CSK in 2018 and 2019. 'They have a history of retaining the vast majority of their squad.'

Chennai were not only more patient with players than Bangalore when they were enjoying success, but also avoided overreacting to defeats. On average CSK made 0.9 team changes after a victory and just 1.6 after a defeat while RCB made an average of 1.2 team changes when they won and a lofty 2.4 when they lost.

Average Team Changes by Previous Result			
Match Result	**CSK**	**IPL Average**	**RCB**
Won	0.9	1.2	1.2
Lost	1.6	2.1	2.4

'Consistency of selection is a big factor in RCB's struggles,' said Kartik. 'RCB do the opposite of what CSK does. CSK is a template that other teams should follow. Every T20 team where I have been successful or where they have won tournaments – places like Middlesex and Somerset – people and captains hardly made any changes. So if we had 12 or 13 players that would be the number of people used during the season.'

The benefits of this consistency of selection were myriad. Firstly, the stability bred familiarity of roles for the players who became accustomed to their job in the team. As players continued to be involved they became better at what they were tasked with doing. At the start of new seasons at Chennai, Hussey recalled that there was no need for big strategy meetings to outline roles and responsibilities: the large majority of players were simply continuing their jobs from the year before. 'Everyone knew each other inside and out so it was a case of just get our heads down and just get into it.'

The trust placed in players also encouraged them to play with freedom – particularly essential in T20 where failure, even for the best batsmen, was wired into the format. In the IPL, where an overseas player's salary was directly linked to the number of games they played, consistency of selection helped avoid situations where players might play selfishly. A batsman fretting about being dropped might, consciously or unconsciously, bat more carefully rather than attack. Sometimes the interests of the player and team might collide.

'There's no way of measuring the confidence that gets instilled in a player from being selected and being around the group and being made to feel comfortable. I think that's a priceless entity that a lot of teams miss,' said Billings.

'They believe in a certain individual,' explained Kartik. 'T20 is a format where players are doing things for you, putting their neck on the line, asked to up the ante, take risks and do well for the team and if they succeed, they succeed but if they fail the belief of the team management, captain and coach is what will make them play well the next time.'

Thirdly, the patience afforded to players at Chennai demonstrated an understanding and acceptance of the format's vicissitudes. Compared to other sports, T20 seasons were very short, with no more than 14 matches in a regular competition. This gave rise to short-termism among coaches, prone to overreacting to defeats because they were fretting about their own jobs.

Chennai took a different approach. 'Even if you miss out in three or four games, if they know you're a good player they'll keep backing you no matter what, whereas you see with a lot of other teams that they really chop and change a lot,' said Hussey. 'In a game like T20 where it can be quite volatile you are going to have a period where you are going to miss out a few times.'

'Other teams are so quick to drop players and make a change and try and find the ideal combination,' added Kartik. 'The ideal combination in T20 is found by giving trust and having trust and giving that feeling that you're our player.'

Dravid believed that CSK's stability came from the very top: their owners. 'India Cements understand the ups and downs of cricket because the company had supported cricket since the 1970s and they've been running a league in Madras. They don't panic as quickly as some of the other teams have.

'Unfortunately in a 14-game tournament a lot boils down to luck. One thing here, one thing there. If you start attributing things or trying to look for reasons, you can't always find them. The team that does a lot of things right can still lose a game, and the team that does a lot of things wrong can still win a game, but it is not perceived that way. 'Sack the coaches, these players weren't good, pick new players.' I find it can get a bit chaotic at times.'

Brendon McCullum, who played for both CSK and RCB, recognised inconsistency of selection as something that hampered teams' ability to play aggressive cricket.

'Franchise cricket is very different to international cricket to try and build an aggressive team. When you try and play aggressive cricket you need an all-in mentality. You need consistent selection policies; you're asking guys to go out there and play at a level that may even be slightly uncomfortable for them and it will become more comfortable the more they do it. But initially it will be uncomfortable and what comes with that is a bit of insecurity and a bit of doubt and often a lot of inconsistencies.

'With New Zealand it was very easy to get that all-in approach because we are from a small country and there's not a huge amount of depth. We had one sort of theme of cricketers who were all able to get on the bus, sitting on the right seats and heading in the right direction. With these franchises it can be a lot more difficult.'

Personal relationships were also stronger in international cricket, where players spent most of the year together, rather than just a few weeks when they were competing for places and potentially salaries.

McCullum believed this created an environment more suited to attacking play at international level. 'I was invested in the people. I knew their parents' names, their kids' names, what motivated them in the game and genuinely they were my friends and I felt like I was fully invested in them and it's very hard to get that level of emotional attachment. You know when you go over the wall they are coming with you.'

Nurturing an attacking philosophy at domestic level was something McCullum grappled with during his time as captain of Brisbane Heat and Lahore Qalandars, where his teams generally struggled. However, his appointment as head coach of Trinbago and Kolkata Knight Riders in August 2019 gave him more power and influence to encourage an aggressive mentality from the top down.

The 2019 IPL season distilled the contrasting approaches CSK and RCB took to selection. Having spent £475,000 at the 2019 auction on the brilliantly talented 22-year-old West Indies batsman Shimron Hetmyer, RCB gave him just four innings – three in the middle order, two of them in the difficult number five position, and one as opener – in which he scored just 15 runs. Having lost all four matches, Bangalore paid little heed to the complexity of Hetmyer's role or the small number of opportunities he had and unceremoniously dropped him, leaving him out for nine matches. Hetmyer wasn't selected again until the final match of the season, when RCB were already out. A match-winning 75 in his first match back, off just 47 balls, underlined Bangalore's mismanagement.

While Hetmyer struggled for RCB, Watson was in similar strife for Chennai, averaging just 18.75 across his first eight innings of the season. Rather than dropping him, CSK persisted with Watson. In his following eight innings he scored 251 runs with three 50s, including one in the final.

'With someone like Shane Watson it is a matter of time,' said Hussey. 'It is a matter of when, not if. When you've got a quality player there then they are going to come good at some stage and it is about keeping the faith in them.'

The start of a new IPL season was often marked by Bangalore scrabbling around for their best combination; Chennai did not have to. 'RCB get it wrong to start with, then chop and change and by the time they have chopped and changed they finally identify the right team but it is too late,' said the RCB insider.

Research by Gain Line Analytics suggested that continuity of selection also had benefits to team cohesion and performance in high-pressure games. Between 2008 and 2018 Gain Line found that there was little correlation between success and the number of games played by players individually, but the more cohesion a team had, as measured by their games played together and stability of the side, the more successful they generally were. This suggested that teams should look to sign players who were used to playing together, and working in tandem with the bat and ball.

By the end of 2019 Chennai had used only 74 different players across 189 matches – easily the fewest of the original eight IPL teams, both overall and on a per-game basis. Their captain, Dhoni and vice-captain Raina, had remained the same in every season. In contrast, Bangalore had been led by six different captains and had used 129 different players across 196 matches, the most of all teams overall. That equated to almost twice as many new players as Chennai for each match.

Players used by IPL Teams, 2008–19			
Team	**Matches**	**Players**	**New Players per Match**
CSK	189	74	0.39
DD	185	114	0.61
KXIP	181	116	0.64
KKR	194	106	0.54
MI	209	109	0.52
SRH/DC	191	129	0.67
RR	154	107	0.69
RCB	196	129	0.66

The difference between the two teams was 'simple,' said McCullum. 'One team gives selection loyalty and works on the team they have; the other chases a perfect team and doesn't have a blueprint for how they are going to play.'

Chennai's stability extended beyond the players. Having represented CSK in the inaugural season, Fleming was appointed head coach in 2009, where he has remained ever since. A number of Fleming's support staff also used to play for Chennai: in 2019, both the batting and bowling coaches had played for CSK in the 2008 final.

Fleming's style of leadership emphasised making players feel comfortable. The IPL was a peculiar environment with a lot of unfamiliar players from different backgrounds and cultures spending an intense six-week period together. Establishing a laid-back team culture allowed his players to thrive despite the chaos.

In an interview with *Cricket Monthly* Fleming recalled a conversation he had with Matthew Hayden, who was one year his senior, in 2009: 'What will be the best thing for you during this IPL in India? What would be the ultimate programme for you?' He said, 'Mate, surfing. I want to surf.' I said, 'Okay, mate. Surf. We will send you wherever you want to go. You surf, obviously you have franchise commitments, but outside that, we will see you game day. Let's see how you go.'

That season, Hayden scored 572 runs at an average of 52.00. 'My philosophy is to empower players,' explained Fleming. 'Empower the player to, one, decide if he wants to train, and then tell me what he wants to train.'

Washington, who played under Fleming at Rising Pune Supergiant, recognised Fleming's ability as a man-manager. 'Fleming knows how to get the best of any individual and understands the individual really well. He's always cool and calm.'

Thirty-nine when he was appointed head coach, Fleming was inexperienced for such a role. However, his task was made easier by the experience within Chennai's squad.

Ostensibly T20 was an action-packed format that demanded youth. Yet this perception belied the importance of experienced players, able to maintain their equanimity during the bedlam of the IPL.

In 2018, Chennai recruited 11 players over the age of 30 years old and four above 35. That season their average age of 34 years and six months was comfortably the oldest in the league: the nickname 'Dad's Army' naturally followed.

'This year we have really valued experience,' explained Fleming in a press conference after the auction. 'M.S. [Dhoni] and I are on the same wavelength that experience counts. So if you look at our side there's a lot of experience through there. Understanding an IPL and what's involved in an IPL.'

It was suspected that fielding would be one area of the game where Chennai's older side would cost them. Fielding standards as a whole were elevated by T20 but CSK's ageing squad was considered ill-suited to the athleticism of the modern game.

Yet fielding was one area of cricket that remained misunderstood. Chennai's older players were slightly slower movers in the field than younger opponents and this did mean they weren't as quick to the ball or as swift across the ground – but generally this might cost them four or five runs per match. The one area of fielding that impacted the scoreboard most significantly was catching, where Chennai's age was no impediment.

According to CricViz, Chennai's successful stop percentage of 63% was the third worst in the 2018 IPL season but their successful catch percentage of 80% was the third best. Across the season CricViz estimated that Chennai's fielding saved three runs per match – the second most of all teams.

Chennai's success with an older, less agile fielding team was a fascinating window into an unexplored area of the game. Dravid, who was considered one of India's finest cricketing thinkers, believed that fielding in T20 was fundamentally overvalued.

'If you go for a better fielder and his inexperience costs you because he bowls three full tosses at the back end of a T20, that's 18 runs,' said Dravid. 'I don't care how good a fielder he is, he is not going to save 18 runs in a T20 game. I am not saying the experienced guy won't go for a six but he might go for two twos and then the inexperienced guy has cost you eight runs and that's still a huge amount to save in the field just to be even.'

Dravid thought that in T20, where boundary hitting tended to be more decisive than strike rotation, it was possible to 'hide' weak fielders, whereas in 50-over cricket, where strike rotation mattered more and therefore more fielders were in the game, fielding had more value. 'In T20 you definitely need a very good long on and long off, you need a good deep point, deep square leg and a guy at deep midwicket. You need four or five guns and you need a good keeper, to take those stumpings or stop edges or take catches. The rest of the five guys, I would not compromise or I would not worry.'

Ultimately Chennai recognised that the impact of better ground fielding in the shortest format was normally very marginal. 'We are well covered in other areas,' said Dhoni in a post-match press conference during the 2019 season. 'We will never be a great fielding side, but we can be a safe fielding side. We might bleed a few runs here and there, but as long as we use our experience, we'll make it up with our batting and bowling.'

Chennai's faith in experience was rewarded with a third IPL title in 2018; Watson, approaching 37, scored a match-winning century in the final. CSK's season was defined by winning tight matches – eight of their victories came in the last over or by a margin of less than ten runs – with their know-how under pressure considered decisive.

'Experience matters under pressure,' said Dravid. 'The ability to handle India, the ability to handle everything that goes on around the IPL franchise and the pressure of it all.'

The very next season Chennai – who had retained 22 players of their title-winning squad – finished second in the league table before losing to Mumbai Indians in the final. Being one year older was no barrier to their success.

***

T20 was designed to be determined by very fine margins. The brevity of the format heightens the role of luck. Such a volatile game increases the need to manage and exploit home conditions. Teams that dominate at home in leagues often only require one or two wins away to ensure qualification.

Some teams can ask groundsmen to tailor pitches and boundary sizes to their strengths – for instance, a team with a strong seam attack might request pitches with pace and bounce. But in the IPL, franchises essentially drop into venues owned by the state associations for two months of the year. Rather than tailor the ground to the team, franchises need to tailor their team to the ground.

Chennai's home venue, the M.A. Chidambaram Stadium in Chepauk, is one of the most spin-friendly venues in world cricket. The hot weather in southern India bakes the soil, producing dry pitches where the ball grips and turns. Ever since the inaugural auction CSK structured their squad around these conditions, where they would play half their matches.

'We break the season into two halves: home matches and away legs,' explained CSK's chief executive Kasi Viswanathan in a 2019 interview with *The New Indian Express*. 'The first and foremost thing is each team plays seven matches at home and you have to maximise it. So our target is to win five of the seven matches we play at Chepauk. Then when we travel outside, we look to win three to four away fixtures which will take the count to about eight wins. That number will mostly put you through to the knockouts.' This was a basic strategy but it was one that was conspicuously underused: only 53% of T20 matches were won by the home team.

In the 2008 auction the off-spinner Ashwin and the left-arm spinner Shadab Jakati were joined by Muttiah Muralitharan to form a spin triumvirate, with Raina providing an occasional fourth option. In 2012 Jadeja replaced Jakati; recruiting quality spinners was a recurring theme of future auctions. By the end of the 2019 IPL, the only team to have bowled a higher proportion of spin overs than Chennai were Kolkata Knight Riders, who also built a bowling attack to exploit turning pitches at Eden Gardens.

Chennai's spin-heavy strategy both exploited home conditions and ensured that the team could use the most successful type of bowler extensively. Spinners boasted lower economy rates than pace bowlers in every single over of the innings, and many analysts believed most teams underbowled them. Between 2008 and 2019, 42% of Chennai's overs were bowled by spin, second only to KKR. In a match against RCB in 2014, Chennai bowled 17.4 overs of spin, the most ever by an IPL team.

To support their spin strategy, Chennai generally recruited Indian batsmen, who were typically more adept at playing spin, in the middle order and focused on overseas players as openers, where less spin was bowled. 'Playing in Chennai the one constant has always been the spinners. It has always turned here so that has been our home ground advantage,' explained Hussey.

'There's such a massive home advantage [at Chepauk],' said one IPL insider. 'More so than Eden Gardens, more so than Mohali. You take ten balls to get yourself in whereas normally you only take four to get yourself in; but the Chennai player takes six balls rather than ten. There's that swing. Other teams take too long to get into the game in Chennai and it's game over.'

Batting in Chepauk in Balls 1–10			
Team	**Strike Rate**	**Balls per Dismissal**	**Average**
CSK Batsmen	113.43	28	31.62
Away Batsmen	107.86	19	20.61

Chennai's success at home was not only founded on their squad building but also on their training methods. In the IPL's early seasons, Chennai and Mumbai – who also had an excellent home record – were the only two teams who regularly utilised 'middle practice'.

'That makes a difference because if you are practising on the square all the time the players are getting used to the pitches, the angles and boundary sizes,' explained Dravid. The difficulty was not all teams could exploit this advantage. 'Other teams are not able to do that because of the paucity of the square [number of pitches] or maybe they don't have that much clout [with the state association].'

By the end of the 2019 IPL, Chennai had won 41 of their 59 matches at the Chepauk, over two of every three they played, meaning they only had to win around one-third of their away games to reach the play-offs. Among all T20 teams only the Rajasthan Royals and Lancashire could boast a better home venue win percentage than Chennai's 69% in Chepauk.

In 2018 political protests in the first match at the venue led to the IPL governing council ruling that all Chennai's home matches should be shifted to an alternative venue. With six frontline spinners and Bravo's slower ball variations, Chennai had structured their squad around playing matches at the M.A. Chidambaram Stadium. 'Making sure we had good spinners to play in Chennai was a big focus at the 2018 auction,' said Hussey.

To most other teams the move away from their home venue – especially having placed it so central to their plans – would have dealt a terminal blow. Not Chennai. 'It was phenomenal,' said Hussey. 'But again I think it came down to the experience and attitude of the players and the leaders, the coaching staff and captain. No one complained about it. This is just what we are doing and we've got to get on with it.'

Chennai's remaining six home games were moved to Pune. Conditions at the MCA Stadium were the antithesis of M.A. Chidambaram Stadium. Instead of slow, low surfaces, Pune offered pace and bounce. Fortunately Fleming, Dhoni and a number of CSK players were able to draw on their experience at the venue with Rising Pune Supergiant where they had played during Chennai's two-year suspension. An injury to the spin bowler Mitchell Santner enabled Chennai to adjust their squad and they recruited South African quick Lungi Ngidi, who excelled. Despite the relocation, Chennai's flexibility helped them top the table after winning five of their six matches in Pune.

While Chennai dominated at home, whether that was in Chepauk or Pune, Bangalore floundered. T20 was played to a very different tempo at the M. Chinnaswamy Stadium. Notoriously flat pitches, tiny boundaries and being at altitude placed an emphasis on destructive batsmen who could utilise the advantages provided by the surroundings and, crucially, excellent bowlers who could nullify the threat of batsmen running riot.

'There is zero home advantage at Chinnaswamy. We tried to create one but there isn't one there because the surface is too good,' said Trent Woodhill, who worked at RCB as a batting and fielding coach. 'It's such a 50:50 playing field.'

In the early seasons RCB misunderstood not only the venue but the format. Their squad bore more resemblance to a Test match fantasy XI than a T20 XI. In the inaugural season Bangalore were regularly outhit by sides with more power.

By 2011 Bangalore addressed this problem, belatedly moving towards players more suited to the T20 format. But their shift to power hitters came at a cost. As RCB splurged money on Gayle, de Villiers and Dilshan they left themselves less to spend on bowlers.

'Looking back on some of the auctions and for RCB you always felt they will be chasing a gun death bowler,' said Dravid. 'Then the first thing you realise is they've spent 15 crores on Yuvraj Singh and you think, "Oh, shit! They aren't in the market for that!" and by the time a death bowler comes round they won't be able to spend any money so we can outbid them on that one.'

This unadulterated focus on batting prowess was a directive that insiders say came largely from Mallya, RCB's majority owner and chairman between 2008 and 2016. 'Mallya was the main decision-maker and he loved the superstars of batting,' said one anonymous source. 'Bowlers like Mustafizur Rahman were shouted down at the auction by Mallya because he wanted batting gurus.

'It started with Dravid, Kallis, and then it went to de Villiers and

Dilshan and Gayle. They were like the Yankees in the last couple of years. They've won nothing but fuck it's a good game to go and watch. They lose but they still hit a lot of home runs.'

The combination of Bangalore's batting might and the Chinnaswamy produced some of the most remarkable displays of batsmanship ever seen in cricket. In 2013 Gayle bludgeoned 175 not out, the highest T20 score of all time; in 2015 de Villiers and Kohli set a new world record for the highest partnership in history by adding 215. In 2016 the pair beat it, adding 229 in 96 balls during a season heralded as the apogee of T20 batsmanship: Kohli scored a season's record 973 runs in 16 innings, including four centuries, while de Villiers hit 687. With Gayle, Watson and Rahul also in the team, RCB's top five was among the most formidable ever assembled in T20.

'Definitely RCB were a batting team,' said the team insider. 'It just worked that way with the big three. They fell into it with Gayle, A.B. and Virat, and then found it difficult to afford the best bowlers.'

'Bangalore have never balanced their team very well,' observed Dravid. 'They had their best year when they had a bowler like Mitchell Starc who was able to close out games for them. But they kept going out and picking gun batsmen.'

The acclaim that followed Bangalore's batting was not reflected in results. While the Chinnaswamy may have produced brilliant entertainment it was such a good venue for batting that it also placed a great emphasis on quality bowling, particularly in the death overs where unchecked batsmen could run amok. 'They have never had a plan to counter the Chinnaswamy Stadium and particularly the difficulty of death bowling at the Chinnaswamy,' said Sundararaman, their former analyst. Teams and their strategies are shaped by their home venues and in this respect RCB deserve sympathy: the Chinnaswamy was a more difficult venue to tame than Chepauk.

RCB's batting-heavy approach was to embrace the fundamental inequity of T20 – a bowler was limited to 24 balls, while a batsman could be there for an entire innings – and prioritise players who could have the greatest possible impact on a game. When it came off, there was nothing quite like it, as anyone who went to the Chinnaswamy and witnessed one of those Kohli-de Villiers partnerships would attest. Bangalore's perfect game could probably beat anyone else's.

The snag was that securing those two required stumping up a lot of cash. In 2019, RCB paid Kohli and de Villiers a combined £3.47 million, over one-third of their entire allocated playing budget. Bangalore's bowling was consistently compromised by this spending imbalance. Across their history their only bowler who consistently excelled was the leg-spinner Yuzvendra Chahal. Pace bowlers in particular struggled.

While tapping into the inequity of T20 could bring benefits, the approach was laden with risk. On a near-perfect day a batsman might face 60 balls but on a bad day they might face just one. In contrast, bowlers could deliver 24 balls in every match. While the match involvement of a batsman was determined by how long they could survive, the match involvement of a bowler was determined by their captain.

This meant that on the very best days, when the batting clicked and everything fell into place, Bangalore could post and chase gargantuan totals. But the vulnerability of their bowling – particularly at home – meant that they found it very difficult to defend even very large totals. Bangalore won 51% of matches chasing but just 40% of matches when defending. The Chinnaswamy demanded a quality of bowler that Bangalore simply couldn't afford.

The problems associated with Bangalore's batting-heavy team were compounded by the way in which they deployed their batting stars. Aside from spending copious cash on batting firepower there was no discernible strategy that defined them. Instead there was something of a Fantasy XI feel about Bangalore: throw together some of the world's biggest hitters and hope for the best.

RCB bore similarities with Real Madrid's *galacticos* in the early and mid 2000s. Then, Real's President Florentino Pérez splurged hundreds of millions on some of the world's best attacking players – Luis Figo, Zinedine Zidane, Ronaldo, David Beckham, Michael Owen and Robinho – while neglecting defence. In 2003, the same summer as they signed Beckham, Real Madrid sold the defensive midfielder Claude Makelele, renowned for his undemonstrative work. 'He wasn't a header of the ball and he rarely passed the ball more than three metres . . . Younger players will arrive who will cause Makelele to be forgotten,' Pérez declared when Makelele was sold. Yet it took Real Madrid another eight seasons to next advance beyond the Champions League's quarter-finals. Their neglect of defence mirrored Bangalore's lack of regard for defence in T20.

Where RCB's batting lacked shape and structure, CSK's was defined by it. While some teams saw the Powerplay as an opportunity to get ahead in the game, Chennai generally saw it as a period to set up the rest of the innings. In run chases Chennai's steady Powerplay ensured they took the game deep; once they took it that far they were clinical. With experience and know-how at the death, Chennai won 57% of run chases that went to the last over, comfortably the highest proportion of any IPL team.

'The goal was always to get 40 or 45 runs for no wickets down in the first six overs,' recalled Hussey, who opened for CSK from 2010 to 2015. 'When I first started playing we knew we had the power to finish with Raina, Dhoni and Morkel. The idea was to keep wickets in hand for the back end.'

This was a strategy informed by Chennai's bowling strength and the lower-scoring nature of their home venue. By taking a measured approach to the first six overs and not risking a top order collapse by attacking too hard, Chennai ensured that, when they batted first, they could at least progress safely and post a respectable total. They could do this because their bowling was capable of defending even sub-par scores; RCB had to score above par to protect their weaker bowling. 'That's where Chennai have always been successful because they've often had stronger bowling than Bangalore,' said Dravid.

Though Chennai's batting had structure, they were not dogmatic in their approach. In 2014 and 2015 they adapted their strategy according to their resources, deploying the aggressive openers Dwayne Smith and McCullum in attacking roles in the Powerplay.

Chennai also showed flexibility with perhaps the most significant strategic decision in the game: the toss. Between 2008 and 2011 CSK batted first in 81% of matches when they won the toss. From 2012, they inverted that strategy, choosing to chase 62% of the time.

CSK's team of the early 2010s was among the first T20 sides to think in terms of roles rather than set positions. Below a solid opening pair – Vijay and either Hayden or Hussey – Chennai had a series of powerful hitters – left-handers Raina and Morkel and right-handers Dhoni and Bravo. These four would move up and down the order depending on the match situation, the opportunity to capitalise on a particularly short boundary or to exploit a favourable match-up.

In the victory in the 2010 IPL final, Dhoni came in at No. 5 and Morkel No. 6; when Chennai retained the title a year later, Dhoni batted at No. 3 and Morkel at No. 5. Sometimes both would bat lower; on other occasions, Morkel would bat above Dhoni.

Badrinath, a classical player with a modest T20 strike rate, was also used adroitly. If Chennai lost early wickets, Badrinath would come in early, often making crucial contributions. He walked in at 27-2 in a winner-takes-all league match in 2010, making 53; and at 1-2 in the 2012 elimination final, making 47. Otherwise he would bat lower down – he batted No. 7 ten times for Chennai, and No. 8 twice. Remarkably for a specialist batsman, Badrinath did not bat in 32 of his 114 games for Chennai. It was no indictment of his worth, merely a reflection that the circumstances did not call for his specific talents.

Roles applied to Chennai's bowling too. In the 2019 IPL Deepak Chahar, a classical seamer who bowled full and swung the ball, was deployed almost exclusively as a Powerplay bowler, regularly bowling three consecutive overs to start the innings. In contrast Dwayne Bravo was deployed almost entirely in the second half of the innings when his variations were most valuable.

This role-based approach to team-building was taken to a new extreme by Islamabad United in the Pakistan Super League. They didn't just adopt middle order flexibility, as CSK successfully did, but extended it to the entire order. Islamabad saw a batsman's position on the team sheet as merely the basis for negotiation. Anyone could be moved based on insights from statistics, observations of how the game was evolving, or simple gut feel.

At Islamabad, Andre Russell was used both as an opener and at No. 8. J.P. Duminy, a middle order player, was pushed up to open in 2018, to his surprise – but adapted well. Hussain Talat batted between Nos. 3 and 8; Asif Ali from opener to No. 8; Sahibzada Farhan from opener to No. 6. In a game in 2018, Shadab Khan batted at No. 10; six days later, he batted at No. 3 – one of six No. 3s Islamabad used in 12 games en route to the title that season.

***

Captaincy is arguably more important in cricket than any other major team sport. The importance of the strategic side of the game may be even greater in T20. In a format with such tiny margins between victory and defeat, the significance of every captaincy decision is amplified. This applies not only to macro-strategies – such as bowling changes and batting orders – but to micro-strategies such as field placements and ball-by-ball tactics.

'The value of every over is much more in T20,' said Dravid, who captained India, RCB and Rajasthan Royals. 'The ability to come back from a bad decision is much easier in 50-over or Test cricket than in T20.'

'In sports like NFL, NBA and soccer there are a lot of plans and strategies made but everything is done by the manager,' explained Sundararaman. 'They play a big role during the game from the sidelines. They are allowed to communicate, they are allowed to chat – they've been given more power. Whereas in cricket that is rarely the case. In franchise cricket you have coaches constantly changing. There's hardly any continuity. Coaches don't play a big role on the field; they play it off the field and during strategic timeouts but more or less it is run by the captain so the captain needs to be the one who makes sure plans get executed.'

There were many structural reasons why Chennai won and why Bangalore lost, but the captaincy of Dhoni and Kohli perpetuated these fundamental differences. Although Chennai's squad was well structured and Bangalore's was not, CSK consistently overperformed what could be expected from their playing strength; RCB did the opposite. The captaincy of Dhoni and Kohli was a big part of this.

To watch Dhoni and Kohli captain was to observe two strikingly contrasting operators. Dhoni epitomised equanimity: from behind the stumps he would calmly marshal his bowlers and his field, he rarely looked flustered and never looked panicked. 'He [Dhoni] is absolutely incredible. He is one of a kind to be honest. What people say about him is what you see. He is a very calm, cool, collected guy,' said Hussey.

Dhoni's phlegmatic leadership was juxtaposed by Kohli, who – often patrolling the boundary rope – was a hurricane of emotion. Wickets would send him into raptures; dropped catches into a frenzy. Boundaries would be met with a kick of the turf and a shake of the head. And, after defeats, he was far more prone to changing the team than Dhoni.

Kohli was an instinctive and impulsive captain, but his status as the game's most iconic player meant he could invigorate his players. 'He gets all the other members in the side inspired and motivated,' said Washington, who played at RCB in 2018 and 2019. 'His pep talks in particular have been very helpful for players to go out there and express themselves.'

Their respective appearances reflected the tactical clarity present at both teams. 'CSK has very little "white noise" around them,' observed McCullum. 'RCB have too much.'

Dhoni's brilliance as a tactician and the stability of his relationship with Fleming established the pair as the primary decision-makers at Chennai. Success on the field entrenched this hierarchy. 'Decision-making will come down to Flem and Dhoni at the end of the day,' said Hussey, batting coach in 2018 and 2019.

While Dhoni was the predominant strategist and tactician, he bounced ideas off Fleming and the pair challenged one another. 'There's a lot of trust between the two of them,' explained Billings.

The value of Dhoni's tactical nous to Chennai was highlighted in 2019; he missed two games with a back injury and Chennai were beaten on both occasions. '[Dhoni is] a great leader and a great player and he's been a constant for us for so many years that you get into the rhythms of having him there and when you take a leader like that out, there are going to be holes to fill,' explained Fleming after the second of CSK's two defeats without Dhoni.

At Bangalore, Kohli was appointed captain in 2013, aged just 24. Yet as the world's premier batsman, the face of Indian cricket and the heir apparent to Dhoni as Indian captain, he was the obvious choice to lead RCB. But in the seven IPL seasons until 2019, Kohli struggled to establish a strong strategic presence; in tight, tactical matches his judgement calls would often backfire. Unlike the stability of Chennai, Kohli worked with three different coaches in seven seasons.

'CSK are so good because Dhoni understands the format so well. But I think Virat doesn't get it at times,' said a former Bangalore player who also asked to remain anonymous.

In 2019, former KKR captain Gautam Gambhir became Kohli's most high-profile public critic. 'I don't see him as a shrewd captain and I don't see him as a tactful captain,' said Gambhir on Star Sports.

'You cannot compare him to someone like Rohit or Dhoni at this stage because he has been part of RCB, and captaining RCB for the last seven to eight years, and he has been very lucky and should be thanking the franchise that they stuck with him because not many captains have got such a long rope where they haven't won a tournament.'

Of course, to a large extent Kohli was hamstrung by RCB's weak squads. But it seemed that his leadership compounded rather than helped alleviate those problems.

Managing Kohli's impulses as captain was a constant battle for RCB's management. 'Virat is such a respectful guy that he is always going to listen to his elders,' said the team insider. '2016 was awesome because there was A.B., Shane Watson, and he was comfortable with them. He was able to trust Dan Vettori. And Vettori was excellent. So those two had a really close relationship.'

However, the insider believed that the appointment of former Indian fast bowler Nehra as bowling coach in 2018 derailed things and tensions rose at the franchise. In 2019, by which point Vettori had been sacked as head coach, Nehra could be seen directing Kohli's bowling and field changes from the sidelines, and his influence illustrated the challenge of nurturing a productive team environment in the IPL. Too many voices could quickly become confusing and overwhelming.

Unlike Kohli, Dhoni appeared to have a preternatural understanding of captaincy. The speed and effectiveness at which he read the game was remarkable. 'His feel for the game is second to none, there is no doubt about that,' said Billings. By the end of the 2019 IPL, Dhoni had played 862 matches at professional level in all formats and captained in 547 of them; only eight players in the history of the game had captained more often. This vast memory bank of experience gave Dhoni a mind unlike any other in the modern game.

'Dhoni is very calm and knows what is needed in the situation of the game and the conditions,' said the off-spinner Washington, who played under Dhoni at Rising Pune Supergiant. 'He knows how to get the best out of every individual. As a bowler if I listen to what he says, half the job is done and things get a little easier because there's no room for confusion.'

Chennai used data analysis behind the scenes but Dhoni was very rarely exposed to it. It wasn't that CSK rejected the premise of calculated decision-making. Instead, Dhoni's mind, fine-tuned by 100s of matches, did the calculations alone, like a cricket supercomputer. 'He quite often goes with his gut and quite often his gut is right. It's amazing sometimes watching him go to work out there,' said Hussey.

Often Dhoni's reading of the game would be supported by data but occasionally his interpretation would challenge the numbers. For example, in a match against KKR in the 2019 IPL the data would have dissuaded most captains from bowling spin to Sunil Narine. Dhoni calculated that Harbhajan was one spin bowler who matched up well with Narine because of his slower speeds. It took Harbhajan just four balls to get his man when a slow, wide tempter beat Narine in the air and took the edge.

'Dhoni knew that if he bowls at this speed on this pitch Narine will get out and that's exactly what happened,' said Sundararaman.

At Chennai Dhoni's influence extended beyond the playing field. Hussey believed Dhoni's calmness informed the franchise's stability and consistency of selection. 'He hardly ever panics and that comes through obviously with all the selections. If there's any thought of chopping and changing things – he will generally take a step back and take a big deep breath and say no, no come on it's okay.' Dhoni's equanimity meant that he understood the uncertainty inherent in T20 and avoided overreacting to defeats, giving Chennai the best chance of enjoying sustained success.

Before the 2020 IPL, RCB enacted a major overhaul of their team management, appointing Mike Hesson as Director of Cricket Operations and Simon Katich as head coach. Although Kohli remained captain, Hesson and Katich embraced significant change, releasing six of Bangalore's eight overseas players. At the auction, Bangalore invested in four overseas quick bowlers, which represented a move away from the batting-heavy approach for which they were renowned. Bangalore even changed their logo to a logo, declaring 'A new chapter begins'. It amounted to belated recognition that their previous imbalanced approach had failed.

***

The cocktail of Dhoni's captaincy, the role clarity produced by Chennai's consistency of selection and the experience in the squad bred a remarkable team environment.

After CSK won their opening two matches in 2019 Dwayne Bravo revealed that Chennai, one of the most successful teams in T20 history, 'don't have team meetings'.

'We don't plan,' said Bravo in a press conference. 'We just turn up, go with the flow on any given day. We just watch the situation and adjust and adapt quickly. That's where the experience comes in.'

The coaches interacted with players on a one-on-one basis and occasionally in small groups but entire team meetings were very rare. 'I guess the Indian culture is a bit different in that respect. It's not like a Western culture where you come together as a team and map things out. It's a bit more fluid,' said Hussey. 'Flem certainly talks to the whole team but it sort of organically evolves. It might be sort of before training or in the dressing room after a game. That's where he addresses things as a whole or as a team. Very rarely would we organise a get-together.'

In many respects this was the acme of T20 strategy. Chennai had built their squad so carefully, defined their player roles so clearly and grooved their method so consistently that very little needed to be said for them to perform. 'Everyone knew their roles pretty clearly anyway so there was no need to confuse things with meaningless meetings,' Hussey explained.

T20 was so young, the seasons were so short and the competition was often haphazard and confused with players and coaches coming and going. Yet in a game as volatile as T20, Chennai's record of progressing to the play-offs in every season was a beacon of sustained excellence.

'In any sport it's very hard to be that consistent,' observed Sundararaman. 'If you look at Premier League football it's very hard to finish in the top four every single year and in T20 it's even harder because it is so volatile.

'It's a great achievement. One of the biggest achievements in sporting history since T20 was created. It's not easy for a franchise to do what they've done. They have a great captain and a great culture.'

Chennai's extraordinary dominance and Bangalore's perpetual struggle carried lessons for teams in different leagues around the world. It affirmed that simply buying the world's very best players would not guarantee success. There was strategy, man-management and nuance to T20 that proved more important than even the most star-studded team in the world.

FOURTEEN

THE DEMOCRATISATION OF CRICKET

'Not just me, but the entire nation is proud of you'
**Nepal's prime minister Sher Bahadur Deuba after 17-year-old Sandeep
Lamichhane was signed by the Indian Premier League in 2018**

When Rashid Khan was born in Afghanistan – officially in 1998, though some suggest it was a couple of years earlier – the International Cricket Council had around 100 members. Afghanistan were not even among them.

Cricket in Afghanistan was a legacy of war. Afghans first came across the game in the 1980s, when they were refugees in Pakistan, principally Peshawar. Many watched Pakistan win the World Cup in 1992. In refugee camps thousands of Afghans forged a love for cricket, playing with a stick for a bat and tennis balls, or even just plastic bags wrapped up to make a ball. They took this new love back with them to Afghanistan.

In 1995, the Afghanistan Cricket Federation was formed. Despite its English origins, the sport was tolerated by the Taliban because of its conservative dress code and its popularity in Pakistan, one of only three states who recognised the Taliban as Afghanistan's official government.

And so when Rashid was born in Jalalabad, the capital of Nangarhar province, the notion that he would become one of the greatest cricketers of his age was completely fantastical. Afghanistan had no cricketing infrastructure, no fixtures and no way of developing players.

Rashid was the sixth-born child in his family; there would eventually be 11 – seven boys and four girls. Shortly after the US attacks on Afghanistan, which began in October 2001, Rashid fled with his family to Peshawar – where, as Afghans had during the Afghan-Soviet Union War in the 1980s, they learned cricket.

Yet Rashid and his family were different to the stereotype of Afghan refugees. They were part of Afghanistan's middle class; their parents worked in a car business, and dreamed of Rashid becoming a doctor.

Rashid spent around a decade in Pakistan. Although he and his family sometimes returned to their home in Jalalabad, it was only at the end of 2013 that they returned there for good. In Pakistan, Rashid and his six brothers all bowled leg spin.

In Peshawar and then back in Jalalabad, Rashid would play cricket with a tape-ball – a tennis ball covered in tape. 'I was playing a lot at home – three, four hours, playing with the brothers every day. That improved my game and my skills.' In the family backyard or on the street, Rashid constantly devised new variations. The environment required experimentation to get ahead, with Rashid even trying to learn from Muttiah Muralitharan.

'I used to bowl sometimes off spin, sometimes leg spin, sometimes the Murali action you know – just having fun. I loved bowling leg spin. I watched Shahid Afridi, Anil Kumble – these two were my favourites, I used to watch their videos a lot. So that's how I was capable of bowling the leg spin very well. I had the skills and I had the talent in the leg spin that could turn the ball both ways.'

More than anyone else, Rashid very deliberately borrowed from Shahid Afridi, Pakistan's leg-spinning all-rounder. Several other international leg-spinners were more renowned than Afridi, but as he hailed from Khyber, along the border with Afghanistan, he was a natural idol for young Afghan cricketers. Afridi's leg spin, unusually quick, was also ideally suited to limited overs cricket. And his celebration – extending himself out to resemble a star after each wicket – was fun to imitate.

Turning a tape-ball on cement is reckoned to be tougher than turning a hard ball on a cricket pitch. 'I got used to the tape-ball and turning the ball,' Rashid said. 'It was really tough to spin the ball but still I was spinning the ball on any surface – on cement and rough areas I was trying to spin it.' The difficulty of obtaining spin encouraged Rashid to bowl quicker than other spinners, as Afridi did, giving him another weapon if the ball did not turn.

Rashid was 14 when he first played cricket with a hard ball, in a game in Peshawar. 'My friend was going to play a hard-ball game. He told me,

"Let's go – we have only ten players so can you please just go and fill the place."' Then mainly a batsman, Rashid scored 65 in his first game. 'I loved the game and I loved the hard-ball. I started thinking that I should play hard ball cricket and improve my skills and practise more and more.' When bowling with a hard ball, Rashid used the 'same grips' he had honed with a tape-ball, and found they transferred well.

As Rashid entered his teens, Afghanistan's national team soared. With a potent bowling attack, initially tailored around pace, and some brutal hitters throughout their batting order, Afghanistan took just six years between their first official international match, in 2004, and their first global event, the T20 World Cup in 2010, where Rashid first saw them play on TV. 'When I saw the international side playing in the international level, then the motivation and everything started. I just tried my best to represent my country.'

When Rashid returned home, 'we hardly had some good facilities, or some good grounds in Afghanistan. It was not green,' he joked. He resolved to pursue his cricket with greater intensity. 'When we came back home I played a lot – it was a little bit serious. And I thought, "Yeah I'm good enough, I just need to give a bit of time to it and improve my skills."' Rashid realised that his leg spin, rather than batting, was more likely to elevate his career; he had noted how leg-spinners were thriving in T20. 'In every net session, I'm just trying my best to learn something new. I'm just experimenting with myself in the net sessions.'

In an age when talent production in elite sport can seem almost industrialised, Rashid is essentially an entirely self-taught cricketer who has reached the apex of his sport. Three months in Afghanistan's academy were the limit of his formal coaching before playing international cricket. And, in the academy, as with Rashid's subsequent teams, the coaches refrained from tinkering with his method. He considers his lack of formal coaching an advantage.

'I think if I would have changed my action I would have lost my consistency, I would have lost my speed and my rhythm and everything. So I think whatever I have is something natural.

'The coaches I've had in the national team have said the same thing – this is your advantage and this is your main weapon. You're getting the success because you're different than others and have a quick arm action, you have the speed so you don't need to change these things. You just need to have something in your mind to be calm and cool and relaxed and enjoy yourself.'

After thriving in Afghanistan's domestic cricket and in the U-19 World Cup, Rashid made his one-day international debut against Zimbabwe in late 2015, aged 17. 'Representing a country, which has faced lots of difficulties – in war, and these things – it really felt something special.' Immediately his combination of accurate leg spin at high speeds, and an almost indecipherable googly, marked Rashid out as a thrilling player. In 2016 he thrived in the T20 World Cup in India. A year later, Rashid was signed up by the IPL.

***

Since its earliest days, cricket has been a sport besotted with hierarchies. From the distinction between 'Gentlemen' (wealthy cricketers who played as unpaid amateurs) and 'Players' (grubby professionals who played for money) which survived in England until 1962, to the distinction between Full and Associate Members of the ICC, and the existence of Test and one-day international 'status' for matches, cricket has always sought to demarcate strictly between those inside its hallowed elite and those locked outside the gates.

The size of its global events embodies cricket's elitism, conservatism and disregard for those on the outside looking in. The 2019 Cricket World Cup – the men's World Cup in the 50-over format – contained only ten teams, a reduction of six from 2007. Perversely the reduction, according to numerous ICC sources, was driven by emerging countries having the temerity to win matches they shouldn't have done, thereby knocking India and Pakistan, and their enormous television audiences, out in the first round of the 2007 World Cup. The men's T20 World Cup, lauded as the globalisation vehicle, was only scheduled to include 12 teams in its main stage in 2012 – the same as kabaddi, eight fewer than rugby union and 20 fewer than basketball. International cricket, with its strict divisions between teams, and the way in which fixtures and money are tied to a country's status rather than their on-field results, has been where meritocracy goes to die.

T20 holds out the hope of shattering this elitist cabal. While the pinnacle of 50-over and multi-day cricket remains in the international game, the ecosystem of T20 much more closely resembles that of football and other sports. The format's World Cup has huge appeal and is the flagship tournament. But besides that event – about a month every two years – the most high-profile T20 is found in domestic leagues.

Such leagues don't care where cricketers are from, or what status their nation is – only their quality. And so for cricketers from outside cricket's elite nations, T20 leagues offer the promise of a path from obscurity to playing with and against the world's best.

A few years earlier, before the T20 boom, Rashid's journey would have been inconceivable. His talent wouldn't have mattered when set against the biggest problem: Rashid was from Afghanistan, and cricketers from outside the Full Members were automatically treated as second rate. Their countries were denied fixtures, funding or a fair chance. However talented a player, he would have scant chance of rising above obscurity.

T20 takes a revolutionary approach to determining what a player may be able to achieve: domestic teams judge players on how they play, not where they come from. The format is cricket's great democratising tool, a unique avenue for players from smaller nations to be elevated to the elite.

At the start of his career, Rashid was still hampered by teams thinking of cricketers through the prism of these old hierarchies. If a cricketer was from outside the old ten Full Members, it followed that they were less good. England, extraordinarily, still bar all players not from Full Member nations from being overseas players.

In the first years of the IPL, the best way to get a contract as an overseas player was to be Australian. It helped that there were so many Australian coaches. From 2008 to 2018, the average Australian coach picked 2.8 Australians among their overseas players each season, according to the T20 analyst Dan Weston; the average coach not from Australia picked half as many Australians. Too often squads in the IPL, and beyond, were determined by who players knew, not what they could do.

'Somebody has to be the first,' said Kabir Khan, then the Afghanistan coach, in 2012. 'Somebody has to be the first to have a contract with a county, or in grade cricket or in the IPL, the Bangladesh league or the Sri Lankan league.

'If the door is open, you can go through it. At the moment the door is shut, and we want someone to start to open it.'

Four years later, Rashid thrived in the T20 World Cup. Yet still he found it hard to get a chance in T20 leagues around the world.

A.R. Srikkanth, the meticulous analyst for Kolkata and in other leagues, was the first to sign Rashid up to a major league, recruiting him to the Bangladesh Premier League at the end of 2016. Rashid excelled, conceding only six runs an over.

Watching Rashid's performance, Srikkanth immediately started messaging Kolkata's senior figures about Rashid over WhatsApp, arguing that Rashid would augment Kolkata's spin-heavy strategy. But Gautam Gambhir, KKR's captain at the time, was unconvinced.

'Gambhir didn't know much about Rashid and didn't quite trust my word at that point of time,' Srikkanth recalled. This was indicative of the wider perception of players from less-renowned nations, even at a time when Afghanistan had already played in several World Cups. 'Teams did not take players from less-known countries from a cricketing perspective seriously. Teams and especially captains did not trust these players' skills.'

A few other Associate players – the Netherlands pair Ryan ten Doeschate and Dirk Nannes, who subsequently represented Australia; and Kenya's Tanmay Mishra, who played as a local due to his Indian parents – had come before Rashid. But he and Mohammad Nabi could be considered the first cricketers born and raised in an Associate country to get an IPL contract as overseas players. And unlike ten Doeschate and Nannes, the Afghan pair earned their contracts through their performances outside the Full Member sphere.

Before the 2017 IPL auction, Sunrisers Hyderabad wanted to recruit an elite spinner to bowl in the middle overs of the innings. The more they scrutinised the numbers, the more they realised that there was no one better than Rashid.

'We specifically went for Rashid Khan because we felt that he was going to have a massive influence in the middle overs of the game,' explained Tom Moody, Sunrisers coach when they signed Rashid. 'We shortlisted, and then once he was on our shortlist we then dug in deeper, and that's when the analyst comes in and gives us some real back-end information that we might not know. He also gave me endless footage of certain situations – not only when he bowled well, but when he was challenged, and who challenged him, and how that comes about. So you slice and dice as much as you can to come to what you hope is going to be the right decision.'

Moody looked beyond Rashid's nationality, and saw only his skills. 'I watched what Rashid was doing to the likes of Ireland and others, through video, and I still felt what he was capable of doing as a bowler was going to challenge anyone,' he recalled. 'People argued at the time, "Yeah, but they're not doing it against the bigger countries" – and all that type of stuff – and to me that wasn't a major issue.

'You saw him bowl and what he was capable of doing and how he was defeating his opponent – whether it was beating him with turn in the air, turn off the wicket, or shape in the air, or batsmen totally misreading him. That was enough for me. Because I'd just seen how T20 had gone up to that point where anyone that could move the ball both ways, and there was a mystery attached to that, became very valuable. The biggest challenge he had to face – I feel, and the only risk we were taking – was how he adapted to the big stage. That, to me, was the only risk. To me, he had the goods. It was just a case of did he have the character. And he had that in spades.'

A few hours before Rashid's name was called in the 2017 auction, the name of Mohammad Nabi, his Afghan teammate was read out. Nabi, an all-rounder who bowled off spin, was picked up by Moody and Sunrisers – thereby becoming the first-ever player to grow up in an Associate nation signed as an overseas player in the IPL. Rashid attracted a bidding war between Sunrisers and Mumbai Indians, and was sold to Sunrisers for four crore (£450,000).

'I always watched IPL on TV, but when you're coming from a country like Afghanistan, playing in the IPL is more than special,' Rashid said. 'It was a special feeling, a proud feeling, for me and my country as well to represent Afghanistan in the IPL – IPL is the biggest league in the world.'

When he arrived in the IPL, Rashid 'was so nervous'. His coach, Moody, spoke to Rashid before his first game. 'He told me, "Don't be stressed about the franchise, don't be stressed about anything, don't think about the money that you got, you're just here, enjoy it – show your skills. Be clear in your mind. We are here to support you – you have enough talent to surprise each and every one. One thing that will test you will be how you control your mood, how you control yourself. We are behind you, so go out and enjoy yourself." That was the message I got from him.'

Rashid got a wicket with his fourth ball on his IPL debut. Ten days later, he played against Kolkata – whose analyst had wanted to sign him but whose captain had not. The first ball that Rashid bowled to Gambhir, the batsman attempted a cut and misread the turn – playing for spin that wasn't there. Gambhir was clean bowled. After he was dismissed, Gambhir turned to Srikkanth in the Kolkata dressing room: 'Good spotting,' he said. Rashid ended his first season with 17 wickets, at a better economy rate than the five bowlers with more, and established as one of T20's most thrilling talents.

By early 2018, Rashid was already officially rated as the number one T20 bowler in the world, and among the most sought-after names in T20 leagues the world over. His real impact went much deeper.

Blast walls are erected to protect people and buildings from the after-effects of explosions. One such wall in Kabul, erected in 2018, was emblazoned with a caption: 'Faces of new Afghanistan'. The mural features leading Afghans trying to shape a new image for the country – women's and children's rights advocates, award-winning journalists and photographers, and female members of an Afghan orchestra who have performed all over the world, defying the threats they receive at home.

Included among this list was Rashid, about to bowl a ball. He was not just a brilliant cricketer, but a cricketer whose impact transcended sport.

'It makes you feel very, very special to be in that stage in that place and have your photo imprinted with people who have lots of achievements for Afghanistan. It's really special to be among them. I feel really blessed – you can't believe to get that sort of achievement in a very short period of time. To be playing four years and getting that sort of success and to a stage like that – it's more than a dream.'

Just as promised on that mural, Rashid believed that cricketing success is giving a new image to Afghanistan. 'Sport is the only thing that brings peace to the country,' he said. 'So it's a wonderful feeling to see the youngsters playing cricket.'

Rashid's schedule took him all over the world; in 2018, he only returned home once. But in his occasional forays back to Afghanistan, he observed how academies and the streets brimmed with children bowling leg spin, inspired by him as Rashid once was by Afridi. 'I really love to watch.'

***

Most T20 bowlers could be placed somewhere on a scale between attacking – taking wickets at a low strike rate – and containing – conceding a low economy rate. Rashid, uniquely, was exceptional on both scales.

Between Rashid's T20 debut in October 2015 and the start of 2019 he was absurdly dominant, snaring an astonishing 214 wickets. Among bowlers to deliver more than 1,000 balls in this period, only four bowlers had a lower strike rate than Rashid's 15.3 balls per wicket – and all of them were quicks who bowled at the death where wickets fell more regularly. Not a single bowler had a lower economy rate than Rashid's 6.04 runs per over. No one came close to matching Rashid's mastery of attack and defence.

'I basically just used him at any time I needed a wicket or it was the hardest over in the game and he absolutely loves it,' said Luke Wright, who captained Rashid in the T20 Blast in 2018, when Sussex reached the final. 'He joined us as an absolute superstar but his enthusiasm is how you'd expect an academy lad to come through and play. Just absolutely was mad for it, excited to play the games, and diving around in the field. I'd say where do you want to bowl and when do you want to bowl? And he said you tell me – I'll bowl any over and I'll bowl from any end. So for a captain that's amazing. Sometimes you get characters who if you ask to bowl into the wind they don't want to do it, so when someone like Rashid Khan turns up it's brilliant.'

At Sussex and elsewhere, Rashid's brilliance lifted his teammates. 'It gives you a lot more flexibility. We'd see that some teams just try to see him out and they aren't worried about runs – they just don't want to let him get four-for but in doing so when you are just trying to defend he still gets people out. Then when some teams try to target him he is so tough to hit that he takes wickets.

'It has a knock-on effect on the other bowlers. They then have to go harder at other people and other people get wickets because they have to go harder and try and target them.'

Rashid was to T20 bowling what Chris Gayle was to T20 batting: a remarkable outlier, both in his statistics and his technique. Other leg-spinners who have reached the apex of the game through traditional techniques – like Australia's Adam Zampa and England's Adil Rashid – have since changed their method to be more like Rashid.

In longer formats of cricket, leg-spinners tried to beat batsmen in the air by tossing the ball up above their eyeline at slow speeds and on full lengths. This attacking philosophy and the unnatural wrist rotations involved in delivery meant that leg-spinners had historically been strike bowlers but also expensive bowlers. The rise of T20 and the growth of power hitting necessitated the evolution of a new breed of leg-spinner. Samuel Badree introduced this new method but Rashid perfected it and was at the forefront of an era dominated by spin bowlers. At one point in 2018 nine of the top ten spots in the ICC T20 international bowling rankings were occupied by wrist spinners. These bowlers generally bowled flatter, faster and shorter, keeping the ball away from the batsman's arc, and they bowled a high proportion of googlies to complicate attacking batting.

A comparison of Shane Warne – an old-school leg-spinner and its most famous exponent – and Rashid, encapsulates the transformation in leg spin across the last decade.

The Evolution of Leg Spin in T20 Cricket		
Shane Warne (2008–13)		**Rashid Khan (2015–19)**
49 mph	Average Speed	57 mph
4.85 metres	Average Length	5.15 metres
3.93°	Average Spin	2.05°
1.02°	Average Drift	0.55°
30%	Full Length	24%
34%	Good Length	26%
36%	Short Length	50%
4%	Googly	40%

'We used to always tell spinners to have more patience than the batsman,' recalled Warne. 'Bowl ball after ball after ball in the right spot. Just keep bowling it. Now, with so much white-ball cricket you are told never to bowl the same ball twice.'

Most spin bowlers, especially leg-spinners, didn't really have a run-up – it was more of a slow gather or at most a bustling walk. Rashid, like Afridi, ran up to and through the crease and this speed created momentum for a rapid delivery motion where Rashid's fast arm speed sent the ball fizzing down the pitch. Warne noted that this fast arm made his action particularly challenging to decipher during day-night matches, when batsmen found it slightly harder to pick out his action closely: indeed, Rashid has a notably better record in day-night matches than day games.

While Rashid's pace remained significantly slower than pace bowlers – so he still benefited from keeping pace off the ball, like all spinners – bowling slightly faster gave the batsmen less time to read the line and the length and play the ball. 'The quick arm action and the speed I'm bowling it makes it tough to work out which way it is going.'

As well as bowling faster than most wrist spinners Rashid also bowled a lot flatter. Firing the ball down out of his hand rather than up. One traditional drill that spin bowlers would use to help with their flight is to bowl a ball over a piece of string suspended about a metre high halfway down the pitch; with Rashid it was more likely that he would look to squeeze the ball beneath the string instead.

Rashid's fast release speeds and flat trajectory caused the ball to skid off the pitch, which allowed him to bowl shorter lengths and keep balls out of the batsmen's arcs, making it harder for them to 'step and hit'.

At Rashid's speed, line was perhaps more important than length. Rashid bowled a relentlessly tight line to both right-handers and left-handers, giving them no room to free their arms; 53.6% of his dismissals were bowled or lbw, the second-highest percentage of any bowler in T20 to have bowled in more than 100 innings. 'The more you bowl wicket to wicket, the more it makes it difficult for the batsman,' Rashid explained. 'If he makes a little mistake he's gone. So mostly I'm looking to bowl wicket to wicket.'

What elevated Rashid wasn't just where he bowled but what he bowled. Rashid's googly was brilliantly controlled and almost impossible to read from the hand; at such a high speed, it was even more difficult to play it off the pitch. Rashid bowled googlies 40% of the time – ten times as many as Warne in T20, and comfortably the highest proportion of any wrist spinner in the world. 'When someone is not reading you and someone doesn't know which way it is going, then if you bowl four or five in an over then that is also fine. If someone is not reading you and someone is not picking it up you should bowl it more.'

Rashid could bowl googlies so regularly without being deciphered because, unlike most leg-spinners, he used his fingers, more than his wrist, so batsmen could not scour his wrist for clues about when he was bowling a googly. Rashid made only the slightest adjustment to his grip, which was barely discernible to the batsman. He disguised his googly like an elite poker player concealing a flush. 'The release point is the same for both wrong one and leg spin. I think that makes it a little bit tough for the batsman. The googly is my main weapon.'

While other wrist spinners generated revolutions on the ball by rolling their wrist in a way that one might turn a door handle, Rashid instead only used his wrist to get into his release position and then imparted revs using his fingers. The wrist rotation of typical leg-spinners allowed them to turn the ball far but compromised their control. By using his fingers to spin the ball Rashid sacrificed his degrees of spin – and he did turn the ball less than typical leg-spinners – but gained essential control.

Rashid's speed harried batsmen; his line and length cramped them. All the while, the direction of spin – into the batsman, away from him or not turning at all – changed almost every other ball. Compared to T20 leg-spinners who had come before him, Rashid was faster, flatter, shorter, straighter, more varied and unerringly accurate. This template rose above the conditions and match situations, allowing Rashid to succeed all around the world on a variety of pitches and in all three phases of the innings.

The Third Era of Spin Bowling – Leading Spin Wicket-Takers, 2015–June 2019		
Bowler	**Spin Type**	**Wickets**
Rashid Khan	Wrist Spin	254
Imran Tahir	Wrist Spin	194
Sunil Narine	Mystery Spin	181
Shakib Al Hasan	Finger Spin	174
Shahid Afridi	Wrist Spin	156
Mohammad Nabi	Finger Spin	156
Yuzvendra Chahal	Wrist Spin	141
Ish Sodhi	Wrist Spin	133
Adam Zampa	Wrist Spin	117
Shadab Khan	Wrist Spin	103
Piyush Chawla	Wrist Spin	102
Imad Wasim	Finger Spin	99
Kuldeep Yadav	Wrist Spin	98

Wisden Cricketers' Almanack occupies a unique place in the sport. It is an annual that doubles as a moral authority on the game it covers. Each year since 1889, the Almanack has selected its five cricketers of the year: a moment that is considered a news event in its own right.

Virtually all of the most famous names in the sport have been selected among the Almanack's cricketers of the year. And yet only players who represented ten countries – the first ten to play Test cricket – have ever been honoured in this way, which speaks of cricket's insularity. (A couple of players raised away from these ten nations, like England's Irish-born Eoin Morgan, have won the award – but only when they were representing one of the old ten countries in international cricket.)

In 2018, Wisden created a new award: the Leading T20 Cricketer in the World award. Rashid was the inaugural winner: a perfect distillation of how T20 has democratised cricket. Unlike traditional international cricket, the IPL doesn't care about hierarchies or status. Only cricketers from 12 countries – ten before 2017 – are allowed to play Test matches. The IPL is a democracy in which everyone is welcome. (Well, not entirely everyone: Pakistani players are banned because of the geopolitical situation between India and Pakistan and some Sri Lankans have been banned due to political tensions.)

One of the greatest virtues of the IPL is its contempt for cricket's traditional hierarchies: a league that doesn't care about a player's passport or history, only their ability to help win cricket matches.

And while Associate players receive scant salaries from their international fixtures – leading Associate players very seldom earn more than £30,000 a year from their penurious national boards – T20 leagues allow them to earn what they're worth. While Rashid had a comfortable home life before – 'We had money, it's not about that we had no home or cars,' he explained – his IPL contract showed how T20 leagues created a stage on which players from emerging nations were equal to those from cricket's traditional powerhouses.

T20 leagues also meant that players from the sport's Full Members could be paid what they were worth, rather than this being determined by the nationality on their passport. In international cricket in 2017, ESPNcricinfo found, New Zealand's captain Kane Williamson earned £0.19 million, while England's captain Joe Root earned £1.05 million – even though Williamson is ranked a better batsman in Tests and T20 internationals. Yet in the 2018 IPL, Williamson was sold for three crore (£330,000) while Root went unsold. That season, Williamson was the top run-scorer in the competition, captaining Sunrisers to the final.

In his debut season in the IPL Rashid did more than just enjoy stunning success. By showing what talent existed beyond the sport's traditional outposts, he served as a gateway for all players from beyond cricket's old ten Test nations to enter the hallowed world of T20 leagues.

Rashid's remarkable impact – he proved even more effective in the Caribbean Premier League, where he got a hat-trick just with his googlies, and in Australia's Big Bash than in his first season in India – led to leading T20 minds actively scouting Afghanistan in search of similarly precocious talents.

Teams focused especially on mystery spinners. Spinners had shown themselves the most valuable bowlers of all in T20; those spinners who, like Rashid, were uncoached and had unique actions, were especially potent. One of the joys of T20 has been that, especially among spinners, the format has encouraged individuality of style; the less identikit a spinner's action, the more effective they tend to be. T20 has placed a premium on bowlers nurtured away from the almost industrialised talent production systems in countries like Australia and England, where cricketers can appear as if mass-produced. Such idiosyncratic talents are more likely to be found outside the sport's traditional economic and sporting powerhouses.

After Rashid and Nabi, scouts kept returning to Afghanistan, and kept finding more talent. 'In Afghanistan, everyone loves spin, it's like a natural talent they have,' Rashid said. 'They just need to be polished up to come into international cricket and show their skills. They have enough talent, they have enough skills. It's all about something natural – naturally they have good power in their fingers in the schools. That's how I think we're getting more spinners from Afghanistan rather than the fast bowlers.'

In the 2018 IPL, three Afghan teenage spinners – Rashid, the left-arm wrist spinner Zahir Khan and Mujeeb Zadran, who possessed so many different variations he was best classed simply as a mystery bowler – had contracts.

***

The ascent of T20 led to, for the first time in cricket history, Associate nations creating high-profile domestic leagues, featuring overseas players and televised around the world, either on TV networks or over YouTube. The economic landscape for such leagues was challenging; like many T20 leagues the world over, they consistently made a loss in their first years, while attempting to build up an audience and their commercial worth. But for players in Associate nations such leagues created an avenue for them to learn from established players, showcase their talents and ultimately be picked up by more prestigious leagues.

In 2016, Cricket Hong Kong, the sport's governing body in Hong Kong, created the Hong Kong Blitz, a short franchise T20 competition that featured private investment and five overseas players per team. It was the first of its kind in an Associate nation.

In March 2015 Nepal's coach Pubudu Dassanayake was on his way to the wedding of Nepal cricketer Basant Regmi. Halfway through the six-hour drive from Kathmandu, Dassanayake stopped in the city of Bharatpur. Dassanayake was invited to check out the local talent. 'I went to the small cricket grounds next to the main road and there were about ten youngsters training inside a net,' he recalls. Dassanayake's eyes were drawn to Sandeep Lamichhane, a leg-spinner who was 14 at the time and had learned how to bowl leg spin following Shane Warne. 'I used to watch him on TV and follow him on YouTube,' Lamichhane recalled. 'I used to watch his videos and follow his action in my childhood.'

A few weeks later, Lamichhane was included in an U-19 camp. In November 2015, he played an unofficial match for Nepal against a touring MCC team. One MCC player, Hong Kong's Scott McKechnie, then recommended that Kowloon Cantons, a side in the Hong Kong Blitz, recruit Lamichhane in the first year of the competition.

In Hong Kong's inaugural T20 Blitz tournament, Lamichhane impressed the former Australian captain Michael Clarke, who joked at training he should move to Australia as they need a good leg-spinner. Clarke helped Lamichhane get a contract for Western Suburbs, his club side in Sydney. 'Playing in Hong Kong was the biggest turning point in my career because I went there and met Clarke,' Lamichhane said. 'When I went there I had nothing with me.'

Lamichhane's experiences in Hong Kong and Australia helped him thrive in lower levels of international cricket for Nepal. Rashid had shown that this could be the catalyst for wider recognition. 'When Rashid can do it why can't I? That's what I asked myself.'

As word of Lamichhane's talent spread, the agent Talha Aisham enlisted Mushtaq Ahmed, a former Pakistan leg-spinner, to look at footage of his bowling. Aisham subsequently signed Lamichhane, helping to put him into the draft list for T20 leagues, and get him a contract in the Bangladesh Premier League in 2017. 'It was a difficult job to convince the T20 leagues around the world to give him a chance, especially when he was from an Associate cricket nation,' Aisham said, suggesting that franchises are still less willing to entrust in players from emerging countries.

In January 2018, Lamichhane was training with Nepal in Dubai, when one of the team officials interrupted the practice session with the news that he had been signed by Delhi Daredevils, who picked him up for INR 20 lakh (£23,000) in the final round of the IPL auction. 'Everyone came to me and congratulated me – they were really happy everyone. I was so excited.' In the new world of T20, domestic leagues in Associate countries had now become a pathway to the biggest leagues.

'Not just me, but the entire nation is proud of you,' Nepal's prime minister Sher Bahadur Deuba said after Lamichhane was signed at the age of 17. Few expected Lamichhane to play a game but, after Delhi endured an abject season, he was thrust into the final throes of their campaign.

In his very first match, Lamichhane was entrusted to bowl to Virat Kohli and A.B. de Villiers: a Nepalese teenager suddenly on the same field as two giants of the sport. 'Something you have been dreaming of – bowling against them and playing against them.' Lamichhane proved he was not just a signing for show, conceding just 25 runs in four overs on debut and then excelling in two more games that season. By the time 2018 was out, Lamichhane had thrived in the Caribbean Premier League, the Big Bash and Canada's new star-studded Global T20 tournament too.

'It's really amazing, someone from Nepal getting chances in the biggest leagues of the world – IPL and all the other leagues,' Lamichhane said. 'People from Nepal always text me good luck for the game and you have been doing really well for our country – keep doing the fantastic work. That gives me a lot of motivation.

'We've got a huge fan base back home and everyone there is really enjoying this moment. You can't even describe in words how happy right now watching me on TV and against the big players.'

**

Other T20 leagues in Associate nations had a similar democratising effect. By 2019, there were established leagues in Afghanistan and Nepal, which both attracted a good calibre of overseas player, while the Netherlands, Scotland and recently promoted Ireland were about to launch a joint T20 league.

That venture was to be bankrolled by Mercuri, an Indian investment company who funded the Global T20 Canada league, which debuted in 2018. This was a stunningly ambitious venture: it had no restrictions on overseas players in each XI at all, and thus could, in theory, assemble a player pool to make it the highest-quality T20 league in the world. Things did not quite work out like that in the first year, though the money available to overseas players was such that many players preferred playing in Canada to England's T20 Blast tournament, which was played at the same time. The first year was marred by poor pitches and crowds – not helped by all 22 matches taking place at the Maple Leaf Cricket Club, a ground in King City, 30 kilometres from Toronto.

Yet, for all these challenges, the Global T20 also provided a vehicle for the advancement of North American talent of the sort unthinkable in the pre-T20 age.

In 2010, when he was 19, Ali Khan moved to the US from Punjab in Pakistan. His uncle, who already lived in Greater Dayton, Ohio, sponsored Khan and his family to get a green card. Khan had a job lined up working for a telecommunications firm there. The company was called Cricket Wireless, though it had nothing whatsoever to do with cricket.

Khan had been an enthusiastic tape-ball player in his youth, but seldom played with a hard ball. Assuming that there would be no possibilities to play cricket in Dayton, where Khan was moving with his family, he didn't take any cricket equipment on his flight.

'I didn't think there'd be any cricket when I got here, so I didn't pack anything. I was pretty much giving up on cricket when I was moving,' he recalled. For all his excitement about moving to the US, he had 'mixed feelings' because he would have to abandon cricket completely.

A few weeks later, Khan learned about Greater Dayton Cricket Club. His uncle was actually a significant figure in the club, though he hadn't mentioned it to Khan before. Khan, a fast bowler, bowled well in his first evening practice session and was invited to play in a game on the Sunday. The standard was mixed, but Khan relished playing. His success led to the chance to play for a side in the Midwest Cricket Tournament too, a competition for sides from across Ohio, Kentucky and Indiana. Here the standard was better, because the talent was more concentrated, but it would often take Khan hours to travel to games.

In 2013, when he was 22, Khan messaged 'Maq' Qureshi, who ran the US Open cricket tournament: a short annual competition which took place at the end of the year in Florida and paid enough to attract a number of West Indies international players. Qureshi said, 'You can buy a one-way ticket and come down here. If we like you we'll pay you back,' Khan recalled. 'I went down there, bought my own ticket and we lost in the quarter-final but I got four wickets.' He had done enough to persuade Qureshi to buy his return ticket home, and get him opportunities to play elsewhere in the US. In his determination to further his cricket however he could, Khan used to drive five hours each way to play in Chicago's 40-over league, and even flew to Washington DC to play in the Washington league.

'It was very difficult,' Khan recalled. 'Especially when you're living in the US and working five or six days a week and then only able to play cricket on the weekends and that too on AstroTurf because we didn't have proper facilities. It was very hard but it's just always believing in yourself and working towards your dream. I knew it's tough right now but maybe down the road it would pay off so I never gave up on it and just kept playing – every day after work I went straight to the gym, did my workouts. I continued doing the work. I always believed I could become something.' Even though Khan was normally paid small match fees, these were less than the amount he earned at Cricket Wireless. As Khan was paid by the number of days he worked, he effectively lost money when he played two games a weekend.

Khan came through open trials for the USA to be selected in the USA squad which played in the Caribbean 50-over tournament for the first time in 2016. He also earned a contract in the Caribbean Premier League, which mandated that all franchises had to select one North American player. Khan dismissed Kumar Sangakkara, the great Sri Lankan batsman, with his first ball in the Caribbean Premier League while playing for the Guyana Amazon Warriors.

Two years later, he hadn't played another CPL game, and was finding it increasingly hard to justify the amount of time he was devoting to cricket. 'It was starting to get tough for my boss as well. He was saying, "You're starting to get too much now, you're getting too many days off,"' he recalled. Khan was told that he could become a logistics manager if he stopped playing, and considered giving up cricket altogether.

In December 2017, Khan returned to Florida for the US Open tournament. One of his teammates was Dwayne Bravo, who was impressed, telling Khan, 'Don't give up,' when he said goodbye at the end of the tournament.

Soon afterwards, Bravo was selected in the Global T20 league in Canada, and recommended Khan be signed by his side. Khan thrived and, again on Bravo's recommendation, then joined the Trinbago Knight Riders in the CPL. Khan, who regularly bowled at speeds in excess of 90 mph, was outstanding for Trinbago; he was named in ESPNcricinfo's team of the tournament as they won the title, and was signed by the Bangladesh Premier League shortly afterwards. Once again, a domestic league in an Associate nation had helped elevate an Associate cricketer to the big leagues – even if, as with Lamichhane, Khan's tale showed the importance of contacts in the T20 ecosystem, something many Associate players still lacked, hampering their chances of earning an opportunity.

While playing in Canada, Khan was signed by the cricket agency Insignia, who specialise in representing T20 players. Khan's agent, Eddie Tolchard, 'made me a promise that if we keep working hard I don't have to go back to my regular nine-to-five job again,' Khan said. 'He promised me that you won't have to sell another phone again.' And so in 2018, after eight years at Cricket Wireless, Khan left the firm to become a professional cricketer.

He believes that his circuitous journey to becoming a full-time cricketer, just before turning 28, would have been impossible before T20. 'It would have been really hard if there were no leagues or T20,' he said. 'T20 has given me an opportunity to showcase my skills in front of a wider audience. Associate players running shoulder to shoulder with known international stalwarts has given us an opportunity to show that we can stand with the best in the world.'

Like Mujeeb Zadran, Zakir Khan and Sandeep Lamichhane before him, Ali Khan was in Rashid's debt. Where once teams looked down on players from emerging nations, Srikkanth said, 'Rashid Khan changed that mindset for good.' Rashid and T20 have begun to make cricket a sport for those from Kabul, Kathmandu and perhaps even Kansas City, not just Kent and Kolkata.

As players, agents and teams alike search for any competitive advantage they can find, so they will increasingly scour the globe in search of talents from outside cricket's traditional heartlands. Thanks to T20, cricket is at the onset of a great revolution: of finally becoming a game open to all the talents, regardless of the nationality on their passport.

FIFTEEN

THE FIRST INTERNATIONAL T20 DYNASTY

'Gents, let's go and take what's ours'
Marlon Samuels, before the 2016 T20 World Cup

On weekends and weekday evenings in Trinidad and Tobago, games of windball cricket are dotted throughout the country. Matches are played to a backdrop of live music, free-flowing beer and healthy crowds, often into the hundreds for league matches, rising to four figures for finals. Some forms of windball cricket are played year-round in Trinidad.

These matches share much with T20 cricket, yet the game itself is organised differently. In Norman's Windball League, one of the most popular leagues, each innings only lasts 12 overs, so the matches take about an hour and a half. Matches are played, usually on concrete, with a windball – a tennis ball, sometimes covered with extra tape. There is no lbw rule. And bowlers can choose whether to bowl normally – or 'pelt', which means they can throw the ball, contravening the normal 15-degree limit for bowlers to straighten their arms in professional cricket.

Windball cricket is played throughout the Caribbean; the annual West Indies Windball Cricket Championships, played over ten overs a side, ran from 1991 until the mid 2000s. But the beating heart of windball is found in Trinidad, which has underpinned the West Indies' T20 glories, both in lifting two World Cups and in dominating leagues around the world.

'Windball cricket is a backyard sport in Trinidad,' explained Azad Ali, one of the founders of a league called the QPCC Windball Tournament, which plays matches at the famous Queen's Park Oval in the capital Port of Spain. 'Your parents would put a bat and a ball in a car trunk and take you to the beach or your aunt or uncle. When you go into the back of the yard everybody plays windball cricket. After school they go to the savannah, or they go to their neighbour's house and play it in the yard.'

The format can be adapted to any circumstance: 'We designed it to play on the streets of Trinidad.'

Trinidad and Tobago is T20's talent gold mine; nowhere on earth has produced so much T20 royalty per head of population. Windball cricket has turned into a nursery for international cricket's first T20 dynasty.

***

Norman Mungroo is the founder of Norman's Windball League, an 11-a-side competition which has grown from 12 teams in 2004 to 54 in 2019. There is a picture that Mungroo cherishes, in which he is standing in the middle of five men. To his left are Kieron Pollard and Rayad Emrit; to his right are Sunil Narine and Lendl Simmons. All four played T20 for the West Indies; three – Pollard, Narine and Simmons – won the T20 World Cup.

In between their sojourns in lucrative T20 leagues, Trinidad and Tobago's T20 stars have still made time to play windball. Narine, Pollard and Dwayne Bravo all continued to play after winning the World Cup; Nicholas Pooran, considered one of the coming West Indies stars, played windball cricket in 2019, a week before leaving for that season's IPL. These players continued playing windball because it is fun, and the prize money – $14,000 shared between the team winning the premier division, and sums for those lower down – is a nice side-earner. They also play it because, in the skills it demands, windball is like a more intensive version of T20.

'People come out to see superstars. It's right in the backyard here so it's really, really awesome to see the guys playing,' said Mungroo. 'All the big guns in the Trinidad team who played with the West Indies and in all the different franchises over the world come to play. It keeps them fit and they're learning a lot from windball to T20 cricket. It's even faster than T20 . . . That's why so many of the better T20 players are from Trinidad.'

As captain of Trinidad and Tobago from 2001 to 2011, across all three formats of the sport, Daren Ganga was sometimes concerned about the amount of windball cricket that players including Simmons, Narine, Pollard and the Bravo brothers, Darren and Dwayne, would play, even during the professional seasons. 'I as captain would hear that these guys were playing softball cricket in the night and it came to the point where I had to talk to them seriously about the wear and tear on their body and how it can negatively impact their hard-ball game.'

Yet, for T20, windball was advantageous: 'There were no rules, you could reverse sweep, you could swing as hard as possible.'

Windball taught batsmen not to value their wicket too greatly. For players nursed on longer versions of the sport, T20 posed a fundamental challenge: how to learn to fear for their wicket less. Yet players reared on windball did not need to attempt to unlearn these new ways, as distilled by Narine's success as a T20 opener attacking with alacrity from his first ball. Ganga recalled often 'driving through the area where Sunil is from and you see him playing on a concrete strip with all the community members'.

As a batsman, Narine became among the most feared in all windball cricket. 'He's a devastating batsman when he bats in windball. He will hit you for five sixes, six sixes – easy,' Ali said. 'He's just a natural to the game. Most of his technique came from windball – especially outside the off stump.'

Windball developed both batsmen's attitude and skills to thrive in T20. The balls move considerably in the air, forcing batsmen to adjust to late movement and get in position fast, Mungroo explained.

'The windball will be doing all kinds of things so if they can hit that windball, hard ball comes like nothing for them. So it's a good training. This windball moves a lot, it comes through fast, so these guys need foot movement, eyesight.

'Some of the coaches might say this windball might spoil you or whatever. I would say no – this windball cricket give them good eyesight, give them a lot of foot movements.'

The lack of the lbw law in windball, Mungroo said, encouraged players to use their feet innovatively and move around their stumps, especially to open up the leg side, as they then might in T20. 'This is why the guys have such a free way of batting, because there's no lbw, so they move fast across the wicket to pick up the line and length.

'If you notice how Pooran and Sunil club this ball, Pollard . . . These fellas when you see them batting with the windball it's the same way as with the hard ball.'

More condensed versions of windball elevated the need for big hitting even further. Ali created an eight-over, eight-a-side league called the QPCC Windball Tournament. Two-a-side windball cricket would also be played in a cage, with batsmen awarded runs depending on where they hit the ball. The only way to get a six was to hit the ball straight over the bowler's head – something that Narine and Pollard became particularly adept at in windball and T20 alike, Ali said.

'That's why Pollard is so effective with his sixes because in windball cricket, the easiest boundary, that gives you the most amount of runs, is straight back over the bowler's head. In cage cricket if you hit to the sides you have to run your runs. So windball cricket encourages you to play correct, straight back over the bowler's head.'

Ganga, who captained Pollard for Trinidad and Tobago at the start of his career, believed that this aptitude of hitting the ball straight set Pollard apart. 'The big difference with Kieron Pollard as against many of the big hitters in world cricket is that, although now he seems to choose the leg-side option as his most favoured option, when he was a teenager his power option was always down the ground. He was always looking to hit the ball very straight and that stood out.'

For bowlers, windball cricket forced them to adapt to survive. In windball, 'players who would never make it professionally were developing adaptations to their deliveries like a knuckleball where you pressed on the soft ball and it dipped and gripped off the surface,' Ganga recalled. 'All these sorts of subtle variations allowed our hard-ball players to be exposed and they started implementing that in their hard-ball game.

'The prime example of that is Sunil Narine . . . Playing softball cricket I think his variations, his uniqueness in terms of his grip – all those things would have also contributed positively to his development.'

Batsmen, in turn, became more adroit at recognising and adapting to variations. And the nature of windball meant that fielders became well versed in spectacular catches on the boundary rope, which Pollard and others from Trinidad became renowned for.

Playing against some of the world's best T20 players in windball – as the young Pooran did against Narine, for instance – then developed the next generation at an accelerated rate. 'So when we know Sunil Narine and Kieron Pollard are playing in a match, plenty of people will go there to see them,' Ali said. 'A lot of people like to play against them, a lot of people like to challenge them.'

***

After Allen Stanford's imprisonment for 110 years for presiding over an extraordinary Ponzi scheme, the Coolidge ground he built in Antigua for his tournaments – unkempt, overgrown and disused – looked scarcely more appealing than Stanford's Florida prison cell. It seemed like a sad encapsulation of the West Indies' whole tawdry entanglement with Stanford. Yet the competition's legacy was altogether more complicated.

When Stanford created and funded the Stanford 20/20 tournament in 2006, it was acclaimed as a tool to reinvigorate Caribbean cricket. 'We thought cricket was fading away. People's focus was starting to shift. That brought everything back,' reflected Ramnaresh Sarwan, who enjoyed a distinguished West Indies career and captained Guyana to the first title. Sarwan also played in the game between Stanford Superstars and England.

With the Stanford 20/20, Sarwan noticed an immediate shift. Players began doing more weights, to improve their six-hitting ability, at the expense of endurance training. 'That's why they've become even stronger,' he reflected. 'The majority of the guys are in the weights room; there's not much running these days. For Test cricket it was more endurance work we had to do, just very light weights. Now guys are doing much heavier weights and I think that's one of the reasons guys are hitting the ball so far.'

Heightened professionalism – Sarwan considered the Stanford tournament more professional than the West Indies team at the time – abetted this shift. 'It was the first time we were really introduced to the types of food that would allow you to perform at a certain level. It was a whole new beginning for us in terms of understanding nutrition.'

The Stanford 20/20 'was a competition and a format of the game that brought a totally different perspective on our cricket,' said Ganga, who captained Trinidad and Tobago in the first final. 'Our cricket back then – mid to late 2000s – was going through a tumultuous time. There were issues with the board at national level, that's well documented. The first-

os Brathwaite, who would later become the West Indies T20 captain,
rved: 'It started the whole T20 revolution. So thanks to Stanford for
'

***

s the million-dollar shot. In the first Stanford 20/20 final, Narsingh
narine hit the penultimate ball for six, securing Guyana the title, and
1 million prize.

t, for all the pain of Deonarine's million-dollar six, Trinidad and
ago glimpsed a shape of their future in the 2006 Stanford tournament.
08, they won the second Stanford 20/20 – and then beat Middlesex
e Stanford international club championship, earning $400,000.

n opportunity to play T20 cricket was handed down to us and we had to
ally develop our own approaches towards this format,' Ganga recalled.
ers trained with certain things in mind. We strategically decided how
anted to play the game. We had some physically strong players and
new it was about risk-taking and managing it from a batting, bowling,
ng perspective. We adopted an approach that was very similar to the
ankan national team that won the World Cup in 1996.'

that competition, Sri Lanka's buccaneering batting at the start of
nnings left an indelible mark on 50-over cricket. Now, the West
es were about to do the same for the 20-over game. 'They were very
ess and fearless in their approach and that is exactly the approach
we adopted in T20 from the onset.'

ter the 2009 Stanford 20/20 was cancelled, the West Indies board
not organise a replacement. Trinidad and Tobago qualified for
naugural Champions League, in October 2009, by dint of their
rmances a full 20 months earlier. Competing against sides who had
d much more T20, had overseas players and more heralded domestic
ms, they were considered rank outsiders.

anga did not share this belief. While his classical batting was not
ally suited to the format, Ganga emerged as the West Indies' first
T20 thinker. 'He understood how to build a T20 team,' reflected
Bishop, a former West Indies Test player from Trinidad. 'He was
d of his time.'

anford gave Trinidad and Tobago a 'competitive advantage' in the

class cricket standards needed to improve from the quality of the venues, the arrangement and remuneration that went with first-class cricket.'

The financial incentives were totally out of kilter with the norm in Caribbean domestic cricket. Each winning team in a match shared $30,000; the man of the match received $25,000. The 'play of the day' – the best single moment in a game, normally a six, brilliant ball to get a wicket or spectacular catch – received $10,000 for essentially one ball's work. 'That was mind-boggling,' Ganga said. 'Nowhere could a first-class player get the opportunity to earn money to that sort of level. So it brought a certain seriousness, it brought an intensity.

'The equipment, the clothing – everything contributed positively to the players and them wanting to express themselves and be part of the national team and excel in this competition. So the standard of playing rose as well.'

The tournament 'really allowed a lot of West Indians and Trinidadians an opportunity to learn the game and develop approaches way before any of the other players in world cricket,' Ganga recalled.

'I think the opportunity to play it from the onset would have contributed positively to our players being more competent than all the other players around the globe because we had those experiences a lot earlier than other international players.' This 'led to our players developing variations in their bowling, being innovative in their batting and showing more power than anything else'.

Greater financial rewards also kept players in the game. Samuel Badree, who would rise to become the number one T20 bowler in the world, was 25 at the time of the first Stanford tournament; struggling to break into domestic cricket in longer formats, he might have given the game up for good without the fillip of the tournament.

For penurious boards, T20 offered the only plausible route to receiving substantial corporate sponsorship. 'Territorial boards poured resources into T20,' said Ganga; it was pragmatic to prioritise the format.

The same logic extended to the grassroots game. 'T20 is simply more affordable, and affordable is often the deciding factor in many things in the Caribbean,' explained Julian Cresser, an academic from the Caribbean specialising in West Indies cricket. 'Schools, clubs, communities, even the West Indies cricket board, simply can no longer afford the money, or time, to play longer cricket.' Many regional youth tournaments are now played just in the limited overs formats. 'The result is that from very early, players who have the skills to succeed in the shorter formats are promoted to the front and other players fall by the wayside.'

T20 was a natural fit for the West Indies' traditional strengths. If the notion of calypso cricket was easily exaggerated – West Indies also produced fine but more cautious Test match batsmen, like Larry Gomes and Shivnarine Chanderpaul – it contained some truth.

'Young boys and girls develop their athleticism from an early age,' said Cresser. 'T20 cricket draws on this athleticism – many of the best sportspersons are multi-sport athletes in their youth.'

Sarwan was 'not surprised' by the West Indies' subsequent success in T20. 'The build and striking of the ball – it was like it was tailor-made for us, the majority of our players. I mean Dwayne Bravo, Pollard, Russell, Gayle who dominated T20 cricket. If you take a look at those guys, they're built like machines to play T20.'

'It is the style of cricket that West Indians play – it's very instinctive, it's very natural, it's got a lot of flair,' Ganga said. 'A cavalier style sort of approach to the game and different formats. The West Indian style fits perfectly with the requirements for T20 cricket because it requires you to be fearless as a cricketer and that's why you see a lot of West Indian and Trinidad and Tobago players in particular warm towards this format.'

The game also showcased the skills honed in grassroots level – often through windball, especially in Trinidad, but sometimes in local T20 competitions. In Jamaica, which has also produced a number of leading T20 players, the local SDC T20 competition, which is community-based, features around 300 teams.

'There are intense, but for the most part friendly, rivalries and players take great pride in representing their communities,' Cresser said. 'Culturally, T20 is in many ways a better fit. People want to play.'

Sean Newell, a cricket coach at Calabar High School in Jamaica, said there is a direct link between the nature of pop-up grassroots matches and T20 success. 'It's basically from our nature. The flamboyance is a result of the type and style of cricket that is played in our backyards and schools. It is more on an individual basis where we would rather hit boundaries rather than run singles. We pride ourselves on power hitting so the T20 would fit the West Indies more. We like to show off our strength, power and individualism.'

The Stanford 20/20 permeated even the remotest a While there were only six West Indies teams in first-islands were banded together to form teams – th the first year of the Stanford tournament, giving op from hitherto ignored territories. 'He exposed a lo by allowing every single island in the Caribbean t team in his Allen Stanford tournament,' Ganga sai

'Man, it was great because what he did too opportunity to win,' recalled Virgil Browne, part o despite the island's population of just 11,000, reac the first Stanford 20/20 tournament. Nevis had the d first team to top 200 in the competition: they made 2 against Antigua. 'Everybody was thinking 160 . . . barrier against Antigua we were like yo, you gotta lo

Every team had bespoke coaching and fitness tra the 14 'legends' on the panel Stanford assemble diffused across the region.

The tournament involved 'more training as [individual,' Browne remembered. 'It's just the fact in a professional set-up. Every day you're going o cricket – you never had that before. You are now in you money.'

When Nevis reached the semi-finals in 2006, the one of the competition's developmental teams, mea around £1,700 a month for a year. 'People were c opportunity to have cricket as a career and get paic

For some players, the money they received from Several members of the Stanford Superstars who th notorious winner-takes-all $20 million match in 2 $1 million winnings in Stanford. Like others conn got any of their cash back.

After years of neglect, the Coolidge Cricket G later revived. But even while the weeds reigned, th it was a symbol of criminal activity on an extraordi claim to have planted the seeds of a new dynasty.

'The investment made by Allen Stanford in tha to West Indies dominating T20 cricket around th

first Champions League, Ganga said. 'We were a lot more comfortable playing in pressure situations.'

This confidence was married with intense preparation. 'We were more prepared than most other teams,' Ganga recalled. 'We were able to analyse our benchmarks that were playing T20 cricket and we set our standards a little bit higher than what was happening globally so we were always a step ahead of the game in terms of benchmarks for batting, for bowling. We knew trends and it worked in our favour.

'We were meticulous. We analysed what other teams were achieving in T20 cricket from the point of view of dot balls, where they were after six overs, how they approached the middle overs, and where they scored in the death overs. We used that information to suit our style of play.'

In India, Trinidad and Tobago unveiled their radically different approach to T20 on the world: embracing boundary hitting at the expense of all else, even if this meant playing out more dot balls. 'We knew that we could afford to consolidate in the middle overs and set the game up so that [Kieron] Pollard and [Dwayne] Bravo could play with freedom at the back end.'

Ganga liberated the belligerent hitters around him in the batting order, instilling an approach that emphasised boundaries over reducing dot balls. He also innovated in the field – notably embracing using Samuel Badree as a leg-spinner who would routinely bowl all the way through the Powerplay, a role unique in T20 history.

Opening with Badree, who scarcely turned the new ball but generated bounce and skid, recognised how spinners, contrary to 150 years of received cricket wisdom, could be most effective at the start of an innings. The decision had its roots in club cricket, where Badree thrived with the new ball in T20. Trinidad's players knew that the Champions League was a route to the IPL. Their play was stunning, twice chasing scores over 170 comfortably – including in Pollard's epochal heist against New South Wales – and scoring 213, the competition's lone total over 200, against the South African team Diamond Eagles.

The upshot was that, having initially been almost ignored by the IPL – just eight players appeared in the first two seasons compared to 30 Australians – soon West Indies players became among the most coveted in the league. By the end of 2019, only Australia and South Africa had featured more as overseas players in the tournament.

Rise of the West Indies and Trinidad and Tobago in the IPL		
IPL Season	**WI Players to Appear**	**T and T Players to Appear**
2008	4	1
2009	4	1
2010	6	3
2011	4	2
2012	8	4
2013	12	6
2014	13	7
2015	8	5
2016	9	4
2017	9	5
2018	8	4
2019	13	5

Uniquely, players from the West Indies had access to all three of the Stanford tournament, the Champions League and the IPL. And so Caribbean players had both especially strong reasons to prioritise T20, and an unrivalled opportunity to develop their skills in the format. For all that the IPL benefited local Indian players, the BCCI barring them from playing in overseas T20 leagues prevented them from enjoying the same learnings in foreign conditions as the West Indies.

'Once there was that initial success in the Stanford tournaments, it has just steamrolled,' observed Bishop. 'More and more young players have idolised Gayle and Pollard, who were the early trendsetters in the format.'

The ascent of T20 'definitely encouraged them to specialise, because most of these players are looking to take their skills into bigger and more lucrative markets like the IPL,' explained Sean Newell, the cricket coach at Calabar High School in Jamaica. 'West Indies will continue to have a super-strong T20 team as our team consists of all the skill sets for the shorter and more exciting format.'

The relative importance of T20, compared to the other formats, was greater in the West Indies during a formative stage in the game's development. This advantage underpinned the West Indies' T20 World Cup victory in 2012, the team's first World Cup victory in any format for 33 years. Six of the victorious XI, and eight members of the 15-man squad, were from Trinidad and Tobago. All of these had been in Trinidad's squad for the 2009 Champions League. When the West Indies pulverised Australia in the semi-final, Pollard and Dwayne Bravo hit three sixes apiece to lift the total to 205; then, Trinidad's bowlers claimed nine Australian wickets.

After Stanford and the Champions League, which was scrapped in 2014, the West Indies gained a more durable T20 competition: the Caribbean Premier League, which launched in 2013. With only six teams in the region, and franchises permitted four overseas players per team, even competition to gain spots in the squads could be fierce. This was especially the case in Trinidad, who won three of the four CPL titles from 2015 to 2018.

In a sense the CPL completed the revolution that Stanford, and then the Champions League, started: for the first time, domestic West Indies players could play with and against foreign stars in the region. Thanks to T20, Caribbean players could be well paid even without playing for the international side or foreign teams.

'I think the CPL and T20 – you could put it as a by-product of what Stanford started,' said Virgil Browne. 'It's a great thing for the region in terms of bringing back interest in the game of cricket.'

***

The theory of desirable difficulty holds that there are some problems no one would ever want, but can actually be a help in the long run. For instance, the most successful individuals are more likely to lose a parent young.

In the years after Stanford, a cocktail of the inequities in cricket economics and the toxic relationship between the West Indies players and board pushed a number of their best cricketers to become T20 specialists at home and abroad. From 2012 to 2016, the seven cricketers in the world who played the most T20 matches were all West Indian. And so they came to understand the intricacies, skills and tactics of the format more than anyone else.

Most T20 Matches in the World, 2012–16	
Player	**Matches**
Dwayne Bravo	250
Kieron Pollard	218
Andre Russell	211
Chris Gayle	194
Dwayne Smith	193
Darren Sammy	190
Sunil Narine	188

'From playing around the world, we know about playing T20 cricket,' said Ravi Rampaul, a Trinidadian fast bowler who played in the Champions League and the T20 World Cup-winning campaign in 2012. 'We have experience in all the team because of all the franchises.' When put to him that the frequently poisonous relationship between the West Indies' players and board had been an advantage for their T20 because it encouraged players to specialise, he laughed. 'That's true.' While the West Indies often struggled to field anything like their best team in bilateral T20 cricket, with leading players unselected or unavailable due to the relations with the board and being able to earn more in T20 leagues – contributing to their surprisingly underwhelming performance in bilateral cricket – their full-strength squad came together for the T20 World Cup.

Deleterious relations with the board, 'in a way worked out well for the players,' said Badree, a long-time representative on the West Indian Players' Association. 'As the T20 leagues came aboard, the players had more opportunities to go outside and represent different franchises, different teams, and make an honest living – a decent living at that.

'We've got so many experienced players that form the core of our T20 team – guys like Gayle, Bravo, Narine, Pollard and so on – who have played so many competitions around the world. The knowledge and the experiences that they've gained – when they come together as a team they bring that and they share it with the other guys. I think that's really the reason why we are successful: that experience and that knowledge that we have of the other teams, having played in the same dressing rooms with these guys and played in different conditions.'

West Indies in T20 Internationals, 2012–19 (Excluding No Results)			
Tournament	**Matches**	**Won**	**Percentage Won**
T20 World Cups	17	12	71%
Other T20	51	22	43%

A few months before the 2016 T20 World Cup, the West Indies toured Australia for a Test series. The West Indies' performances were egregious. All the while, seven of the best Caribbean players, who were all part of the triumphant 2012 T20 World Cup squad, were in Australia playing in the Big Bash instead. Six of them would then be in the 2016 World Cup squad.

'That was a massive help,' said Phil Simmons, who was West Indies head coach then. 'You look at the players who controlled the team – [Darren] Sammy, Chris [Gayle], Bravo – they'd played international T20 and T20 leagues around the world. It's not a case where they've always smashed it, they've played proper cricket in different teams in different ways. So they brought their experience to the team and realised that we had to play this way because of the team we had.'

At the 2016 T20 World Cup, five of the West Indies side had played exclusively T20 in the preceding year, compared to none from any of their opponents during the tournament. Where once the West Indies used their players' experience in county cricket to help them dominate Test cricket, now they used their multifarious experiences in domestic leagues around the world – the different conditions; the cutting edge analysis; the world-beating coaching – to help them dominate T20. So although the team itself had a puny support staff and sporting infrastructure compared to rivals like India, leading players had benefited from the totality of intelligence about T20.

All the while, the West Indies affirmed that T20 was a game that rewarded experience. In the 2007 WT20, the average player age was 27.38 years. By the 2016 tournament, the average age in the main stage had risen to 28.94, according to the statistician Ric Finlay. The West Indies were the oldest of the lot, with an average age in the final of 31.94.

T20 Records Held by West Indian Players (2019)	
Most Matches	Kieron Pollard (475)
Most Runs	Chris Gayle (12,808)
Most Wickets	Dwayne Bravo (490)

Most Catches	Kieron Pollard (272)
Best Economy Rate (minimum 100 wickets)	Samuel Badree (6.02)
Best Strike Rate (minimum 2,500 runs)	Andre Russell (169.83)

'The game is about decision-making under pressure,' said the former Australia Test batsman Simon Katich, who coached many West Indies players as head coach of Trinbago Knight Riders. 'Generally experienced players are going to make good decisions when they have a vast amount of experience to draw on given all the game situations they have found themselves in.'

Skill, style and experience, honed everywhere from windball games in Trinidad to the IPL, combined to make the West Indies some of the most sought-after T20 players in the world. Tom Moody, who has worked as head coach for Sunrisers Hyderabad in the IPL and tournament director of the CPL, observed how hard the Caribbean style is to mimic.

'When teams and coaches and analysts look at trying to build a side, it's very difficult to be able to build a side that is just the West Indian model. Generally in franchise cricket, every team is looking for a couple of players of those capabilities – the power hitters – but there's only so many of them around.

'What West Indies cricket have done very successfully, is that they have embraced their strengths – and their strength is power and speed. And they have embraced that and they have allowed their players to play with freedom with that . . . If they block three balls and hit three balls over the ground, well, 18 off an over's pretty good, isn't it? But not everyone is capable of doing that.'

***

For all that the broader financial situation in the sport is weighted against the West Indies – the board's total revenue from broadcasting contracts is around £12 million a year, compared with England's £220 million, from 2020 onwards, and India's £750 million – their T20 pedigree appears built to last. In the 2019 IPL, 13 West Indies players appeared – including nine who did not play in the final of the 2016 T20 World Cup, and six who were 23 or younger. They played in the same spirit as their forebears.

A year earlier, a new T20 tournament had been created in Canada, which allowed teams to field an unlimited number of overseas players.

The tournament had the financial clout to attract many leading cricketers – including Gayle, Russell, Narine, Dwayne Bravo and the Australian pair of Steve Smith and David Warner, fresh from being banned for their role in a major scandal when a cricket ball was doctored with sandpaper. And so the West Indies B team who entered the tournament passed by largely unnoticed. With good reason: 23 other West Indians had been picked up in the draft ahead of them, and only those left behind were eligible.

Yet this coterie of unheralded players ended up reaching the final. They did so playing in the spirit of the great Caribbean T20 sides, including chasing 216 in the semi-finals against an attack that featured the New Zealand fast bowler Tim Southee, the Australian leg-spinner Fawad Ahmed, Russell, and Sheldon Cottrell, a left-arm pace bowler who has represented the West Indies in all three formats. The victory was sealed, naturally, with a six off the last ball; Sherfane Rutherford, a 19-year-old Guyanese left-hander, had blitzed 134 not out off just 66 balls. A year later, he was in the IPL too.

'I remember looking at the team that went to the Global T20 Canada – very young team but the fearlessness with which they played their cricket, it blew me away,' said Bishop. 'There's a fearlessness about them and I think that has been built as a philosophy from the days of the Champions League, Trinidad and Tobago, the Stanford tournament when Trinidad and Guyana did so well.

'T20 they've seen it – I like that, three weeks' work. That fits well with me wanting to socialise in between and they gravitate towards it a lot more and it's having an impact on batting in the longer forms of the game but I'm not complaining. The guys are excellent at it. I think really to sum it up, each generation in the Windies has built on the previous T20 marketers – led by Pollard, Bravo, Narine, Badree, who were at the forefront – because it sits so well with our athleticism and attention spans.'

***

The West Indies squad gathered in Dubai at the end of February 2016 in turmoil. The relationship between the players and the board had disintegrated so much that the players had considered pulling out of the looming T20 World Cup. In an age of teams preparing for T20 ever more meticulously, the West Indies had only played two T20 internationals in the previous year – the fewest of any side in the tournament.

Yet they still retained a belief that they would thrive in India. 'Marlon Samuels doesn't talk very much,' recalled Phil Simmons, then the West Indies coach. 'I remember early on, in the camp in Dubai, we had a chat as a team. He said: "Gents, let's go and take what's ours."'

Shortly afterwards, on the eve of their opening game in the tournament, Dwayne Bravo even dared to compare the current side with esteemed teams of yore. 'The way the West Indies goes about its T20 game, the manner in which we like to dominate the format, is much how we dominated Tests in the 1980s . . . We see it as our baby.'

The West Indies weren't just damaged by their relations with the board. They also suffered from missing Kieron Pollard and Sunil Narine, two T20 greats, from the tournament. And while Chris Gayle eviscerated England with a century in the opening game, he only contributed 13 runs in the remainder of the tournament.

Ordinarily, players of such calibre being absent or out of form would have been debilitating. Yet, while most countries had two or three power hitters, the West Indies had almost a squad's worth.

Omitted from the original squad, Lendl Simmons, another Trinidadian – and Phil's nephew – landed in Mumbai two days before the semi-final against India. He had already thrived on the ground in the IPL, and was the top run-scorer for Mumbai in their IPL victory in 2015.

At the start of his innings, Simmons had a confrontation with Virat Kohli. 'When he fielded, he said something to me, and I said to myself, "I'm going to show you you're not the only good batsman,"' Simmons said, believing that Kohli kept throwing the ball to his end to try to get under his skin. 'That's the way he is. He's very arrogant, he's very aggressive when he fields, and when he bats as well. He's just a very aggressive person.'

The feud 'really urged me to bat the way I did – to show him that he's not the only one who can do it,' Simmons said. 'When India chase, one of their top batsmen bats deep – that was my role, batting in the middle overs, especially because I play spin well. I knew they didn't have any good death bowlers, so with Russell, Bravo and Sammy to come once we passed the middle overs, those guys could always come out and finish.' Russell marmalised India's death bowlers, after Simmons – who made

82 not out, abetted by twice being caught off no-balls – had set up the Mumbai heist.

'I had some chances going my way, but such is life: every cricketer has his day and you just need to cash in when it is your day.' This distilled the West Indies' approach to T20 innings building: with so many players capable of playing in such an ebullient way, they avoided over-dependency on any individual, and liberated each other to attack.

The West Indies had shown themselves not just a better T20 team than their opponents, but a radically different one. India's approach was built upon minimising dot balls and maximising twos; Ajinkya Rahane was recalled to the side to provide solidity and did exactly that, taking 35 balls over 40 runs as opener, setting up India's 192 for 2, but the West Indies recognised that it was under par.

Before the semi-final, the West Indies' data analysis found that the pull shot was the most effective shot at the Wankhede Stadium. These findings led the West Indies to focus on bowling full, outside off stump and take the pace off the ball to cut off India's supply of boundaries. While India's total was ostensibly imposing, the West Indies realised this was not the case on such a high-scoring ground.

It showed the shrewdness of the West Indies' bowling attack – an easily overlooked, but indispensable, component of their success. This had the adaptability to suit all conditions but, with a preponderance of spinners and bowlers adept at bowling slower balls, was particularly well suited to conditions in Asia, where the 2012, 2014 and 2016 T20 World Cups were all played. Across these three tournaments, West Indies ranked among the three most frugal sides during the first six overs and the middle overs, and in the final five overs they were the very best. Here, perhaps, was another legacy of Caribbean windball and grassroots culture: bowlers were uniquely prepared to maintain a semblance of order amid all the bedlam at the death of the innings.

When it was their turn to bat at the Wankhede, in defiance of all received wisdom, the West Indies' batsmen played out 50 dot balls to India's 27. They made up for it by hitting 146 runs in boundaries to India's 92, with 11 sixes to India's four. These exposed how India had overvalued wickets, and left their batting resources unused.

As balls whizzed off Caribbean bats like fireworks set off into the night sky it reflected a batting approach that prioritised strike rate over average.

'It's calypso cricket,' Lendl Simmons said. 'It's because of the way we play our cricket – we are aggressive, very sprightly and that's how we are . . . T20 is right up our alley.'

***

In a preview of the 2016 T20 World Cup, the English commentator Mark Nicholas denigrated the West Indies' chances. 'West Indies are short of brains but have IPL history in their ranks,' he wrote for ESPNcricinfo.

'That comment really set us off,' captain Darren Sammy said before the final. 'It's really emotional, for somebody whom I respect and have a good rapport with generally, to describe our team – who two [four] years ago were world champions – as guys with no brains. That's really out of order.'

Nicholas's words illustrated how the West Indies' shrewd thinking was widely overlooked. While their extraordinary capacity to hit boundaries created the seductive impression that their success was simply a triumph of raw talent, that obscured the deep planning underpinning the team.

'T20 is such a fast game that it needs sharp thinking. In Test cricket you come off at lunchtime and you talk to the players,' explained head coach Phil Simmons. 'You have to be a lot more precise because you have no time for adjustments. In Test matches you assess by sessions; in one-day cricket you assess by overs; in T20 now you assess by balls. Every ball is an event. Every ball, you have to assess what is the situation for the next ball.'

In 2015, the Caribbean Premier League enlisted the analyst Gaurav Sundararaman, who had previously worked for IPL teams, to be a consultant for all franchises in the competition, providing data for teams who requested it. The Barbados Tridents coach Desmond Haynes, a leading member of the great West Indies team during the 1980s, was particularly enthusiastic. 'Desmond Haynes was the man who backed me. He's a big believer in data and analytics.' Haynes used Sundararaman's findings to inform strategies, like uncovering that all the sixes in St Kitts tended to be hit in one direction, leading to spinners only bowling from one end. Barbados reached the final.

During the CPL, Sundararaman met Phil Simmons, who was also taken by his work. At Simmons's suggestion, the West Indies hired Sundararaman for the T20 World Cup in 2016.

Every day during the tournament, Simmons would chat to Sundararaman. They discussed 'match-ups' – the best and worst player v player combinations between West Indians and the teams they were playing – the ground characteristics, a par score and second-guessed what the opposition would do, and how best to counteract it.

'He was a very good help in going through the opposition and things that we could try on different grounds. The thing about data is it's how you use it. Our players used it very well,' Simmons reflected. 'The main thing is to assess the opposition and know that we as a team know where their strengths are and where they want to score their runs and where they will bowl to us. The second part is you can look back and see what we've done in the past games and how people bowl to us, helping us to see what we needed to improve on.'

Data informed the West Indies' decisions during the tournament. They knew that South Africa struggled against spin, so played an extra spinner and used Chris Gayle's off spin for three overs against their left-handers; the West Indies spinners bowled ten overs in this match. Andre Russell's poor economy rate at the death led to him bowling earlier in the innings. When batting, Russell was told to anticipate the slower ball, which had dismissed him 15 times in T20 in 2015; he did so spectacularly during the epic semi-final run chase against India. They also opened with a spinner, Samuel Badree, in every match; spinners are consistently more economical than quicks in the opening overs.

While Simmons acted as a funnel for the data – telling the players only what was really important and actionable information – some players used data particularly extensively. 'What needed to be shared they took it on board and used it well.

'Everybody's different. I have some players who live by it and now they have it on their phones – you could put all the data to their phones and they would sit at it and look at it at night. You have some players who just back their talent and come up on the day and say, "I'm going to bowl wide yorkers and bumpers and it's going to go how it goes."'

One player who looked at data on his phone was the belligerent all-rounder Carlos Brathwaite. 'Obviously you do your homework, you set your plans, and you try to think of what plans they have for you and how you would counter-attack that.'

Simmons found analysis especially useful for their bowlers. 'It's got to the stage where bowlers look at batsmen – he always moves on the first ball, or he always goes deep in his crease after three dot balls.'

'We just looked at the data for the grounds and tried to match it to the wickets and what the pitch looked like to work out a par score,' Simmons recalled. 'I think 187 or something was the par score for the Wankhede so we had no issues with that. In the dressing room we said they need to score 210 for us to be in trouble. So we were very calm.'

Paradoxically, perhaps the biggest triumph of data lay in six hitting. As teams were seldom bowled out in T20, embracing a higher degree of batting risk – by trying to hit more sixes – was prudent. The West Indies recognised how batting brutality could render dot balls or sharper running irrelevant. The six trumped all else.

'People say we don't rotate our strike well – we will talk about that,' Sammy said before the final in 2016. 'But first thing is you have to stop us from hitting boundaries. That has been difficult for oppositions once we get in that swing.

'I think since the inception of T20, you've seen West Indies is a boundary-hitting team so that's no surprise for me.

'We built a big-hitting team with the players that we had. Because of the way we played we had to score more boundaries than the other teams,' Phil Simmons explained. 'We have always been known to be boundary hitters and we knew that we had boundary hitters down to number eight.

'In the grounds in India especially where we played the semi-finals, we backed our strength which is boundary hitting . . . At the beginning we decided that we were good at chasing because when we batted first there was a lot of pressure on us to go big early on. But when we chased we could do that later on because of our ability to hit boundaries – with the likes of Russell, Sammy and Bravo lower down, we had a lot of firepower so we just nailed it on that we were going to chase as much as we could.'

The team were unconcerned about allowing far more dot balls than their opponents. 'We didn't worry about it too much because we knew we could make it up. If Chris Gayle plays out 20 dots in 60 balls he'd still have 100.' For the West Indies, Simmons said, 'The T20 game has made ten an over for the last six or ten overs a walk in the park now.'

The trade-off inherent in the West Indies' batting style – accepting a high number of dot balls, reasoning that the number of boundaries would more than make up for it – is 'a high risk and high reward approach. They're very rare players,' said Sundararaman. 'They don't worry too much about wickets. They were able to hit sixes. The way T20 has evolved, if you're not able to hit sixes, you're not in the game.'

Shortly after their semi-final victory, coach Simmons tweeted: 'Awesome display by this group [of] men with no brains, imagine if we had some'.

What came together in the tournament, he said, was 'the want, the desire, the experience and the knowledge that this is the way we have to play.'

***

In the final at Eden Gardens, Gayle was out to his second ball, and Simmons to his very first. In a game that oscillated as wildly as a classic Test match, Samuels played magnificently, evoking his match-winning innings in the 2012 final, driven by a feud with Ben Stokes. During Samuels's 85, Simmons kept being reminded of his words in Dubai before the tournament: 'It stays in my mind, just that statement from him.'

But Samuels was lacking for support. Enter another replacement in the squad – Brathwaite, who arrived at the crease with the sum total of 25 international T20 runs in his entire career, and with some guffawing at his new £420,000 IPL contract. From only his fourth ball Brathwaite demonstrated he had finesse to match his power when he scooped a ball from David Willey for four.

Six balls later, in the cauldron of a steamy Eden Gardens, England had 19 to defend from the final over, entrusted to regular death bowler Ben Stokes.

'We are standing at the end of Stokes's mark talking about the three balls that he can bowl,' England captain Eoin Morgan recalled of the conversation they had before Stokes's first delivery. 'So with the field that was set he could bowl a straight yorker, wide slower ball or a bouncer. And he bowled really well at the death throughout the whole tournament and he went to start with a yorker.'

Stokes 'was just thinking about me, what I wanted to do,' he later told the *Daily Telegraph*. 'I knew if I got six yorkers in the blockhole they were only going to get eight or nine runs maximum and we would win.'

As he prepared to face the final over, Brathwaite 'was numb. It was a state that I've only reached a couple times since . . . I had a clear mindset, I just watched the ball and allowed my instincts to react.'

Stokes missed his first yorker by a fair way, and Brathwaite swatted it over the fine leg boundary for six.

'It can happen to any bowler,' Morgan said. 'So once that happens, we are at the end of his mark and we talk about what he is going to bowl next and you can always tell a bowler is in the right space when he says, no, that's my fault I need to get it right. I'll go again. And that's nice and you run away and watch again.

'And the second ball wasn't that bad a ball, it was a great shot.' Stokes had missed his yorker again, but only fractionally this time and Brathwaite – with a perfect swing of the bat – dispatched it over wide long on for six. 'And then you meet before the third and then it's 12 off two [in this over] and so they need seven off four. So it was a matter of trying to take a wicket then so we took his length back and went into the wicket. And that didn't work out and he hit it out of the ground again.'

With the West Indies' analysts, Brathwaite had been planning for this moment for weeks, going back to before the opening group match with England. 'We knew Ben Stokes and Chris Jordan bowled very good yorkers – sometimes straight, sometimes wide – and in that situation it was about repeating that again. So I knew the long boundary was to the leg side, and if he did bowl a yorker it would be straight, or the plan would be into the wicket.'

A millimetre too short here; a millimetre too wide there. It was enough for Brathwaite to plunder four imperious strokes that were beautiful in their brutality.

Three of the four sixes smoked off Brathwaite's bat were to the leg side. Deliberately targeting the *longer* boundary: it was a novel approach that epitomised the audacity of the West Indies' T20 cricket.

SIXTEEN

HOW TO WIN IN T20

*'Given the constraints with budgets in a
draft or auction you are always compromised'*
Tom Moody, IPL Winning Coach

Around selection tables, selectors and coaches of national teams and franchises alike are tasked with building a T20 team. They are, essentially, discussing, the six main trade-offs of how to build a T20 side.

Batting v Bowling
The most fundamental decision on the auction table or in the selection room is whether to prioritise batting or bowling. Naturally, every team wants to be strong in both – but most sides end up stronger in one of the two disciplines.

In the 2017/18 Bangladesh Premier League, Rangpur Riders made a decisive choice: they were going to plump for batting strength. Their top three included Chris Gayle and Brendon McCullum, two of T20's most iconic players, with Johnson Charles – another belligerent hitter who played 34 T20 internationals for the West Indies – nestled in between. Rangpur's game-plan was patently obvious: to out-muscle the opposition, and make up for their relative deficiency in bowling.

Initially, this plan regularly failed. Rangpur stumbled through the league stages, winning just six of their 12 games and sneaking into the final play-off slot. On relatively slow pitches that produced scrappy, low-scoring games, Rangpur's strategy often floundered – their bowling wasn't strong enough to restrict teams, and the grounds neutered the big-hitting prowess of their top three, who were less suited to steady accumulation. When two batsmen command a huge proportion of a team's budget struggle, as Gayle and McCullum did, it was rare that the team could withstand them struggling.

After Rangpur twice collapsed for under 100 on the tacky wickets at the Shere Bangla National Stadium in Dhaka, they took to blaming the conditions. 'It was a very poor wicket,' said McCullum, Rangpur's stand-in captain. 'I think the tournament can benefit from better surfaces.'

So could Rangpur. 'It is very hard to come into the tournament as a stroke-maker when you can't trust the pitch,' McCullum lamented. 'You can't trust the bounce and pace . . . It will be nice to have a surface that is more consistent and has more pace.'

After their underwhelming performances in the league stage, Rangpur finally got their wish in the play-off matches: pitches that allowed their players to hit through the line of the ball with freedom.

What followed was a remarkable distillation of how, at their best, top-order batsmen have a unique ability to shape T20 games to their will. In their first play-off match Rangpur needed 168 to win; Gayle scored 126 on his own. In their second play-off Gayle made only three – but Charles hit 105, and McCullum 78, to lift Rangpur to an insurmountable 192-3. In the final, Gayle managed a century of runs in sixes alone; his remarkable 146, supported by another McCullum 50, set up a comfortable Rangpur victory.

Sometimes it was said that bowlers win you tournaments and batsmen win you matches. Perhaps a more accurate maxim would be: you need bowlers to get you through the group stage, and then batsmen to win you tournaments. Despite a poor bowling attack, Rangpur edged through the group stage before their batsmen had three big days out and took them to the title. Across the two play-off games and the final, Rangpur's top three scored 94% of their runs and faced 90% of their balls – dominating in a way that bowlers are prevented from doing by how T20 limits each bowler to 24 balls.

In the three knockout games, Gayle faced 130 balls – the equivalent to more than seven overs per game, or close to the full allocation of two bowlers in an innings. In these 130 balls, Gayle scored an absurd 275 runs, including 32 sixes. This was the ultimate strong-link performance: a reminder that, for all the strategising in T20, the format lends itself to being defined by a dominant batting performance.

Rangpur were coached by Tom Moody, the former Australian international cricketer and regular presence on the T20 circuit. Normally, Moody sides deliberately focus on bowling but, partly because of the owners' wishes, Rangpur adopted a different approach.

Four months after Rangpur's victory, Moody coached Sunrisers Hyderabad in the 2018 IPL. At full strength, three of Sunrisers's overseas players – Rashid Khan, Shakib Al Hasan and Billy Stanlake – regularly bowled out their full allocation of overs. Sunrisers also targeted strong local bowlers, with Indian seamers Sandeep Sharma, Bhuvneshwar Kumar and Siddarth Kaul all outstanding during the season.

Prioritising bowling was a deliberate choice – albeit one that became more pronounced after David Warner's ban from the season. The upshot was that Sunrisers challenged the orthodoxy of the essence of T20: attack, boundaries and excitement. There are certain parallels between the 2018 Sunrisers approach and *catenaccio*, the Italian style of football that emphasises defence. Sunrisers aimed to keep games as low-scoring as possible; the Rajiv Gandhi Stadium, their home ground, was far less conducive to rapacious scoring than, say, the Chinnaswamy Stadium.

'We put a lot of importance on the 120 balls we've got to defend,' explained Moody. 'On wickets where it's challenging I think your bowlers are more important. You'll be able to absolutely strangle your opponents in challenging conditions and your batsmen will be able to find a way, even if it's a conservative way, to be able to make a competitive total or chase down a modest total.'

Much discussion around T20 games concerns the idea of a 'par score': a score by the team batting first that, all things being equal, gives them a 50-50 chance of defending. Sunrisers showed that all things didn't have to be equal. They could score totals that would, by conventional thinking, be sub-par – but their bowling strength was such that they could win anyway. And so 'par' for Sunrisers was less than it would be for another team facing the same attack at the same ground. In 2018, Sunrisers defended scores of 132, 118, and 151. They kept their opponents to under 150 seven times during the 2018 IPL; no other side managed this feat more than three times.

'When people talk about a par score it's like a negative – as in they've only got a par score of 150,' said Moody. 'As long as you put the other pieces of your game together, in the field and with the ball, that 150 might be 20 too many – and that means it's way over par.'

Moody's comments were revealing: they showed how, more than any other decision that a team made, whether they prioritised batting or bowling informed the rest of their strategy. Being content with what other teams might have regarded as sub-par meant that Sunrisers did not need to pack their side with as much batting – and the batsmen they did have, notably Shikhar Dhawan, Kane Williamson and Shakib, played relatively sedately. Because they did not need as many runs, bowling dominant teams batted in a way that reduced risk – preferring minimising dot balls and scampering ones and twos over a high six-hitting percentage, especially in the first 15 overs.

Unlike Rangpur a few months earlier, Moody's team were consistent: Sunrisers came top of the group stages. Yet, just as Moody had benefited from batsmen dominating games in Bangladesh, so he suffered from the same during the IPL final. Sunrisers made 178-6 against Chennai Super Kings, which seemed to set them up for victory until Shane Watson's wonderful 117 not out.

While Moody favoured strong bowling sides, he believed that they could be more vulnerable when batting conditions were better – just as at the Wankhede during Watson's century. In 2018, Sunrisers lost six of the seven highest-scoring matches they were involved in.

Moody's perspective was backed up by analysis from CricViz that found in leagues that were traditionally higher scoring: the Blast and the IPL, batting-heavy teams were more successful than they were in lower scoring leagues such as the CPL and PSL where bowling-heavy teams were dominant. However, notably – even in the Blast and the IPL, batting-heavy teams could not match win percentages of bowling-heavy sides.

So the ideal balance of a side was to be strong in both areas. But, though more batting-orientated teams may have had a higher ceiling, as that remarkable Rangpur sequence attests, more bowling-orientated sides were more likely to be consistent.

Strong bowling attacks were better-suited to coping with the vagaries of the toss. Between 2014 and 2020 there was a growing movement to field first, with 60% of toss winners electing to chase.

But if a side were comfortable defending, losing the toss and being put in to bat was far less of a handicap. Some teams with outstanding bowling attacks were so confident in their bowlers that they chose to bat first – meaning that, given they are likely to be asked to bat if they lose the toss too, they could do what they wanted to regardless of the toss. In the

2017/18 Big Bash, Adelaide Strikers won the toss six times, including in their victories in the semi-final and final, and chose to bat every time. Like Sunrisers – and Sussex, who would later adopt a similar strategy – Adelaide had Rashid, imbuing them with belief that nothing was undefendable.

Strong bowling attacks were also particularly adept at exploiting home advantage. Preparing home wickets that play to a team's strength – Perth's fast, bouncy tracks or Guyana's slow turners – set a team up to be dominant at home. A side winning six of their seven IPL home games, say, only needed to win two matches away to reach the knockout stages. Teams with formidable batting were less adept at exploiting home advantage: short boundaries and excellent batting conditions were close to the norm everywhere.

Any T20 team strived to be balanced and the importance of bowling over batting was perhaps overstated at times. But when making decisions around the margins – between, say, a stronger batsman and stronger bowler at number seven – generally teams were slightly more consistent when they prioritised bowling.

The trade-offs in squad construction – Stability v Flexibility; Concentrated v Dispersed; Domestic v Overseas

If batting v bowling broadly represented what a team will look like; the second question was how? How were we going to pursue our strategy and build our squad?

There were various fundamental trade-offs that teams had to consider at this stage before they moved onto who they actually wanted to sign.

Should we build a small squad or a large squad? Should talent be concentrated or more evenly spread? Should we prioritise overseas or domestic stars? Should we focus on youth or experience?

In leagues like the PSL, CPL and BPL that use drafts, many of these trade-offs are imposed on teams. Most fundamentally, drafts prescribe how many players should be in each squad; what each player is paid is governed by which round of the draft they are signed.

In the IPL, with its auction, and the Blast and BBL, with their traditional contracting, these very fundamental issues were left unresolved. Squads for the 2020 IPL could range from 16-25 players and teams could spend up to the salary cap of £8.95 million however they wished.

In the 2018 IPL auction Kolkata Knight Riders and Royal Challengers Bangalore demonstrated two very different approaches to squad construction.

Kolkata Knight Riders eschewed this logic, and signed just 19 players in their squad, which was the smallest in IPL history. They even left one overseas slot empty. One of their seven overseas spots was given over to an experimental pick from their sister franchise Trinbago Knight Riders, essentially giving them six legitimate overseas options in their squad.

A trimmer squad allowed a team to plump for quality over quantity and so develop a stronger first-choice 11. KKR extended this logic to overseas players, spending a large proportion of their purse on Andre Russell, Chris Lynn, Sunil Narine and Mitchell Starc who they planned to play in most matches. They then spent frugally on their other overseas players, who were essentially viewed as back-ups.

The snag was that a slimmer squad is less flexible, and more vulnerable to the vagaries of form and injuries. When Starc and the young Indian quick Kamlesh Nagarkoti were ruled out of the season with injury, KKR had no replacements who could seamlessly slot in.

RCB's auction approach was almost the antithesis of KKR's. They filled 24 of the 25 slots in their squad, all eight overseas slots and – aside from a big outlay on one overseas player (AB de Villiers) their money was spent relatively evenly on the remaining seven overseas players. While KKR had opted for quality, RCB plumped for quantity. By having a larger squad and various overseas options they gave themselves more choice and greater flexibility.

Neither KKR or RCB's approaches were illogical. But both had distinct pros and cons.

Tellingly, after the auction it was fairly easy to identify what KKR's strongest team would be, with the main four overseas players locked in before Starc's injury and only 19 players to choose from. The same could not be said of RCB whose big squad and more dispersed spend made it far harder to identify their structure and set-up.

RCB's flexible approach certainly had merit: their bowling attack comprised right-arm quicks, a left-arm quick, a leg spinner, multiple off spinners and a left-arm spinner, enabling them to exploit match-ups and adapt to different conditions and opponents. But this approach required strategic and selection clarity that RCB had lacked historically. Adjusting a team regularly made sense in many respects but required careful management of players who could slot in and out, which could damage players' form and role clarity. With a stable XI, said AR Srikkanth, the KKR analyst, 'players can play freely, play their natural game and according to the situation. 'KKR's smaller squad established stability and consistency of selection that saw them finish third in the points table while RCB failed to replicate such stability and finished sixth.

To what extent teams prioritised overseas or domestic players was also a very fundamental trade-off. Overseas players brought star quality and rare skills, but their availability was less guaranteed than domestic players, who also brought familiarity with local conditions and would in all leagues represent the large majority of a team's squad. Some teams built their squad with overseas players at their centre while others prioritised domestic talent and used overseas players to plug gaps around them.

The 2020 PSL encapsulated two contrasting approaches to overseas players. The exceptional supply of domestic pace bowlers meant sides often prioritised overseas batsmen. Islamabad took this approach to its extreme, signing just one overseas pace bowler (Dale Steyn) and *four* overseas top order batsmen (Luke Ronchi, Dawid Malan, Colin Ingram and Colin Munro). Steyn was unavailable for United's early matches so they picked all four overseas batsmen, filling spots one to four in the batting order.

In contrast to Islamabad, Peshawar Zalmi had a healthy supply of domestic batsmen, including Kamran Akmal and Shoaib Malik, two of the top five run-scorers in PSL history. Before 2020 they also signed the talented youngster Haider Ali, meaning three of their top four spots in their order were filled by local batsmen. With Wahab Riaz, Hasan Ali and Rahat Ali, Zalmi's domestic pace bowling was also well-stocked. These twin strengths gave Zalmi greater flexibility with their overseas players with just one specialist batsman (Tom Banton) signed at the draft and the remaining spots going to all-rounders (Kieron Pollard, Liam Livingstone, Liam Dawson and Dwaine Pretorius).

The differences in squad construction between United and Zalmi manifested themselves in the raw statistics for each team: 34% of Islamabad's balls were faced or bowled by overseas players, while only 22% of Zalmi's were – comfortably the fewest of all teams. Indeed, in some matches Zalmi chose to only pick three overseas players.

There were benefits to both approaches – overseas players were often the best players available in a competition so building a strategy around them could produce remarkable results: in that same PSL season Lahore

Qalandars enjoyed these benefits with the Australian pair of Ben Dunk and Chris Lynn winning matches single-handedly. Yet if these overseas players fell out of form it could expose the weaker domestic players. From Chennai in the IPL to Perth in the Big Bash, the most successful teams were generally those with the best domestic players, with overseas players the condiments.

Age was another factor in squad construction. The short contract cycles in many leagues made it difficult for teams to hoard young talent across a long period.

Often the average age of a squad was little more than the product of the players already contracted to the team. However, sometimes there were clear examples of teams pursuing older or younger squads. The CSK team of 2018-2020 – mocked as 'dad's army' – prioritised experience. So did the 2017 Islamabad United squad – at times, eight of their starting XI were at least 33, with seven over 35. Like the 2018 CSK side, Islamabad won the title in 2016 after coming through a number of tense finishes.

Yet younger sides also had benefits. Most obviously younger teams were generally fitter and more athletic and they often incorporated players at the cutting edge of the format. Most significantly, young teams had the benefit of having greater scope to build dynastic success. In 2018 the Delhi Daredevils, perennial strugglers in the IPL who had not reached the play-offs since 2012, made a clear move to target youth in an effort to build for long-term success. Ahead of the auction Delhi opted to retain two of India's brightest young talents: Rishabh Pant and Shreyas Iyer, making Iyer captain. At the auction itself Delhi continued to prioritise youth, signing the teenagers Prithvi Shaw, Abhishek Sharma and Sandeep Lamichhane. Their young squad was built with a clear eye on the future and the following season they reached the play-offs for the first time in seven seasons.

Perhaps the most nuanced trade-off was the extent to which teams opted for specialists – batsmen who batted and bowlers who bowled – over all-rounders. This trade-off could be seen as a proxy for the idea of batting and bowling depth. Generally teams who focussed on specialists were likely to have less depth in both departments but higher quality overall, while teams who liked all-rounders would generally have more depth but slightly lower quality. Two of the world's foremost T20 teams in 2020, England and India, embodied these two different approaches.

In Ben Stokes and Moeen Ali England had two batsmen capable of batting in the top seven and contributing with the ball. Many of their bowlers, like Tom Curran, Chris Jordan and Sam Curran, were also able batsmen. The upshot was that England had excellent depth in both departments – with useful batsmen at nine or even ten and six genuine bowling options.

India often followed the opposing tactic. Once Suresh Raina and Yuvraj Singh had been moved on, very few of India's T20 batsmen could even occasionally contribute with the ball; most their bowlers were fairly weak batsmen. These resources made Hardik Pandya essential: he was a good enough batsman to bat in the top seven and a good enough bowler to bowl four overs.

While the dominance of specialists over all-rounders compromised India's depth, the quality of the players in the respective departments was very high. India's strategy revolved around the idea that their batsmen would do the batting and the bowlers would do the bowling.

The contrast in strategies was evident in the 2018 T20 series between the sides. In all three matches India only used five bowlers – each bowling their allocation of four overs – while in two of the three matches England used six bowlers. India number seven batsman only faced 10 balls across the three matches and the rest of their order wasn't required; England's numbers 7 to 11 faced 46. With good batsmen in the lower order, England's top order were more inclined to bat aggressively, while India were forced to be slightly more circumspect.

A specialist strategy places huge importance on the balancing player who is asked to fulfill two roles to a high standard. The pressures on this system were exposed in early 2020 when Hardik was injured and India were forced to adapt their strategy because they could not find a player of sufficient quality to balance the team. Their response therefore was to select two all-rounders in Ravindra Jadeja and Shivam Dubey. Essentially they feared that just one all-rounder would leave them exposed in one department.

Genuine all-rounders – who could get into the team for their batting or bowling alone – were as rare as Faberge eggs. So teams often made significant compromises around their batting or bowling depth or picked multi-skilled players who lacked sufficient quality with either bat or ball. Teams with good batting depth were often weaker in bowling and vice versa; only genuine all-rounders could help bridge the divide. No element of a T20 side reflected their broader strategy more than how they approached the trade-off between specialists and all-rounders.

Platform Laying v Powerplay Maximising

The Powerplay is arguably the most interesting period of a T20 game. During this phase wickets are at their most valuable – but the fielding restrictions encourage the batting team to risk wickets in pursuit of quick runs while the ball is hard and the field is up. This trade-off was one of the most significant in reflecting the character of a T20 team.

For seven years Brisbane Heat deployed Brendon McCullum and Chris Lynn – the 'bash brothers' who both liked a beer, a punt and to belt the ball out the ground – in their top three, often opening together, to exploit the fielding restrictions. This was the inverse of Perth Scorchers's approach.

If the Big Bash was a party, Scorchers were the designated drivers. While many opponents began their innings with all the self-restraint of overexcited teens, Scorchers began with a steely determination to resist the allure of excess. This platform-laying approach was led by Michael Klinger – an orthodox and phenomenally consistent top-order batsman who, across his T20 career averaged 35 runs, with a strike rate of 123: no opening batsman with more than 2500 career runs averaged more at a lower strike rate. Klinger was the embodiment of a very specific Powerplay strategy of prioritising wicket preservation over scoring rate.

Often, Perth's entire top order channeled Klinger's spirit of cautious accumulation. In 2017, Perth signed Ian Bell – a classical Test batsman – as an overseas player. With Shaun Marsh, Adam Voges, Sam Whiteman and Cameron Bancroft, Perth often fielded a top order who all had a strike rate of under 130.

Unsurprisingly given the top-order they assembled, the Scorchers had the lowest run rate in the Powerplay among the eight BBL teams – just 6.97 between 2012/13 and 2017/18. But they lost the fewest wickets per Powerplay of any side in this period. Their average Powerplay score was 42 for 1. It sounds like a dreary formula – but it was part of a system that worked, and spectacularly well. Perth won three titles in four seasons with this approach, and came in the top three in seven consecutive years, one of the most impressive T20 dynasties.

Starting cautiously allowed Perth to accelerate in the middle overs, when they had the second highest run rate of any side, and at the death. Most importantly, Perth didn't need to score that quickly, because their bowling attack was among the strongest in T20 history, often comprising five international bowlers. David Willey, who was England's regular T20 opening bowler, was sometimes used as third change behind the likes of Jason Behrendorff, Mitchell Johnson and Nathan Coulter-Nile. With comfortably the league's best bowling attack, low-risk accumulation in the Powerplay was ideally suited to Perth because it set them well on their way to at least posting a defendable total or chasing a target that often did not require fast scoring rates.

'Bowlers win you games,' explained Voges, Perth's captain during their storied run. 'That's what our success has been built around. We haven't always scored 180 or 200 runs in a game, but we're the group that can defend 130 or 140.'

The use of an anchor like Klinger could also depend on the maturity of the team. From 2008-2012, Gloucestershire's inexperienced side finished bottom of their T20 group in three out of five seasons. So John Bracewell, Gloucestershire's head coach in 2013, identified Klinger as an ideal fit to take the county to the next stage. For the next seven seasons, the team's entire batting strategy would essentially be built around Klinger.

'We had some extremely optimistic young hitters who loved the T20 environment and Maxi able to consistently bat half the overs allowed the rest to target 60 balls per match. This was more about adapting to our strengths and recognising our potential flaws,' Bracewell explained. In the context of Gloucestershire's limited budget, the strategy worked: in Klinger's seven seasons, they made the T20 Blast quarter-finals three times, and topped their group once. Gloucestershire increased their win percentage from 29% between 2008 and 2012 to 47% in Klinger's time at the club.

The answer to the question of whether a team needed an anchor – or sometimes multiple anchors – depended on the individual character of their side.

This was nicely illustrated by Babar Azam, who returned contrasting impacts with two notably different teams. Babar's attractive technique and wonderful timing earned him acclaim, but he was at times guilty of scoring too slowly. When playing for Pakistan – a strong bowling team who often played in low-scoring games – Babar's steady anchoring method proved an excellent fit: he contributed +5.7 runs more than the average player when playing for them, according to CricViz's match impact model. Yet when playing for his PSL side Karachi Kings – who were not as strong a bowling team and generally played in higher scoring games – he was less valuable, only contributing around half a run more than an average player. His game-plan was ideal for lower scoring matches but could be exposed when higher run rates and more power was required.

Much as Klinger's approach was emblematic of platform-laying, McCullum was similarly representative of the Powerplay-exploiters. From Brisbane to Lahore Qalandars and Gujarat Lions, McCullum was a common thread in many of the most aggressive top orders. These teams were prepared to risk early wickets in pursuit of quick runs, viewing the Powerplay as a unique opportunity to get ahead in the game.

Across their two IPL seasons Gujarat partnered McCullum with a combination of the hard-hitting Bajan Dwayne Smith, Australia's Aaron Finch, England's Jason Roy, and the Indian pocket-rocket Ishan Kishan. The Lions scored at 8.62 runs per over in the first six overs – second only to Kolkata Knight Riders who partnered Lynn with the pinch-hitter Sunil Narine – another common player among Powerplay exploiters.

Powerplay-exploiters generally saw a greater variance in their returns than the platform-layers. For instance, Gujarat lost three wickets in five of their 30 Powerplays but scored at more than 10 runs per over on eight occasions.

As data analysis evolved, the debate about a team's approach to the start of their innings meant sides looked beyond a player's overall strike rate when assembling their line-up. A team who prioritised maximising the batting Powerplay also focussed on players who started their innings rapidly, who better-exploited the fielding restrictions than players who absorbed balls before accelerating.

In early 2020, England dropped Dawid Malan, despite a phenomenal start to his T20 international career. While Malan had shown that he could score at an ample rate, he was hampered by his strike rate in his first 10 balls – 110 across his T20 career. The players England preferred for a place in their top three – Roy, Jos Buttler and Jonny Bairstow – all had strike rates of at least 137 in the first 10 balls during the same time period.

The decision not to select Malan, then, was rooted in how England wanted to approach the Powerplay. Having Ben Stokes and Moeen Ali allowed England to bat deep. This made Malan's consistent scoring, while beginning relatively sedately, less valuable than it would have been for teams like Perth who did not bat as deep as England. England's non-selection of Malan in their first choice T20 side – just like that of anchor Joe Root – illustrated how teams' styles meant they had no need for players who would be valuable in an equally good team who adopted different tactics. The question for teams was not just about a player's individual qualities, but one of team balance.

Different teams had profoundly different approaches to the Powerplay – between maximising runs and laying a platform – but it was too simplistic to say one approach was inherently right or wrong. Rather, the optimal approach was specific to each team, particularly dependent on whether they were stronger in batting or bowling and how deep their batting order was. Teams like Gujarat, Kolkata Knight Riders, Brisbane Heat and Nottinghamshire thrived by attacking the Powerplay with elan and routinely being, say, 65 for two or three after six overs; those like Sunrisers Hyderabad, Perth Scorchers and Gloucestershire succeeded after regularly being around 40-1 off six overs.

So while a team's approach to the batting Powerplay reflected the broader composition of their side, perhaps the optimal approach was a hybrid that sought to retain what was best about the two styles. Batting teams could attack in the Powerplay – using aggressive pinch-hitters, like Narine or perhaps Rashid Khan, alongside an assertive specialist batsman. Yet, to help them rebuild after losing early wickets or adapt to playing on pitches that make clearing the boundary harder, they could also use a player like Kohli or Williamson as an anchor – aiming to use them in a set role, not a set position in the order. Such a player, ideally, would come in around the seventh over to bat during the middle overs and set up a team for their final assault. In this way, perhaps, batting teams could avoid making any trade-offs: they could simultaneously attack with gusto at the start of an innings, and have insurance if these gung-ho tactics went wrong.

Boundary-Hitting v Activity Rate

Most batsmen can be thought of as existing somewhere on a continuum, between aiming to hit as many sixes as possible and aiming to score off every ball. The contrast is encapsulated by the batting styles of two of T20's most iconic players. Chris Gayle failed to score off 45% of deliveries but scored a six every nine balls – brutality that rendered dot balls of scant importance. Virat Kohli was Gayle's antithesis; he only allowed 32% dot balls and built a game defined by efficiency. During one of Kohli's most famous T20 innings, in a virtual quarter-final against Australia in the 2016 World Cup, he scored four twos in five balls at one stage, such was his meticulous placement and the intensity of his running between the wickets. By 2020, Gayle scored a two every 30 balls, Kohli one every 13 balls.

Ultimately, the difference in these styles was one of priorities. The Gayle approach centred on the idea that the currency that mattered in T20 batting was the boundary – above all, the six. A higher boundary-rate, with a particular emphasis on sixes, was what mattered above all else; after all, an over with four dot balls could still yield 12 runs. Thinking in multiples of four and six turned the quick single into an undesirable risk – especially as, inverting the traditional logic that batsmen were most vulnerable when they allowed themselves to be bowled at for a whole over, big hitters could particularly relish facing a bowler for a whole over.

The Kohli approach was built on a very different notion. With only 120 balls an innings, allowing a multitude of dot balls amounted to a flagrant waste of resources. Instead, players should use subtle placement and aggressive running to minimise dot balls, turning dots into quick singles and ones into twos and so maximising their activity rate – the proportion of balls from which they scored. In the process players could score quickly while minimising risks, and still hit the worst deliveries for four. Even if a side only managed a four every two overs, if they scored a single off every other ball they would still score at 7.5 runs an over.

Naturally, the batting style of teams themselves was determined by their mix between these styles.

The West Indies came closest to extending Gayle's style to the entire team. With Gayle opening – rendering it much harder for his team-mates to scamper singles – the West Indies emphatically embraced the Gayle approach from 2012-16.

They did so in full knowledge that the strategy would lead to an alarming number of dot balls. The trade-off, as they saw it, was worth it, because no side could score sixes with such reliability. Even Marlon Samuels – at number three, nominally the anchor player – smote six sixes during the 2012 World Cup final.

At their best, the West Indies's brutality rendered extra singles trivial. Across the semi-finals and final of the victorious 2012 and 2016 campaigns, the West Indies scored 39 sixes while conceding 14 – an 150-run advantage over their opponents that scotched the notion that 'smart cricket' in T20 was about minimising dot balls.

'We knew that we had boundary hitters down to No. 8,' Phil Simmons, the West Indies coach in 2016, explained. 'We didn't worry about dot balls too much because we knew we could make them up.' Carlos Brathwaite's four thunderous sixes at Eden Gardens were the perfect end point for a T20 team that were not merely among the best of all time but also the most distinctive.

Five months after winning the World Cup, the West Indies arrived in the UAE for a three-match T20 series against Pakistan. While the West Indies were missing a couple of their World Cup winning stars, notably Chris Gayle and Andre Russell, they had Kieron Pollard and Sunil Narine, two titans who had missed the World Cup, available again.

Pakistan planned to neuter the West Indies's six-hitting strength. They deliberately prepared slow and low wickets in Dubai and Abu Dhabi, preventing batsmen from hitting through the line of the ball. The boundary ropes were moved right out. Effectively, Pakistan were trying to change the terrain on which the battle was fought – from being a game about power, which Pakistan would lose, to a game of strike-rotation and placement.

The West Indies were emasculated. They only mustered seven sixes across the three games Instead, Pakistan's strong bowling attack and superiority in hitting fours and rotating the strike – scoring off 67% of their deliveries compared to just 57% for the West Indies – underpinned a crushing 3-0 victory. Six months later, they defeated the West Indies 3-1 away, benefiting from slow wickets in Trinidad & Tobago.

'Conditions played into our favour,' Pakistan's head coach Mickey Arthur said reflecting on these twin series victories. 'That allowed our guys to bowl cutters, there was a little bit of reverse swing on offer. It suited our spinners and it suited our game plan. They were hard wickets just to come in and take the attack – the wickets weren't that true, it was tough to hit solid cricket shots, you almost had to roll your sleeves up and work as a batsman, instead of just walking in and just enjoying it from ball one. We played very smart cricket.'

This success was the template for Pakistan building one of the finest international T20 teams, even if the quirks of the T20 World Cup scheduling denied them a chance to take this team to the world stage. From 2016 to 2018 they won 29 out of 33 games, easily the most sustained run of success ever recorded at the top echelons of international cricket.

They achieved it with a simple formula. Smartly exploiting home conditions – 'boundaries out suited our game a lot,' said Arthur – Pakistan played on wickets that maximised their comparative advantage in bowling. Unusually, Pakistan chose to bat first most of the time, such was the prowess of their wonderfully varied attack.

'Particularly in Dubai, and in Asian countries, we knew that if we got above 155, we could defend. Stats told us we defended that over 90% of the time. So we set out every innings to get 155,' Arthur said.

'The batting unit set up around very, very defined roles. And we knew that on a good day we get 170, on a bad day we probably get 145. But we were pretty consistent in getting around that 150, 155 mark. And then our bowlers did us proud all the time by defending it.'

The pragmatism of this batting approach – typical of many strong bowling sides – maximised Pakistan's consistency. Hitting the ball along the ground was favoured. Rather than try to imitate the Caribbean style, which Pakistan lacked the batting heft to do, they charted a different course, built around the dexterous wrists of opener Babar Azam and the shrewdness of middle order accumulators Shoaib Malik, Mohammed Hafeez and Sarfaraz Ahmed.

'Our mantra was always we're doing it our way,' Arthur reflected. 'We didn't have power hitters. We didn't have guys that could come in in overs 15,16, 17 and whack it out the ground. So we had to do things differently.

'We looked to run hard which is why we worked so much in our fitness. From overs seven to 15 it was a case of hopefully we had a batsman in and then it was a case of running hard.'

The graceful Azam was Pakistan's pivotal batsmen: between the end of the 2016 World Cup and the end of 2018 Babar averaged 54, the best in the world and only faced 28% dot balls – second only to his teammate Shoaib Malik who faced just 25%. 'The minute we got outside the Powerplay, then Babar knew he had to be there for the long haul – he had to get us to over 15 or 16,' Arthur explained.

One statistic that Arthur focused on embodied Pakistan's emphasis. He aimed to ensure that Pakistan's bowlers returned a dot ball percentage of at least 40% with the ball and less than 33% with the bat. Across the 33 game streak, Pakistan's bowlers returned a dot ball percentage of 40% and their batsmen 31% – matching both targets.

'We had dot-ball percentage goals that we wanted to achieve every game,' he said. 'We always measured dot-ball percentages. Dot-ball percentage for me was an area that we improved on drastically.'

Where the West Indies's hitting mocked the marginal value of an extra single here or there, Pakistan treasured the single, with Arthur's focus upon fitness maximising Pakistan's ability to pinch extra runs. 'In cricket the one is one of the most important shots because the one takes the pressure off you, it rotates the strike.'

Yet the macro-forces in the sport – of rising run rates and falling balls per wicket – seemed to favour boundary-hitters. All told, sides with a higher boundary percentage won 82% of matches, but those with a higher activity rate only won 52% of matches. The future of batting, perhaps, belongs to those rare few players and teams who can simultaneously do both, turning the biggest trade-off in T20 batting into no trade-off at all.

Pace Bowling v Spin Bowling

When assembling a bowling attack, perhaps the most fundamental question faced by a T20 team is how much pace do they want to bowl, and how much spin? Between 2015 and 2020, the average team bowled eight overs of spin and 12 overs of pace. All sides sought to find the right balance based on a combination of conditions, resources and opposition match-ups.

In the 2019 Caribbean Premier League, Guyana Amazon Warriors won 11 consecutive games, only slipping up in the final. They did so through unabashedly embracing spin, bowling 131.2 overs of spin – 57% of their overs – during the competition. In the process they also became the first ever side to bowl more overs of spin than pace in the Powerplay over a season, delivering 60 overs of spin in the Powerplay but just 12 overs of pace.

This was only an extreme version of the approach Guyana adopted from the CPL's creation. Exploiting the natural turn at Providence, their home ground – and, grumbled some opponents, taking home advantage to an unfair degree – Guyana bowled spin with 52% of their overs from 2013-19, the highest figure of any major domestic T20 side in the world. At home, that rose to 56%, also the highest figure in the world. Providence's slow, low, dry pitch and vast boundaries were perfectly suited to a spin-heavy attack.

This approach exploited how, in all phases of T20, spinners had a better economy rate than seamers. Guyana had an array of different types of spinners: off spinners Chris Green and Shoaib Malik; leg spinners Shadab Khan, Imran Tahir and Qais Ahmed; and left-arm finger spinner Chandrapaul Hemraj. The attack had contrasting strengths: for instance Green bowled a very tight line, often barely turning the ball and routinely opened the bowling. Tahir was a prodigious turner who operated less in the Powerplay but was more accomplished bowling at the death.

'With pace the ball can go everywhere – if you're not express pace or don't have huge skill then it's basically a bowling machine set-up and guys are comfortable,' said Johan Botha, the head coach for Guyana in 2019. 'I definitely think spin is still underused. Teams can use it more aggressively – but you've got to have quality.

'With our team structure and the make-up of the wicket, it just suits our attack perfectly. With the Caribbean players, they've obviously got a lot of power – if you're not express pace or don't do anything with the ball or have great skills it's just there to be hit. So we need to use the spinners – guys who make the ball move off the wicket. And with the leg spinners, you've got to pick the ball out the hand which way it's going and that obviously gives them the edge – so you've first got to see it before you commit to the shot.'

Such spin depth compensated for a distinctly unremarkable pace attack. But while spin domination underpinned Guyana's phenomenal home record, playing away from Providence required Guyana to 'change our mindset a little bit,' Botha reflected.

In the 2019 final against Barbados Tridents, staged in Trinidad & Tobago, Guyana's spin quartet returned combined figures of 1-77 from their ten overs, allowing Barbados to reach an insurmountable 171-6. It was Guyana's fifth defeat from five finals; all were away from Providence.

Embracing spin seems particularly well-suited to maximising home advantage. Many T20 sides with the best home records were among the teams who bowled the most spin, and had pitches that offered unusual turn. Guyana were the torchbearers for this style of play but Chennai at Chepauk and Kolkata at Eden Gardens both found sustained IPL success through this method. So too did Lancashire at Old Trafford, Hampshire at the Ageas Bowl and the Sydney Thunder at Spotless Stadium. Afghanistan's national side also pursued a spin-heavy strategy.

The lesson from Guyana, perhaps, was that relying upon spin could be a brilliant way to reach the knockout stages, but a less effective tool for actually winning competitions. Tournament organisers often prepared wickets for knockout matches that were conducive to high-scoring and nullified spin, making high-quality pace essential.

Yet if bowling an abundance of spin has generally been a successful template, the decision about whether to prioritise pace or spin should reflect a team's home conditions and the supply of players. The Perth Scorchers team who won three BBL titles and reached the semi-finals every year from 2011/12 to 2017/18 bowled an unusually small amount of spin – less than 30%, and even less at home.

This strategy was perfectly suited to exploiting Perth's two distinguishing qualities – the conditions at the WACA: a bouncy pitch aided the quicks and short straight boundaries neutered spinners; and the phenomenal supply of high-quality local quick bowlers. Perth fielded an combination of the left-arm pace of Mitchell Johnson, the left-arm swing of Jason Behrendorff, the right-arm swing and seam of Nathan Coulter-Nile and Jhye Richardson and the knuckleballs and savvy of Andrew Tye, who took a world-record three T20 hat-tricks in a calendar year. These local pace bowlers, all born in Western Australia, were augmented by overseas recruits: Alfonso Thomas and Yasir Arafat – a pair of high-quality death bowlers – the left-arm Powerplay specialist David Willey and the versatile Tim Bresnan. Even the spin attack, small that it was, provided quality through the wrist spin of Brad Hogg and wily finger spin of Ashton Agar.

While spin bowlers outperformed quicks by most metrics, pace bowlers did have certain advantages, as Perth illuminated. The best pace bowlers – who had an array of cutters and slower balls, as well as the traditional weapons of the bouncer and yorker, so could vary their pace – often had a greater range and variety of deliveries, making them more adaptable when confronted with different wickets and boundary sizes.

The world's fastest bowlers also had the option to simply take conditions out of the equation entirely by bowling at very high speeds. Ultimately, it mattered little what the pitch was doing when the bowler was hurling down 150 kph thunderbolts. Bowling at this speed gave pace bowlers an element of physical intimidation that spinners lacked.

Both Guyana and Perth stood as extreme templates for how to ruthlessly exploit home advantage; they just did so in completely contrasting ways. Ultimately, the utopia that all teams chased was an attack that could simultaneously dominate at home and adapt away.

Wicket-Taking v Run-Saving

Over 16 games in the 2018/19 Big Bash, the Melbourne Renegades hit just two half-centuries. Ordinarily this would be a template for T20 failure – except the Renegades wound up champions. This was a triumph for a batting style that emphasised selflessness and depth over stars, and a strong bowling attack. But, more than anything, it was vindication for a particular style of play, which could be best surmised as defensive bowling. Melbourne Renegades had such control that they could restrict opponents to manageable scores without depending on the most proven way of keeping runs down: taking wickets. Here was a bowling attack – if it could be called that – built on the principle of defence.

The work constructing the line-up began before the Renegades's campaign. The side had several fine right-arm pace bowlers, led by Australian international Kane Richardson, but lacked variety – so they were ill-equipped to exploit match-ups. To remedy this, head coach Andrew McDonald targeted signing a left-arm pace bowler, recruiting Englishman Harry Gurney over glitzier options. The Renegades also signed leg spinner Cameron Boyce, who turned the ball the opposite way to off spinners Mohammad Nabi and Tom Cooper. A monochrome attack was now technicolour.

Many coaches claimed that the best way to slow the scorecard was to take wickets. While this was true, the more attacking a team was the more they compromised control – McDonald's primary focus was defence for the sake of defence. Rather than hunting for wickets, the Renegades viewed wickets as a natural by-product of defending well enough.

'I see bowling as 120 balls to defend,' McDonald explained. 'If you can defend every ball it will probably bring about wickets anyway so we definitely had a defensive mindset around our bowling. We put a lot of time and effort into planning; it's one thing planning but it's having the ability to execute as well. The bowlers that we had on that list were able to execute as well – so yes the attitude of defending 120 balls is a philosophy that we went with.' The Renegades's gambit, essentially, was that even if opponents got off to a good start and had well-set batsmen, their bowling in the last stages of an innings was still sufficiently robust to rein them in.

Often, the attitude was detectable from the very first over. On several occasions, the Renegades opened with Nabi or Cooper, an auxiliary bowler who was not in their main five main bowlers. Getting one over from their sixth bowler out the way gave the Renegades more flexibility.

'We tried to sneak that first over, hoping it would sort of go for less than a run a ball – there's one gone, and it gives us one extra over at the death,' McDonald said. 'Against certain teams we felt like we were going to be vulnerable at the back end so an over from our key bowlers was more valuable at the back end rather than the front end. So that was the trade-off and Cooper did an amazing job up front. He was clever enough to defend those first six balls and disappear one over pretty quickly. And then it helped us set up our bowling distribution for the rest of the game.'

The deployment of Cooper symbolised the Renegades's approach. The first over of the innings was when the ball swung most and batsmen were most vulnerable. But so committed to the idea of defence were the Renegades that they were happy to forgo the benefits of first over swing to protect their death overs and reinforce their run-saving options.

'There's one thing that's a given – you've got to bowl 20 overs. And the stronger bowling line-ups tend to be able to manage the 20 overs a lot better,' McDonald said. 'The way we started our strategy meetings was our bowling distribution and then that lent itself to the selection of the team. So, we were more concerned about how that 20 overs looked and then worked out our team from there.

'Our game plan was built upon really making sure that we had great defensive options from 15 overs onwards. We felt as though that could be our point of difference if we were able to close out games.'

With such potency at the death, the Renegades could defend middling totals even without bowling the opposition out. In one league match, they set Sydney Thunder an underwhelming target of 153, yet restricted Sydney to 140-5, with Sydney's Jason Sangha left on 54 not out from 49 balls; he had batted deep, as chasing teams want one frontline batsman to do, yet been unable to discover a final flourish against Gurney, Richardson and Dan Christian. It was a prelude to one of the most remarkable T20 games of all time.

The 2019 Big Bash final was an organiser's dream: the first ever all-Melbourne final, pitting the Renegades against the Stars, whose star-studded top five, including Marcus Stoinis and Glenn Maxwell, befitted their team name. When the Renegades recovered to 145-5 from their 20 overs, the Stars were still favourites to win; when the Stars advanced to 93-0 in the 13th over, Renegades's home fans were making for the exit.

At which point the Renegades produced one of the most stunning comebacks in T20 history. Over 14 balls, Boyce dismissed both openers and Chris Tremain snared Australian T20 players Maxwell and Peter Handscomb. The entire attack was relentless: Gurney did not concede a boundary at all from his four overs. In a surreal half hour, 53 from 43 balls with all ten wickets in hand became 28 required off the final over. For the first time, the Renegades were Big Bash champions.

Even when their position seemed futile, the Renegades maintained a disciplined defence: they only conceded three boundaries, and 36 runs, from the Powerplay. 'You can kill the game in the Powerplay when you're only chasing 145. None for 36 is great, we had 10 wickets in hand but you probably needed to go a bit harder,' Maxwell, the Stars' captain, lamented. 'They bowled pretty well and kept us around 7.5 an over and as soon as you lose a wicket that can really sky-rocket.'

The Renegades had no right to win from the Stars being 93-0 – but their strong defensive attack meant that the game was not already completely out of sight. For the Renegades, the skill to restrict boundaries was their elixir. Their stuttering innings had contained an unspectacular 12 fours and four sixes – 72 runs in boundaries. But they only allowed the Stars seven fours and three sixes – 46 runs in boundaries, including none at all for an extraordinary 45-ball period from the end of the 12th over to the middle of the 20th. By this point the home crowd at the Docklands were delirious: the trophy was already mathematically won.

The pitfalls of the Renegades' approach were illustrated in their ill-fated title defence. Building a bowling strategy so totally around defence left little margin for error. If one or two bowlers lost form or suffered injury, as they did in the following campaign, opponents could capitalise on weaker links. Under a new coach, the Renegades lost their opening nine fixtures and finished bottom.

The antithesis to the controlled, almost regimented style of the Renegades was in teams who attacked with the ball, risking conceding runs in pursuit of wickets. In 2020, Multan Sultans – coached by Andy Flower and using England's analyst Nathan Leamon – believed that wickets were the most effective means to quell scoring, shaping their bowling strategy.

The Sultans' approach was perfectly illustrated in a match against Quetta Gladiators – who were primed to launch an assault at 99-1 after 11 overs chasing 200. A more defensive-minded team may have opted to squeeze Quetta; the required run rate was over 11 per over. But Multan were not as strong as the Renegades at the death and recognised the destabilising value of wickets through the middle overs. They threw the ball to left-arm spinner Khushdil Shah, who was in the team for his batting and had not yet bowled a single over in the season.

Khushdil's direction of spin – away from the two right-handers – made attacking him risky, but with the required rate spiralling Quetta's batsmen had no choice. Three balls into his over, Ashan Ali picked out long on. Quetta's launch never came and Multan emerged as winners by 30 runs. It was this spirit of attack that defined the Sultans' campaign and they finished top of the table before the Covid-19 pandemic prematurely ended the season.

Defensive teams like the Renegades often back-loaded their bowling, placing an emphasis on the death overs. Attacking teams like Multan generally front-loaded their attack, knowing that early wickets would make squeezing the innings at the death far easier, whoever bowled then.

In the Powerplay the Sultans were pace-heavy and had a varied attack with the beanpole Mohammad Irfan, swing bowlers Sohail Tanvir and Junaid Khan and the skiddy Muhammad Ilyas operating together. This contrasting group were all encouraged to attack. No team found more swing in the Powerplay than Multan. This strategy produced high-octane cricket. In four of eight matches Multan conceded more than 10 runs per over in the Powerplay but in four they took at least two wickets in the phase; in two games they both happened together. These returns encapsulated the nature of attacking bowling: it encouraged both more runs and more wickets.

The approach took bravery but was made far easier by the quality of Multan's spinners. In the middle overs, Multan could turn to the elite leg spin of Imran Tahir and Shahid Afridi, the off spin of Moeen Ali and the left-arm spin of Khushdil. This gave Multan an attack that could exploit a variety of match-ups.

Despite not possessing a single death bowler of particular repute, the Sultans recorded the best death overs economy rate in the league. Their aggression earlier in the innings deprived opponents of well-set batsmen; even in the last five overs, Multan took a wicket every 8.6 balls.

Watching attacking bowling teams was a very different experience to watching defensive teams. Defensive bowling sides tended to seem in control; generally their matches followed a fairly predictable pattern. Attacking bowling teams often produced far more volatile cricket. Attacking bowling, by definition, compromised defence – so the Powerplay, especially, featured an abundance of both runs and wickets.

The team that defied trade-offs
While the West Indies team that won two World Cups in 2012 and 2016 were widely regarded as the first international T20 dynasty, by 2019 they were, in the eyes of many, eclipsed as T20's greatest side by the Mumbai Indians. 'Given the constraints with budgets in a draft or auction you are always compromised,' explained Moody. 'If you go all out for that impact player in one discipline you find yourself being slightly limited in other areas.' Yet no T20 team so effectively avoided these compromises as Mumbai.

By the end of the 2010s the IPL was often thought to be the highest standard of T20 outside a select few match-ups between international cricket's strongest sides: Australia, India, England and – when at full strength – the West Indies. The combination of an open market, India's vast talent pool and the wealth of IPL sides meant the league's best sides would be considered favourites against most international teams.

In the 2019 IPL final, with a heart-stopping one-run win over Chennai Super Kings, Mumbai sealed their fourth IPL crown in seven years, to go with their two Champions League titles. The basis for this remarkable haul lay in Mumbai's ability to navigate the trade-offs faced by T20 teams the world over.

By their 2017 and 2019 title victories, it was impossible to say whether Mumbai were a batting team or a bowling team – they were both. The nature of drafts, auctions and salary caps in domestic leagues meant that there was generally an inverse relationship between batting and bowling strength. Escaping this trade-off made Mumbai a remarkable side.

The basis of any great team is the composition of their squad. By 2019, Mumbai's squad balanced bat and ball, pace and spin, youth and experience, attack and defence, dominance at home and adaptability away.

The roots of Mumbai's trade-off defying squad were in 2010, when the franchise had the foresight to establish a scouting network comprising six scouts, which would be led by the former India and Mumbai head coach John Wright from 2015. The network was astonishingly effective at identifying brilliant young talent. The biggest success story was the 19-year-old Jasprit Bumrah, plucked out of age-group cricket in Gujarat before becoming the world's best quick and the spearhead of Mumbai's pace attack. The all-rounders Hardik and Krunal Pandya were also products of Mumbai's scouting and also would become the fulcrums of Mumbai's team.

The Pandya brothers and Bumrah were the three headline recruits of a stellar list of players unearthed by the scouts. Mumbai could also credit identifying Yuzvendra Chahal, Mayank Markande, Rahul Chahar, Shreyas Gopal, Suryakumar Yadav, Kuldeep Yadav, Axar Patel and Nitish Rana to their network. This stellar group – all identified by Mumbai, though some later thrived for different franchises – were the dividend on Mumbai's scouting investment.

By identifying high quality Indian players early in their development Mumbai effectively found a way to pay well below the true market price for players. This freed up budget to spend elsewhere, enabling them to chase the more in-demand Indian players – such as Rohit Sharma in the 2011 auction who would become the team's captain and figurehead – and overseas players, including Kieron Pollard and Lasith Malinga, who both represented Mumbai for more than a decade.

Mumbai recognised the areas of traditional strength in the Indian market were primarily middle order batsmen and spin bowlers. Once they'd exploited the domestic supply chain through their scouting network they then supplemented this Indian core with overseas players who filled gaps with skill-sets that were harder to find in the Indian market.

The franchise's commitment to this idea was such that, across the first 12 years of the IPL, they only contracted two specialist overseas spinners: South Africa's Robin Peterson and Sri Lanka's Akila Dananjaya. Neither bowled more than ten overs for the club. This tactic reflected how good Indian spinners were – it was simply not worth using an overseas pick on them.

Instead, Mumbai focused their overseas picks on the three types of players produced less readily in India. First, they targeted powerful top order batsmen like Dwayne Smith, Jos Buttler, Evin Lewis, Quinton de Kock and Chris Lynn. Second, they recruited hard-hitting finishers -Pollard, Glenn Maxwell and Ben Cutting. Most significantly, Mumbai had a penchant for overseas quicks, particularly left-armers, who could bowl with the new ball and at the death – Mitchell McClenaghan, Mitchell Johnson, Jason Behrendorff, Mustafizur Rahman and Trent Boult.

After the 2019 auction the only discernible hole in Mumbai's squad was the lack of an off spinner. Mumbai remedied that with a smart post-auction trade, bringing in Jayant Yadav from Delhi Capitals. Yadav was an unremarkable bowler but Mumbai recognised he could be a crucial role player.

Building such a well-rounded squad with an excellent spread of skills and a healthy mix of youth and experience provided Mumbai with a superb base. In Pollard, Hardik and Krunal, Mumbai had three all-rounders, enabling them to maintain batting and bowling depth simultaneously. This trio gave Mumbai the basis to find a way to avoid the trade-offs inherent in building a T20 side.

The strength of their Indian batting, led by Rohit, meant Mumbai often only felt the need to use one overseas spot on a batsman – typically an opener. With Pollard's all-round skills, Mumbai could dedicate two spots to overseas pace bowlers – Malinga, partnered by a new ball specialist.

The small boundaries and true pitch at the Wankhede meant Mumbai's home conditions favoured pace bowlers, making their acquisitions of Malinga and Bumrah so important. At home Mumbai would only ever play two spinners. Instead Mumbai went pace-heavy with their elite quicks sandwiching spin overs from Krunal and a second spinner.

Yet Mumbai had the spin resources, and the pragmatism, to adapt when required. In the 2019 IPL no team except Mumbai won their away match against Chennai Super Kings – and Mumbai won there twice. Compared to the other six visiting teams, Mumbai significantly altered the amount of overs they bowled with spinners in Chennai compared to their previous match. Ultimately, they recognised the significant difference in conditions presented by Chepauk and altered their bowling strategy accordingly. One spinner brought in for the Chennai match was the new trade Yadav – he only played two games in 2019 but contributed to victories both times, exploiting favourable match-ups and conditions.

Such flexibility was apparent throughout Mumbai's strategy. Most their team was fixed but a couple of spots were rotated. This marriage of stability and flexibility saw Mumbai enjoy the benefits of consistency of selection while exploiting match-ups and favourable conditions.

Mumbai could be radical with their batting order, using McClenaghan and Harbhajan Singh as pinch-hitters. Even their two most celebrated batsmen were used flexibly. Rohit's position constantly shuffled between opening and the middle order, depending on the needs of the team. In Mumbai's four IPL final victories, he was used at four, then three, then four and then as opener. Pollard was used similarly shrewdly, batting as high as four or as low as number eight.

Boundary-hitting, which suited the high-scoring Wankhede, was the focus of Mumbai's batting, but players also had the savviness to adapt. In the 2019 qualifier the dynamic Ishan Kishan adjusted on a slow, low Chennai pitch to score 28 off 31 balls and then in another low-scoring match 23 off 26 in the final. Both innings were ranked as slight negative contributions by CricViz but the way he tempered his natural instincts illustrated the capacity to evolve and both would've been more damaging had he got out early.

Mumbai's bowling attack was similarly complementary. Malinga and Bumrah were supreme death overs bowlers while Krunal was an excellent defensive spinner who could operate in the Powerplay. Together these three locked down 12 of Mumbai's 20 overs, forcing teams to take on the remaining bowlers: attacking quicks like McClenaghan and Behrendorff or wrist spinners Chahar and Markande. These bowlers were often expensive – but picked up regular wickets. This combination of attacking and defensive skills made Mumbai's 20 overs fiendishly difficult to combat.

The upshot of Mumbai's excellent squad and pragmatic, open-minded deployment of it meant that they built a team to win in all climes, and in a myriad of different ways. More than any other team in T20's first 17 years, Mumbai defied trade-offs.

EPILOGUE

31 PREDICTIONS FOR THE FUTURE OF T20

For all its evolution since 2003, T20 still has a very long way to go. The tumult of the early years of the IPL has given way to acceptance of T20's place. This has precipitated a rise in advanced thinking around the format that has represented the beginning of a strategic and technical revolution. Yet the speed and efficiency of change is only going to accelerate in the years ahead, as teams, management, coaches, players, the media and fans become more familiar with the game and its subtleties – and the financial incentives to win increase. All the while, there will continue to be innovation off the pitch in how the sport is structured. Here are 32 predictions for the years ahead.

Greater specialisation in formats

As understanding of T20 deepens it will become increasingly acknowledged that T20 and Test cricket are so different that they are essentially different sports. Although there are still 22 players on a 22-yard pitch with six stumps and a leather ball, the offensive and defensive players are inverted.

As awareness of these differences becomes increasingly apparent and as the game – particularly T20, still in its nascent years – continues to evolve, the gulf is likely to widen. Very few players will be able to master the skills required to succeed in both Tests and T20. The ODI format, meanwhile, is likely to represent the middle ground.

This divergence is already clearly apparent in spin bowling: almost no spinners since the advent of T20 have maintained consistent performances in all three formats. Shane Warne and Muttiah Muralitharan, the two greatest spin bowlers in the history of the game, are arguably joined by only left-arm spinners Daniel Vettori and Shakib Al Hasan in being able to excel in all three formats.

Pace bowlers are increasingly finding cross-format success almost as elusive. For batsmen there has remained more of a crossover, helped by their physiological advantage which enables them to train more. But as pressures are placed on power hitting and 360-degree scoring, many will be forced to choose between the defence-orientated red-ball game and attack-focused white-ball formats.

Teams will be bowled out more but also make more runs
Many T20 teams still use their resources poorly: in general, they systematically overvalue wickets, meaning that they leave hitting power untapped because they are too cautious for too much of their innings. The T20 World Cup semi-final in 2016, when India cruised to 192 for 2 off their 20 overs and were then defeated by the West Indies, is a classic of this genre.

T20 sides are still often governed by thinking from 50-over cricket about keeping wickets in hand – even though this matters far less in T20, whether a side is batting first or chasing. An enlightening statistic by the ESPNcricinfo writer Kartikeya Date showed that, when T20 teams lost in run chases, they were bowled out just 37% of the time – half as much as in ODI cricket – and lost fewer than eight wickets 32% of the time, compared with 10% in ODIs. This exposed the deep failings in much T20 strategy.

As T20 sides become shrewder, the slow increase in the number of runs per innings in recent years is likely to continue. Paradoxically, proof of smart thinking may be losing more wickets – unlike in other formats of cricket, the volume of run scoring and the frequency of wickets being lost could rise in sync.

Rather than build an innings in the conventional way, more teams are likely to use expendable players at the top of the order, like Sunil Narine, to target the fielding restrictions. Teams will move to more bespoke batting orders, embracing thinking in terms of positions rather than set positions, following on from the examples of CSK and latterly Islamabad United. The general improvements in the standards of bowlers' batting will augment this shift by giving sides more flexibility.

For instance, teams could have essentially separate batting orders in the Powerplay and afterwards: two or three low-value players who would be deployed to target the fielding restrictions, followed by players to control the middle of the innings and then those to target the end of the innings. If a team lost a wicket to be, say, 40 for 2 after four overs, they could send out a player in the team largely in for their bowling to continue attacking; even, say, 12 off six balls while the fielding restrictions remained might be viewed as a good result. Top order batsmen, who would value their wicket highly during the fielding restrictions and so be likely to begin slowly, could then be saved until after the Powerplay.

This could all help create a paradigm shift in the expectations placed on individual players. So, rather than top order batsmen aiming to bat for half or more of the innings and sides aiming for at least one member of their top three to score a half-century, teams could be set up looking for, say, any six of the top nine batsmen to score 35 from 20 balls.

There will be a rationalisation of T20 leagues

The future may well involve more T20 teams, with other national, regional or even intrastate tournaments popping up. But the economics of the sport – so far, most teams and leagues have lost money – points to a rationalisation in the ambitions of leagues, and the hierarchy between leagues solidifying. So while the IPL is likely to expand, in both its number of teams and length, from 2023, or possibly even sooner, other leagues will have to spend less, aiming for less glitzy overseas players and perhaps occupying less time, if they are to be commercially viable. The future of T20 leagues may be simultaneously of more leagues but distinct tiers between the leagues, as in, say, football. And the IPL is only likely to become more dominant.

'Most signs point towards the IPL strengthening its position as the Premier League or NBA of cricket,' said Jon Long, the former head of strategy for the ICC. 'There will be a handful of leagues that will remain broadly similar to their current structures – perhaps incrementally increasing the number of teams and matches – while several other competitions will have gone through changes in terms of ownership, structure, duration and player eligibility criteria. It will remain challenging for leagues outside the three to four major markets to become financially sustainable but entrepreneurs and investors will continue to experiment with competitions.' But some leagues which are popular today may not be able to survive in their current guise.

Greater use of data

It is likely that at the heart of greater strategising will be greater use of data. While cricket has already made strides in integrating more sophisticated data analysis into decision-making, the sport has only scratched the surface of its potential.

'We haven't anywhere near reached peak data,' said Trent Woodhill, a coach in the IPL and other leagues. 'We have the data. We just don't have enough people being able to drive it and buying into it. You're still going to get push-back. Cricket is still a game played by experienced players with allegedly good instincts. We're still a long way behind American sports.'

A key growth area will be fielding where a combination of fielder tracking and advanced fielding metrics will not only enable analysts to prescribe a more accurate value to fielders, but will also help enhance coaching by identifying very specific fielder strengths and weaknesses.

'I think you'll see a bigger and bigger focus on fielding performance,' explained England lead analyst Nathan Leamon. 'I think fielding is the area of the game with the biggest headroom to improve. If you compare our skills in certain areas with other sports, there's definitely evidence that we're not close to the limits of how well you can field.'

The arrival of reliable fielding maps will greatly enhance analysis of all facets of the game. It will become possible to identify the batsmen who are best at finding gaps in the field, bowlers who are most effective at bowling to their field and the captain who utilises his fielders most efficiently, among many other things.

More football-style sackings

Before the 2017 season, Daniel Vettori was unveiled as Middlesex coach. The club stressed his IPL experience with Bangalore; they made no reference, and didn't seem to notice, that his actual win-loss record in the IPL and elsewhere was mediocre. It embodied the lack of care paid to many coaching appointments, with jobs awarded largely on the basis of who looked the part and networks.

At Middlesex, Vettori won a derisory seven games out of 27. By the end of 2018, he had lost both his Bangalore and Middlesex jobs. It was a window into how, slowly, as the actual business of winning becomes more important to T20 teams, so coaches are becoming more accountable. This is begetting more job insecurity. The future of T20 coaching is likely to see more football-style sackings, including in mid-season.

The T20 World Cup will expand

The ICC often declare that T20 is the globalisation vehicle, but the number of countries permitted to play in the main stage of the men's World Cup remains pitiful compared to sports that cricket likes to consider itself bigger than. But the decision in 2018 to open up T20 international status to all men's and women's international sides, bringing cricket in line with other sports, hinted at a desire to grow the sport less tepidly.

One of the next steps will be to increase the size of the T20 World Cup. From 2020, this comprises 12 sides in the main stage, with a further four playing a preliminary round (effectively another qualifier) immediately before, an increase from ten sides in the main stage in previous tournaments.

In the years to come this number is likely to grow. Sanjog Gupta, the executive vice-president of Star TV Network – and, as such, a crucial member of the cricket ecosystem – said that he supports a more inclusive format.

'I do see room for the T20 World Cup to be a big platform for new nations to come in and new nations and new viewers to be inducted in cricket and for it to become the tournament that's the real first handshake for viewers around the world,' Gupta said.

He suggested two potential models for expansion. The first option would include 14 teams: 'You could potentially look at two groups of seven, which gives you 42 games followed by an extended play-offs.'

The second option would include 15 teams, followed by a subsequent stage. 'You could potentially look at three groups of five each, with two from each group qualifying and playing in the Super Six. That gives you a good mix of new teams, more regions but also great games at the Super Six and league stage.'

Recent progress made by the US men's team, who are now ranked among the world top 20 in ODI cricket, is likely to crystallise the desire to grow the T20 World Cup.

Greater emphasis on home advantage

T20 is an inherently volatile game that can be won or lost on the finest of margins. It is this fragility that means teams should seek to control every possible variable because they could easily end up being the difference between victory and defeat.

Teams play half their league matches at home. This offers the opportunity for teams to either adjust their conditions to suit their squad, which is more likely in leagues with less player turnover, like the T20 Blast in England, BBL in Australia and competitions in South Africa and New Zealand. Another option, more likely in leagues with greater player turnover such as the IPL, PSL and CPL, is to adjust their squad to suit conditions. If teams can dominate at home and win, say, 70% of their home fixtures, they will typically only require a handful of wins away to progress to the play-off stages.

So far there is only the faintest hint of home advantage in T20: 53% of matches are won by the home team, a lower advantage than in basketball, football or ODI cricket, where home teams win 59% of games.

Yet sides such as Chennai Super Kings in Chepauk, Rajasthan Royals in Jaipur and Perth Scorchers at the WACA have given a glimpse of what is possible. Perth won 69% of all their matches at the WACA, but their home form then dipped markedly when they moved to a new ground.

As T20 continues to mature it will become more results-orientated. Shrewd team managers will come to prioritise devising a strategy to dominate at home.

Formats will get shorter at amateur level

Time pressures have not only squeezed the professional game to produce shorter and shorter formats but these challenges are even more acute at amateur level. Playing cricket at club level across 50 overs a side takes an entire day out of someone's weekend. In England in particular, participation numbers in amateur cricket are falling.

In response to this participation crisis it is likely that more midweek evening games will be played after work. In Asia and the Caribbean these matches will be played under lights as part of vibrant local leagues. These matches will take less time than traditional weekend fixtures and mirror the professional game's prioritisation of T20.

Agents will continue to become more important

Agents have been among the first winners of the first age of T20. With T20 leagues from Afghanistan to Australia and Canada to the Caribbean, agents are more prevalent, and influential, than ever before. As of 2019, there were 40 in England alone, about double the number five years ago; worldwide, the number has risen to 110 registered agents. The shifting terrain has created a new need for agents – and so a new source of cash, with players using agents to get into T20 leagues while teams use agents to identify who is available and fulfils the league's eligibility requirements.

Agents act like career planners. When considering offers from T20 franchises, agents routinely look at ground dimensions – smaller grounds are better for boundary hitters and worse for spinners, for instance – as well as the players and coaches they'd work with. And, rather like in football, agents are becoming a way of players voicing their discontent, and trying to assume a more prominent role in their teams. James Welch, a former Durham academy player who has run the agency Quantum Sport since 2007, once emailed Yorkshire's director of cricket with David Willey's lofty strike rate in the Powerplay to try to convince him to use Willey higher up the order. 'Players want to see that you're adding value.'

Yet as cricket's wealth has snowballed, so the war for talent between agents has intensified. 'Player poaching is a serious issue,' said Talha Aisham from the agency Saya Corporation. 'As this profession is getting popular, a lot of people are coming to it without any background and training.'

After the Afghan Premier League draft in 2018, one insider reported, several young Afghan players who had just earned contracts were messaged by a former team official, saying that they needed to give 10% of their money to the official to finalise their contracts. This was a complete lie, but a window into the opportunities for gluttony and malfeasance opened up by T20 leagues.

In some T20 leagues insiders whisper that captains or coaches seem to push specific players whom their agent also represents. The potential for conflict of interest, with agents representing coaches and players alike, is obvious.

There is broad agreement in the sport that there should be greater regulation. As of 2019, agents were unregulated everywhere except England, Australia, South Africa and New Zealand. If regulations do not become more common – the ICC supports more member states introducing regulatory systems but a blanket global agent registration system is considered unlikely – then stories about the malign influence of agents promise to become more common in the sport's new landscape.

Batsmen retiring out

In a CPL match in 2017, just 12 days after hitting an innings of 121 not out, Andre Russell – one of the most destructive T20 players of all time – was unused by Jamaica. Chasing 157 to win against Barbados, Jamaica ended up on 154 for 3, somehow contriving to lose by two runs despite having seven wickets in hand. Yet Russell did not bat at all – the T20 equivalent of having Lionel Messi on the bench but not being able to bring him on.

It was a perfect case study of how teams could benefit from retiring out struggling batsmen, rather than allowing them to continue to consume deliveries at the crease and prevent other players from getting to bat.

Retiring a batsman out has negative connotations attached to it partly because cricket is obsessed by the concept of 'fair play'. Many believe the battle at the crease is part of the game, rather than something that can be tactically ended.

It is not, however, against the laws of the game to retire a batsman out. And, on occasion, it could be prudent for a team to do so, to ensure they didn't leave one of their best batting resources unused. Similarly, fielding teams may employ 'tactical drops', making little effort to get to a high ball simply to keep a weaker batsman at the crease, and leave as few balls as possible for a player like Russell to impact the game.

Innovation in this area came from an unlikely source. In September 2018, Belize became the first team in an official T20 cricket game to retire a batsman out when they withdrew Howell Gillett who was 8 not out off 23 balls in a match against Panama.

Match-ups will become more sophisticated

One of the buzzwords of the first era of T20 has been match-ups: that is opposition teams targeting certain types of batsmen with certain types of bowlers.

'It happens every game,' said England's captain Eoin Morgan. 'The one where it has worked best was the World Cup Final in 2016 where we opened the bowling with Joe Root to Chris Gayle. We had an under-par score on the board, we needed early wickets and the ball wasn't going to swing because it didn't swing the first innings so we decided to take a bit of a left-field call and again it was calculated but it came off.'

As data analysis of T20 improves, the level of detail in these match-ups will grow. For example, not all right-arm pace bowlers are the same. Indeed, two right-arm bowlers such as Lasith Malinga – with a low, slingy release – and Jason Holder – with an unusually high release point – could scarcely be more different. The same applies to batsmen: traditional anchor Michael Klinger is a right-handed batsmen but to group him as the same kind of player as, say, Jos Buttler would be inaccurate.

Advanced analysis is beginning to reflect this. CricViz have built a model that groups players using detailed shot type, footwork, scoring zone and ball-tracking data, separating players into sub-categories and then identifying strengths and weaknesses within these. As a result, Klinger might have a positive match-up against Malinga but a negative match-up against Holder, despite them both being right-arm quicks.

More set plays

Field settings generally are dictated to by the ball that a bowler is wanting to bowl. If he is looking to bowl a wide yorker, for example, then third man will be back; if he is looking to bowl a slower ball then third man and fine leg will be up. These settings are typically managed by the captain and bowler and are now a fundamental part of basic T20 tactics.

Yet, as the game and as planning around the game develops, it is possible that these field settings will become more predetermined. Fielding teams may employ something akin to set piece routines in football. A code signal from the coach or captain might be all it takes for the field to snap into a certain shape and the bowler respond with the relevant delivery. This might become particularly pertinent if more stringent over-rate penalties are applied through the use of ball clocks, counting down the time permitted in between deliveries.

As analytics of field settings – perhaps the most underappreciated aspect of the sport – grows, the detail that goes into these set plays will rapidly evolve. Teams will be able to identify subtle differences in shot location of different batsmen against different deliveries and they will manage their set plays accordingly.

Hybrid spin bowlers

Just as Rashid Khan transformed leg spin, another Afghan teen threatens to transform spin bowling entirely. Mujeeb Ur Rahman's bowling style is distinctive because it cannot be categorised as either a finger spin or wrist spin. Mujeeb bowls off breaks, carrom balls, doosras, leg breaks and googlies – he is a hybrid bowler and the first of his kind. By straddling different bowling techniques, not only is Mujeeb harder to read and has a wider arsenal at his disposal, but he is able to exploit batsmen's weaknesses even more specifically. Mujeeb's success inspired other bowlers, most notably Mujeeb's teammate at Kings XI Punjab the off-spinner R. Ashwin to start bowling occasional leg breaks and googlies as well.

The innovation is unlikely to stop there. On 27 October 2018 the Sri Lankan Kamindu Mendis bowled right-arm and left-arm finger spin in the same over in a T20 international against England. To the right-handed Jason Roy, Mendis bowled left-arm finger spin, taking the ball away from the bat and then mid-over changed to bowl right-arm finger spin to the left-handed Ben Stokes, taking the ball away from the bat once more. The amount of practice needed to reach an elite standard with both arms is a roadblock to many others doing the same, but Mendis embodies how bowlers will explore new and previously unimagined avenues.

'You need to be constantly evolving,' said Samuel Badree. 'Anything that is different will become successful, at least initially.'

As match-ups become increasingly salient in T20, bowlers such as Mujeeb and Mendis are capable of two different styles of bowling and therefore of targeting both right- and left-handed batsmen.

In spin bowling, the smallest changes in grip or release can have profound consequences for how the ball behaves. Not only will the future involve major shifts in technique such as hybrid spinners and, occasionally, ambidextrous bowlers but the art will continue to become ever more intricate as bowlers push to stay one step ahead of the batsmen.

The rise of general managers

In recent years, football clubs have empowered directors of football, who are responsible for player recruitment and strategy that outlasts the mere head coach, who tends to survive far less long. Largely unknown, general managers have become increasingly important in T20 leagues; with head coaches typically working simultaneously for several sides, general managers are charged with planning for the longer term, negotiating player contracts or conducting auction strategy (depending on the rules of the league) and arranging preseason schedules.

Clubs that are serious about winning will focus more on making sure they are planning for the long term. That will mean more general managers, mirroring similar figures in football and US sports who are ultimately responsible for hiring and firing the head coach. Given the multifarious demands of the role, that is likely to mean more outside voices without experience of playing the sport professionally.

In 2015, Mohammed Khan, an American with his own marketing and consultancy agency, sent an unsolicited email to a private equity and investment firm, about a sponsorship opportunity in Formula One. This led to a meeting with the chairman of the Chalak Mitra Group, who also owned Jamaica Tallawahs, where the two bonded over cricket. A few months later, Khan was hired to run the team as general manager. Khan was responsible for the player auction, and promptly won the Caribbean Premier League in his first season, with the team displaying a new preference for roles over rigid positions and Khan making extensive use of data analytics. His next few years were altogether more taxing, leaving Jamaica after a change in ownership and then having an ill-fated brief stint with the St Lucia Stars. But Khan had hinted at the new importance of general managers in T20.

Bowlers will be paid more
As totals in T20 will rise, so the difficulty of preventing teams from haemorrhaging runs will intensify. But the few able to prevent carnage will become more valuable than ever, and they will be paid accordingly. Far from the brutality of T20 hitting putting bowlers off, the incentives of the market may mean that bowlers have never had it so good.

'I've captained guys in the T10 format and it's just not a pretty place – 60-yard boundaries with guys teeing off from ball one,' said Eoin Morgan. 'It's an unbelievable challenge but also it presents a huge opportunity for somebody to be really, really good and make a good living and life around it. I think that's a huge carrot.' A.R. Srikkanth, Kolkata's analyst, predicted: 'Bowling hasn't taken precedence so far but it will eventually,' envisaging that the price for bowlers relative to batsmen would increase.

International cricket will gain a new structure

The paradox of international T20 cricket is that it is the most popular format of the sport but, after the creation of new leagues in ODI and Test cricket, it is the one format lacking any overarching context in between World Cups. The problem with most international T20 cricket is its structure: there isn't one. T20 internationals in between World Cups are essentially friendlies.

From 2018, football replaced a large number of international friendly matches with the new Nations League, a competition that placed teams in groups of four, with promotion and relegation, creating a dynamic competition. The format generated far more interest than the friendly games it replaced.

T20, with smaller margins between teams, ideally lends itself to a Nations League-type format – with, say, a series of groups of four teams each in different divisions, and the competition potentially doubling as part of the T20 World Cup qualification structure. Such a format could lend itself to short and snazzy competitions – say, of four teams playing each other twice each in their division, with the entire tournament lasting ten days and played in one or two countries.

Whatever the solution, insiders believe that international T20s, in their current form, do not do the format justice; many international T20s are played by virtual shadow sides, with countries resting their leading players, especially fast bowlers. Such matches, without clear consequences, mean that potential fan interest – and so economic value – is left untapped.

'When we have context in the ODI league going forward and the World Test Championship as well it may isolate T20 internationals a little in the sense that they're all friendlies,' said Harrison. 'Bringing context into all international cricket except T20 internationals is going to put pressure on international T20. We don't want it turning into exhibition cricket, we want it to be top-drawer, high-intensity T20 cricket played with the very best T20 players in the world. Maybe in order to introduce that kind of jeopardy into that we need to introduce context. Qualification gives you a definite potential hook to provide that so maybe we need to create that peril around qualification for World T20.'

Super-fast bowlers
Traditionally bowling actions have been a product of a compromise between competing factors – broadly: speed, accuracy, movement and endurance.

The reduced physical workload of four overs per match and the challenges posed by balls that don't swing and pitches that don't seam, opens up the possibility of a new breed of pace bowler: concerned almost entirely with bowling at high speeds.

These bowling actions will likely look and feel very different to traditional bowling actions. They will probably be slingy and more round-arm, resembling a javelin thrower as much as a cricket player. Such bowlers will also be built differently too. They will have distinct training regimes, with high strength and power development emphasised to develop short bursts of explosive movement to attain extreme high ball speeds over 24 balls.

Producing bowlers such as these will require 'a completely different approach to developing fast bowlers' according to Marc Portus, head of movement science at the Australian Institute of Sport and a bowling biomechanics expert.

Cricket has already produced a handful of bowlers in this mould. The Australian Shaun Tait and the Pakistani Shoaib Akhtar, who played in the early 2000s, are the most famous examples. Both Tait and Shoaib were clocked at 100 mph and regularly operated in the high 90s. Tait and Shoaib employed bowling actions with enormous pivoting delivery strides and a slingy, round-arm release that echoed the Australian Jeff Thomson in the 1980s who was also capable of electric speed. Both Tait and Shoaib battled injuries throughout their careers: the sheer physical burden placed on their bodies by their bowling actions was too much to withstand bowling more than a dozen overs at a time. In T20 though, with only 24 balls permitted per bowler, this barrier no longer exists.

Batsmen more like baseball hitters
The emphasis on boundary hitting in T20 will give rise to a new subset of batsmen, more aligned to baseball hitters than traditional cricketers. These players will have techniques designed to maximise shot power and distance with minimal footwork and a strong, stable base and a still head. Their bat swing will be long and clean and they will generally be big,

powerful men. They will typically target the leg side because it is the most natural hitting zone but they will evolve to hit over the off side as well.

'I think guys are going to get bigger and stronger like baseball where the fielders don't matter,' envisaged Brendon McCullum. 'You'll just take the fielders on. Andre Russell is like that, isn't he? He doesn't play sweeps or ramps, he just hits in his area.'

The physique of batsmen will change – and so will the risks of performance-enhancing drugs
As T20 places a greater premium on the physique of players, so an increasing number of batsmen will appear tailor-made to hit sixes. Batsmen will get stronger, with training programmes specifically designed to augment six hitting.

The lessons of the world's other great bat-and-ball sport, baseball, suggests that some cricketers will be tempted by performance-enhancing drugs. This risk is heightened by the lax standards of drugs testing in T20 leagues around the world. Unless there is a concerted uplift in both the quality and quantity of drugs testing in cricket, the fear will be that cricket will sleepwalk into a doping crisis of the sort that has already befallen baseball.

Spinners will bowl more
Traditionally pace bowlers have bowled at the start and the end of the innings in white-ball cricket and the spinners have operated through the middle. But in T20 where the emphasis is on boundary hitting, spinners returned a lower economy rate than pace bowlers in every single over of the innings. This suggests that spinners have been systematically underbowled – perhaps because captains whose spinners were hit at the start or end of an innings could expect to face far more criticism than captains who bowled pace bowlers then, in accordance with traditional cricket thinking.

The great CSK and KKR teams have already shown what is possible by building spin-heavy attacks, particularly in spin-friendly conditions; so have the CPL's Guyana Amazon Warriors. Gradually more teams will break with convention and seek to take advantage of this fundamental imbalance between pace and spin. Teams who are set up to deliver at least 16 overs of spin – especially in home conditions – will become commonplace. One team may even make history by delivering all 20 overs by spin.

Spin power hitters will be very valuable

The continued rise of spin bowling and its greater usage will place huge value on those batsmen capable of power hitting against spin. The lack of pace on the ball and the different directions of turn have traditionally made consistent hitting of spin bowling very difficult. Yet the likes of India's Hardik Pandya – with long levers and rapid hand speed – have shown that it is possible. Until spin power-hitting techniques become a more established part of youth coaching, these players will remain very rare and very valuable.

Innovations to help incoming batsmen

Incoming batsmen can sometimes be seen shadow batting by the dugout, often wielding two bats to help with bat speed when they then have just one in their hand at the crease, and occasionally they'll be on exercise bikes. Ultimately though, this kind of preparation doesn't happen nearly enough and is barely adequate as it is.

Innovations like batting cages – essentially pitchside nets or nets in the bowels of the stadium – and virtual reality headsets are tools that could be used to help prepare incoming batsmen. By hitting balls before arriving at the crease or by visualising facing certain bowlers, batsmen can better prepare themselves for arriving in the middle. Installing batting cages might provide logistical challenges to smaller venues but newer stadiums in particular should engineer space for them; nursery grounds and indoor schools could also be used.

Batsmen will start faster

The first era of T20 batsmanship was defined by batsmen expanding their power game, by elevating strike rates from around 130 towards 150. The next era will be defined by batsmen reaching these scoring rates more quickly. Currently many batsmen still take time to 'play themselves in' – an approach embodied by Chris Gayle who scores very slowly at the start of his innings before accelerating rapidly later. Higher scoring rates, deeper batting orders and the evolution of the format more generally will place pressure on this approach and greater emphasis will be put on the need for batsmen to start more rapidly. Shorter formats such as the Hundred and T10 will illustrate how players can score with alacrity from their first ball. The signs of improvement are already there: strike rates in the first ten balls of the innings rose from 105.83 between 2010 and 2015 to 112.41 since then.

Greater safety precautions

It is reflective of the changed balance of power in the game that where helmetless batsmen once feared hostile fast bowlers, now – as helmets have come into the game and power hitting has developed – the relationship has been inverted.

In 2017 Nottinghamshire's Luke Fletcher bowled a full toss to Birmingham's Sam Hain who smashed the ball straight back towards Fletcher and clattered him on the head. Fletcher was fortunate – he suffered a small bleed on his brain but did not lose consciousness and, after being ruled out of the season, resumed playing again the following year. The incident embodied the dangers facing bowlers, who have traditionally worn no form of protection, and led to the New Zealander Wayne Barnes bowling with a face mask in T20. Umpires have also begun wearing helmets and arm shields.

The years ahead will see bowlers and umpires better protected. Fielders could also be helped by cushioning around the outfield to protect them as they attempt athletic boundary saves and catches. Netting around the boundary edge, as used in baseball, would be a straightforward way to ensure against serious injury or perhaps even a fatality in the crowd. Cricket should not wait until it is too late.

Home and away kits

Unlike other team sports such as football and rugby, the players on the pitch cannot be distinguished from their equipment, with spectators instead relying on which players are using bats to distinguish them from the fielders. But for casual fans the introduction of home and away kits in T20 when teams' home strips are the same colour would be a simple way to make the game more accessible. Having a second kit could also increase a team's merchandising revenue.

Owners will become more important

As cricket has been unusual in having such a comparatively unlucrative domestic game, compared with other sports, so it has had relative refuge from team owners who try to bend the sport to their will, as is common in US sports, European football and European rugby. Indeed, while the names and motivations of owners in these sports is a common point of discussion among fans and the media, owners of specific teams have largely been ignored in cricket. But one by-product of the growing strength of club, compared to country, cricket is likely to be more interventionist owners.

'More pressure will come from franchise owners to have a stake in decision-making,' said Jon Long, former head of strategy at the ICC. 'Cricket has been remarkably effective in keeping its major leagues under the control of its national governing bodies. This might not change in the coming five years but if it does change then private investors will start to exert greater influence over scheduling, player salaries and income, which will bring the leagues into greater conflict with the international game and change the landscape more dramatically.'

Owners could provide yet another source of conflict in a game already brimming with tensions between different factions. Sports owners are overwhelmingly motivated by a desire to make cash for themselves – as with any business – so will be inclined to push for more matches and longer league seasons, so that they can sell the broadcasting rights for more. The tensions familiar to other sports, between member boards and private owners, may come to cricket too.

A T20 World Cup will be played in the US in the 2020s

Cricket's administrators have looked wistfully to the US market for years. But the climate there has never been more promising. The number of immigrants from India alone rose to 2.4 million by 2015, buttressed by others from cricket-playing areas in the Caribbean and the rest of the Asian subcontinent. The USA team secured one-day international status in 2019, opening up new sources of funding. The ICC has overseen a transformation in the quality of governance of US cricket. So the chance to galvanise – and monetise – the sport in the US has never been greater. Indeed, huge amounts could be made from the existing US market, even without growing it – the US is the second biggest market for ESPNcricinfo, for instance.

Compared to other global sports, cricket has been extraordinarily insular in where it has staged its global events. While Japan hosted the 2019 Rugby World Cup, China the 2019 Basketball World Cup, and the 2018 Football World Cup was staged in Russia, all major men's global events from 2016 to 2023 were awarded to Australia, England or India.

The T20 World Cup represents the best chance of opening up events to new frontiers. While much work would need to be done on infrastructure, at some point in the 2020s the ICC could dare to stage the T20 World Cup in the US in the hope of unlocking new cash and globalising the sport. But the idea has burgeoning support among some of the most influential countries in the sport. 'I would love to take a T20 World Cup to the US – I think it would be a brilliant thing to do,' said Tom Harrison, England's chief executive.

The system of drafts and auctions will evolve

The IPL's auction system is not designed to spread talent around most efficiently. Instead, it is designed to be compelling entertainment – compelling TV – something in which it succeeds spectacularly. But among some franchises, there is a wish for the system to evolve.

'I hope we'll get away from these auctions,' said Venky Mysore, chief executive of Kolkata Knight Riders. 'As the league has reached the stage of maturity the weightage that one has to give to continuity is very high – the connection with the team, the city, the fan base and everything else. I'd like to see a different system perhaps – maybe a mini-draft, more trading and loans, rather than a full-scale auction where you undergo significant churn of the team. We have to get to that next phase now I think.'

A new system – say, of elite international players still taking part in the auction, but lesser players being recruited separately by teams – would change the dynamics of the IPL, and other T20 leagues which use a draft system. This would create more continuity in teams, and prevent teams losing all bar a handful of their players during the big auctions, every three or four years, which would encourage teams to focus more on improving the players they already had, rather than merely signing better ones. If teams could retain more players they would be more inclined to develop their contracted players. An intimation of this was hinted at after the 2019 IPL season when Mumbai Indians' injured fast bowler Alzarri Joseph spent close to four months recovering in Mumbai where he was nurtured by the team's support staff.

Teams will become more sophisticated in their talent identification

Since the creation of the Pakistan Super League, the Lahore Qalandars team have conducted trials for young players throughout Pakistan, which several hundred thousand players are believed to have taken part in. They have uncovered talented overlooked players, including the exciting fast bowler Haris Rauf, in this way.

Only, there is a snag: teams are only allowed to sign players who don't play in the Pakistani professional system before the draft. That creates an incentive problem: one team could do all the talent scouting, and rivals could benefit from this by picking up these players in the draft. Similar handicaps impede teams from ambitious talent identification and development programmes in other leagues, including the IPL.

Some teams in the biggest leagues already employ scouts full-time, like football clubs, to scour emerging talent. If the recruitment system is tweaked to allow clubs to be sure to benefit from the talent they uncover then teams would have more incentive to invest in finding new talent. That could mean a surge in academies and innovative talent identification schemes within the countries that teams are based.

More elite players from non-traditional countries

With the auction system as it stands, one IPL team could build a swanky academy in Nepal, say – but the talent produced would be equally open to all teams. If the system is tweaked, it would incentivise teams to invest in proactively developing and improving talent in foreign countries to improve their side.

An alternative model is also possible. The NBA has academies dotted around the world, in Australia, China, India, Mexico and Senegal, funded centrally by the league. With imagination, cricket's biggest T20 leagues could do the same. The IPL creating academies in, say, Canada, the US and Germany could unearth talent that would grow the league in these markets, and so make the league's economics even more profitable.

T20 will develop its own language

During this first era of T20 the format has suffered both in media perception and in tactical reality because of comparisons to longer forms of cricket. So far T20 has almost exclusively been described and understood using a framework and a language inherited from longer forms of the game.

As a result there is a chasm between the level of conversations that happen in teams and the more simplistic conversations about decision-making that take place outside the changing room.

Conveying T20's messages and stories will be greatly enhanced by the development of a separate strategic and tactical vocabulary specifically for T20, similar to that now common in football coverage. While we have begun to see this in T20 with concepts such as 'front-loading' which means to adopt an aggressive, top-heavy batting strategy in the Powerplay, these terms are rare and scarcely used. An evolution of T20 terminology will showcase the format's nuances, complexities and skills.

T20 will be cricket's gateway to the Olympics

In 1900, Devon and Somerset Wanderers, representing Great Britain, beat the French Athletic Club Union in a cricket match in Paris. Twelve years later, this game was officially recognised as being part of the 1900 Olympic Games. It remains the only game of cricket to take place in the Olympics.

In 2009, rugby sevens rejoined the Olympics, effective from the 2016 Games. The benefits have dwarfed all of World Rugby's expectations: rugby has received around an extra £25 million every four-year cycle from national Olympic committees since rejoining, as well as extra sponsorship and support from local government. Most significant has been the exposure gained through being an Olympic sport – both in the Games themselves and in qualification for it – which has boosted participation in the men's and, especially, women's game around the world.

Rugby's surge has highlighted cricket's curious position as being the only major sport not in the Games. For a long time it was this way because it didn't want to be, with England historically staunchly opposed, arguing that it would cause disruption to their home summer once every four years. England are now declared supporters of joining the Games. 'T20's got a huge role to play in the future,' said Harrison. 'I'd like to see the ICC – and we're huge believers in this – adopt a proper strategy to get into the Olympic Games.'

That just leaves India as a potential obstacle. Virtually every other board – even Scotland and the West Indies, whose cricket players would be represented under different banners at the Olympics – are strong proponents of joining the Games, convinced of the potential to galvanise the sport in emerging nations. In Germany, for instance, cricket would receive £750,000 a year just by dint of being an Olympic sport, compared to about £150,000 a year from the ICC. And the International Olympic Committee, who are keen to grow the Olympics in South Asia are also known to be keen.

T20 is the most probable avenue for cricket to join the Games. The most likely format, in both men's and women's cricket, seems to be of two groups of four – with the identities of the nations decided by pre-qualifying – progressing to the semi-finals and finals. It could be a seminal moment for cricket.

APPENDIX I

AN INTRODUCTION TO T20 CRICKET

Twenty20 (T20) cricket is a format of cricket established at professional level in 2003. It has since transformed the way the game is played on the pitch and the economics of the sport off it.

T20 is named as such because each team bats for 20 overs. In cricket, an over is made up of six balls, meaning each team has an allocation of 120 balls. Each team bats once and the team with the highest score wins. A team in T20, as in other formats of cricket, is made up of 11 players.

T20 is a game defined by resources and trade-offs.

The resource for the batting team is balls – they have 120 balls in which to score as many runs as they can. However, as attacking intent increases, the risk of the batsman getting out also increases. This means that the batting team have to manage risk appropriately to ensure that their pursuit of runs does not come at the cost of losing wickets so regularly that they are bowled out inside their 20 overs. This balance between run-scoring (attack) and wicket-preservation (defence) is the trade-off facing the batting team.

The resource for the bowling team is their bowlers. In T20, bowlers are not permitted to bowl more than four overs each. So for a bowling team to complete their 20 overs they need to use at least five bowlers. As with the batsmen, the bowlers are faced with a similar trade-off between looking to take wickets (attack) and looking to save runs (defence).

Generally certain lengths – very full or very short – take wickets at a faster rate but concede runs at a faster rate.

The difficulty with the bowling team managing their resource of bowlers is that players who are good at both batting and bowling are often difficult to find and, therefore, players who can do both well – known as all-rounders – are rare and precious. Picking five strong bowlers typically compromises the depth of the batting. This effort to find the best balance between batting and bowling depth is at the heart of T20 strategy.

T20 matches take about three hours to play and it is this shorter time period which makes the T20 format the most accessible form of the game for fans because it can be played, for example, in an evening after work, whereas longer forms of cricket typically take all day and can be played across multiple days.

T20 matches are generally thought to consist of three phases. The first is the Powerplay phase which lasts for six overs at the start of the innings. During this period, the fielding team are only allowed two fielders outside the 30-yard fielding circle – these fielding restrictions are designed to encourage the batsmen to attack and take risks in search of early runs. Generally fast bowlers operate in this phase, although the proportion of overs bowled by spinners in the Powerplay has risen through T20 history.

After the end of the Powerplay, the fielding team are permitted five fielders outside the 30-yard circle. Although these field restrictions remain in place for the remainder of the innings, the last 14 overs are typically thought of in two phases: the middle-overs, between overs 7 and 15; and the death-overs, from overs 16 and 20. Generally the middle-overs see the batsmen take slightly fewer risks than in the Powerplay, adapting to the new field restrictions and typically an increase in the proportion of overs bowled by spinners. From around the 15th over, the batting team begins to increase their attacking intent in the death-over phase, at which point the proportion of overs bowled by quick bowlers increases once more. These patterns are not fixed, of course, and different teams adopt different methods – but they are broadly reflective of the shape of a typical T20 innings.

Pace bowling lengths

```
┌─────────────────────────────┐
│         FULL TOSS           │
├ ─ ─ ─ ─ ─ ─ ─ ─ ─ ─ ─ ─ ─ ─┤
│          YORKER             │
├ ─ ─ ─ ─ ─ ─ ─ ─ ─ ─ ─ ─ ─ ─┤
│        HALF VOLLEY          │
├ ─ ─ ─ ─ ─ ─ ─ ─ ─ ─ ─ ─ ─ ─┤
│           FULL              │
├ ─ ─ ─ ─ ─ ─ ─ ─ ─ ─ ─ ─ ─ ─┤
│       GOOD LENGTH           │
├ ─ ─ ─ ─ ─ ─ ─ ─ ─ ─ ─ ─ ─ ─┤
│     BACK OF A LENGTH        │
├ ─ ─ ─ ─ ─ ─ ─ ─ ─ ─ ─ ─ ─ ─┤
│         BOUNCER             │
├ ─ ─ ─ ─ ─ ─ ─ ─ ─ ─ ─ ─ ─ ─┤
│          SHORT              │
│                             │
└─────────────────────────────┘
```

Fielding positions (right-handed batsman)

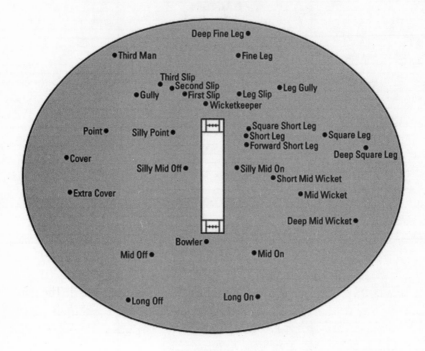

APPENDIX II

A TIMELINE OF T20 HISTORY

April 2002 – England's 18 first-class counties narrowly vote to create a new 20-over format, in response to dwindling interest in the game.

June 2003 – The first season in T20 history begins in England. The rain stays away – all 48 matches in 2003 were played to a conclusion – and the crowds flock to games, vaulting past the organisers' hopes. Other countries soon create T20 leagues of their own.

August 2004 – The first women's T20 international is played, between England and New Zealand in Hove.

February 2005 – The first men's T20 international is played, between New Zealand and Australia in Auckland. New Zealand's players dress up in retro kits and outfits for the occasion. 'I think it's difficult to play seriously,' Australia's captain Ricky Ponting says after scoring 98 not out.

September 2007 – The first T20 world championship – initially called the World Twenty20, and later named the T20 World Cup – is held in South Africa. India initially did not want to take part, but beat Pakistan in a memorable final.

September 2007 – Two days into the first WT20, the Indian board announce the creation of the Indian Premier League, featuring eight new teams in India, and a Champions League for the best T20 club sides from around the world.

February 2008 – At the first IPL auction – a made-for-TV spectacle – £21 million is spent on players on the first day alone. Even before the teams have any players, the Indian board sell the TV rights for £500 million, over 10 years, and the eight teams for £367 million, payable to the board over a decade.

April 2008 – Brendon McCullum scores 158 not for Kolkata Knight Riders in the first-ever IPL game. The great Australian leg spinner Shane Warne captains Rajasthan Royals – the team with the smallest budget – to the inaugural IPL title.

November 2008 – The full England team play a $20 million, winner-takes-all, match against the Stanford Superstars, a team created by Texan billionaire Sir Allen Stanford, which England view as an alternative to their players featuring in the IPL. England lose by 10 wickets. Three months later, Stanford is charged with fraud on a huge scale, leading to his 110-year imprisonment in the US.

October 2009 – The first Champions League tournament is held, a year late after being rescheduled due to the Mumbai terrorist attacks. New South Wales beat unfancied Trinidad and Tobago in the final.

December 2011 – The first season of the Big Bash League begins in Australia, as the eight-team T20 tournament replaces the previous domestic T20 league, run on traditional state lines and featuring only six sides. It proves a great success; by 2018/19, the league has increased from 31 games to 59

April 2013 – Chris Gayle hits a record 175 not out playing for Royal Challengers Bangalore in an IPL match in Bangalore.

June 2015 – The owners of Kolkata Knight Riders buy the Trinidad and Tobago franchise in the Caribbean Premier League, who they later rename Trinbago Knight Riders.

July 2015 – The Champions League is scrapped with immediate effect. The tournament had struggled to generate viewing figures to justify broadcasters' outlays, with figures for games not involving Indian sides consistently poor.

July 2015 – Chennai Super Kings, IPL champions in both 2010 and 2011, are suspended from the league for two years, along with Rajasthan Royals, by the Indian board, after being found guilty in a probe into illegal betting and match-fixing.

January 2016 – A record 80,000 fans watch the Melbourne derby between Melbourne Stars and Melbourne Renegades in the Big Bash League, breaking the previous record for any Australian domestic match by 28,000.

February 2016 – After two failed launches, the inaugural Pakistan Super League is played. In the first season all matches were contested in the UAE due to security concerns in Pakistan, but that started to change over the coming seasons.

April 2016 – West Indies become the first team to win two T20 World Cups, after Carlos Brathwaite hits four consecutive sixes during an extraordinary final over in Kolkata.

February 2017 – Rashid Khan is one of two Afghan players signed in the first IPL auction, the first-ever time that Afghans have been signed by a major league. Rashid excels in his first season.

September 2017 – The new broadcasting and digital rights for the IPL sell for £2 billion over five years – an annual increase of about three times on the worth of the previous contracts. This means that, from 2018–23, 71% of the Indian board's total broadcasting rights come from the IPL, and only 29% from their home internationals. For the first time ever, each IPL match costs more per game than each Indian home game.

April 2018 – The England and Wales Cricket Board, who had failed to get an elite English Premier League featuring nine T20 teams passed in 2008, announce the creation of a new eight-team competition. It will be played in a new 100-ball format, launching in 2020.

April 2018 – The International Cricket Council announces that all men's T20 international games, beginning in January 2019, will have full international status, putting cricket in line with other sports and helping such games attract more attention. All women's T20 internationals are granted full international status immediately.

APPENDIX III

ALL TIME T20 XI, 2003–2019

---

1) Chris Gayle

The Bradman of T20, Gayle is the most prolific batsman in the format's history and a monolithic presence in the first age of T20. The hulking left-hander had a penchant for starting his innings slowly but with thunderous hitting against pace and spin he was easily capable of catching up at a rapid pace. His awesome power – both through natural timing and sheer strength – enabled him to clear even the largest of boundaries with apparent ease. His destructive batting more than made up for his below-par fielding.

2) David Warner (captain)

Warner is arguably the only player who could challenge Gayle as the greatest IPL opener of all time. At full capacity, the Australian left-hander was not quite as dominant as Gayle but he would get up to speed far quicker and was more consistent. Warner's rapid running between the wickets gave his game versatility that Gayle's sometimes lacked. He was also an astute captain, guiding Sunrisers Hyderabad to the IPL title in 2016 and particularly adept at defending low totals; Cricket Australia's ban on Warner assuming a national leadership role need not apply here.

3) Shane Watson

At his best, Watson was one of the most dominant batsmen in the world and a superb fifth bowler with deceptive pace and an array of slower balls.

Watson's role in teams evolved through his career: bowling less as he grew older, he became more of a specialist batsman in his twilight years. When he did bowl he was a capable operator in all three phases. With the bat, Watson was most at home near the top of the order but fulfilled roles in the middle and lower order as well. Unusually for an Australian, Watson was a supreme player of spin, as reflected in him twice being named the IPL player of the tournament – something only Sunil Narine could match – as well as being player of the tournament in the 2012 T20 World Cup in Sri Lanka.

4) A.B. de Villiers (wicketkeeper)
Gayle was statistically the most dominant batsman but de Villiers was the most versatile. His classical technique, astonishing hand-eye coordination and spirit of élan produced remarkable results. De Villiers combined the power of the likes of Gayle and Warner with the 360-degree dynamism of Glenn Maxwell. He played the large majority of his innings at number three or lower; although this middle order role was the most complex position in T20, he could adapt to all circumstances and climes. De Villiers was also one of the world's best fielders and could keep wicket.

5) Glenn Maxwell
Maxwell was a freakish batsman whose daring and risk-taking approach compromised his consistency but bred a high-octane method defined by wristy flicks, reverse sweeps, ramps and scoops. Not only was Maxwell's technique unusual, but so was his mentality: a no-fear attitude, bordering on the reckless, enabled Maxwell to start in rapid-quick fashion, barely wasting balls before he got up to speed. The haste of Maxwell's starts made him ideally suited to the middle order. Useful off spin and livewire fielding made him a superb all-round package.

6) Kieron Pollard
Pollard redefined the role of a finisher, transforming the position from one previously shaped by touch and placement to one founded on strength and power. A huge muscular frame, a clean bat-swing and an uncomplicated approach of hitting straight, hard and long combined emphatically. The destructiveness of Pollard's approach did not make it any less calculated – with over 400 T20 matches, the Trinidadian grasped

the nuances of the format better than most and chose his moment to attack clinically. Early in his career, Pollard was also a useful medium-fast bowler and throughout it he was a spectacular fielder, particularly on the boundary.

7) Andre Russell

Russell took what Pollard did to death overs hitting and then improved it. He was slightly leaner than Pollard which gave him greater dynamism around the crease which in turn widened the hitting arc to include cover point and shrunk the margin of error for the bowlers even further. Russell's slightly smaller frame made him a better bowler than Pollard too – capable of speeds of more than 90 mph, he was a bona fide fifth bowling option when fully fit. With the ball, as with the bat, Russell was a risk-taker: he would bowl attacking lines and lengths in pursuit of wickets and could bowl in all phases of the game.

8) Sunil Narine

The only man who can rival Gayle's longevity and consistency in T20 is the Trinidadian spin bowler Narine. After bursting on to the scene with an array of mystery deliveries which spun in different directions with no discernible change in action, Narine slowly evolved into a less mysterious but no less brilliant bowler. A suspension for an illegal bowling action forced Narine to adapt his methods, spinning the ball less but increasing his control with fast speeds, flat trajectories and short lengths. For close to a decade Narine's four overs regularly cost only slightly more than a run a ball, lending his team precious control. His late-career development into an effective pinch-hitter, exploiting the fielding restrictions by hitting up and over the ring elevated his impact even further.

9) Rashid Khan

Before he had even played T20 cricket for half a decade, Rashid had established himself as a legend of the format. Rashid took the techniques of leg-spinners Shahid Afridi and Samuel Badree and fused them with a unique finger and wrist-spinning action to obtain the holy grail of bowling: a low economy rate and a low strike rate, dominating in leagues around the world. Rashid's action made it nearly impossible to pick which way the ball would spin and his speed made it nearly impossible to play even if the batsman did. Rashid was also a very useful lower order batsman and a superb fielder.

10) Lasith Malinga

The king of T20 fast bowling. Malinga's unique round-arm action enabled him to perfect the yorker delivery to an extent unmatched by any bowler to ever play the game. His low release point also contributed to his skiddy bouncers which targeted the head and neck of the batsmen, which in turn made the yorker delivery all the more effective. Early on in his career Malinga was capable of high speeds but as this side of his game dwindled he made up for it with experience and cunning. His dipping slower ball and late swing made his full and straight lengths even more dangerous.

11) Jasprit Bumrah

Malinga's apprentice at Mumbai Indians, Bumrah found success with the yorker using an action almost polar-opposite to Malinga's – underlining the scope for different techniques in the sport. Rather than a low-arm action Bumrah employed a high-arm release that speared the ball in towards the stumps and pads. Bumrah did not swing the ball like Malinga but he got movement off the pitch and was arguably even more accurate. A menace to face with the new and old ball.

12th man) Shahid Afridi

Afridi was in many respects the prototypical T20 player. He made his professional debut in the 20th century but was perfectly suited to cricket's 21st century format. His fast, fizzing leg breaks inspired Rashid's transformative method while his kamikaze batting of unadulterated attack was totally in sync with the 20-over format. For much of his career Afridi was good enough to be selected for his bowling alone but his batting, although inconsistent, could also be match-winning as well.

ACKNOWLEDGEMENTS

Writing this book – my first and Tim's second – was an enormous challenge, not least because the very motivation for writing it was the relative scarcity of literature and analysis on the Twenty20 format.

We were led, therefore, to search for answers and stories not from old books and accounts, but instead directly from the protagonists themselves. Writing *Cricket 2.0* has seen us conduct more than 80 interviews with players, coaches, analysts and the game's administrators. For this we are deeply thankful to those individuals who were not only generous with their time but pleasantly forthcoming and candid. Too often sportsmen are criticised for their interactions with the media but in writing this book we encountered nothing but warmth and an infectious passion for the game we all love.

This book is defined by the contributions of our interviewees, both on and off the field: Talha Aisham, Azad Ali, Jim Allenby, Manoj Badale, Samuel Badree, Trevor Bayliss, Sam Billings, Ian Bishop, Carlos Brathwaite, Dwayne Bravo, Virgil Browne, John Buchanan, Jos Buttler, Hassan Cheema, Aakash Chopra, Julian Cresser, Carl Crowe, Charles Dagnall, AB de Villiers, Cameron Delport, Jade Dernbach, Paul Dimeo, Ryan ten Doeschate, Rahul Dravid, Anthony Everard, Darren Ganga, Jason Gillespie, Sanjog Gupta, Martin Guptill, Joe Harris, Desmond Haynes, Tom Harrison, Joe Harris, Brad Hodge, Brad Hogg, Adam Hollioake, Benny Howell, David Howman, Mike Hussey, Tony Irish, Chris Jordan, Murali Kartik, Simon Katich, Ali Khan, Rashid Khan,

Lance Klusener, Sandeep Lamichhane, Justin Langer, Nathan Leamon, Evin Lewis, Jon Long, Chris Lynn, Richard Madley, Shuaib Ismail Manjra, Dimitri Mascarenhas, Brendon McCullum, Tom Moody, Peter Moores, Eoin Morgan, Norman Mungroo, Venky Mysore, Mohammad Nabi, Sunil Narine, Sean Newell, Paul Nixon, Jeetan Patel, Kieron Pollard, Ricky Ponting, Rovman Powell, Dean Plunkett, Ravi Rampaul, Stuart Robertson, Luke Ronchi, Pete Russell, Krishmar Santokie, Owais Shah, Renee Anne Shirley, Ryan Sidebottom, Lendl Simmons, Phil Simmons, Jeremy Snape, Washington Sundar, Gaurav Sundararaman, AJ Tye, Alex Tudor, Rehan Ul-Haq, Paddy Upton, Adam Voges, Ivan Waddington, Shane Warne, Dan Weston, Andrew Wildblood, Kane Williamson, Chris Woakes, Julian Wood, Trent Woodhill, John Wright, Luke Wright, Adam Voges and Mike Young. Sincere apologies to anyone we have unintentionally omitted. A few others also spoke to us on condition of anonymity; we are equally grateful.

While most of these interviews were done specifically for the book, some were previously conducted as part of our journalism and are reused here. Any interviews that we used which were conducted by others are credited accordingly in the main body of the text. The websites ESPNcricinfo and CricBuzz have been particularly valuable, as well as various editions of *Wisden Cricketers' Almanack* and newspaper archives.

Both Harsha Bhogle and Michael Vaughan contributed fascinating, contrasting, forewords and we are hugely grateful for their time and insights.

We would like to give particular thanks to the sports management company Insignia Sports International and their managing director Eddie Tolchard whose willingness to help organise interviews with the many players his agency represents and efforts to put us in touch with additional players and coaches proved to be an invaluable part of this project. The same goes for Danny Reuben, the head of team communications for the England & Wales Cricket Board, who went above and beyond arranging interviews with those inside the England team.

Warm thanks are also due to the numerous friends, colleagues and family members who not only had the patience to listen to our musings but who were kind enough to read various chapters in their myriad different forms. So thank you to Adam Collins, Bertus de Jong, Ben Jones, Aleks Klosok, Jono McCrostie, Patrick Noone, Matt Roller, Izzy Westbury, Richard Wigmore and Simon Wilde for their help. We have also enjoyed reading, and discussing, T20 with journalists including David Hopps, Jarrod Kimber, Kartikeya Date and Peter Miller.

We are very thankful to my employers at CricViz and Tim's at *The Telegraph* for allowing us to pursue this venture alongside our day jobs. The CricViz team – and especially their data scientist Sam Green – are due thanks for responding to countless requests for statistics and analysis. The CricViz database and the exhaustive global cricket website ESPNcricinfo were two indispensable tools, without which the book would have been considerably more difficult.

Some of the book builds on ideas previously explored in our journalism. Tim would particularly like to thank Rahul Bhattacharya, his brilliant editor on several articles about T20 for *The Cricket Monthly*, ESPNcricinfo's digital magazine; ESPNcricinfo's features editor Leslie Mathew; and Andy Fifield, the sports editor from *The Daily Telegraph*, who has always encouraged him to explore new avenues.

Tim and I are both very grateful for the support of our literary agent David Luxton who first believed in the idea before helping sell it to our publishers Polaris and to our editor Peter Burns for his ideas and enthusiasm driving the project forward. Naturally, any mistakes that remain are ours alone.

Finally, we would like to thank our family and friends whose support kept us going when perhaps even we doubted the sanity of this undertaking and who will hopefully now be pleased that we both have more time for them once again!

Freddie Wilde and Tim Wigmore